DANIEL WEBSTER

VOLUME I

A.W.Elson & Co.,Boston.

DANIEL WEBSTER

*From a study by Gilbert Stuart
in the possession of Mr. Henry Parkman*

DANIEL WEBSTER

By

CLAUDE MOORE FUESS

VOLUME I
1782—1830

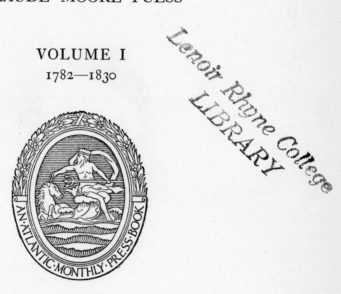

With illustrations

BOSTON
LITTLE, BROWN, AND COMPANY
1930

Copyright, 1930,
By Claude M. Fuess

———

All rights reserved

Published October, 1930
Reprinted October, 1930
Reprinted December, 1930

THE ATLANTIC MONTHLY PRESS BOOKS
ARE PUBLISHED BY
LITTLE, BROWN, AND COMPANY
IN ASSOCIATION WITH
THE ATLANTIC MONTHLY COMPANY

To my Wife

FOREWORD

WHEN, several years ago, I first conceived the project of a comprehensive biography of Daniel Webster, I resolved to begin by reading everything in existence by or about him. This I have failed to do, for his letters are still widely distributed, and there are some which are inaccessible to the investigator. I have, however, done my best to trace all that he ever wrote and all that has been said concerning his character and achievements.

It is, perhaps, superfluous to state that the available sources are very extensive; and I have been fortunate in being able to utilize a considerable amount of material which was not at the disposal of earlier biographers. The basis of research is the imposing National Edition of Webster's Writings and Speeches, published in 1903, in eighteen large volumes. This is supplemented by original documents in the New Hampshire Historical Society, the Massachusetts Historical Society, and the Congressional Library, not to mention smaller collections in private libraries and in the papers of Caleb Cushing, Edward Everett, and others. Not a few letters to and from Webster are owned by individuals and are scattered widely through the United States.

No statesman of that era was discussed more frequently or frankly in the public press; and the newspapers, not only in Washington, New York, and Boston, but also in such communities as Portsmouth, Keene, and Concord, are filled with references to him. While I have lacked time for going through all the journals of that period, I have examined many of them in various sections of the country, and have found the labor profitable.

Of other first-hand material, diaries, such as those of John Quincy Adams, Philip Hone, James K. Polk, and Ralph W. Emerson, have been of incalculable assistance; and reminiscences and memoirs, like those of Harvey, Lanman, Poore, Wentworth, Plumer, Hoar, and many others, have been helpful, not only with facts, but also with impressions of contemporary society and politics. There are naturally countless monographs covering in detail special phases of Webster's career and of the historical events in which he participated. It is not an exaggeration, furthermore, to say that, in the biographies of nearly all the eminent Americans of the first half of the nineteenth century, mention of Webster may be found. The list is long and formidable, including not only such giants as Clay, Calhoun, Jackson, the Adamses, Douglas, and Lincoln, but also lesser figures, like Benton, Van Buren, Sumner, Garrison, Tyler, Buchanan, Everett, Cushing, and Choate. The names of the more important books will be found at the close of this volume.

During Webster's long life, he was compelled again and again to take sides on controversial questions. Even his most ardent eulogists can hardly approve every one of his decisions, and I have occasionally been obliged to be critical of his attitude and his conduct. Whenever this has happened, I have attempted to sustain myself by logic and by ample authority. But there will always be honest disagreements arising from differences in temperament, geographical location, and political philosophy. There is also a wealth of mythical stories which have accumulated around Webster's name, and which can now be neither confirmed nor disproved.

It is not easy to express adequately my gratitude for the aid which I have received from numerous acquaintances and friends. My colleagues, Archibald Freeman, Roy E. Spencer, Arthur W. Leonard, Horace M. Poynter, and Charles H. Forbes, have read several of the chapters and have made helpful suggestions. In the proof reading I have been aided greatly by Mr. and Mrs. Alan R. Blackmer. Among those upon whose knowledge I have most relied are Charles Warren, Esquire, of

Washington, D. C.; Worthington C. Ford and Mark A. DeWolfe Howe, of the Massachusetts Historical Society; Judge Elias B. Bishop, of the Superior Court of Massachusetts; President Ernest M. Hopkins, Professor Leon B. Richardson, and Mr. Gilman D. Frost, all of Dartmouth College; Reverend Alfred R. Hussey, of Plymouth, and Reverend Alfred Gooding, of Portsmouth; Clarence E. Carr, of Andover, New Hampshire; Wilson Olney, of Boston, who placed at my disposal his interesting collections of manuscripts; Charles S. Tyler, of Beverly, who allowed me to inspect his unequaled collection of Websteriana, and Edwin A. Bayley, of Boston, who consented to let me reproduce some of his Webster engravings and daguerreotypes; Major Otis Hammond, of Concord, who granted me many privileges in the New Hampshire Historical Society; Foster W. Stearns, of Hancock, New Hampshire; and Howard S. F. Randolph, of the New York Genealogical and Biographical Society. Laurence M. Crosbie, of Exeter, has allowed me to profit by his extensive researches into New Hampshire history and has read a good share of my manuscript. Judge A. W. Cozart, of Columbus, Georgia, has also read the book and has given me the benefit of his legal experience and his sympathetic counsel. My friend, Markham W. Stackpole, of Milton, has kept me from many verbal indiscretions and infelicities. Lewis A. Armistead, of Boston, Webster's great-grandson, permitted me to use the unpublished manuscript diary of his grandmother, Julia Webster Appleton. Many other persons have advised me on matters of detail. I wish also to acknowledge my obligation to the staffs of the Congressional Library, the Boston Public Library, the New Hampshire Historical Society, the Massachusetts Historical Society, the Keene, New Hampshire, Public Library, the public library of Charleston, South Carolina, the Dartmouth College Library, the Phillips Exeter Academy Library, and the library of Phillips Academy, Andover, and, above all, to the Boston Athenæum, where much of my reading has been carried on. To Mr. Edward A. Weeks, of the Atlantic Monthly Press, I am under great obligation for a searching reading of my manuscript, and many fruitful suggestions. My wife, patient under my moods and abstractions, has sustained my courage during long hours of toil and meditation.

It is futile to expect that a work of this scope will be absolutely accurate or complete. There will be blunders and omissions, no matter how much pains has been taken to correct them. Nor will the treatment of the hero please everybody. Webster's versatile activities as lawyer, orator, and statesman were so broad in scope that some of them have undoubtedly been neglected. It is my hope, however, that Daniel Webster will emerge from these pages, not a legendary figure, but a human personage, with weaknesses and shortcomings, perhaps, but also with something of the glorious magnetism which thrilled those whom he met. No one can read his utterances and look long at his portraits without being in some degree overwhelmed by the power and majesty of the man.

C. M. F.

CONTENTS

ILLUSTRATIONS

DANIEL WEBSTER

VOLUME I

I

THE BACKGROUND

Born the wild Northern hills among,
From whence his yeoman father wrung
By patient toil subsistence scant,
Not competence and yet not want,
He early gained the power to pay
His cheerful, self-reliant way.
— WHITTIER, *Snow-Bound*

Heaven bless this goodly land of our fathers! Its rulers and its people may commit a thousand follies, yet Heaven bless it! Next to the friends beloved of my heart, these same hills and glens and native woods and native streams will have my last earthly recollections.
— WEBSTER, Letter to James Kent, June 5, 1832

ON a summer afternoon in 1790, a frail, black-eyed boy, barefooted and dressed in a tow shirt and coarse cassimere trousers, stepped out of his father's tavern at Salisbury Lower Village, in the upper valley of the Merrimack River. Across the highway was the general store kept by his school-teacher, William Hoyt, filled with tempting things to eat and wear. There his glance fell on a novelty, — a large cotton handkerchief, crudely printed on both sides, — and, having already a passion for literature, he bought it with the coins which were jingling in his pocket. What he saw was the text of the Federal Constitution, which had recently been ratified by the states and was being circulated in this quaint fashion. Then and there he sat down under a spreading elm and read it through.

More than sixty years afterward, within sight of the spot where he made this significant purchase, Daniel Webster dictated an account of it to his friend, Blatchford. "From this," he said, "I first learned either that there was a Constitution, or that there were thirteen states." "I remember to have

read it," he added whimsically, "and have known more or less
of it ever since."

When that lad was born, on January 18, 1782, the American
colonies were functioning under the Articles of Confederation,
adopted early in the previous year. Whether the thirteen
states, with their jealousies and rivalries, could be moulded
into a coherent nation was yet to be determined. Only three
months before, the surrender of Cornwallis at Yorktown had
dissipated England's last hope of retaining her American possessions; but she had not yet recognized their independence,
and the exhausted patriot leaders had lapsed into lethargy,
with economic and political disorganization everywhere around
them. At Paris, the tactful Franklin was patiently awaiting
an opportunity to negotiate a peace. Lord North, still stupidly
obstinate, refused to resign, and it was not until the autumn
of 1783 that a treaty could be wrung from the British cabinet.
So far as New Hampshire citizens knew, they were still rebels,
at war with the mother country, and their future was dark
with hazards.

Of the builders of the young republic, several were already
on the stage. George Washington, his campaigns over, was
soon to retire at a little over fifty into what he hoped might be
the undisturbed placidity of Mount Vernon. John Marshall,
a budding lawyer of twenty-seven, had lately taken his seat
in the General Assembly of his state; and Thomas Jefferson,
his kinsman and political foe, was revising his *Notes on Virginia*
after two terms as Governor. The precocious Alexander
Hamilton, later the leader of the Federalist Party, was as yet
more of a soldier than a statesman. John Quincy Adams was
in Paris, a lively assistant secretary to the American Mission.
In North Carolina, a raw-boned youth named Andrew Jackson
was mastering the humble trade of saddler. Somewhere in the
"Slashes," south of the Potomac, little five-year-old Henry
Clay, in homespun, was astride a horse on his way to Daricott's
Mill. Four men destined to be Webster's most relentless
opponents were also born in 1782 — Thomas H. Benton, on
March 14, John C. Calhoun, on March 18, Lewis Cass, on

3a £350

Ebenezer Webster & Mehitabel Smith wer
Married Jan'y ye 8th 1761

Olle Daughter of Ebent Webster by Mehitabel
his Wife Born Janry ye 28th 1762

Ebent son of Ebent Webster by Mehitabel his
Wife born July ye 16th 1764

Susanna Daughter of Ebent Webster by
Mehitabel his Wife born October ye 25th 1766

David son of Ebent Webster by Mehitabel his Wife
Born May ye 1st 1769

Joseph son of Ebent Webster by Mehitabel
His Wife born March ye 25th 1772

Mehitabel Webster Wife of Ebent Webster
Departed this Life March ye 28th 1774

Ebent Webster & Abigail Eastman were
Married October ye 13th 1774

Mehitabel Daughter of Ebent Webster by
Abigail his Wife born Septr 21st 1775

Abigail Daughter of Ebent Webster by Abigail his
Wife born February ye 8th 1778

Ezekiel son of Ebent Webster by Abigail his Wife
Born march ye 11th 1780

Daniel son to Ebent Webster by Abigail his
was born January ye 18th   1782

Sarah Daughter to Ebent Webster by Abigail his
Wife was born may 13th 1784

THE ENTRY OF DANIEL WEBSTER'S BIRTH IN
THE SALISBURY TOWN BOOK

October 9, and Martin Van Buren, on December 5. Edward Everett and Rufus Choate and Caleb Cushing, whose fates were to be so inextricably interwoven with those of Webster, were still in "the realm of the unborn."

Four generations of Websters before him had tilled the soil of New England and were buried within its borders. There he received his education and won his first successes. He was to be more than once New England's candidate for the Presidency. His career of over seventy years divides itself with mathematical precision into two periods of almost equal length, the first belonging to New Hampshire, the second mainly to Massachusetts. From Salisbury he moved to Boscawen, and from there successively to Portsmouth and Boston. Even when he was officially in Washington, his real home was either at The Elms, near his birthplace, or at Marshfield, on the shore of the Atlantic. Webster loved New England, and she, in return, bestowed upon him nearly every honor within her gift.

His family was of what genealogists call "sturdy New England stock," and believers in eugenics will find in his ancestry much to sustain their faith. Most of the many Websters in the United States to-day trace their line back to Thomas Webster, a shadowy figure who died in April 1634, at Ormsby, near Yarmouth, in Norfolk County, England.[1] At a more remote period, the family was probably lowland Scotch, and the name itself means a male weaver.[2] Thomas's widow, Margaret (or Margery), came to this country with her infant son, Thomas, about 1635 and settled at Ipswich, Massachusetts, later moving north to Hampton, New Hampshire. Of this son we know little, except that he married Sarah Brewer and died, in 1715, at Hampton, at the age of eighty-three.

Among Thomas's five sons and four daughters, the most aggressive was Ebenezer (1667–1736), who, pushing a few miles to the west, was one of the grantees of the town of Kingston,

---

[1] See Dearborn's *History of Salisbury, New Hampshire*, p. 828 ff. This book, published in 1890, is full of interesting material, but must be used cautiously because of its numerous inaccuracies and inconsistencies.

[2] Burns uses the word in his poem, "Willie was a wabster guid," and Stevenson employs it in a sentence in *Catriona* — "Tom was a wabster to his trade."

New Hampshire, where he settled at the opening of the eighteenth century. He became an intrepid Indian hunter and a guide in the company of Captain John Gilman which set out in 1710 in pursuit of marauding redskins. By his wife, Hannah Judkins, he had nine children, of whom the eldest son, also named Ebenezer, was born at Kingston in 1714. This second Ebenezer did not inherit his father's energy and has been described as "poor, versatile, and witty, obtaining a scanty living by hatcheling flax, cutting cord wood, shearing sheep, etc." [1] He was, however, fortunate in his marriage, for, on July 20, 1738, he took as his wife Susanna Batchelder, who brought into the family a fresh and vigorous strain.

The true Websters, according to Daniel's testimony, had "light complexions, sandy hair, a good deal of it, and bushy eyebrows," and were "rather slender than broad or corpulent." [2] But Susanna was the descendant of the Reverend Stephen Bachiler (1561–1660), the first settled clergyman in the province of New Hampshire, an enterprising and obstinate man, tall, with very swarthy skin, black coarse hair, and sultry eyes, — "like sloes," — quite different from the blonde and freckled Websters. He was a refractory personality, with some unclerical weaknesses of the flesh. His great-great-granddaughter, Susanna, was a woman "of remarkable strength of character, robust in form, with black hair, a piercing black eye, and dark complexion." [3] Writing to his son, Fletcher, Daniel Webster once said : —

I believe we are all indebted to my father's mother for a large portion of the little sense and character which belongs to us. Her name was Susannah Batchelder ; she was the daughter of a clergyman, and a woman of uncommon strength of understanding. If I had had many boys, I should have called one of them "Batchelder." [4]

[1] *New England Historical and Genealogical Register*, VI, 1.
[2] National Edition of Webster's Writings and Speeches, XVII, 3.
[3] Dearborn, *Salisbury*, p. 829.
[4] See the *Batchelder-Batcheller Genealogy*, by Frederick Clifton Pierce, published in 1898, which, however, cannot be entirely relied upon. Several eminent persons trace their lineage back to the Reverend Stephen Bachiler, but the statement frequently made that John Greenleaf Whittier and Caleb Cushing were among his direct descendants has no foundation in fact, and their supposed physical resemblance to Webster was not due to heredity.

Her oldest son, Ebenezer, born on April 22, 1739, at East Kingston, was Daniel Webster's father. His childhood was spent on the farm, but he was then bound out to a tyrannical master, and, at the age of fourteen, ran away to live with his benefactor, Colonel Ebenezer Stevens.[1] While still a boy, he enlisted as a private in the famous "Rangers," led by Major Robert Rogers,[2] and saw active military service with General Jeffrey Amherst during his invasion of Canada in 1759. Returning with the rank of captain, he married Mehitable Smith, of Kingston, and with a party of discharged veterans, headed by Colonel Stevens, pushed north up the Merrimack to a district designated as Stevenstown, which their patron had obtained by grant from Governor Benning Wentworth. On the northern boundary of the new township — which was christened Salisbury and still bears that name, although somewhat altered in shape and size — Captain Webster was allotted, in 1762, some 225 acres of land.

At first, he had no roof to shelter him. He and his companions had to dig a well, clear the virgin forest, and sow and plant the soil. Soon he built for himself a log cabin on high ground three miles west of the Merrimack, close to a foamy stream which he called Punch Brook. He was indeed of pioneer stuff, just as rugged, just as inured to hardship, just as patient under adversity, as any "Forty-Niner" or early settler on the bleak Iowa prairies.

By 1767, the population of Salisbury was 210, and the growing town was incorporated a year later, in the name of His Majesty George III. The New Hampshire clearings, hewn out laboriously from the pines which clothed the hills, were dotted with outcroppings of rock, and the soil at its best was thin. Some of the farms at the base of Mount Kearsarge were styled "Little Gains," "Hard Scrabble," and "Dungeswamp" — the last being an Indian word to signify the poorest land in

---

[1] Dearborn, *Salisbury*, pp. 829–30.
[2] These troops, enlisted from the hardiest and boldest young men in New England, carried both snowshoes and skates during the winter months, and achieved some brilliant military exploits. It was a mark of distinction to belong to Rogers's company.

creation.[1] But soon, in the midst of the wilderness, could be seen charred stumps, with a few fruit trees here and there, and some scanty wheat peeping up after the spring rains. The forest abounded in black and brown bears, lynxes, and gray wolves, and Captain Webster killed many a fat buck for his larder. The beaver had built a dam within a few rods of his cabin. It was a wild country in the " 1760's," and there are sections of it which are almost as wild to-day.

In front of Ebenezer's house, to the southwest, rose Searle's Hill, called by Webster Mount Pisgah, on the summit of which the first settlers erected their church, a large, two-storied structure, without a steeple. Because of its commanding situation, it served also as a watchtower. But the ceaseless snows of winter blocked the road to the top, and it was also discovered that the more fertile tracts lay on lower ground. To-day that meetinghouse, with its adjacent cemetery, has vanished, and its very site, like the other land on the side of Searle's Hill, has reverted to timber. The scars cut by the pioneers have been obliterated by dense underbrush. Nature has triumphed over man. Ebenezer Webster, however, did not easily abandon the conflict. On the fringes of civilization, with hardly a white man's habitation between him and the St. Lawrence, on debatable ground where Indians frequently alarmed his wife and children, he slowly won a temporary advantage over climate and soil, and eked out a subsistence for himself and his family.

Ebenezer's wife, Mehitable, about whom little is known except that she bore him five children,[2] died in March 1774, leaving him with an eight-year-old girl and two small boys,

---

[1] See Webster's speech "On the Opening of the Northern Railroad to Grafton, N. H., August 28, 1847" (National Edition, IV, 107-11).

[2] There is some confusion as to the birth dates of the children of Ebenezer Webster by Mehitable Smith. Olle, or Olivia, born January 28, 1762, died in infancy; Ebenezer, born July 16, 1764, died of the same epidemic which struck down his older sister; Susanna, born October 25, 1766, later married John Colby, of Andover, New Hampshire, and died in that town, March 23, 1804; David, born May 1, 1769, became a farmer in Canada, married a widow, Rebecca Huntoon, and left a large family; and Joseph, born March 25, 1772, died unmarried, January 20, 1810. No one of them seems to have displayed marked ability of any kind.

the youngest a mere infant. Several stories have been handed down regarding his second marriage, the best authenticated of which states that Captain Webster, in his masculine perplexity regarding his motherless family, consulted "Aunt Ruth," the wife of his brother, William, who lived on the slope of Searle's Hill. When he had explained his problem, she thought a minute and replied, "Eben, have n't you heard of Nabby Eastman? She's a tailoress by trade and knows what life is. In every respect she's a most excellent person. She's up from below right now, visiting her relatives here. Go home, put on your Sunday suit, and ride over and see Nabby." [1] This counsel had the ring of common sense, if not of romance. Captain Webster accepted it, and, in August of that year, Abigail Eastman, of Salisbury, Massachusetts, was united to him in marriage by Parson Jonathan Searle. When the two came down from the hilltop to Ebenezer Webster's log house, the bridegroom said simply, "These, Nabby, are my children."

Abigail Eastman, the mother of Daniel Webster, was thirty-seven years old at the time of her wedding and had undoubtedly long been classed as an "old maid." [2] She was one of the "black Eastmans," of Welsh origin, her immigrant ancestor having been Roger Eastman (Easman), who came to America in 1638 in the ship *Confidence* and settled at Salisbury, Massachusetts. [3] Abigail's father was Major Roger Eastman, "a

---

[1] This story is told in fuller detail in Dearborn's *History of Salisbury*, pp. 746–47, quoted from an article in the *New York Evangelist* for March 1, 1883, giving the recollections of Mrs. Betsey Webster, who died at Palmyra, New York, in 1880, aged eighty-seven years. It doubtless came down to her as a family tradition. Another version, slightly different in minor respects, is to be found in Towne's *Birthplace of Daniel Webster*, published in 1927, on page 4.

[2] She was born on July 19, 1737, the youngest of four children, and was two years older than her husband.

[3] Webster's ancestry, while neither Pilgrim nor Puritan, was nevertheless largely Anglo-Saxon and Celtic, with hardly a trace of the Latin element. Those who are curious to follow out in detail the ramifications of Webster's ancestry and kin should examine *The Genealogy of the Webster Family to Which Daniel Webster Belonged*, an unpublished manuscript by Mabel Fern Faling, a bound typewritten copy of which is deposited with the New England Historical Genealogical Society, in Boston. On the general subject of family pride, Webster expressed himself in the Plymouth Oration: "There may be, and there often is, indeed, a regard for ancestry, which nourishes only a weak pride; as there is also a care for posterity which only disguises an habitual avarice or hides the workings of a low and groveling vanity. But there

soldier bold," who was bred a house carpenter, but, having
"a noble and lofty soul," went out to fight the French and lost
a leg;[1] and her mother was Gerusha (Jerusha) Fitz, described
by Daniel as handsome, with "dark, beautiful eyes, inimitable
teeth, and hair as black as a coal." [2]   Soon after their daughter's belated matrimonial venture, her parents came to live with
her in New Hampshire, where they died in Captain Webster's
house.[3]   A neighbor of "Nabby" Webster's once said that she
had "a dark complexion, with strongly marked features, indica-
tive of a strong mind and sound sense,"[4] and another acquaintance remembered that her countenance wore "the expression
of strength rather than beauty."   There is in existence a sil-
houette showing her as a decidedly plain, rather large-nosed
woman, of ample proportions.   Although Daniel referred to her
with affection, he did not seem drawn to her as he was to his
father; but she was a conscientious mother to Ebenezer's
children and a faithful helpmeet to her husband.

Captain Webster had qualities which made him a leader in
the scattered community around the headwaters of the Merrimack.   As early as 1764, when his cabin had just been completed, he was named Highway Surveyor.   Five years later,
he was chosen for the first of many terms as Moderator of Town
Meeting — a position which, in New England, is seldom accorded to a citizen who cannot compel the obedience of even
the most unruly voter.   He also served intermittently as Town
Clerk, Selectman, and Coroner.   But it was the outbreak of
another war which offered him his real opportunity.   He ob-

---

is also a moral and philosophical respect for our ancestors, which elevates the character
and improves the heart.   Next to the sense of religious duty and moral feeling, I hardly
know what should bear with a stronger obligation on a liberal and enlightened mind,
than a consciousness of alliance with excellence which has departed; and a consciousness, too, that in its acts and conduct, and even in its sentiments and thoughts, it
may be actively operating on the happiness of those who come after it."

[1] National Edition, XVI, 663.

[2] Webster's statement to Charles H. Warren, *Proceedings of the Massachusetts Historical Society*, XV, 280–81.

[3] Daniel Webster wrote that Major Eastman planted trees for fruit on the Webster
farm, "and among others planted a pear tree about 1770, which is now in full bearing."
(Letter to Warren, September 19, 1852, National Edition, XVI, 663.)

[4] *Ibid.*, XVII, 60.

tained in 1774 a commission as Captain in the militia, and, as
soon as the news of Lexington and Concord penetrated to Salisbury, he marched with some of his men under "forced draft"
to Cambridge to meet with the Massachusetts Committee
of Safety. While stationed at Dorchester Heights, he was
assigned to guard duty around Washington's tent. The
Commander-in-Chief summoned Captain Webster to his
headquarters, consulted him regarding patriotic sentiment
in New Hampshire, offered him some refreshment, and closed
the interview by warmly shaking his hand.[1]

As one of the Salisbury Selectmen, Captain Webster signed
the famous "Association Test," engaging, for the citizens of
the town, "that we will, to the utmost of our power, at the
risque of our lives and fortunes, with arms, oppose the hostile
proceedings of the British fleets and armies against the United
States."[2] He was quite ready himself to undergo the hazards
of battle. At Bennington, on August 16, 1777, he conducted
himself with conspicuous valor, being among the first to scale
the Tory breastworks; and he emerged from the hand-to-
hand conflict with his features so besmeared with powder as
to be hardly recognizable.

Like many of the colonial officers, Captain Webster usually
came back to his fireside for the winter months, setting out
in the spring, after the roads were cleared of snow and mud, to
join his command. As a volunteer without pay, he was welcomed by General Washington. In August 1778 he participated in the expedition to Rhode Island, and in 1780 he was
in charge of a company in the regiment of Colonel Moses
Nichols, assigned to the protection of West Point. When he
and his men were posted on guard over Washington's tent on
the evening after Arnold's treason had been disclosed, the
General said to him earnestly, "Captain Webster, I believe

---

[1] Harvey, *Reminiscences*, pp. 5–6.

[2] According to a story told by Harvey, Webster was appointed on a committee to
determine the amount which each citizen ought to contribute to the condu~t of the
war. When the richest man in the community objected that his share was too large,
Webster said, " Sir, our authorities require us to fight *and* pay. Now, you must pay
or fight." (*Ibid.*, p. 7.)

I can trust you." [1]   It is easy to understand why Washington was idolized in the Webster family.

Writing of him as he was in his prime, Daniel described his father as "tall, six feet, or six feet within a half an inch, with a broad and full chest, hair still of an unchanged black, features rather large and prominent, a Roman nose, and eyes of brilliant black." [2]   General John Stark, referring to Daniel's Moorish complexion, said that it was like that of Ebenezer Webster, which burnt gunpowder could not change. [3]   He had a martial bearing, and once, at Exeter, when a mob gathered at the Court House, he merely stepped to a balcony and, in a stentorian voice, shouted, "I command you to disperse." [4]   The rioters melted away.   Daniel said of him that he had a heart which "he seemed to have borrowed from a lion," [5] and he kept his intrepid spirit to the end of his days.   Although he had never been to school, he taught himself to read and write; and his letters are good in handwriting, and no worse in spelling than those of some college graduates of that generation.   Everything which we hear of Ebenezer Webster shows him to have been a man of native common sense, strong tenacity, and forceful character. [6]   It is regrettable that no portrait of him was ever painted.

Although Captain Webster could be stern, he had also a grim humor which made him an agreeable companion.   Daniel spoke of him as "deeply religious, but not sour," and he was for many years an elder in Salisbury Church.   Even in his

[1] Harvey, p. 7.
[2] National Edition, XVII, 4.
[3] *Ibid.*, 5-6.
[4] This incident occurred in 1786, coincidental with Shays's Rebellion in Massachusetts.   Want of money and business depression led about two hundred men, armed with muskets and clubs, to march into Exeter from the surrounding country and send in a petition to the Legislature for the redress of their grievances.   Surrounding the Court House where the Legislature was then in session, they demanded an immediate answer.   It was then that Ebenezer Webster appeared, with General Sullivan and others, and issued his command.
[5] National Edition, XVIII, 229.
[6] Ebenezer Webster is listed among the subscribers from New Hampshire to Jeremy Belknap's *History of New Hampshire*, in 1792.   This list, numbering over a hundred, includes most of the distinguished men in the state at that period.

old age, when he was crippled by rheumatism, he enjoyed his joke and had an infectious laugh. His readiness to efface himself and make sacrifices for his children is a trait which will become evident later in this narrative.

There were moments when a wider field of activity seemed about to open for Ebenezer Webster. He served capably in the Legislature,[1] and he was chosen in 1788 as a delegate to the State Convention for considering the proposed Federal Constitution. Although he himself is supposed to have favored the Constitution, he was hampered by the opposition of an advisory committee of his townspeople, who objected to it on the ground that it tolerated slavery. It was then, according to Daniel Webster, that his father made the following speech : —

Mr. President, I have listened to the arguments for and against the Constitution. I am convinced such a government as that Constitution will establish, if adopted, — a government acting directly on the people of the states, — is necessary for the common defence and the general welfare. It is the only government which will enable us to pay off the national debt, the debt which we owe for the Revolution, and which we are bound in honor fully and fairly to discharge. Besides, I have followed the lead of Washington through seven years of war, and I have never been misled. His name is subscribed to this Constitution. He will not mislead us now. I shall vote for its adoption.[2]

Whatever the actual views of Ebenezer Webster may have been, these words sound suspiciously as if they had been put into his mouth by his son — *aut Cæsar aut nihil*. There is a further difficulty. The State Convention, after assembling at Exeter in February, adjourned because a majority of the delegates had been instructed by their towns not to favor the Constitution. At its second session, held at Concord, in June, Ebenezer Webster was one of four delegates present but not

[1] In 1778–80, he was Representative from Salisbury and Boscawen, and he was the Representative from Salisbury in 1790–91. In 1788, he was chosen by the Legislature as Senator from Hillsborough County, no Senator having been elected by the people of that district, and he took a conspicuous part in the committee work of that session.

[2] Curtis, *Life of Daniel Webster*, I, 9–10.

voting when the issue was finally presented.[1] He did, however, as one of the presidential electors from New Hampshire,
cast his vote in 1789 for Washington. He once said that, if
he had had a broader education, he might have been a Congressman under the new Federal Government. His ambition had
to be satisfied, however, with a commission in 1791 as Justice
of the Inferior Court of Common Pleas — a position which
brought him some distinction and a small annual salary.

"Nabby" and "Eben" Webster had five children. The
oldest, Mehitable, named for Captain Webster's first wife,
was born in 1775, became a "noted teacher," and died unmarried at the age of thirty-nine. Abigail, born in 1778, later
married William Haddock and died at twenty-seven. Then
came two sons, — Ezekiel, born on March 11, 1780, and Daniel,
— and finally Sarah, the youngest, born in 1784, who married
her cousin, Ebenezer Webster, and died in 1811.

The first three were born in the log cabin. Towards the
close of the Revolution, however, Captain Webster built for
his family a small frame dwelling only a few rods distant, and
in this Daniel first saw the light of day. A drawing of this
structure made by Charles Lanman, Webster's private secretary, while the latter was bending over his shoulder, was reproduced as a woodcut for the frontispiece of Lanman's *The Private Life of Daniel Webster*, published in 1852 a few weeks after
Webster's death. According to Lanman, it was one-storied,
with a high gabled roof, a single chimney, one front door with a
window on either side, three windows at each end, with four
rooms and an addition in the rear for the kitchen.[2] The sketch
shows a well-curb and sweep at the eastern end, with a noble

[1] Captain Webster's part in this Convention is still something of a mystery. There
is a tradition that the four delegates not voting were detained not unwillingly at a
dinner given by a certain Timothy Walker. Those interested will consult *A History
of the New Hampshire Convention for the Discussion and Decision of the Federal Constitution*, by Joseph B. Walker, published in 1888. A clear statement of the problems
involved is presented by Fisher in *The True Daniel Webster*, pp. 26–28. New Hampshire was the ninth state to ratify the Constitution, and her acceptance of it made the
Federal Government a reality. Lewis Cass, a native of Exeter, remembered the
bonfires which blazed in the streets on the evening of the day when the Constitution
was adopted.

[2] Lanman, *The Private Life of Daniel Webster*, p. 11.

elm towering above. Behind the house was a large barn in the midst of partly cleared pasture. Directly in front was a meadow sloping gradually down to Punch Brook and degenerating into a bog at the edge of the alder-bordered stream.

When this building was removed or destroyed cannot be ascertained, but General Lyman, visiting the spot in 1849, reported that nothing was left of it except the cellar.[1] This testimony was corroborated by Edward Everett, who wrote, "It has long disappeared, but the spot where it stood is well known, and is covered by a house since built."[2] Everett doubtless referred to the Sawyer house, erected in the late eighteenth century and still extant.

Local tradition, however, maintained that a portion of the first frame dwelling had been preserved as an ell, or shed, incorporated in the larger Sawyer farmhouse.[3] In 1904, a group of public-spirited citizens formed the Webster Birthplace Association, later expanded into a larger organization for restoring the place where Webster was born. Some investigations revealed what was assumed to be the site of Ebenezer Webster's home, and, after the ell had been removed to this stone foundation, the remainder was reconstructed in general conformity with the original design.[4] The title was transferred in 1917 to the State of New Hampshire, by which it is now

[1] " Not a vestige of that habitation remains, to mark the place, unless it is the cellar, now partly filled up, and the trunk of an ancient apple-tree, the top of which is dead, but from which, near the earth, are sprouting forth a few thriving branches." (Lyman, *Life and Memorials of Daniel Webster*, I, 170.)

[2] National Edition, I. 8. Everett's *Biographical Memoir*, published first in 1851, was unquestionably read by Webster himself, and can, therefore, be relied upon in most essential particulars.

[3] In 1894, the New Hampshire Historical Society made a pilgrimage to Franklin and visited " the room in which the famous lawyer, orator, and statesman first opened his eyes to the light of day, as established by indisputable evidence of Dr. J. J. Dearborn, the historian of Salisbury, who was present and gave the company much interesting information."

[4] The model selected by the architect was a drawing by H. Billings, engraved by E. A. Fowle and printed as the frontispiece to the first volume of Webster's *Works* in 1851. According to Lanman, this sketch represents, not the birthplace, but the property adjoining it, and " was engraved by mistake, or, at any rate, without Mr. Webster's sanction." Lanman added, " The authentic drawing was given to the engraver, but he strangely thought proper to substitute the handsome but false picture for the homely but accurate one." (Lanman, p. 65.)

maintained. The birthplace in its restored form does not to-day altogether correspond to the description given by Lanman, but it is probable that the older portion is part of the original Webster dwelling.

As one to-day looks south from the birthplace, there is not another roof visible, and the seclusion is impressive. A farmer and his son still mow and rake and load the hay in the pasture along Punch Brook as Captain Webster and his children used to do, and they unhesitatingly admit that Salisbury has a stubborn soil. Jagged boulders dot the meadow, and there are boggy patches in the hollows. From its edges one may step directly into dense bushes, and from them into what seems like primeval forest. Searle's Hill, its summit now inaccessible except to the pedestrian, stands out as it did when the alarmed settlers kindled their beacons at the top; and the peak of rocky Kearsarge, nearly three thousand feet in elevation, still dominates the western landscape. Punch Brook, formed on the Webster farm by the mingling of two smaller streams, has its foamy pools where trout lie hidden. On its banks just below the bridge have been uncovered the foundation walls of what must have been Captain Webster's sawmill, and a section of an old "up-and-down" saw, together with a rusty axe dug up from the cellar, are preserved in the Birthplace Museum. Giant elms, which were saplings when Daniel roamed the country side, stand guard over the clearing.

In the new frame house, which must have seemed very luxurious to the Websters, Daniel Webster was born, in the very midst of a bleak New England winter, assisted into the world by the local midwife. He was a "crying baby," of whose life the sturdy mother often despaired.[1] In the lofty church on the hill, during the summer following his birth, the child was baptized by Parson Jonathan Searle, wearing his customary powdered wig, deerskin breeches, long silk stockings, with silver knee and shoe buckles, and an ample surplice

[1] Webster remembered having a long illness, and hearing his father say to Abigail Webster, "We must give him up; we never can raise this child." (Harvey, p. 397.)

BIRTHPLACE OF DANIEL WEBSTER, FRANKLIN, NEW HAMPSHIRE

and gown.[1] There had never been a Daniel in the Webster family, but the mother christened her sons after her two brothers, Ezekiel and Daniel.

When he was barely two years old, Daniel was moved with all the family treasures to a new farm in the valley of the Merrimack, at Salisbury Lower Village, about three miles to the east. On his military expeditions, Captain Webster had seen agricultural land which made him realize the poverty of the soil at the base of Searle's Hill; and he had also to consider the second Mrs. Webster, who preferred a less isolated place of residence. He bought sixty acres, and one-half of a hundred-acre lot, from Sarah Call, for 155 pounds, reckoned at the rate of three shillings per bushel of Indian corn — a transaction indicating some of the financial difficulties of those precarious days at the close of the Revolution. The area thus acquired was about two and one-half miles south of the junction of the Pemigewasset and the Winnepesaukee, in the fertile intervale. On the farm were the remains of a log fort, one of the last of the stockades constructed along the frontier as a protection against the Indians. In a cabin in the valley, a Mrs. Philip Call had been massacred by a band of marauding redskins, while her daughter-in-law, with a tiny baby, managed to escape death by hiding behind the chimney.[2] The land was then in Salisbury, but in 1828 was made a part of the township of Franklin.

The new dwelling of the Websters was a frame building of considerable size, with two stories and garret. There, for the next fifteen years, Captain Webster maintained a tavern for passing travelers. It occupied a strategic position where the highway, — the earliest one laid out within the town limits, —

[1] Daniel used to tell with gusto the story, related to him by one who saw the incident, of how, after the baptism, Mrs. Clay's ample bonnet, bedecked with ribbons, blew off and was carried down the slope by the wind. At her request, the parson strutted after it, but too slowly, refusing to unbend his dignity. Finally the exasperated lady shouted. "Searle, you devil, you, why don't you run?" This appeal was irresistible, and the clergyman, throwing off his pride, hastened his pace, captured the bonnet, and restored it to the wearer. (Lyman, I, 184–85.)

[2] The story, as Webster used to relate it, is told in Lyman, I, 155–56. See also National Edition, XVI, 525–26, and XVIII, 536.

after turning west from the Merrimack for perhaps a third of a mile, curved sharply again to the north.   Recently this portion of the road has been straightened, and the old thoroughfare is little more than a grass-grown path; while the broad modern boulevard, bearing the name of the Daniel Webster Highway, is traversed daily by thousands of automobiles on the way to White Mountain resorts or to mill cities along the Merrimack. Webster described it as "a spot of absolute quiet," [1] but the railroad, laid across it in 1846, transformed that district, and the automobile has completed the metamorphosis which the locomotive began.

The Merrimack at this point is rather deep and narrow, with steep banks rising perpendicularly from its eastern shore. On the western side, however, where the Webster farm was located, lies a level stretch, an alluvial deposit of an earlier period, fully half a mile wide, and, when properly cultivated, very productive.   Behind it to the west the hills rise gradually to the Center Road Village and Salisbury Heights.   When Captain Webster transported his family, he followed a rough road down Punch Brook to the spot where it falls into the Merrimack, and then turned south for some rods until he reached his new acres.

Except when the summer foliage softens its contours, the landscape in this section of New Hampshire seems stern and pitiless.   Bleak ridges, gray with outcroppings of granite, rise from a sombre forest.   If you wander far from the main motor highways, you find yourself on "ribbon" roads, lined with tumble-down stone walls, with an occasional deserted farmhouse, its roof open to the rains and its blinds hanging loose upon their hinges.   In the more solitary places, the pastures are reverting to undergrowth, and the farmers who have clung to them have almost forgotten how to smile.   The scenery is not unlike that in the English Westmorland or the Scottish Highlands, but no Wordsworth or Scott has immortalized it. [2]   Writing of it towards the close of his life, Webster

---

[1] Webster to Fillmore, July 13, 1852 (National Edition, XVIII, 535).

[2] Robert Frost, especially in *North of Boston*, has caught more of the spirit of the New Hampshire countryside than any other poet.

said, "This is a very picturesque country. The hills are high, numerous, and irregular — some with wooded summits, and some with rocky heads as white as snow. . . . I really think this region is the true Switzerland of the United States."[1]

The climate is subject to disconcerting extremes of heat and cold. Winter sets in early and continues long,[2] and in some years the snow does not melt until the end of April. Frosts have been recorded there in July, and in February the rural roads are packed with colossal drifts. Readers of Whittier's *Snow-Bound* have in their imaginations a perfectly drawn picture of what Daniel Webster must often have experienced when he looked out and saw

> No cloud above, no earth below, —
> A universe of sky and snow!

In midsummer, on the other hand, there are likely to be periods of intense, oppressive heat, terminated by thunderstorms of extraordinary violence. And then, for compensation, there will come in July and August afternoons of amazing beauty, with a light breeze tempering the sun's rays and a romantic glow investing the hills. The chief quality of the climate is its infinite variety. Any weather, good or bad, may be expected at any time.

A post-rider made the trip on horseback once a week between Boston and Concord, New Hampshire, sometimes carrying farther north copies of the *Columbian Centinel* and the Concord *Gazette*. Writing of the year 1805, Webster said, "Stage-coaches, then, no more ran into the center of New Hampshire than they ran to Baffin's Bay."[3] But biographers have somewhat overemphasized the isolation of the youthful Webster. The tavern on the valley highway was an oasis where travelers

---

[1] Webster to Mrs. Cheney, September 29, 1845 (National Edition, XVI, 675). He added, " I am attracted to this particular spot by very strong feelings. It is the scene of my early years."

[2] Thomas W. Thompson, writing from Salisbury Lower Village in October 1804, described a storm which deposited snow a foot deep in the woods and wreaked immense damage upon the neighboring orchards. (*Ibid.*, XVII, 190.)

[3] National Edition, XVII, 22.

paused for rest and refreshment; and, as the eighteenth century drew to a close, the population along the Merrimack was rapidly increasing.[1]   The Websters had communication with the outside world.   Captain Webster's political activities drew him frequently to Concord, the capital of the state, less than twenty miles to the south.   Probably Daniel never felt the loneliness attributed to him by historians.

It is not easy, in these days of rapid and cheap transportation, of readily obtainable comforts and luxuries, and of entertainment furnished by motion pictures, magazines, and radios, to imagine what life was like in Salisbury in the last decade of the eighteenth century.   Of the 150,000 people in New Hampshire, a large proportion, including even clergymen, lawyers, and physicians, practised husbandry, and each farmer was virtually self-supporting.   He raised all his own food, and his womenfolk spun and wove their own clothes.   Hulled corn, hominy, hasty pudding, pork and beans, and beef were all products of his estate, and he even manufactured his own cider and rum, which he consumed in large quantities on festival occasions.[2]   Stoves were not introduced until well into the nineteenth century.   Joints were roasted either in the "tin kitchen" in front of the huge open fireplace or in the spacious brick oven heated by wood.   Vegetables were boiled in kettles suspended on the adjustable iron hooks at the corner of the hearth.   Corn was pounded in a rough wooden mortar, and the dishes were either wooden or pewter.   At night, the only illumination came from candles or from the open fire, fed with pine-knots, which was the centre of household activity.

> And, for the winter fireside meet,
> Between the andirons' straddling feet,
> The mug of cider simmered slow,

---

[1] Even in 1767, there were 752 people in Concord, 285 in Boscawen, 502 in Canterbury, — on the other side of the Merrimack, — and 210 in Salisbury.   The population of New Hampshire in 1800 was 183,868.

[2] " Among husbandmen, cyder is their common drink.   Malt liquor is not so frequent as its wholesomeness deserves." (Belknap, *History of New Hampshire*, III, 265.)

The apples sputtered in a row,
And, close at hand, the basket stood
With nuts from brown October's wood.[1]

The blaze on the hearth had to be covered with ashes before the master of the house went to bed, for there were no matches, and the rekindling of the fire could not be neglected. Carpets were still unknown, but the floors were sometimes sprinkled with white sand. Outdoors each thrifty housewife had her mash-tub, in which ashes were leached for making soap.

Some flax was then grown in the township, and there are still hidden away in garrets the odd-looking implements once used for its breaking, swingling, carding, and spinning. Ezekiel and Daniel probably wore suits colored from the dye-pot which stood in the chimney corner. The women went about their homes in petticoats, but "dressed up" when visitors came. On Sunday, people donned their best garments and rode to church, not merely to sing hymns and listen to the tedious sermons, but also to learn what had happened during the week; and the lunch at noon was a welcome opportunity for gossip. Everybody was up and stirring on week days before sunrise, and nobody was awake long after sundown. Traveling was uncomfortable, and there were women who never, from the cradle to the grave, went outside the limits of the town. Wagons were just coming in, but they had no springs, and the roads were very rough. The first sleigh in Salisbury was owned by Ebenezer Webster.

Agriculture was carried on under what seem to us primitive conditions. The soil was turned by a huge plow, twelve or fifteen feet long, which it took six yoke of oxen to draw, with one man riding on the beam to keep its nose in the ground. Shovels were wooden, shod with iron, and the pitchforks, made by the local blacksmith, were very heavy. Captain Webster brought to Salisbury, in 1765, the stones for a grist-mill, dragging them in on an ox-sled. In the Webster household, as in those of their neighbors, specie was rare, and a system of barter

[1] Whittier, *Snow-Bound*, Cambridge Edition, p. 401.

had to be adopted. Although he labored incessantly, Captain Webster was never prosperous and was seldom free from the menace of debt.

For all the ordinary ailments simple remedies sufficed, and the physician was summoned only in the most serious emergencies. The death rate, especially among children, was exceedingly high, but those who survived infancy were likely to be of such tough fibre as to withstand most diseases. This explains many cases of remarkable longevity. The fact that all but two of Ebenezer Webster's ten children reached maturity indicates that the stock had unusual vitality.

Daniel was the thinnest and feeblest of "Nabby" Webster's flock, and she once rode with him on horseback to Little Boar's Head, on the seacoast, in order to test the effect of salt-water bathing upon him. Whenever he told this story, his eyes filled with tears, and he would end, "There was a mother for you!" [1] He was not allowed to do any of the heavy chores, but was permitted to spend his time largely in play. There were, of course, light tasks for him to perform. He yoked the oxen, curried the horses, drove the cows to pasture, followed the mowers with a wooden spreader, and rode the horse to harrow between rows of corn at weeding season. In after life, he liked to reminisce about those boyhood days. In 1837, he said proudly to an audience in St. Louis, "I am a farmer, and on the yellow sands of the east, many a time have I tilled my father's field, and followed my father's plough." [2] His fondness for Gray's *Elegy* was due to such realistic stanzas as : —

> Oft did the harvest to their sickle yield :
> Their furrow oft the stubborn glebe has broke :
> How jocund did they drive their team a-field !
> How bow'd the woods beneath their sturdy stroke !

As is inevitable with the youngest boy in a large household, Daniel was a family pet. He liked to pitch quoits and to

[1] Harvey, p. 317. According to Harvey, Webster could find nothing away from home that equaled his mother's cooking, and once wrote her from Hanover a poetical letter heralding his arrival and asking her to have ready for him his favorite dish of chickens and pork.
[2] National Edition, XIII, 80.

wrestle, and on winter afternoons he coasted down the long hills or skated on the river. Of the period until he was fourteen, he said, "A great deal of the time I was sick, and when well was exceedingly slender, and apparently of feeble system." [1] This frailty was the excuse for giving him more schooling than had been accorded his older brothers and sisters. And yet, in 1839, thirteen years before his death, he noted that, at the age of fifty-seven, he had outlived them all.

Taught his letters by his mother, Daniel could not remember a time when he was unable to read. His first Bible was her gift, and his copious quotations from it in after years prove that its style and substance were well assimilated. Of its influence upon him Webster once said to Lanman: —

My father had a sonorous voice, an untaught but correct ear, and a keen perception of all that was beautiful or sublime in thought. How often after the labors of the day, before twilight had deepened into obscurity, would he read to me his favorite portions of the Bible, the Book of Job, the Prayer of Habakkuk, and extracts from Isaiah! It was doubtless his impressive manner on such occasions, his suffused eye, his broken voice, and reverential intonation, that gave me a taste for the inspired authors, and preserved me from that danger of neglect into which our early familiarity with these books — a familiarity in the meantime rather with the sound of the words than with their sense and beauties — too often threatens to precipitate us. [2]

In this description we are reminded of how in "The Cotter's Saturday Night"

> The priest-like father reads the sacred page,
>   How Abram was the friend of God on high . . .
> Or Job's pathetic plaint, and wailing cry;
>   Or rapt Isaiah's wild, seraphic fire;
> Or other holy Seers that tune the sacred lyre.

When he was well enough, he was sent at irregular intervals to the migratory schools which even the least enterprising communities in New England established as soon as their churches had been organized. His teachers were semi-itiner-

---

[1] National Edition, XVII, 9.   [2] *Ibid.*, XIII, 572.

ant and usually poorly qualified for instructing others. "Nothing was taught but reading and writing," said Webster in his Autobiography.[1] Sometimes the school was kept in the Lower Village, close by his home; at other seasons he had to walk two or three miles each way, morning and afternoon, carrying his luncheon with him; and when it was being held even farther from his home, he was "boarded out" at the house of a family friend. His first master was Thomas Chase, of whom Webster made the comment, "He could read tolerably well, and wrote a fair hand; but spelling was not his forte." [2]

When the lad had learned his letters, he proceeded to borrow every volume within his reach. His father had joined with Thomas W. Thompson, the local attorney, and the Reverend Thomas Worcester, the Salisbury clergyman, in starting a circulating library, small but carefully selected, in which the bookish Daniel found his chief delight. Long afterwards, Webster sometimes astonished his legal companions by quoting at length from the *Essay on Man* or *Paradise Lost*, or even from Watts's hymns, most of which he could recite by the time he was twelve. His guests at Marshfield used to hear him singing in the early morning such stanzas as: —

> Our lives through various scenes are drawn,
>   And vexed with trifling cares;
> While thine eternal thoughts move on
>   Thine undisturbed affairs.

Almost unconsciously, he acquired a thorough knowledge of the English classics, including such writers as Samuel Butler, Addison, Swift, Pope, and Dr. Johnson. He was much affected by the papers from the *Spectator*, particularly the essay on the ballad of "Chevy Chase." Through this intensive reading

---

[1] National Edition, XVII, 7. Webster's Autobiography is a fragment, written out in 1829 for Mrs. Eliza Buckminster Lee, and extending only to 1817. Brief though it is, it is of great value because of its recollections of his childhood.

[2] Another teacher was William Hoyt, who kept the general store in Salisbury Lower Village. Still another was James Tappan, who lived to an advanced age, surviving his famous pupil. Webster wrote him an interesting letter on July 20, 1852. (National Edition, XVIII, 541.)

came a feeling for style and rhythm which had a beneficial effect upon his speeches.

When the yearly almanac arrived, he and Ezekiel usually memorized before nightfall the verses at the tops of the pages devoted to the months. Once the two brothers, differing as they lay in bed regarding the rendering of a line in April's poetry, stole out in their nightshirts to the chamber where their aged grandmother was sleeping and brought back the precious pamphlet, only to discover that Ezekiel had won. Just as he was dropping off to slumber again, Daniel noticed a flickering light in the room which they had just visited, and springing out of bed, found that flames were spreading from an overturned candle. He shouted to arouse the family, and Captain Webster, hastening to the rescue, seized everything that was ablaze and wrapped it in blankets. It was a fortunate escape from a disaster which would have been blamed on an overscrupulous attention to accuracy of quotation.[1]

Literature was even then an indispensable source of stimulation to Daniel Webster. "We had so few books that to read them once or twice was nothing," he wrote. "We thought they were all to be got by heart." [2] But he was also a friendly boy, who liked people, especially those of marked individuality. He enjoyed talking with old John Bowen, who had been a prisoner among the Indians, and with George Bayly, "a yeoman of humor and mimicry," [3] who had seen the first tree felled in northern New Hampshire. In a tiny cottage on a corner of the Webster farm lived Robert Wise, a Yorkshireman who had survived a career of miraculous adventures as soldier and sailor, who had been twice a deserter, and had at last, after fighting under the Union Jack at Bunker Hill, joined the colonists and served under Stark in later campaigns.[4] His

---

[1] National Edition, XVII, 8.　　　　[2] Ibid.　　　　[3] Ibid., XVIII, 296.

[4] Ibid., XVII, 16–17. Henry A. Wise, in his Seven Decades of the Union, 195–96, tells of a conversation with Webster about Robert Wise, but the account is filled with minor errors. It says that Webster's early home was " along the New Hampshire coast," that the name of the old pensioner was Daniel Wise, and that he was a bachelor. Webster, in his Autobiography, expressly states that Robert Wise had a wife, but no child.

fantastic tales held the credulous, imaginative lad in a mesmeric spell; and the veteran also took him as a companion
on his walks, paddled him up and down the river, and taught
him the art of angling.[1] An odd playmate he must have been,
and a diverting tutor. In return, Daniel read the newspapers
to him, for he could neither read nor write.

Although Daniel was fond of nature and could beat a path
through the woods with Wise for hours at a stretch, he had no
love for farm labor. In his sixty-fifth year, writing at the
spot where he had been brought up, he said : —

This fair field is before me. I could see a lamb on any part of it.
I have ploughed it, and raked it, and hoed it; but I never mowed it.
Somehow, I could never learn enough to hang a scythe. I had not
wit enough. My brother Joe used to say that my father sent me to
college in order to make me equal to the rest of the children.[2]

Something about him made an impression on strangers.
He often entertained guests at the tavern by reading aloud
from the Bible; and teamsters, as they pulled up at the door,
would say, "Come, let's go in and hear a psalm from Dan
Webster." Many years later, when Senator Webster had
just ended one of his political speeches, a man came up to him
and asked in amazement, "Is this the little black Dan that used
to water the horses?" His teacher, James Tappan, remembered that Daniel "was always the brightest boy in school."
On a Saturday morning, Master Tappan held up a shining
new jackknife, promising it as a reward on Monday to the
pupil who would commit to memory the greatest number of
verses from the Bible. Many of the boys and girls did well,

---

[1] Daniel's passion for fishing, if not instinctive, was at least created in him very
early. At the age of five, according to Lanman, the boy was riding on horseback with
his father along a road near his birthplace, when Captain Webster, passing near Punch
Brook, suddenly exclaimed, " Dan'l, how would you like to catch a trout?" They
dismounted, and Ebenezer, cutting a hazel rod, attached to it a line and hook which
he had in his pocket, baited it with a worm captured under a stone, and then told the
youngster to creep up on a boulder and cast carefully into the deep pool below. The
little fellow, obeying instructions, hooked his fish, and then, in his excitement, lost his
balance and tumbled into the water, over his head. He was drawn out, still clutching
the improvised rod, with a good-sized trout trailing from the hook. (Lanman, p. 135.)

[2] Webster to Blatchford, May 3, 1846 (National Edition, XVIII, 228).

for the prize was worth striving for; but Daniel had memorized so many verses that, after he had repeated sixty or seventy, the master stopped him, leaving him to protest that there were several chapters more which he could recite.   At the sawmill on Punch Brook, which Captain Webster still operated even after he had moved to the Lower Village, Daniel was sometimes assigned the not very arduous task of setting the saw and hoisting the gate; and, during the few minutes while the blade was grinding through the timber, he employed the time in reading from the book which he never failed to carry in his pocket.

It was a household in which love of country was instilled into the children with their daily food.   At the tavern fireside, Daniel listened to tales of the Revolution from men who were familiar with the flash of rifles and who had seen Knox and Steuben and Washington.   Captain Webster must have told stories of his campaigns under Rogers and of the debates in the New Hampshire Convention of 1788.   As Parton said, Daniel learned political history at town meetings, on election days, from the actors themselves — not from the cold and uninviting pages of textbooks.   And always before him was the figure of George Washington, his father's hero, as the model of what a patriot ought to be.

The three hundred dollars which Ebenezer Webster received, after 1791, as annual compensation for his services as Lay Justice of the Court of Common Pleas, was chiefly responsible for his decision to give his youngest son an education.   At the close of the century he exchanged houses with his son-in-law, William Haddock,[1] and moved to The Elms, a comfortable dwelling still standing, with some additions, only a short distance from the site of the tavern.[2]   It was this farm which

[1] William Haddock (1769–1828) came to Salisbury from Haverhill, Massachusetts, before 1794, being by trade a tanner and currier, as well as a shoemaker.   For his first wife, he married Daniel's sister, Abigail, and accumulated a small fortune, most of which he later lost through poor investments.   His son, Charles Brickett Haddock (1796–1861), was Daniel's favorite nephew.

[2] For a useful and accurate map of The Elms farm and its environment, see the drawing by F. N. Hancock in Fisher's *The True Daniel Webster*, facing page 42.   The house is now occupied as the office and residence of the Superintendent of the New Hampshire Orphans' Home.

Ebenezer Webster occupied until he died in 1806.   It was then taken over by his son, Ezekiel, at whose death in 1829 it was bought by Daniel, who kept it mainly for raising cattle.   But at the time when Judge Webster transferred to The Elms, Daniel was a student in Dartmouth College.   It was the tavern which was his boyhood home, and to which his recollections invariably turned.

Certain events of his childhood were indelibly stamped on Webster's mind.   Struthers Burt has written : —

> No one knows the countryside,
> Sweet and deep and amplified,
> Until he's watched it day by day,
> Month by month from frost to hay.

This Captain Webster's sons had done.   Daniel never forgot how, when the Merrimack was teeming with fish in the spring, the shad, on reaching the junction of the two streams which form the larger river, went up the Winnepesaukee to the warmer waters of the lake, while the salmon sought the colder Pemigewasset rushing down from the mountains.   He vividly recalled that during an April freshet a great barn went sailing down the valley, swept along by the torrent.   Writing of his affection for New Hampshire, he said, "For my part, I shall continue to love her white-topped hills, her clear running streams, her beautiful lakes, and her deep shady forests, as long as I live." [1] More specifically he described The Elms as follows : —

This house faces north.   Its front windows look towards the River Merrimack.   But then the river soon turns to the south, so that the eastern windows look toward the river also.   But the river has so deepened its channel, in this stretch of it, in the last fifty years, that we cannot see its water without approaching it, or going back to the higher lands behind us. . . .   Looking out at the east windows at this moment (two P.M.), with a beautiful sun just breaking out, my eye sweeps a rich and level plain of one hundred acres.   At the end of it, a third of a mile off, I see plain marble gravestones, designating the places where repose my father, my mother, my brother Joseph,

[1] Webster to Coffin, June 11, 1840 (National Edition, XVIII, 86).

and my sisters Mehitable, Abigail, and Sarah, good scripture names, inherited from their Puritan ancestors.[1]

In almost the last letter which he wrote, Webster said to Charles H. Warren: "But you never saw Salisbury, nor the sources of the Merrimack, nor Kearsarge, nor the Ragged Mountain, nor my Punch Brook Pasture, of 500 acres, where 100 cattle graze along the glades and glide through the bushes like so many deer. My! I do not think you ever saw anything." His New Hampshire home was his solace to the end of his days.

There was little of the prodigy about the youthful Webster. Except for his physical weakness, — which he later entirely outgrew, — he seems to have had a normal, healthy childhood, free from morbid influences and without Freudian complexes. His parents, although straitened in their resources, were refined people, with a Puritan respect for learning and law, and with rigid standards of conduct. The forces to which Daniel was susceptible came from nature, from humanity, and from books, and he profited by them all.

[1] National Edition, XVIII, p. 228. The railroad and the attractive new brick buildings of the New Hampshire Orphans' Home have considerably altered the view which Webster described, but the little cemetery is still carefully kept. A bronze tablet on a boulder commemorates the fact that the Superintendent's Residence — or rather one section of it — was once the home of Daniel Webster's father and later of Daniel himself. In 1925, a Daniel Webster Memorial Building was dedicated at the Orphans' Home, with an address by Senator George H. Moses. In 1852, Webster wrote, "There are seven houses in the village, of which two are mine, one for our use and one for the tenants." Both the houses which he mentions are still standing, but the old tavern has long since disappeared, and its site is unmarked.

II

EXETER AND DARTMOUTH

The duty of man to his Maker, to his fellow-men, and to himself have ever been here inculcated.
— WEBSTER, Address at the Abbot Festival, Exeter,
August 23, 1838

It is doubtful if the name of any educational institution in the land is so inseparably blended with the name of a graduate, or even of a founder, as is the name of Dartmouth with that of Daniel Webster.
— PRESIDENT WILLIAM J. TUCKER, Address at the Webster
Centennial of Dartmouth College, September 25, 1901

ONCE, in the broad meadow at The Elms, "Dan'l" Webster was set to mowing by his father, but made awkward work of it. His wayward scythe was sometimes on the ground and sometimes over the tops of the grass — never where it should have been if it had been swung by competent hands. When he complained that the tool was not properly balanced, unsuccessful efforts were made to adjust it. At last the vexed Captain Webster cried, "Well, hang it to suit yourself." Quickly the boy threw it over the limb of a tree, saying, "There, that 's just right." The father, laughing in spite of his irritation, told him to let it remain where it was.

But Daniel might have been obliged to settle down as a farmer if his alertness of mind had not attracted the notice of a man who had the inclination and the power to help him. Thomas W. Thompson,[1] an intimate friend of the Webster

[1] Thomas White Thompson (1766–1821), born in Boston, early moved with his parents to Newburyport, attended Dummer Academy, and graduated from Harvard College in 1786. With notable versatility, he studied theology, acted as a tutor at Harvard, and read law under Theophilus Parsons. What drew him to New Hampshire is not known, but he opened an office in 1791 at Salisbury Center, and moved in the following year to the Lower Village, where he became the leading citizen. He was later Member of Congress (1805–07), and, after removing to Concord in 1809, was State Treasurer (1810), Speaker of the New Hampshire House of Representatives

family, maintained a law office near the tavern; and, when
Daniel was not more than thirteen, the attorney, lacking a
clerk, hired the lad to sit at his desk while he was away on
business and explain to prospective clients where he had gone.
The duties of the position were so slight that the boy investigated the books on the shelves around him, and, when Thompson casually tossed him a Latin grammar, Daniel, hoping to
please his employer, committed it to memory. This feat so
stirred Thompson's interest that he suggested to Captain
Webster the wisdom of encouraging the youngster by sending
him to an academy, with the idea of preparing him to be a
teacher. Ebenezer Webster, neither then nor later, had any
superfluous funds. On the other hand, Daniel's physical
deficiencies seemed to indicate that he could never earn a living
by manual labor. The only alternative was to equip him
with as much schooling as the family finances would allow.
Consciousness of this fact, joined with pride in the impression
which his son had made on Lawyer Thompson, led Captain
Webster to come to a definite decision. The announcement
of his plan, so important to Daniel's development, was made
under circumstances best told in the latter's own words: —

Of a hot day in July, it must have been in one of the last years of
Washington's administration, I was making hay with my father, just
where I now see a remaining elm tree. About the middle of the afternoon, the Honorable Abiel Foster, M. C., who lived in Canterbury,
six miles off, called at the house, and came into the field to see my
father. He was a worthy man, college learned, and had been a minister, but was not a person of any considerable natural power. My
father was his friend and supporter. He talked awhile in the field,
and went on his way. When he was gone, my father called me to
him, and we sat down beneath the elm, on a haycock. He said,
"My son, that is a worthy man, he is a member of Congress, he goes
to Philadelphia, and gets six dollars a day, while I toil here. It is

(1812–14), and United States Senator (1814–17). He was elected a trustee of Dartmouth College in 1801. Thompson was described as "an accomplished gentleman,
distinguished for the dignity and urbanity of his manners, for integrity and piety."
His political career served as a stimulus to Daniel Webster, who admired and respected
him, and was influenced by his unadulterated Federalism.

because he had an education, which I never had. If I had had his early education, I should have been in Philadelphia in his place. I came near it as it was. But I missed it, and now I must work here." "My dear father," said I, "you shall not work. Brother and I will work for you, and wear our hands out, and you shall rest." And I remember to have cried and I cry now at the recollection. "My child," said he, "it is of no importance to me. I now live but for my children. I could not give your elder brothers the advantage of knowledge, but I can do something for you. Exert yourself, improve your opportunities, and when I am gone, you will not need to go through the hardships which I have undergone, and which have made me old before my time." [1]

The pathos of this incident is heightened for us by the fact that, only seventeen years later, Daniel Webster was elected to Congress from New Hampshire, attaining with little effort the office which Captain Webster had struggled vainly to secure. This conversation in the hayfield opened an unexpected future to the barefooted country lad. Before that date no one among the American Websters had been in any sense a scholar. Gaining a precarious livelihood by tilling the soil, they had belonged to the yeoman class. Daniel and his brother, Ezekiel, were the first to become "learned" men.

The plan upon which Captain Webster had resolved was put into operation the following spring. On May 25, 1796, he lifted the youngster on a horse with a side saddle and, mounting his own steed, started with him for Exeter, one of the most important New Hampshire villages and the seat of the Phillips Exeter Academy. The route was familiar to him, for Exeter had been the capital of the state, which he had often visited on legislative business. The travelers stopped for the night at Allenstown, continued their journey on the next day as far as Poplin, and reached their destination early on the following morning.[2]

The Phillips Exeter Academy, now one of our greatest preparatory schools, — comparable with Eton and Harrow in

<hr>

[1] National Edition, XVIII, 228–29, Letter to Blatchford, May 3, 1846.
[2] Lyman, I, 203.

England, — had then been in operation about thirteen years.[1]
Founded mainly through the liberal endowments of Dr. John
Phillips, it had been incorporated in 1781, and opened to pupils
two years later. Its first Principal, William Woodbridge, had
been succeeded by Benjamin Abbot,[2] one of the most brilliant
of American teachers, who governed the school for half a
century, leaving it "famous for scholarship and the devotion
of its graduates to church and state." [3]

The first small school building was soon outgrown, and a
new and beautiful main hall, on Front Street, was completed
just before Webster's arrival. In 1796, the enrollment was
not far from ninety, of whom about half were from New
Hampshire. In Webster's day, Dr. Abbot had only one assistant, usually a young and inexperienced man who remained
for but a year.

Father and son rode down the shaded street of the country
village, the boy on the bony horse, in clumsy cowhide shoes
and a homespun suit too tight for him. According to tradition,[4] Captain Webster took the lad to Dr. Abbot to arrange
for his admission. The Principal, in his pompous manner,
donned his cocked hat and said, "Let the young gentleman
be presented for examination." After making the conventional inquiries, he handed him a Bible and asked him to read
aloud the twenty-second chapter of Luke, describing the be-
trayal of Jesus by Judas and the denial by Peter. This was
an easy task for the boy who had so often declaimed the Psalms

[1] It was almost inevitable that Captain Webster should turn to Exeter for the
education of his son. He himself had been born at Kingston, only six miles away, and
he had known Exeter as a boy. As for the school, it was then, as it is to-day, the best
in New Hampshire, its only rival in New England being the slightly older Phillips
Academy, Andover, Massachusetts, established also by the Phillips family.

[2] Benjamin Abbot (1762–1849), a graduate of Phillips Academy, Andover, and
Harvard (1788), spent all his mature life at Exeter. He believed that the burden in
education must be placed squarely upon the undergraduate, and he was a thorough
drillmaster. His discipline was strict, but just, and he pursued a firm policy as Principal. In his character he represented the Puritan virtues of industry, honesty, and
idealism.

[3] Quoted from *The Phillips Exeter Academy: A History*, by Laurence M. Crosbie,
a thorough and readable study of the development of the school. It has an admirable
chapter — No. VIII — on " Abbot's Favorite Pupil: Daniel Webster."

[4] Lyman, I, 204–5.

in his father's tavern, and he went unfalteringly to the close of the rhythmical passage. He closed the book and stood silent. Then Dr. Abbot, taking the volume from his hand, said simply, "Young man, you are qualified to enter this institution."

At that moment, however, Daniel Webster did not look like a promising candidate for greatness. The diffident farmer's son, who had never before been away from home, was thrown without warning into strange surroundings, among lads from the cities, much better dressed than he and far more sophisticated. While waiting for the meal to be served in his boarding house, he at first sat at the table with his knife and fork held upright on either side of his plate; and his father is reported to have said, "Daniel knows no more about holding a knife and fork than a cow does about holding a spade." Squire Clifford, in whose house Daniel roomed and boarded, saw the boy's embarrassment and, realizing his shyness, induced another student to sacrifice himself for the benefit of Daniel. At the next meal, the victim deliberately held his utensils aloft with his fists planted on the table as Daniel had been doing. Squire Clifford then reproved him, and the scapegoat, controlling his laughter only with difficulty, thanked his mentor and accepted the rebuke. Daniel did not miss the hint, and his manners steadily improved.[1] Other vague tales of Webster's uncouthness have undoubtedly some basis in fact, but he was quick to learn and soon took on the color of his environment, as boys have a way of doing.

Squire Clifford's residence — known to-day as the Garrison House — had been built in 1658 as a protection against the Indians, and is still standing in excellent condition at the corner of Water and Clifford Streets, near the "white bridge." Webster's study table, a hinged board which folded against the wall when not required, is shown to visitors.

The routine did not allow the students much leisure. Morning prayers were held at seven-thirty every day in Dr. Abbot's

---

[1] Cunningham, *Familiar Sketches of the Phillips Exeter Academy*, pp. 130–32. See also Crosbie, p. 82.

room, which was plain and bare, with rows of unpainted pine desks and a gigantic cast-iron stove, the heat from which was augmented on cold winter days by the blaze from the logs in the huge fireplace. There was no artificial light except from candles, and it was often so dark that printed letters could hardly be made out. The woodwork everywhere, on desks and walls and railings, was scarred by jackknives, and Webster himself was later to cut a rude "D. W." deep into a panel in the bell tower. The pupils studied and recited from eight until ten, and then, after a recess of twenty minutes, continued at their books until twelve. The afternoon sessions lasted from three to six in summer and from two to five in winter. Each boy was compelled to be in his room at seven o'clock in the evening and had to go to bed at nine. Wednesday and Saturday afternoons were half-holidays.

Because Webster had appeared in the middle of the academic year, the Principal assigned him to the lowest class, where, for a few weeks, he covered familiar ground in English grammar, writing, and arithmetic. Accustomed as he was to the inefficient teachers in the district schools of Salisbury, he had to adjust himself to instructors who knew their business. But at the end of a month, the Principal's assistant, Nicholas Emery, — afterwards a lawyer and judge in Portland, Maine, — placed him at the head of the section. When the term closed, Emery, having ascertained by questioning Webster that the lad might not return, urged him to come back, promising that he should be promoted to a higher class where he could advance more rapidly. "Those were the first truly encouraging words that I ever received with regard to my studies," said Webster later. "I then resolved to return, and pursue them with diligence, and as much ability as I possessed."

Webster had not been altogether happy at the school. His unfashionable garb and awkward manners had excited the derision of some of his mates. The fourteen-year-old lad had not yet outgrown the sensitiveness which had been the consequence or the accompaniment of his physical weakness.

Emery's sympathy filled the boy with a new confidence and induced him to persevere at Exeter a little longer.

On his return in October, Daniel began Latin and public speaking under the precocious Joseph Stevens Buckminster, who, although only in his thirteenth year,[1] was already a Senior at Exeter and was taking Dr. Abbot's place while the latter was recovering from an indisposition. That a child like Buckminster should have charge of instruction in Latin at Exeter may well seem remarkable to present-day students of that institution, but the prodigy was apparently quite equal to the responsibility. Under his guidance, Webster made rapid progress in Latin, and he always regarded his tutor with kindness. It is impossible to ascertain the length of time during which Webster was actually taught by Dr. Abbot, but he must have sat under him, for the Principal later said : —

It was generally believed that Webster was a dull and unsuccessful pupil, but such was not the case. His mind rarely seemed to be occupied with his studies. His large, lustrous, thoughtful eyes were gazing about the room, or looking out of the window; but, at recitation, the pupil who appeared not to be engaged in studious preparation always acquitted himself well.

Webster's only conspicuous failure was in declamation, then an important feature of the curriculum. In the public exhibition held each week, every student was supposed to take part, but the boy who was to become America's most famous orator could not overcome his timidity. His own confession tells the story : —

Many a piece did I commit to memory, and recite and rehearse in my own room, over and over again, yet, when the day came, when the school collected to hear declamations, when my name was called, and I saw all eyes turned to my seat, I could not raise myself from it.

[1] The stories of Buckminster's precocity would seem mythical if they were not so well authenticated. He was born in Portsmouth, New Hampshire, on May 26, 1784, and was thus more than two years and five months younger than Webster. He had read the Greek Testament when he was only five, and, in 1796, was a tall and dignified youth, who seemed much older than he was. He later graduated from Harvard at sixteen, became a clergyman, was appointed Lecturer in Biblical Criticism at Harvard, and died of epilepsy on June 9, 1812.

Sometimes the instructors frowned, sometimes they smiled. Mr. Buckminster always pressed and entreated, most winningly, that I would venture, but I could never command sufficient resolution.[1]

Doubtless much of Webster's embarrassment arose from a dread of further ridicule from his fellows, but there may have been an actual physical inhibition based upon a nervous weakness. It was, at any rate, merely a temporary difficulty, which completely disappeared when he reached college.

Little beyond these meagre details can be learned regarding Webster's brief career at Exeter. The records of his marks in his various studies have long since disappeared. His stay was too short for the formation of many enduring friendships, but among those with whom he was best acquainted were Lewis Cass,[2] later Governor of Michigan, Minister to France, Secretary of State, and candidate for the Presidency; J. W. Brackett, of New York City; William Garland, of Portsmouth; James Hervey Bingham,[3] with whom he was to continue his intimacy at Dartmouth; and Leverett Saltonstall, of Salem, afterwards a noted lawyer and member of Congress. In later life he was thrown into close relations with other Exeter graduates, including Edward Everett, Jared Sparks, and George Bancroft.

On one occasion he walked with a companion to Rye Beach, ten miles away, and there, just before the sun was setting, had a view of the ocean. "I remember distinctly the impression made upon me at that time," he said, "a sensation such as has never since come to me, much as I have looked at, and love to look at, the sea." [4] There he went again in 1845, towards the close of his life, to gaze once more at the Atlantic from the point where his eyes had seen it as a boy.

[1] National Edition, XVII, 10.

[2] Webster remembered Cass as " a clever fellow, good-natured, kind-hearted, amiable, and obliging."

[3] Bingham later said of Webster as he remembered him at Exeter: "He had an independent air and was rather careless in his dress and appearance. He did not join much in the plays and amusements of the boys of his age, but paid close attention to his studies." See National Edition, XVII, 55.

[4] Harvey, p. 346.

Webster may not have made a deep impression at Exeter as a leader, but the time came when he was welcomed back as his Alma Mater's favorite son. He was elected a Trustee in 1835, and remained nominally a member of the Board until his death, although he was recorded as being present at only two meetings — one in 1836 and another in 1838. At the Abbot Festival in 1838, he presided and delivered an eloquent address, at the close of which he said, in presenting a silver pitcher, the gift of the alumni, to the Principal, "Some men have wrought on brass, some men have wrought on marble, but Abbot wrought on mind." The applause at the conclusion of this sentence was described by one of the guests as "like a sudden peal of thunder." [1] It was the orator's sincere tribute to a great teacher of young men.

There is little remaining to-day of the Exeter which Daniel Webster knew, but he is still remembered there. His portrait hangs in the Academy Auditorium; the marble mantel over the fireplace in the lecture hall was taken from Webster's law office in Boston; and one of the newest dormitories bears his name. The school still maintains its ancient traditions of liberality and democracy, and continues to offer an exceptional opportunity for boys of the Webster type.

In June 1834, Webster sent his youngest son, Edward, to Exeter, and afterwards wrote him an excellent letter of advice, which has been preserved. [2] Only four months before his own death, he wrote, on June 7, 1852, to the Golden Branch literary society, of which he had been made an honorary member, enclosing copies of a speech which he had recently delivered in New York, and ending: —

My Brothers! let us do honor to the Founder of our academy! Let us cherish, affectionately, the memory of the venerable and beloved Benjamin Abbot! And let us labor to repay to the cause of

[1] Quoted by Crosbie from an article by " G. O.," in the *Boston Advertiser* of July 20, 1881. For a good account of the Abbot Festival, see Crosbie, pp. 70–72.

[2] Crosbie, p. 85. See Van Tyne, *Letters of Daniel Webster*, p. 587, for a letter from Webster to his son, Fletcher, asking the latter to take his brother to Exeter and enroll him in the Academy.

Learning, what a most excellent Institution for Learning has done for us. My Brothers, Farewell![1]

This was his last communication to the school.

At the close of the fall term, in December 1796, Captain Webster came for his son and took him back to Salisbury. The reasons why the boy did not return to complete his course can only be surmised. The legend, perpetuated by undergraduate tradition, that he was dismissed by the authorities has no foundation. The suggestion that his health had been impaired is not supported by the evidence. It is more likely that the expense of maintaining the lad away from home was becoming a strain upon the father's financial resources.[2] For the moment there was some uncertainty as to what it would be best for him to do. On his fifteenth birthday, he was teaching a district school, composed of both girls and boys, — many of them older than he, — in a room in the farmhouse of his uncle, William Webster, on the eastern slope of Searle's Hill. He must have been a strange pedagogue, this youth with the gleaming eyes, whose only experience with the world outside of Salisbury had been nine months at Exeter. But he had in his boyish head more sound knowledge of the three R's than any of his own early instructors could have claimed. When school hours were over, he was the companion of his pupils at "apple peelings" and "straw rides" and other rural diversions.[3]

It was probably the Reverend Samuel Wood,[4] of Boscawen, who rescued Daniel Webster from a career as a schoolmaster.

[1] Crosbie, p. 87.

[2] This view was accepted by the late Professor Herbert D. Foster, of Dartmouth College, who had accumulated a large amount of material on Webster, and was expressed by him in a letter to Laurence M. Crosbie, March 11, 1926.

[3] Lyman, I, 212–13.

[4] Samuel Wood (1752–1836) was a man of wide influence in the Merrimack Valley. Graduating from Dartmouth in 1779, as Valedictorian of his class, he had settled in Boscawen, six miles southeast of Salisbury, in 1781, where he was a clergyman for almost fifty years. His house still stands on the road between Salisbury Center and Boscawen, about two miles west from the Merrimack River and Boscawen Plain, on a hill commanding a broad view over the valley. Here, with characteristic enterprise, he planted a large orchard of choice fruit trees, and undertook also the cultivation of the silkworm, with no great success. Under his tutelage, more than a hundred young men were prepared for college, many of them gratuitously.

Having been thrown into contact with the boyish teacher, he was struck by his ability and ambition, and, going to Captain Webster, offered to prepare Daniel for Dartmouth College. The generous proposal could not be rejected. The necessary arrangements were completed, and, as the father and son drove in a "cutter" to Boscawen, the former revealed to the boy his plan to give him a college education. In recollecting that dramatic moment, Daniel afterwards wrote : —

He said he then lived but for his children, and if I would do all I could for myself, he would do what he could for me. I remember that I was quite overcome, and my head grew dizzy. The thing appeared to me so high, and the expense and sacrifice it was to cost my father, so great, that I could only press his hands and shed tears. Excellent, excellent parent! I cannot think of him, even now, without turning child again.[1]

From February to August 1797 Dr. Wood did his best to get Daniel ready to meet the Dartmouth entrance requirements. The task was both congenial and familiar, but was made unusually difficult by the necessity of covering so much work in such a short time. Although the boy knew only a little Latin grammar, Dr. Wood set him at once to reading Virgil and Cicero. "I conceived a pleasure in the study of them, especially the latter, which rendered application no longer a task," he wrote in his Autobiography.[2] With the coming of spring, he took up Greek grammar under David Palmer, a young Dartmouth Senior who happened to be staying with Dr. Wood. For Greek he had no great fondness, but he was diligent, and, after he had been working only six weeks, Dr. Wood urged him to try to enter college at the opening of the regular fall term. It is not astonishing that he went to Hanover, according to his own confession, "miserably prepared, both in Latin and Greek." [3] He was not yet sixteen, and the

---

[1] National Edition, XVII, 10. It is interesting to notice how much Webster's career was affected by external forces. He was, no doubt, eager to secure an education, but the stimulus seems to have come first from Thomas W. Thompson and then from Dr. Wood. It was unquestionably their advice which persuaded Captain Webster to send his son away from home for an education.

[2] *Ibid.*   [3] *Ibid.*

only systematic instruction which he had received had been at Exeter and at Boscawen, in each case for a short period.

He had never outgrown his aversion to farm labor. During the haying season, Captain Webster, in need of hands, sent for him to come back and help in the fields. Finding the turning over of the hay to be a lonely and dull process, the boy inveigled his younger sister, Sally, into wandering off with him to pick whortleberries. They rode away on horseback together and did not return to the tavern until sundown reminded them of supper. When Captain Webster, who had been away at a neighboring village on business, returned and, through questioning, found out what had happened, he could not hold back his laughter; and on the following morning after breakfast he quietly handed his son a compact bundle containing the clothes which the latter had brought from Boscawen. "I believe," said Ebenezer Webster, with a grim smile, "that you may as well go back to Dr. Wood's." So Daniel was destined to use his brain instead of his muscles.[1]

In Boscawen he found various forms of diversion, both intellectual and physical. The picturesque village, with a population recorded in the Selectmen's books for 1786 as "827 soles," was a centre for the surrounding agricultural community, and the farmers drove in frequently for business and gossip. In the Boscawen Social Library, Webster discovered about two hundred books, classified as theological, historical, and miscellaneous, the group including, besides the poems of Milton, Pope, Thomson, and Cowper, *The Fool of Quality*, *Letters on Courtship*, *Coquette*, and *Arabian Nights' Entertainments*, in lighter vein. Here it was that he first turned the enchanting pages of *Don Quixote*, of which he later said : —

I began to read it, and it is literally true that I never closed my eyes till I had finished it; nor did I lay it down for five minutes, so great was the power of that extraordinary book upon my imagination.[2]

[1] The story is told in Lanman, p. 28, and in various other sources. As the boy left the tavern that morning, his patron, Thomas W. Thompson, saw him with his bundle and asked, "Where are you going, Dan?" "Back to school," was the rather shame-faced answer. "I thought it would be so," said Thompson, with a quiet laugh.

[2] National Edition, XVII, 11.

But he did not spend all his time in reading.   He was fond of fishing along Mill Brook and of hunting in the dense forest which could be reached quickly in almost any direction from the Wood farm.   There was about him nothing of the recluse or thin-blooded scholar, and his physical vitality was increasing day by day.   Once, in an introspective mood, he confessed his divided allegiance : —

I must do myself the justice to say that, in those boyish days, there were two things I did dearly love, viz. : reading and playing; pastimes which did not cease to struggle, when boyhood was over (have they yet, altogether?) and in regard to which neither the *cita mors* nor the *victoria laeta* could be said of either.[1]

Neither Ebenezer Webster nor his son had thought of any college except Dartmouth.   It was then the only higher institution of learning in New Hampshire; and Captain Webster had been, in 1789, Chairman of the Legislative Committee which had recommended the Dartmouth College Grant of forty-two thousand acres in the northern part of the state. Dr. Wood was a graduate, although not — as has sometimes been erroneously asserted — a Trustee.   It had the advantage of being easily accessible, for shortly after the Revolution the College Road, four rods broad, had been laid out by surveyors from Boscawen to Hanover, connecting the Merrimack with the Connecticut.   The route was through Salisbury, Andover, Wilmot, Springfield, Enfield, and Lebanon.   It was along this rutted highway, past the rugged slopes of Mount Cardigan and Mascoma Lake, that Daniel Webster, on horseback,

[1] Among the many legends of Webster's mental energy when aroused is one often related by himself, of the occasion when Dr. Wood, noticing how much time the lad was spending in play, suggested that his example might be bad for the other boys. Daniel, sensitive to the suggestion that he was not doing his duty, sat up all that night studying.   On the next morning, he construed his assigned one hundred lines without a mistake.   Dr. Wood was about to leave, but Daniel requested him to listen to a few more pages.   The boy continued, while Dr. Wood sat, impatient for breakfast, which had been announced.   Finally the master asked his pupil how much farther he could go.   " To the end of the twelfth book of the *Æneid!* " was the confident answer.   This story is told in Lyman, I, 218–19.   Doubtless many of the stories of this sort are apocryphal, the product of a lively imagination engaged in retrospection: but Webster, as youth and man, was capable, under stress, of accomplishing an amazing amount of work in a brief period.

carrying with him his feather bed and bedding, together with a few books, some clothes, and provisions for the journey, rode, like D'Artagnan, to seek his fortune. He was now only fifteen years and six months old, but he had matured rapidly at Exeter and Boscawen, and diffidence was no longer one of his handicaps.

On his arrival in Hanover, he fell into the friendly hands of Roswell Shurtleff,[1] then a Junior in the College, who directed him to Ford's Tavern, on the north side of the Green — a building which was afterwards the residence of Squire Mills Olcott and later known as Choate House.[2] Here Webster, with other prospective Freshmen, brushed his clothes and made ready for the entrance examinations.[3] He had to appear in succession before various members of the faculty, — then called the "executive authority," — to be tested in Greek, Latin, English, and arithmetic; and, despite the fact that his knowledge of the classics was, according to Shurtleff, "just to the limit prescribed by law at that period," he was duly admitted, with Dr. Wood's letter of recommendation to support him.

Webster was also obliged to furnish evidence of "good moral character" and to provide a bond of two hundred dollars for the payment of his college bills. When these routine requirements had been met, he doubtless called on President John Wheelock, at the Mansion House, — now the Howe Library,

[1] Roswell Shurtleff (1773–1861), a brilliant student who was much older than his classmates, graduated in 1799 from Dartmouth, and later returned to Hanover as Tutor, Phillips Professor of Theology, Minister of the College Church, Librarian, and Professor of Moral Philosophy and Political Economy. His reminiscences of Webster were used freely by the latter's early biographers.

[2] The house has recently been moved and now stands in a new location on the east side of North Main Street.

[3] According to a story preserved by Lyman, I, 219–20, Daniel left Salisbury dressed in a new suit of blue clothes, including coat, vest, and pantaloons. On his way, just before reaching Hanover, he passed through a violent storm, which drenched him to the skin. When he dismounted at Ford's Tavern, he found that the water had started the color of his suit and that he was " as blue as an indigo-bag." He was called before the faculty without having time to get new attire, and appeared in their presence, as he said, " not only *black* Dan, but *blue* Dan." When he related his mishaps, however, he stimulated their sympathy, and his sad plight may have helped to gain him admission. This picturesque tale has no other authority than that of Lyman, whose inaccuracies in other respects make it exceedingly questionable.

which then occupied the present site of Reed Hall, — and was there formally welcomed to the college. He was enrolled in classes which were probably studying the *Æneid*, Cicero's *Orations*, the Greek Testament, arithmetic, English grammar, rhetoric, composition, and public speaking — a course which, in difficulty and variety, corresponds rather closely to that of the next to the highest year in any of our standard preparatory schools to-day.

Dartmouth College, founded in 1769 through the initiative of Eleazar Wheelock, who became its first President, was still, at the close of the eighteenth century, a "small college," from our present point of view; but it had an average enrollment of a hundred and forty undergraduates, and between 1790 and 1800 its normal graduating class of thirty-six was larger than that of any of its rivals except Harvard. The President, John Wheelock,[1] son of the founder, was a stiff and formal personage, with whom none of the students felt on easy terms. Without any marked intellectual ability or breadth of vision, he had a prodigious store of energy which was often released in ways unfortunate for the college. There were four teachers of professorial rank: Bezaleel Woodward, an unpretentious, friendly person, the sanest and most respected member of the staff, whose field was mathematics and natural philosophy, but who was a collegiate Pooh-Bah; John Smith, known as "Professor Johnny," who taught the languages, and who was so nervous and timid that he was frequently completely disconcerted in the classroom; Nathan Smith, of the Medical School, who offered instruction in chemistry, anatomy and surgery, and the practice of physic; and the President himself, who lectured on Civil and Ecclesiastical History and assumed entire charge of the work of the Senior year. To supplement these there were tutors, young men not long out of college, who were dallying with teaching: John Noyes, later a Congress-

---

[1] John Wheelock (1754–1817), born at Lebanon, Connecticut, graduated at Dartmouth in 1771, as a member of its first class, became a tutor, served as Lieutenant-Colonel in the Revolutionary Army, and, in 1779, at the death of his father, succeeded him through a process of scholastic nepotism. He was deprived of his office by the Trustees in 1815, and died two years later.

man; Stephen Bemis, afterwards a clergyman in Harvard, Massachusetts; and Roswell Shurtleff, who has already been mentioned. All of them were graduates of Dartmouth, and no one of them except Shurtleff remained permanently on the faculty.

The college and the village bore only a slight resemblance to those of to-day. It would, indeed, be difficult to imagine a more striking contrast than that between the Hanover Green of 1797, cut out of a grove of stately pines and bordered with unpretentious residences, and the noble array of brick buildings which now provide for Dartmouth undergraduates every facility which the scholarly life can require. The college was then compact, occupying the low ridge on the east side of the Common. The central structure was Dartmouth Hall, containing not only thirty-six rooms for students, but also quarters for the library and for "philosophical apparatus." It was burned down in 1904, but was almost immediately restored, in brick and stone, on its old location. Directly to the south of Dartmouth Hall stood the Chapel, which dated from 1790, but which was removed in 1828. The Commons Hall, a long, plain wooden structure, had been erected in 1791, on the site now covered in part by Rollins Chapel; but it was not in actual use in Webster's time.[1] The only landmark with which Webster was acquainted is the Meetinghouse, which was built in 1795 on the northeast corner of the square, and which, somewhat restored and remodeled, remains one of the loveliest of New England churches. The historic Burying Ground near the Connecticut, with its simple headstones beneath the pines, preserves the continuity between the past and the present, linking the ancient and the modern Dartmouth as nothing else could do.

Eminent authorities at the college have disagreed with regard to the quarters occupied by Webster while he was at Dartmouth. Professor Charles F. Richardson, in his address

[1] Memorandum from Professor Leon B. Richardson, of Dartmouth, to the author, December 20, 1929. Professor Richardson is an authority on Dartmouth College history.

delivered at the Webster Centennial in 1901, stated positively that Webster lived during his Freshman and Sophomore years in the house of Humphrey Farrar, on South Main Street, citing as evidence a letter written on November 25, 1852, by George Farrar to Professor Edwin D. Sanborn.[1] A portion at least of this original dwelling is still standing, and the owners have marked it with a tablet. Professor Richardson was certain also that Webster, as a Senior, had a room in Dartmouth Hall.

On the other hand, the late Professor Herbert D. Foster, who gave the whole question the most searching scrutiny, asserted that, according to the Treasurer's books, Webster roomed in a college dormitory for the first three years of his course, and, as a Senior, moved to a suite outside of college, probably in what is to-day known as Webster Cottage.[2] A letter from Webster to Bingham, headed "Beechnut Hall, December 28, 1800,"[3] seems to indicate that as a Senior he was then living in a private home, and Professor Foster declared that the proof "rests not merely upon unbroken and uncontradicted traditions, but upon the contemporary record of the careful William Dewey, repeated within the house itself to another cautious witness, Miss McMurphy, and written down by her later." This residence was built about 1780, by Sylvanus Ripley, husband of Abigail Wheelock, President

[1] National Edition, XVII, 53. Farrar's exact words were, " Mr. Webster, Freeborn Adams, my brother William and myself, roomed at my father's house, during the first two years of his college course." It must be kept in mind, however, that this was written considerably more than half a century after the event. Edwin David Sanborn (1801–85), who graduated at Dartmouth in 1832, was long a professor at that college. In 1837, he married Mary Webster, daughter of Daniel's brother, Ezekiel. He was the author of a *Eulogy on Webster* (1853) and a *History of New Hampshire* (1875), and was recognized as an authority on Daniel Webster.

[2] See " Webster and Choate in College," by Herbert D. Foster, published in the *Dartmouth Alumni Magazine* for April and May 1927. These two articles are a mine of interesting information regarding Webster's college days. The Webster Cottage formerly occupied the southwest corner of North Main Street and Webster Avenue, but has lately, in the peripatetic fashion of so many Hanover dwellings, been moved to a new site across the street. There is a charming article in the *Dartmouth Alumni Magazine* for January 1929, by Alice Van Leer Carrick, illustrated with excellent photographs of the old house in the process of removal. Mrs. Carrick, a well-known author and antiquarian, has made the place famous under the name of " Next-to-Nothing House."

[3] National Edition, XVII, 84.

John Wheelock's sister; and Mrs. Ripley, then a widow, occupied the house during the period when Webster is said to have roomed there. The problem is entangled with rumor and belated reminiscences.[1]

The expense of education in that day was moderate as compared with that of our time, and undergraduates apparently had no difficulty in securing credit, even with the college authorities. Professor Foster estimated that Webster incurred a total bill of $88.34, which included three years of room rent, four years of tuition, interest, incidentals, and Commencement tax. His room rent averaged $4.09 annually. For twenty-five months Webster made no settlement with Professor Woodward, the Treasurer. In his Junior year, he paid him $18.40, earned by teaching school at six dollars a month, in Salisbury.[2] In view of his later propensities, it is significant to find him borrowing $26.99 from Richard Lang, the village storekeeper, who had a little square shop near where Webster Hall now stands. His account at Lang's, recently brought to light by Professor Foster, shows that he purchased a candlestick (3/4), with snuffers (2/6), ink-powder (9d.), a hundred quill pens, a "Salmbook (4/6)," and "best laced clock'd cotton hose (15/6)," which must have been an improvement on the stockings which he had worn at the tavern. But even allowing for extravagances not disclosed, it is not easy to see how Daniel could have been then a very heavy burden upon his father, except by depriving him of his assistance on the farm.

Although he was growing more robust, he was still thin-faced, with prominent cheek-bones, and storm-tossed eyes "peering out under dark overhanging brows." So swarthy was he in complexion that the Deweys took him for an Indian as he walked down the aisle on the first Sunday in the College Church, and he was soon given the nickname of "Black Dan." He was interested in politics, and enjoyed fishing, swimming,

---

[1] Professor Foster's conclusions are confirmed by the more recent investigations of Professor Leon B. Richardson.

[2] Webster apparently paid all his bills to the college in full before leaving Hanover in 1801, making a final payment of $5.94 on August 24 to balance his account.

riding, and hunting, although not considered a good shot. "The store accounts and letters," says Professor Foster, "reveal a frank, warm-hearted, sunny, lovable boy, fond of books and friends." When Aaron Loveland, his roommate, brought him to his home in Orford, the grandmother in the Loveland household complained because Daniel put his feet upon the soft soapstone around the fireplace and scratched it. "He was sometimes humorous, always companionable and pleasant," wrote one of his acquaintances. But there is evidence also that he was rather awkward in his bearing, and Loveland said that he was not very popular with the class, owing to his being "so independent and assuming." His closest friend, James H. Bingham, had to confess that Webster was "not intimate with many." But in spite of the fact that "he was, and felt himself to be, a king or oracle," he was recognized as the ablest man in college, and even those who disliked his "unbounded self-confidence" were forced to admit that he was distinguished for the extent and readiness of his knowledge and that his obvious ambition was justified by his ability. He seems to have been free from vices. In a day when everybody, including clergymen and the "best people" generally, consumed considerable quantities of alcoholic beverages, Webster bought and drank them in moderation. Although he refers occasionally in his letters to girls of the neighborhood, his philandering was of an innocuous type, and he had no serious love affair. There are indications in his correspondence, however, that he was not forgotten by some of the local belles, even after many months had elapsed.[1]

After his Freshman year, during which he was busy trying to adjust himself to his new surroundings and to make up for the deficiencies in his preparation, Webster had a creditable scholastic record at Dartmouth. As he himself admitted,

[1] There is a letter, dated February 25, 1802, from Hanover, and signed " C.D.," which would indicate that the writer had a fondness for Daniel. It closes: " Do not forget one who thinks of you with the same tender friendship which causes her to go so far from you only with the greatest reluctance but in so doing follows your better judgment. Yours with the truest affection." (From a letter in the collections of the N. H. Historical Society.)

WHERE WEBSTER ROOMED AS A STUDENT, HANOVER,
NEW HAMPSHIRE

WHERE WEBSTER RECORDED DEEDS, FRYEBURG, MAINE

there were others who read more than he did, but he mastered whatever books he took up.   He once said to Jacob McGaw : —

So much as I read I made my own.   When a half hour or an hour, at most, had elapsed, I closed my book, and thought over what I had read.   If there was anything peculiarly interesting or striking in the passage, I endeavored to recall it, and lay it up in my memory, and commonly could effect my object.   Then if, in debate or conversation afterward, any subject came up on which I had read something, I could talk very easily as far as I had read, and then I was very careful to stop.   Thus greater credit was given me for extensive and accurate knowledge than I really possessed.[1]

Webster evidently possessed to a high degree that faculty of mental concentration which is so often found in men of great genius.   The charge that he was indolent does not seem to be substantiated by the evidence.   "My life was not an idle one," he once broke out.   "What fools they must be to suppose that anybody could succeed in college or public life without study!"[2]   Shurtleff, his fellow student and tutor, wrote of him, "Mr. Webster was remarkable for his steady habits, his intense application to study, and his punctual attendance upon the required exercises."   He rose very early, sat in chapel at daybreak, and often read far into the night.[3]   There were fields in which his scholarship was decidedly deficient.   He once told George Ticknor that, while he was better informed in history and English than any of his class, and was good in composition, he was not strong in Greek and mathematics. He said shortly before his death, "Would that I had pursued my Greek till I could read and understand Demosthenes in his own language!"   But Webster had the gift of making the most of his knowledge, and later when Latin literature was the

---

[1] National Edition, XVII, 51.

[2] *Webster Centennial Proceedings*, p. 35.

[3] When Professor Sanborn once said to him at his own table in Franklin, " It is commonly reported that you did not study much in college," Webster burst out: " I studied and read more than all the rest of my class, if they had all been made into one man.   And I was as much above them all then as I am now ! "   See *Webster Centennial Proceedings*, p. 35.   Webster's classmate, Hotchkiss, wrote, February 25, 1853: " Webster was never an idle student, as some persons falsely and erroneously believe." (National Edition, XVII, 66.)

topic of conversation he held his own with Rufus Choate and Caleb Cushing, two of the most learned men of his generation. He did a good deal of dreaming, and visions of a brilliant future flitted across his mind.

The curriculum which Webster pursued may be examined in the "Laws to be observed by the members of Dartmouth College," enacted by the Trustees on February 9, 1796. As a Sophomore, he continued his Latin and Greek, reading Cicero's *De Oratore* and a collection called *Græca Majora*, but he also studied algebra and geometry (subjects now usually covered in the preparatory school), together with geography and exercises in logic, composition, and speaking. In his Junior year, Latin and Greek were still prescribed, but the course was broadened by the addition of Paley's *Political Philosophy* (first published in England in 1785), the sixth book of which was devoted to political science, a subject peculiarly fascinating to Webster. The Senior work included "Metaphysics, Theology, and Natural Law," some of the books assigned being Locke's famous treatise *On Human Understanding*, Edwards *On the Will*, Stewart's *Philosophy of the Mind*, and Burlamaqui's popular *Principles of Natural Law* (published in Geneva in 1747 and republished in Boston in 1792), which Webster seems to have reread frequently. This curriculum emphasized, besides the Greek and Roman classics, the basic elements of philosophy, theology, and law, and particularly the writing and speaking of our native tongue. It will be observed that there was very little training in scientific methods, and no instruction in the modern languages.

Although Webster did not receive the highest grades in his class, he was not far from the top. He was elected on June 5, 1800, while he was a Junior, to the honorary scholarship society of Phi Beta Kappa, of which twelve out of his class of thirty were members; and some of the extant records of the Dartmouth Chapter are in his handwriting as Secretary. When the time came for Commencement appointments, the faculty could not assign him the Latin Salutatory, for that was automatically given to the foremost scholar, Thomas A.

Merrill, later a clergyman for many years in Middlebury, Vermont. The English Valedictory had usually been awarded by vote of the class, but a feud between the two literary societies — the Social Friends and the United Fraternity — prevented a choice; whereupon the faculty, exercising their authority, ignored Webster — who was the candidate of the United Fraternity — and appointed Caleb Tenney, afterwards a minister at Wethersfield, Connecticut. Webster was offered as consolation either a poem or an oration in English, but, disgruntled at not receiving the English Valedictory, requested to be excused from appearing on the Commencement platform.[1] As a consequence, that member of the graduating class who was later to shed the most lustre upon the college had no part in the programme on August 27, 1801. The story that, in a fit of petulance, he tore up his diploma, crying, "My industry may make me a great man, but this miserable parchment can not!" was told by Charles Lanman, and sponsored by the authority of Theodore Parker; but it was never sanctioned by Webster and is entirely mythical.[2]

A few extant specimens of Webster's composition at this period show how far he had progressed as an author. His earliest attempt at poetry of which we have any knowledge is a passage in couplets sent on December 20, 1798, to his friend, George Herbert,[3] in which "heart" rhymes somewhat loosely with "Clark," and "Time" with "thine." It was his custom to enclose verses in letters to his classmates, but few of them are above mediocrity. Webster was almost devoid of the lyrical and imaginative quality without which such *jeux d'esprit* are of slight value, and he did not then, or later, have any of the gracefulness of phrasing which frequently serves as a substitute for inspiration. In his Junior year he earned part

---

[1] Webster told Rufus Choate that " no disappointment of his whole life ever affected him more keenly." (Parker, *Reminiscences of Rufus Choate*, p. 270.)

[2] The evidence on this subject is discussed with clearness and thoroughness in Professor Richardson's Address, *Webster Centennial Proceedings*, pp. 50–52.

[3] George Herbert (1778–1820), who graduated a year before Webster, became a lawyer in Ellsworth, Maine. Later he was pitifully impecunious and wrote Webster several begging letters, to which the latter responded with characteristic generosity.

of his board at the college by contributing under the pseudonym of "Icarus" to the village newspaper, the *Dartmouth Gazette,* which had been started in August 1799 by Moses Davis, a young printer from Concord.[1] Webster's articles included essays on "Hope,"[2] on "Charity," and on "Fear," poems on "Winter" and on "Spring" (both in blank verse), a metrical epistle on Jefferson's candidacy for the Presidency, and some miscellaneous discussions of contemporary affairs exhibiting a strong Federal bias. In addition to this material, we have also one of his college themes, written on December 15, 1800, and presenting, in about five hundred words, an argument for the acquisition of Florida by the United States. There is a tradition that he wrote a drama which was acted on the commencement stage in his Junior year, but no evidence regarding it can be discovered.

It was in debating and public speaking that Webster was most conspicuous at Dartmouth. The bashfulness and nervous apprehension which had so embarrassed him at Exeter had now vanished, and he was entirely at ease, even before large audiences. The rivalry between the two debating societies — the Social Friends (founded in 1782) and the United Fraternity (founded in 1786) — was intense and stimulating. Webster, who joined the United Fraternity on November 7, 1797, soon became its most active member, holding in succession several honors, beginning with "Inspector of Books" (August 12, 1798), and advancing through the offices of

---

[1] The earliest letter of Webster's which has been preserved was written on August 27, 1799, to Moses Davis, submitting a manuscript and offering himself as a weekly contributor to the *Dartmouth Gazette* (National Edition, XVI, 3). Webster also contributed to a local periodical called the *Literary Tablet,* under the signature of "Monos," but all copies of that magazine have been lost. Manuscript copies of many of Webster's writings at this period are preserved in the archives of the New Hampshire Historical Society in Concord, and there are others in the Dartmouth College Library (see the *Boston Herald,* November 4, 1907).

[2] This, Webster's first contribution to the *Gazette,* was dated August 27, 1799. Beginning as prose, it changed later to blank verse, with opening lines as follows: —

Upborne on Hope's elastic wings, the soul
Scans the dark prospect of futurity,
Opes distant, pleasing objects to the mind
And keeps still burning emulation's flame.

"Librarian," "Orator," and "Vice-President" to that of President (November 25, 1800). The subjects of the weekly debates — in which Webster frequently participated — ranged over a wide field, including such questions as "Are great riches conducive to happiness?" "Ought separate schools to be provided for the education of the different sexes?" and "Does eloquence tend to the investigation of the truth?" [1] We are told that, by the close of his Junior year, "Black Dan" was accounted the best writer and speaker in college. "The powers of his mind," declared one of his friends, "were remarkably displayed by the compass and force of his arguments in extemporaneous debate." [2] His classmate, the Reverend Elihu Smith, spoke of one characteristic which Webster displayed throughout his career: —

In his movements, he was rather slow and deliberate, except when his feelings were aroused; then, his whole soul would kindle into a flame. I recollect that he used to commence speaking rather monotonously and without much excitement, but would always rise, with the importance of the subject, till every eye was fixed upon him. [3]

The testimony as to his effectiveness as a debater is virtually unanimous. "We used to listen to him," wrote the Honorable Henry Hubbard, "with the deepest interest and respect, and no one thought of equalling the vigor and glow of his eloquence." [4] Even with members of the faculty he did not hesitate to express his own views, and they were forced to acknowledge his talents. Professor Woodward, in predicting a brilliant future for young Webster, said, "That man's

[1] For a fuller treatment of the policies and procedure of the two societies, see Professor Charles F. Richardson's address on " Mr. Webster's College Life " in the *Webster Centennial Proceedings* and Professor Herbert D. Foster's article in the *Dartmouth Alumni Magazine* for April 1927, pp. 517–20.

[2] Letter of the Reverend Brown Emerson to Professor Sanborn, November 19, 1852 (National Edition, XVII, 52).

[3] National Edition, XVII, 46. Dr. Smith recalled that Webster was accustomed to arrange his thoughts in his mind in his room or on private walks, and put them on paper just before the exercise was called for.

[4] *Ibid.*, p. 47. Henry Hubbard (1784–1857), who graduated from Dartmouth in 1803, was later United States Senator (1835–41) and Governor of New Hampshire, and his judgment can be relied upon.

victory is certain who reaches the heart through the medium of the understanding. He gained me by combating my opinions, for I often attacked him merely to try his strength." [1]

The citizens of Hanover asked Webster to deliver the Independence Day Oration in that village in 1800, when he was only a Junior and in his nineteenth year. The *Dartmouth Gazette*, in its account, said that "the students first formed a procession at the college and moved to the President's house, where they were joined by the officers of the college, and immediately after by a respectable number of the neighboring citizens." The oration itself was delivered in the meeting-house, and the *Gazette* declared that, though composed on very short notice, it "would have done honor to gray-headed patriotism, and crowned with new laurels the most celebrated orators of our country." It was published "by request of the subscribers" in a small pamphlet, and is worth examination as the first of a long series of occasional addresses. It must be judged with his youth and lack of experience always in mind; but it will not suffer by comparison with most of the Fourth of July orations delivered to-day in small towns of the United States. The biographers who have condemned it because of its floridity and bombast would have done well to remember, not only that Webster was not yet of voting age, but also that the trend of the times was towards an exuberant nationalism and a highly ornamental phraseology. It would have been astounding if the Dartmouth undergraduate, with all his native genius, had not been affected by the smugness and boastfulness of his generation.

Considering the period and the occasion, it was natural that the speech should denounce Great Britain and glorify the United States. The orator referred to England as "imperious Britain" and "haughty Albion," and, in defiance of natural history, announced : —

America, manfully springing from the torturing fangs of the British lion, now rises majestic in the pride of her sovereignty, and bids her eagle elevate his wings.

[1] Knapp, *Life of Webster*, pp. 9–10.

With undisguised satisfaction, he contrasted the peace which our country was enjoying with the sufferings of continental Europe, then being overrun by Napoleon: —

We can now sit down beneath the shadow of the olive, while her cities blaze, her streams run purple with blood, and her fields glitter, a forest of bayonets.

Even in the pursuit and dissemination of education, he claimed superiority for America: —

Yale, Providence, and Harvard now grace our land; and Dartmouth, towering majestic above the groves which encircle her, now inscribes her glory on the registers of fame! Oxford and Cambridge, those oriental stars of literature, shall now be lost, while the bright sun of American science displays his broad circumference in uneclipsed radiance.

Like most of his countrymen in 1800, he was quite ready to defy the world, and, if necessary, to fight France as well as England: —

But Columbia stoops not to tyrants; her sons will never cringe to France; neither a supercilious, five-headed Directory, nor the gasconading Pilgrim of Egypt will ever dictate terms to sovereign America.

Despite its noisy provincialism and inflated style, this Hanover oration is significant in the emphasis which the youthful Webster lays on the need of a truly national spirit and of a staunch fidelity to the principles of the Federal Constitution. Like most of the faculty and the undergraduates, he was strongly Federalist in his political beliefs, and he was a member of a "Federal Club" which had been formed in the student body.[1] In speaking of the Constitution, he used a sentence which perhaps first publicly expressed the veneration for it which was later to mark him as a statesman: —

But, in the adoption of our present system of jurisprudence, we see the powers necessary for the government voluntarily springing from

[1] See the letter from Mrs. George Herbert, March 16, 1856, printed in National Edition, XVII, 74, in which she speaks of a " Constitution of the Federal Club," with several signatures appended, among which was that of Webster, and adds, " These were doubtless intimate friends and choice spirits, of that early period of life; and probably not one of them now survives."

the people, their only proper origin, and directed to the public good, their only proper object.

This has much of the tone of Daniel Webster at his finest, and would have fitted perfectly into the *Reply to Hayne*. The dominating theme of the oration was what Lodge called "the necessity and the nobility of the union of the States," and this, in varying tones and degrees of emphasis, was Webster's text from youth to age.

Another oration of this period was the funeral eulogy delivered in honor of one of his classmates, Ephraim Simonds, who died at Hanover on June 18, 1801, at the age of twenty-six. It is difficult, in such a production, to avoid emotional exaggeration, and Webster yielded to the temptation. He said, for instance, in one paragraph : —

Simonds shall never be forgotten. The future child of Dartmouth, as he treads o'er the mansions of the dead, with his hand on his bosom shall point, "There lies Simonds !" and however careless of his eternal being, however immersed in dissipation or frozen in apathy, he shall check for a moment the tide of mirth, and while an involuntary tear starts in his eye, shall read

Hic jacet, quem religio et scientia condecoraverunt.

Simonds's monument, set up by the United Fraternity beneath the noble pines in the Hanover Burying Ground, still stands, bearing some verses probably composed by Webster : —

Science, religion, in our Simonds shone,
And all the manly virtues were his own.
With anguished hearts we mourn his early doom,
And pay affection's tribute at his tomb.

In August, the spot is charming, and the visitor is sure to look with curiosity at the row of headstones marking the graves of dead Dartmouth students. But Simonds's slaty memorial has begun to crumble, and the letters of the inscription are almost indecipherable. Even if they could easily be read, it is doubtful whether any "child of Dartmouth" to-day knows or cares what they mean. Webster mouthed sonorous phrases and culled skillfully the flowers of rhetoric. The feeling which he displayed was genuine.   But the world would have lost nothing if the eulogy had been forgotten and its words had died upon the air.[1]

Although Webster, as we have explained, took no part in the Commencement exercises of 1801, he did deliver during that week an oration before the United Fraternity, which was later published from a manuscript copy which, by vote of the members, had been deposited in the society archives.[2]   The subject was "The Influence and Instability of Opinion" — by which he meant "Public Opinion," or the *Vox Populi*, which he did not believe to be identical with the *Vox Dei*.   It was, like so many Federalist utterances of the early nineteenth century, an attack on the theories of that dangerous Democrat, Thomas Jefferson.   After expatiating on the pernicious effects of public opinion in the fields of literature, science, religion, and politics, Webster concluded that the truly great man was he who could stand firm "amidst the turmoil of passion and prejudice, amidst the conflict of the winds and waters of party and opinion."   He named Locke, Newton, and Washington as men who possessed this quality of internal greatness, and said, in conclusion : —

Let our sentiments be immovable by any other powers than truth and conviction; and let neither tergiversation nor seduction attach us to the systems of those opinionated visionaries who mistake the fantastic dreams of their own minds for the oracles of philosophy.

Rufus Choate, in reading this production, was struck by its "copiousness, judgment, and enthusiasm," and the sentence just quoted is, in its vocabulary, remarkable for a young man still under twenty.

[1] When George Ticknor, in 1820, told Webster of finding a copy of the *Oration on Simonds*, as it was printed in pamphlet form, Webster seemed disturbed, and said: " I thought till lately that, as only a few copies of it were printed, they must all have been destroyed long ago; but, the other day, Bean, who was in college with me, told me he had one.   It flashed through my mind that it must have been the last copy in the world, and that if he had it in his pocket it would be worth while to kill him, to destroy it from the face of the earth.   So I recommend you not to bring your copy where I am."

[2] See the *New York Herald*, August 16, 1853.

Webster himself had later only regret for these early performances and spoke of them disparagingly.[1] In commenting upon them, he once said, with clear discernment: —

I had not then learned that all true power in writing is in the idea, not in the style, an error into which the *Ars Rhetorica*, as it is usually taught, may easily lead stronger heads than mine.[2]

But those who have taken the pains to read these orations with care will not be disposed to be too severe upon them. With all their defects, they show Webster's later style in the making: the effective use of short and crisp sentences following balanced periods; the fondness for adjectives, verbs, and nouns in series of three, such as "For us they fought, for us they bled, for us they conquered"; the mingling of polysyllabic Latin derivatives with briefer Anglo-Saxon words; and the complete clarity of utterance, even in the discussion of abstruse topics. Compared with the Plymouth Oration of 1820, these youthful discourses seem verbose and bombastic, but they are fully as mature as similar efforts of other collegians, such as Edward Everett and Charles Sumner, who afterwards developed into great orators.

It is a pity that we know so little about Webster's inner life at Dartmouth. Most of the stereotyped reminiscences of his friends seem to indicate that he was something of a prodigy and prig. But here and there in the midst of the formal letters of himself and his coterie of friends we get a touch of humanity. Professor Sanborn tells us that for two years he garbed himself in homespun like the other farmers' sons, but that, after the opening of the Junior year, he became more fastidious in his attire and dressed rather better than the average undergraduate.

[1] Webster, in conversation with Professor C. C. Felton, said that Joseph Dennie, the journalist, wrote a review of the Hanover Oration, which was printed " in a literary paper which he then edited " — presumably the *United States Gazette*, of which Dennie had charge in 1800. Webster went on: " He praised parts of the oration as vigorous and eloquent; but other parts he criticised severely, and said they were mere *emptinesses*. I thought his criticism was just; and I resolved that whatever else should be said of my style, from that time forth there should be no *emptiness* in it." (National Edition, XIII, 582, reprinted from the *American Whig Review*, December 1852.)

[2] Autobiography, National Edition, XVII, 11.

We are told that he and his group of friends, like the early Christians, "had all things common," and that the first one to rise in the morning clothed himself in the best that the apartments could offer, the last one out of bed being the one to suffer most.[1] There is a story of his carrying off with him on his vacation a new and glossy beaver belonging to his chum, Benjamin Clark, leaving in its stead a battered old felt hat, which Clark, lacking other headgear, had to wear for some weeks.[2]

There were, of course, social events in the village of Hanover, and the place probably seemed very gay to the boy who had been brought up in the rural simplicity of Salisbury Lower Village. Many of his classmates and friends were initiated into the Masonic order, but neither he nor Ezekiel ever joined a lodge. Some allusions in his letters indicate that he had learned to dance and was no recluse. One of his friends remembered that he joined in games of ball and other physical exercises,[3] but he was certainly no athlete. During the winter, like many of his impecunious college mates, he became a schoolmaster. In the winter of 1797–98 he taught at the house of his Uncle William, for four dollars a month, and during the ensuing winter he was engaged at the schoolhouse at Shaw's Corner, near his birthplace, for six dollars a month, the period of employment being ordinarily three months. Writing from Salisbury, on February 5, 1800, he tells Bingham that he has fifty pupils, including "five English grammarians, I mean students in English, and two Latin scholars." [4] Special allowances were made for cases like his, and he had no difficulty in keeping up with his class.

Chase, in his *History of Dartmouth College and Hanover, N. H.*, says that the moral tone of the college deteriorated from 1790 to 1800, and that there was, at the close of the century, a "wave of irreligion." Only a single member of the class of 1799, we are told, was publicly known as a professing Christian. This may well have been true, but there is nothing to show

---

[1] National Edition, XVII, 76.   [2] *Ibid.*
[3] *Ibid.*, p. 66, Letter from Hotchkiss.   [4] *Ibid.*, p. 79.

that this alleged laxity had any effect on Webster, and it is worth noting that eight of the thirty members of his graduating class became clergymen. Certainly the existing correspondence between Webster and his friends offers no evidence of either dissipation or what used to be called with horror "infidelity."

Even after graduation, Webster kept in touch with Dartmouth and his friends in Hanover. He frequently returned to it at Commencement and made sentimental journeys to his former haunts. The story of how, in the Dartmouth College Case, he saved his Alma Mater from dissolution will be the theme of a later chapter. . . . The college, on her part, has rejoiced to do him honor. In 1882, a Daniel Webster Professorship of Latin was founded. In 1901, there was an impressive celebration at Hanover, with addresses by President William Jewett Tucker, Samuel W. McCall, Frank S. Black, George F. Hoar, and Chief Justice Melville W. Fuller, commemorating the centennial of Webster's graduation. At this time the corner stone of Webster Hall, a beautiful modern auditorium in brick and granite, was laid by Samuel Appleton, Esquire, the only living grandson of Daniel Webster. One may visit the house where he once lived and study his portraits hanging on the walls and walk a street which bears his name. Indeed, it is of Daniel Webster that every intelligent visitor thinks first when he stops at Hanover and strolls about among the college buildings.

During Webster's four years at Dartmouth, he made steady progress towards maturity. Although mathematics aroused his dislike and Greek did not stir his interest, he became something of a scholar in Latin, and extended his acquaintance with English literature, modern history, and philosophy. His most noticeable advancement intellectually, however, had come from his wide reading in history and politics. This mental growth produced a keen interest in governmental affairs, both in Europe and in the United States, and some of his comments on the contemporary situation indicate that he was fascinated by what was going on. In the midst of the intense party antagonism which preceded the election of 1800, Webster, appalled by the iniquities of the Jeffersonians, wrote his friend, Bingham, that he feared "intestine feuds" and could see in his imagination the time "when the banner of civil war shall be unfurled" and when "American blood shall be made to flow in rivers, by American swords." [1] Already, moreover, he was a firm believer in a strong central government, and he burst out, in the letter just quoted, "Heaven grant that the bonds of our federal union may be strengthened . . . that traitors may be abashed, and that the stars and stripes of United Columbia may wave triumphant." This is the sort of language with which Daniel Webster was later to make his countrymen familiar.

Webster had also developed amazingly in courage and self-confidence. The timid, uncouth rustic who had been so bewildered at Exeter had now acquired poise and an assurance which sometimes could not be differentiated from conceit. He had had an opportunity of measuring himself in competition with other youths of the same age; he had suddenly exhibited that facility and forcefulness in speaking which were to be so large a part of his equipment in statesmanship; and he had discovered that he had a gift for leading others. He was moody, sometimes lethargic, but never negligible. As other important assets, he had displayed a tenacious memory, a remarkable capacity for intellectual concentration, and a talent for writing. His health, meanwhile, had improved until he was a fairly robust man. Those who knew Webster at Dartmouth — both undergraduates and teachers — were impressed by his potentialities and did not hesitate to predict his future eminence, although few could have prognosticated the heights which he would reach.

[1] National Edition, XVII, 79. A portion of this interesting letter was later printed as a contribution to the *Dartmouth Gazette*.

III

MATURING YEARS

I cannot control my fortune: I must follow wherever circumstances lead.
— WEBSTER, *Letter to Bingham, October 6, 1802*

I really often despaired. I thought I never could make myself a lawyer and was almost going back to the business of school teaching.
— WEBSTER, *Autobiography*

THE seven years following Webster's graduation from Dartmouth were a probationary period during which he was serving his apprenticeship to the law. To this profession, which he chose without enthusiasm and with some misgivings as to his qualifications, he was not absolutely devoted, and he had hours of indecision when he felt that he had embarked on the wrong career.[1] There was, however, no escape in any other direction. Meanwhile, with crucial problems to settle and routine duties to fulfill, he wisely made the most of his spare time by reading as widely as possible. Deprived of the personal stimulus of teachers and of college competition, he generated his own energy, storing up a fund of knowledge, both legal and literary, which later was to be very serviceable to him.

While Daniel had been at Hanover, Ezekiel, one year and two months older, had been shackled to the farm as his father's most dependable helper. The two brothers, unusually sympathetic in their tastes and opinions, had been playmates during their childhood. But Ezekiel, although more robust than

---

[1] Webster had been one of eighteen men in his class to register in the Medical School during his Junior year, and this has led certain people to believe that he actually intended at one time to become a physician. As a matter of fact, he, like the others, did this merely so that he might take courses in natural science which the Medical School offered in its curriculum. There is no evidence whatever that Webster ever thought seriously of medicine as a career. See the *Dartmouth Alumni Magazine*, May 1927, p. 606, and April 1929, p. 383.

Daniel, had grown less rapidly to mental maturity and did not seem to have his brother's aptitude for books. Captain Webster's older sons were all established in life, and there was no one to take care of him, his wife, and the two unmarried daughters, unless Ezekiel carried on the farm work. It was an exigency which often arose in rural New England, and in this case Ezekiel seemed likely to be the unfortunate victim.

It was the boys themselves who took the situation into their own hands. Ezekiel had had his ambition kindled by Daniel's success, and the two invariably talked matters over whenever the latter was home for his vacations. The crisis came in May 1799, when the brothers, lying side by side on their pallet at the tavern, held an all-night conference, as a consequence of which they resolved to ask their father to let Ezekiel go first to school and then to college. It was the plausible Daniel, of course, who advanced the arguments, offering on his part to earn money by teaching and to take more than four years, if necessary, to secure his Dartmouth diploma. Captain Webster's reply, which must have required some courage, was recorded in Daniel's Autobiography as follows: —

He said at once he lived but for his children; that he had but little, and on that little he put no value, except so far as it might be useful to them. That to carry us both through college would take all he was worth; that for himself he was willing to run the risk, but that this was a serious matter to our mother and two unmarried sisters; that we must settle the matter with them, and if their consent was obtained, he would trust to Providence, and get along as well as he could.[1]

A family council was called, at which the mother, proud of Daniel's unselfishness and Ezekiel's ambition, is reported to have said: —

I have lived long in the world and have been happy in my children. If Daniel and Ezekiel will promise to take care of me in my old age, I will consent to the sale of all our property, at once, and they may enjoy the benefit of what remains after our debts are paid.[2]

[1] National Edition, XVII, 12.   [2] *Ibid.*, p. 33.

A feasible plan was at once outlined. Captain Webster exchanged houses with his son-in-law, William Haddock, leaving the tavern and going to live in the Elms House, where he resided for the remainder of his life. Ezekiel was entered immediately in Salisbury Academy, and completed his preparation for college by spending nine months under Dr. Wood, at Boscawen, as Daniel had done before him. In the spring of 1801, he matriculated at Dartmouth only a few months before Daniel graduated. Despite the deficiencies of his early education, Ezekiel claimed and held the position of leading scholar of his class.

The praiseworthy sacrifice which the parents underwent for their children was matched by the tenderness with which the two boys later cared for their mother and father. The promise of future support was faithfully kept, and Daniel's interposition in his brother's behalf was one of the most unselfish acts ever recorded to a man's credit. Abigail and Ebenezer Webster's confidence was rewarded by the devotion of their sons and justified by their accomplishments in public life.

The young Dartmouth alumnus, fresh from his oratorical triumphs, now came back to Salisbury Lower Village to live with his parents at The Elms. There, not very ardently, he began the study of law with his patron, Thomas W. Thompson, whose office was diagonally to the northeast across the old highway.[1] In those days, more than 90 per cent of Dartmouth's graduates entered one of the four professions — law, medicine, teaching, or the ministry. Daniel had already tried teaching, and did not fancy it as a career. He was not fitted by temperament to become either a physician or a clergyman. By a process of elimination, therefore, he turned towards the law. He wrote in the autumn to a friend, "I fell into a law office, pretty much by casualty, after Commencement, where I am at present."[2] His letters of the period

[1] Thompson's office was a small wooden building, one story in height, containing two rooms and a narrow hall — the front room being used for general business and the back room for study and private conferences with clients. It was adjacent to Thompson's house, which could be reached from a side door.

[2] Letter to Nathaniel Coffin, October 3, 1801 (National Edition, XVII, 94).

indicate that he was often dissatisfied, apathetic, and despondent, and that he was much disturbed by his father's financial
difficulties.[1]

It was a period when Webster's avid mind was roving from
one project to another. He took some part in local affairs;
indeed, he once said: "My first speech after I left college
was in favor of what was then regarded as a great and almost
impracticable internal improvement, to wit, the making of a
smooth, though hilly road from Connecticut River, opposite
the mouth of the White River, to the Merrimack River at the
mouth of the Contoocook." [2] He pored restlessly over the
masterpieces of Vattel, Burlamaqui, Robertson, and Montes-
quieu; he studied Blackstone assiduously, though without
much interest; and, when ennui assailed him, he turned to
fiction and poetry. That he gained some practical legal experience is indicated by his casual remark, "I have made some
few writs, and am now about to bring an action for trespass
for breaking a violin." [3] There is a dubious tradition that his
first case concerned a bankrupt tradesman in New Chester.
Thompson sent Webster, with the Sheriff, to seize the property,
but they found the establishment closed. Webster then picked
up a log of wood and hurled it against the door, demolishing
the panels, but did not walk inside, for that would have been
the offense of "breaking and entering." The Sheriff, stepping
across the threshold, then served the attachment.[4]

Some of his letters show him in a whimsical mood as he
meditated on the charms of the young ladies from whose society
he was cut off. "My heart always overflows with affection

[1] See his letters to Bingham, National Edition, XVII, 92–94 and 98–99. James
Hervey Bingham (1781–1859), whom Webster addressed as " My best friend " and
" Jemmy," became an attorney in Lempster, New Hampshire, from which village he
frequently wrote to Webster. He served creditably in the Legislature as Representative and Senator and enjoyed an excellent reputation. In 1847, through Webster's
good offices, he was appointed a clerk in the Department of State, and he died in Washington. With no one of his college mates was Webster on more intimate terms.

[2] National Edition, IV, 108. The road was later the Fourth New Hampshire Turn-
pike. Webster, holding the proxies of several absent subscribers, attended the first
meeting of the proprietors in 1801, at Andover, New Hampshire.

[3] Letter to Bingham, October 26, 1801 (National Edition, XVII, 96).

[4] Coffin, *History of Boscawen*, p. 444.

for the sex," he wrote to Bingham.[1]   When he was bored with
law's aridities, he strolled into the woods to shoot partridges
or squirrels, or sauntered with a fishing rod along one of the
Salisbury brooks.   But he was habitually unsettled, and complained, "I never was half so much dispirited as now.   Though
I make myself easy as I can, yet I am really very unpleas-
antly circumstanced." [2]

In January 1802 the precarious financial affairs of the
Websters reached a crisis — a contingency which Daniel had
foretold.   Money was indispensable, and he was pledged to
provide it.   Through a college friend, Samuel A. Bradley,[3]
he had been offered a teaching position at Fryeburg, Maine,
then a part of Massachusetts, and he finally engaged to go for
six months, at a salary of $350 a year.   After his experience
as a pedagogue in Salisbury, he had no misgivings as to his
qualifications, and he set out confidently for his destination,
not far from the New Hampshire border, at the foot of the
White Mountains.   The snow must have been deep and the
thermometer low when Daniel Webster arrived in Fryeburg,
but he was glad to have a change from the monotony of The
Elms, and, after he had sold his horse, he settled down gladly
to his new responsibilities.

Fryeburg, which has been agreeably described under the
name of Equity in the opening paragraphs of William Dean
Howells's *A Modern Instance*, is one of the most charming of
New England villages.[4]   Once a favorite hunting ground of
the formidable Pequawket Indians, it is only a mile from
Lovewell's Pond, where, in 1725, a company of colonial scouts
ambushed by the redskins defended themselves in one of the
bloodiest conflicts of pioneer days.   The settlement itself lies
along a broad, elm-bordered avenue, at the eastern end of which

---

[1] National Edition, XVII, 101.   [2] *Ibid.*, p. 97.

[3] Samuel Ayer Bradley (1774–1844), born in Concord, New Hampshire, had graduated from Dartmouth in 1799, and had become an attorney in Fryeburg, where he spent
the remainder of his life.

[4] For a description of Fryeburg and for poems dealing with it, see *The Illustrated
Fryeburg Memorial*, a small pamphlet published in 1882.   The town was named after
Chaplain Jonathan Frye, who died heroically in the battle at Lovewell's Pond.

rises like a sentinel the Jockey Cap, an odd-shaped granite mound forming a conspicuous landmark. To the north in a long sweep are the Pequawket mountains, and, farther off to the west, is Chocorua Peak, the monarch of the Sandwich range. From any point in the village the residents can lift up their eyes to the hills. The Saco River, more winding than the Meander, flows back and forth across the valley, crossed here and there by picturesque covered bridges. Fryeburg was a centre for farmers and lumbermen, and its stately residences, shut off by white fences from the street, made it seem a prosperous community.

Fryeburg Academy occupied an insignificant, square, one-storied building, erected in 1791, at the foot of Pine Hill, near the corner of Main Street and the East Conway road. Here it was that Master Webster taught the youth and maids of the village. Despite his inexperience, he was "always dignified in deportment," and "usually serious, but often facetious and pleasant."[1] The solemn manner in which he opened and closed the sessions with extemporaneous prayer made a lasting impression on several of his pupils. Naturally his pedagogical duties occupied most of his days, and he attended to them conscientiously, winning "the universal respect of both scholars and villagers."

Webster found in Fryeburg another friend, James McGaw, who had graduated from Dartmouth in 1797 and had afterwards read law in Thompson's office at Salisbury. The two were inseparable, and McGaw, who had some facility of expression, left a vivid description of Webster at twenty: —

Neither the physical nor intellectual expression of his countenance had become so striking as in subsequent life. His cheeks were thin and his cheek bones prominent. There was nothing especially noticeable about him then except his full, steady, large, and searching eyes. Nobody could see those eyes and ever forget their appearance or him who possessed them.[2]

When Charles Lanman asked him about his appearance at

[1] Samuel Osgood to Professor Sanborn (National Edition, XVII, 58).
[2] National Edition, XVII, 50.

that period, Webster replied, "Long, slender, pale, and all eyes; indeed, I went by the name of *all eyes* the country round." [1] He was still very slight in figure, a mere stripling weighing less than one hundred and twenty pounds.

Much to his satisfaction, he was able to add to his income by outside work. He and McGaw boarded and roomed with James R. Osgood, the Register of Deeds for Oxford County, who employed Webster to copy in longhand the documents which came under his jurisdiction, at the rate of one shilling and sixpence each.[2] Although it was a tedious task, Webster toiled at it faithfully during the winter months. In writing about his labors, he said: —

Four evenings in a week earned two dollars; and two dollars a week paid my board. This appeared to me to be a very thriving condition; for my three hundred and fifty dollars salary as a school-master was thus going on, without abatement or deduction for *vivres*.[3]

Almost half a century later, in 1851, when Webster was serving his second term as Secretary of State, he spent some hours in Fryeburg, where he hunted out the volumes of deeds in his own handwriting, still neat and legible, as indeed his chirography always was; and he declared, as he gazed at the yellow pages, that the ache was not yet out of his fingers. But he made no complaint in 1802, for he was helping his brother; and in May, during his spring vacation, he pocketed his first quarter's salary and rode across country to Hanover, where he placed his savings in the hands of "Zeke." [4] In

[1] Lanman, p. 31.

[2] The small brick structure in which Webster did his copying still stands on the south side of the main street, not far from the centre of the village. The curious may find in Vol. II of the bound records of the Commissioner the deeds which he copied.

[3] National Edition, XVII, 13.

[4] George Ticknor, then preparing for Dartmouth, saw Webster in Hanover on this occasion and recalled that the undergraduates were " very proud and very fond of him " and " treated him very caressingly and very very affectionately." Ticknor remembered that Webster at this time " was thin and had not the appearance of being a strong man." He remained in Hanover two or three days, enjoying the company of Ezekiel and the latter's friends, and calling upon the young ladies of the village, and then spent a week with his parents in Salisbury. For Ticknor's account of the visit, see Curtis, I, 51–52. Webster himself described his experiences in a letter to Bingham, May 18, 1802 (National Edition, XVII, 107–10).

his Autobiography, Daniel called this "the first earnings of my life," forgetting his earlier wages as a teacher during his winter absences from Dartmouth.

At Fryeburg, Webster found himself in lively society, surrounded by "men of information and conversable manners," and he did not lack diversion. In a poetical epistle to his friend, Porter, he described his lot as follows: —

> Where Saco rolls, (a name so rough and fierce
> It frights the Muse to bring it into verse,)
> Tied to my school, like cuckold to his wife,
> Whom God knows he'd be rid of, runs my life.
> Six hours to yonder little dome a day,
> The rest to books, to friendship, and to tea;
> And now and then, as varying fancies choose,
> To trifle with young Mary, or the Muse.
> This life, tho' pleasant of its kind, is yet
> Much too inactive, I'm resolved to quit.[1]

He amused himself by scribbling and produced a number of essays and poems which he grouped under the title, *Sports of Pequawket*, but he did not publish them. There were young ladies in Fryeburg who inspired him to be "a little romantic and poetical." "I have seen nearly thirty white muslins trail across a ball room on an evening," he wrote to his friend, Merrill. He did not, however, take either love-making or verse-writing too seriously.

At this period he began to smoke, and there are several references in his letters to his lighting a cigar or drawing comfort from his pipe. He even composed an ode beginning: —

> Come, then, tobacco, new-found friend,
> Come, and thy suppliant attend
> In each dull, lonely hour.[2]

In his account at the Bradley store, the item "Cigars, 9d."

[1] National Edition, XVII, 114.
[2] *Ibid.*, p. 93. In later life, Webster abandoned smoking because of what he thought to be its injurious effect on his throat.

recurs frequently, along with "Raisins, 9d." [1] His favorite outdoor pastime was trout fishing, to which he devoted Wednesday and Saturday afternoons in spring and summer, but always with a copy of Shakespeare in his pocket in case the fish proved unresponsive.

Many years afterwards, Webster wrote that he found in Fryeburg "most of the elements of a happy New England village," and spoke especially of the local clergyman — "a learned, amiable, and excellent minister of the gospel." [2] He continued to be an omnivorous reader, and secured from the local attorney, Judah Dana, permission to use his library. There he browsed, renewing his study of Blackstone, and poring over such works as Adams's *Defense of the American Constitution*, Mosheim's *Ecclesiastical History*, Goldsmith's *History of England*, Williams's *Vermont*, and other historical and political treatises. One of the greatest of American orations, Fisher Ames's speech in 1795 on the Jay Treaty with Great Britain, fell into Webster's hands, and he memorized it, with full approval of its strongly Federalist doctrines. As for *belles-lettres*, McGaw speaks of their reading aloud alternately all of Pope's poetry and the *Tatler* and the *Spectator*, which they procured at the circulating library in the village; and Webster was much struck with the *Pursuits of Literature* — that quaint poem by Mathias, richer in prose annotation than in couplets, but always a boon to bibliophiles.

Webster was complimented by an invitation to deliver the Independence Day Oration, which he spoke in the old Fryeburg Church on July 5, the actual anniversary coming in 1802 on a Sunday. It was a sound exposition of those Federalist principles which he had absorbed at his father's fireside and which labeled him, even in his youth, as a conservative. In one notable paragraph, prophetic of many of his later ad-

---

[1] These items are excerpted from an interesting monograph, *John Adams and Daniel Webster as Schoolmasters* (1903), by Elizabeth Porter Gould. From January 9 to September 3, 1802, Webster ran up a bill of $33.89 at the Bradley store. He paid $24 on account in June, but the balance was not settled until April 29, 1804, when Samuel A. Bradley paid $9.64, doubtless at Webster's request.

[2] National Edition, XVIII, 147.

dresses on the same theme, he stressed the importance of guarding the integrity of our government: —

To the preservation of this Constitution every system of policy should ultimately tend. It should be considered as the sacred and inviolable palladium, ready to wither the hand which would lay hold on it with violence. . . . Whoever does not wish to perpetuate our present form of Government in its purity, is either weak or wicked; he cannot be the friend of his Country. . . . If the Constitution be picked away by piecemeal, it is gone, — and gone as effectively as if some military despot had grasped it at once, trampled it beneath his feet, and scattered its loose leaves in the wild winds. . . . To alter the instrument which ties together five millions of people, on which rests the happiness of ourselves and posterity, is an important and serious business, not to be undertaken without obvious necessity, nor conducted without caution, deliberation, and diffidence.

The young man who spoke these words was already the "Defender of the Constitution," distrustful of change, suspicious of innovation. The oration, we are told, "was greatly admired by the Federal party and much disliked by the Democratic" — a verdict which Webster probably expected. Of perhaps more immediate importance to the orator of the day was the five dollars with which he was presented as an honorarium.

When his six months were over, Webster was urged to remain at Fryeburg, the inducements offered being a salary of five or six hundred dollars, a house of his own, a piece of land to cultivate, and ultimately a remunerative position as Clerk of the Court of Common Pleas.[1] If he had at that time any premonition that he was to become great, he kept it carefully concealed. In discussing his prospects with Bingham, he wrote: —

The talent with which Heaven has intrusted me is small, very small, yet I feel responsible for the use of it, and am not willing to pervert it to purposes reproachful or unjust, nor to hide it, like the slothful servant, in a napkin.[2]

[1] National Edition, XVII, 110.   [2] *Ibid.*, p. 111.

This may have been affectation, but he made statements to his roommate, McGaw, which would indicate that he was entirely sincere in his declaration that he had only "moderate expectations of his eminence in future life." [1]

But teaching school was not his goal. His father and friends were agreed that he ought to continue with the law. Mr. Thompson was ready to accept him again as a student, without charge, and had promised to make him his successor at Salisbury. Captain Webster, moreover, was getting feeble and needed one of his sons close at hand. Accordingly, in September 1802, after Ezekiel had come to Fryeburg for a visit, the two brothers made a short excursion into Maine and then returned together to Salisbury.[2] The mood in which he resumed his accustomed place in Thompson's office is revealed in a sentence in one of his letters : —

To the winds I dismiss those hopes of eminence which ambition inspired and vanity fostered. To be "honest, to be capable, to be faithful" to my client and my conscience, I earnestly hope will be my first endeavor.

For the next year and a half Webster was a fairly assiduous student in Thompson's office, where the prospects of his distinguished success did not seem bright to him or to anybody else in the vicinity. He was planted, it seemed almost irrevocably, in a small rural community, among people whose interests must have appeared very narrow, as compared with even Fryeburg and Hanover. Confessing to Ezekiel that he had no cash to send him, he went on, "We are all here just now in the old way, always behind and lacking; boys digging potatoes with frozen fingers, and girls washing without wood." [3]

---

[1] National Edition, XVII, 51.
[2] Webster revisited Fryeburg in 1806, — at which time he stood godfather to William Pitt Fessenden, — 1831, and 1851. The site of his schoolhouse was purchased, in 1809, by Samuel A. Bradley, who would never allow anyone to build upon it. In 1902, Fryeburg observed the centennial of Webster's residence there with appropriate exercises. Senator George F. Hoar, regretting that he could not be present, wrote, " It lends a dignity to the streets of our town that his feet have been familiar to them."
[3] National Edition, XVII, 123.

As for Ezekiel, he was even worse off, as a letter to Daniel proves : —

Money, Daniel, money. As I was walking down to the office after a letter, I happened to find one cent, which is the only money I have had since the second day after I came on. It is a fact, Dan, that I was called on for a dollar, where I owed it, and borrowed it, and have borrowed it four times since, to pay those I borrowed it of.[1]

There was, indeed, a pitiful lack of ready cash in the Webster family, and allusions in his correspondence indicate that Daniel, forced against his will to apply for loans, had already accumulated debts — small, but beyond his capacity to pay back. Importuned by the unfortunate Ezekiel, with his exhortation, "Whenever you meet, let money be the object of your consultation," and only too well aware of Captain Webster's straitened condition, it is no wonder that Daniel wrote to Bingham : —

This is a cold, poor, comfortless place. If the hill of difficulties be so high we cannot climb over it, yet perhaps we can make a shift to creep around it. At all events it is worth a trial.[2]

No pessimism is so profound as that of the young, and Webster was seldom again so despondent as he was in 1802 and 1803. His gloom was accentuated by occasional minor illnesses. Uncertainty regarding the future kept his mind overwrought, and he could not leave off speculating on the projects which rushed in on his teeming brain. Driven by surging energy and conscious power, he was "cabin'd, cribb'd, confin'd," with no chance of escape from his captivity.

Probably he would have been less disgruntled if he had been more sure that he had chosen the right profession. When he completed Blackstone's *Commentaries*, Thompson prescribed *Coke upon Littleton*, in those days the universal elementary textbook for law students in this country. With this abstruse volume, Webster was soon completely disgusted. He wrote later in his Autobiography : —

[1] National Edition, XVII, 124. [2] *Ibid.*, p. 137.

A boy of twenty, with no previous knowledge of such subjects, cannot understand *Coke*. It is folly to set him upon such an author. There are propositions in *Coke* so abstract, and distinctions so nice, and doctrines embracing so many distinctions and qualifications, that it requires an effort not only of a mature mind, but of a mind both strong and mature, to understand him.[1]

The ancient black-letter edition was not at all inspiring, and Webster would have agreed with Justice Story, who complained of "the intricate, crabbed, and obsolete learning of *Coke upon Littleton*," and with John Quincy Adams, who called it "a very improper book to put into the hands of a student just entering upon the acquisition of the profession." What Webster needed was a practical explanation of such matters as the kinds of writs issued in a suit and the ordinary papers required in legal transactions; instead he was occupied with theoretical questions which could never arise in the experience of a New Hampshire attorney.[2]

Relief came when Webster, prowling through Thompson's library, picked up Espinasse's *Law of Nisi Prius*, in two musty volumes which resembled "a couple of psalm-books." To-day this treatise is virtually obsolete, but Webster, thoroughly bored with Coke, found it to be "plain, easy, and intelligible." Soon he discovered for himself that the most economical way of studying law is "in relation to particular points," by accumulating information around some definite theme or case. Other students since that day have learned through wasteful experience that it is always best to read with some clear purpose in mind.

Webster did not neglect to lighten the heaviness of the law with some general reading. While he was acquiring a knowledge of special pleading through a perusal of Bacon's *Elements* and Saunders's *Reports*, he was completing Hume and Gibbon, as well as other historians, and memorizing whole pages of the Latin classics. Some of his verse translations of Horace's

[1] National Edition, XVII, 14.
[2] For Webster's candid opinion of the system, see Lyman, II, 8–9. See also National Edition, XVII, 129–31.

Odes were printed in New Hampshire newspapers, but have
never been resurrected.

But this young, full-blooded man, hardly out of his teens,
had also his livelier pastimes. The essence of his philosophy
was expressed in a paragraph of a letter written to Bingham : —

It is not he who spends most hours over his books that is the most
successful student. It is impossible to keep the mind on the stretch
forever; it will sometimes relax; and though we may keep our eyes
on our books, it will steal away to easier contemplations, and we may
run over pages without receiving an idea. I know this is the case
with myself, and believe it is with others. The true science of life is
to mingle amusement and business, so as to make the most of time.[1]

We hear, through his letters, of trips to Concord, — where
he "had fine times, singing and dancing, and skipping," — to
Hanover, to Woodstock, Vermont, and to other places nearer
by. He still bantered his friends about the ladies and had
them — or one or two of them — on his own mind. But his
chief recreation was taken by himself, among the hills and along
the streams of Hillsborough County, where he could roam and
meditate undisturbed. In his Autobiography, there is a most
significant passage : —

At this period of my life, I passed a great deal of time alone. . . .
I like to let thoughts go free, and indulge in their excursions. And
when *thinking* is to be done, one must of course be alone. No man
knows *himself* who does not thus, sometimes, keep his own company.[2]

The thoughts of the solitary walker ranged over an extensive field, uncircumscribed by space or time. Often, in depression of spirits, he would rebel against his lot, as he did
in a letter to Merrill : —

Accuracy and diligence are much more necessary to a lawyer, than
great comprehension of mind, or brilliancy of talent. His business
is to refine, define, and split hairs, to look into authorities, and com-
pare cases. A man can never gallop over the fields of law on Pegasus,
nor fly across them on the wings of oratory. If he would stand on

[1] Letter to Bingham, December 23, 1803 (National Edition, XVII, 154).
[2] *Ibid.*, p. 15.

terra firma, he must descend; if he would be a great lawyer, he must first consent to be only a great drudge.[1]

Yet he was still expecting to become a country lawyer and was considering where to settle. After conducting a case at Woodstock, he thought of opening an office in Vermont; and he made inquiries regarding prospects in Washington, in Westmoreland, and in Chesterfield, all of them villages in Cheshire County. He told Bingham that he was looking for a place "where the practice of the bar is fair and honorable,"[2] and intimated that he preferred a location near the Connecticut River. Mr. Thompson, who discerned his protégé's ability, suggested Portsmouth, but Webster wrote, "At present, I do not feel that Portsmouth is the place for me." As spring arrived in 1804, his restlessness increased, and he was eager to get away from too familiar Salisbury. Although he had at least a year more of reading before he could be admitted to the bar, he was convinced that he ought to study for a few months in some other environment. . . . And then, at a moment when he declared that his life was marked with "dark traces and heavy shades," the miraculous happened. An avenue of release was opened up!

As the winter closed in, it was obvious to Daniel and Ezekiel that one of them must earn some money, and it seemed to be the latter's turn. In January 1804, therefore, Daniel went to Boston, — probably his first trip to that city, — found an opening in a school then being conducted by his college friend, Cyrus Perkins,[3] and secured the position for Ezekiel, who, although in his Senior year at Dartmouth, had been teaching at Sanbornton, five miles from The Elms, during the winter. Arrangements having been made with the college authorities, Ezekiel was soon in sole charge of Perkins's small private

---

[1] Letter to Merrill, November 11, 1803 (National Edition, XVII, 151).

[2] *Ibid.*, p. 163.

[3] Cyrus Perkins (1778–1849), born in Middleboro, Massachusetts, graduated from Dartmouth in 1800, as a member of Phi Beta Kappa, and, after some years of teaching, became a physician, later returning to Hanover as Professor of Anatomy and Surgery (1810–19). He was at one time president of the New Hampshire Medical Society.

school on Short Street — since renamed Kingston Street — in Boston. His contract with his predecessor specified that Ezekiel was to receive no money from the students already in attendance until that "quarter" was over; hence his income did not really start until July, and meanwhile he could do nothing for Daniel. He did, however, write him on April 4, 1804, urging him to come to Boston: —

I would have you decamp immediately with all your baggage from Salisbury, and march directly to this place. . . . Consult father, the family, and your friends, and start for Boston immediately after receipt of this letter. Another such opportunity may never occur. Come, and if you don't find everything to your liking, I will carry you back to Salisbury with a chaise and six, and pay you for your time. I must say again, consult father. If he approves, take the patriarchal blessing, and come.[1]

Because the necessary funds were not then forthcoming, Daniel was unable to adopt his brother's suggestion. Furthermore, he was awaiting the outcome of negotiations which seemed likely to gain him an appointment as Clerk of the Court of Common Pleas of Hillsborough County, and he was in a vacillating mood. Fortunately the clerkship evaded him,[2] and he wrote, on June 10: "For cash I have made out. Perhaps in three weeks you may see me in Short Street." [3] It was not, however, until July 17 that he presented himself at Ezekiel's lodgings, confident that the Fates, hitherto malign, were at last to beam upon him.[4]

It soon appeared that the too sanguine Ezekiel was not really in need of an assistant, but was ready to pay Daniel's expenses if the latter could obtain a place in a reputable law office. Whether through carelessness or ignorance, he had brought with him no credentials, and he called unsuccessfully upon two or three well-known firms. Then, with inspired audacity, he went with his college chum, Samuel A. Bradley,

[1] National Edition, XVII, 165.   [2] *Ibid.*, p. 174.   [3] *Ibid.*, p. 173.
[4] In one of the last letters before leaving Salisbury, he wrote to his brother: " Zeke, I don't believe but that Providence will do well for us yet. We shall live, and live comfortably."

to see the eminent lawyer, Christopher Gore,[1] an aristocratic gentleman of wealth and worldly experience. It was at the door of his office on the third story of "Scollay's Building," on Tremont Street, that Daniel Webster knocked on July 20, with his heart beating fast in trepidation.

Bradley, who himself barely knew Gore, had volunteered an introduction, but Webster soon took control of the situation, explained his ambitions, and secured the lawyer's attention. The very ingenuousness of the appeal must have tickled Gore's sense of humor, and Webster's personality even then was magnetic. Soon the frown faded from the attorney's face. He listened courteously, made some inquiries as to Webster's previous training, and finally said: —

My young friend, you look as though you might be trusted. You say you came to study, and not to waste time. I will take you at your word. You may as well hang up your hat at once; go into the other room; take your book and sit down to reading it, and write at your convenience to New Hampshire for your letters.[2]

The timorous Bradley, meanwhile, had disappeared, but Webster's embarrassment had been relieved by Gore's tact, and he lost no time in obeying these instructions. It was more than a week before Gore knew the name of his new clerk; but before very long the latter was writing from "Dear Boston" describing himself as sitting comfortably in Gore's office — a large room on the third story of a brick building in the heart of the city — with a sea-coal fire burning and near by "a most

---

[1] Christopher Gore (1758–1827), whose father had been banished as a Tory during the Revolution but had been restored to American citizenship by legislative act in 1787, graduated from Harvard in the class of 1776, and studied law with Judge John Lowell. He acquired a lucrative practice in Boston and was appointed by President Washington in 1789 as the first District Attorney of the United States for Massachusetts. From 1796 until 1804 he resided in England, fulfilling the duties of his office as Commissioner under the Jay Treaty, and, in 1803, he acted for a time as our *chargé d'affaires*. In 1809 he was chosen Governor of Massachusetts as a Federalist, but was defeated for reëlection by Elbridge Gerry, a Democrat. In 1813, he succeeded James Lloyd as Senator from Massachusetts, but retired in 1816 to private life. At his death, he left valuable bequests to Harvard, and Gore Hall, formerly the home of the Harvard Library, was named after him. He was a staunch conservative and held political principles of which Webster thoroughly approved. See the sketch of him by Lawrence S. Mayo in the *Dictionary of American Biography*.

[2] Autobiography, National Edition, XVII, 18–19.

enormous writing-table with half a cord of books on it." [1]
Webster had been fortunate, for Gore was one of the inner
circle of Boston Federalists, who knew everybody worth while
in New England, and whose legal reputation was such as to
make him the envy of an aspiring young attorney. Undoubtedly Webster's Federalism was strengthened by association with a man of Gore's conservative tendencies.

For the next nine months, except for some unavoidable
absences, Webster read law under Gore's supervision, making
what he modestly called "respectable progress." In August,
while Ezekiel went back to Hanover to receive his diploma from
Dartmouth, — awarded to him after only three years of actual
residence, [2] — Daniel took charge of his brother's school for a
few days, [3] one of his pupils being Edward Everett, later among
his closest friends. [4] Meanwhile, at his boarding house, — Mrs.
Whitwell's, in Court Street, — he had met a Mr. Taylor
Baldwin, an eccentric and wealthy gentleman, who took a
fancy to Webster and asked him to be his companion on a
pleasure trip to the Hudson River. On November 5, — Election Day, — the two set out "in a hackney coach, with a pair
of nimble trotters, a smart coachman before, and a footman
on horseback behind," [5] on a journey which took them to
Springfield, thence to Hartford, through the Berkshires to

[1] National Edition, XVII, 198.

[2] Daniel had used all his influence with his friends at Hanover to secure this concession to Ezekiel. In spite of his shortened period of residence, Ezekiel was one of the
highest scholars in his class.

[3] Paul Revere Frothingham, in his *Edward Everett*, makes the mistake of saying that
Ezekiel Webster was taken ill and " sought the temporary assistance of a younger
brother who had recently completed his law studies." The truth is that Ezekiel was
at Hanover, in excellent health, and that Daniel had by no means finished his legal
preparation.

[4] Edward Everett (1794–1865) was, in 1804, in his eleventh year, and was soon to
embark on that career of remarkable precocity which has probably never been equaled
in this country. He remained in the Webster school for only a few months, going to
Boston Latin School in the autumn. Webster never forgot that Everett had once been
his pupil, and, only a few months before his own death, he wrote him, " We now and
then see, stretching across the heavens, a long streak of clear, blue, cerulean sky, without cloud, or mist, or haze, and such appears to me our acquaintance, from the time
I heard you for a week recite your lessons in the little schoolhouse on Short Street to
the date hereof."

[5] National Edition, XVII, 198.

Albany, and then down the Hudson and back through
Connecticut and Rhode Island to Providence. In Albany,
Webster made some desirable acquaintances, including Abraham Van Vechten, the Schuylers, and Stephen Van Rensselaer.[1]
When he reached Mrs. Whitwell's again at the close of the
month, he had jingling in his pocket what he described as
"one hundred and twenty dear delightfuls," paid to him by
Mr. Baldwin in addition to his expenses, and most acceptable
to the impecunious Webster. Shortly afterwards, Daniel
made a trip to Salisbury to see his father, who was recovering
from a siege of illness and who, as his pathetic letters show,
was much worried about his finances.[2]

In Gore's office, Webster's chief study continued to be the
common law, particularly those portions relating to special
pleading; and he actually took the pains to go through an
old folio edition of Saunders's *Reports*, translating from Latin
and Norman French into English and making abstracts of all
the important arguments. During the winter he was "earnest
in the study of the French language,"[3] which he recognized
to be indispensable. His Journal shows that he read carefully
such standard volumes as Ward's *Law of Nations*, Evans *On
Insurance*, Viner's *Title of Pleadings*, Abbott *On Shipping*,
Bacon's *Elements of Common Law*, and Vattel (for the third
time). He attended regularly the sessions of courts, summarizing all the decisions and observing closely the methods
of the advocates. Placed for the first time where he could
watch in action such first-rate lawyers as Harrison Gray Otis,
James Sullivan, Theophilus Parsons, Daniel Davis, and Samuel
Dexter, as well as his own patron, Christopher Gore, he had an
unusual chance for criticism and comparison; and he left in
his Diary shrewd comments on Parsons, Sullivan, and Dexter.

Once, as he was sitting alone in the office, a little man dressed
in a plain gray suit entered, and, when he was told that Mr.
Gore was out, sat down to await his return. Observing that
Webster was reading Roccus's *De Navibus et Naulo*, he talked

---

[1] Lyman, pp. 16–17.   [2] Van Tyne, pp. 14, 18.   [3] National Edition, XVII, 202.

with him on problems of maritime law, displaying an amazing knowledge of that intricate subject. The stranger was Rufus King,[1] the eminent Federalist, who had just come back from England, where he had been Minister at the Court of St. James's. Within ten years, the two were to be in Congress together, and on the most intimate terms.

Webster's admiration for Gore increased as he grew to know him better, and he wrote: —

He is a lawyer of eminence and a deep and varied scholar. Since I left John Wheelock, I have found no man so indefatigable in research. He has great amenity of manners, is easy, accessible, and communicative, and, take him all in all, I could not wish a better preceptor.[2]

For relaxation, Webster continued to read with his usual assiduity. He found Gifford's *Juvenal* "worth perusing on more accounts than one," but he did not care for Gibbon's *Autobiography*, regarding that author as "a learned, proud, ingenious, foppish, vain, self-deceived man." Among other volumes which he mentions are Moore's *Travels in Italy and France*, Paley's *Natural Theology* (which he must have read in his college days), Boswell's *Hebrides*, and Puffendorf's *Latin History of England*. He contributed some communications to the newspapers, but no one has as yet been able positively to identify them.[3]

Webster, although still reserved, had little difficulty in making friends, and there were several whom he saw frequently, including Cyrus W. Perkins, Augustus Alden, and others with

[1] Rufus King (1755–1827), a native of Maine, had graduated at Harvard in 1777 and studied law in Newburyport with Theophilus Parsons. He had been a member of the old Continental Congress and was a delegate from Massachusetts to the Constitutional Convention of 1787. He moved to New York in 1788, and was soon chosen a United States Senator from that state. He was appointed Minister to Great Britain in 1796. Politically, he was an unswerving Federalist. See the sketch in the *Dictionary of American Biography*.

[2] National Edition, XVII, 194. Letter to Merrill, November 30, 1804.

[3] Thomas W. Thompson wrote to him, October 17, 1804: " I am much pleased with the communications signed Mass. and W. and I can assure you that they have excited a very interesting inquiry for the author. The former I recognized: the latter I had not seen till after the receipt of your letter. Go on. Catch every leisure moment. If pecuniary compensation should not follow, you will have a compensation of a higher nature." (National Edition, XVII, 189.)

whose names his correspondence is sprinkled. Occasionally he played backgammon with the young ladies in the Whitwell boarding house, "in order to keep off the glooms," and there were numerous homes in which he was welcome, including that of Gore. Now and then he scribbled rhymes, such as: —

> What nonsense lurked within the pate, oh!
> Of definition-making Plato,
> Who sang in philosophic metre
> "Man is a rational and biped creature"?
> Many do think, and so do I,
> Old codger, that you told a lie;
> And, yet, perhaps, you surly lout,
> There is a hole where you 'll creep out;
> Males you call rational, but no man
> E'er heard you say the same of woman.[1]

For the most part, however, he kept hard at work, realizing that it would be unwise for him not to improve his opportunities while he was in Boston.

It was at this period, according to the story related by Philip Hone, that Webster first began to drink wine. His patron, Gore, noticing that his clerk looked pale and feeble from the effects of hard study, asked him how he lived. Webster confessed that he was obliged to depend on corned beef and cabbage and to drink water. "That will not do," said the kindly Gore. "You must drink a glass of good wine occasionally, and eat an apple after dinner to promote digestion." "But," replied Webster, "I cannot afford to drink wine." "I will take care of that," replied Gore; and from that time Daniel received occasional presents of Madeira, by which he benefited greatly. "I recovered my health and was enabled to pursue my studies and perform my task with renewed ardor," he concluded, as he related the tale.[2]

In January 1805, when his apprenticeship to the law was almost completed, Webster had to make a crucial decision. For some months Captain Webster had been using his influence

---

[1] National Edition, XVII, 196.   [2] Hone, *Diary*, II, 296–97.

with his friends on the New Hampshire bench to secure for his son an appointment as Clerk of the Court of Common Pleas for Hillsborough County. When Chief Justice Timothy Farrar offered the position to Daniel, his father was overjoyed. The fees accompanying the office amounted annually to at least $1500, and to Captain Webster, whose farm was mortgaged and who had seldom known what it was to be solvent, it looked like a wonderful opening for an inexperienced youth. Even Daniel, realizing that he would be able not only to clear up the family indebtedness but also to help Ezekiel, felt as if his fortune were made. There was not the slightest doubt in his mind that he should accept what seemed like a rich prize. . . . But once again, as so often in Webster's career, an outside influence intervened. When he exultantly informed Mr. Gore of the news, the latter took it for granted that his protégé would decline the offer. "Why," said he, "you don't mean to accept it, surely!" Webster was staggered. Then Gore, seeing the young man's embarrassment, sat down with him to talk it over. He stressed the fact that Daniel was nearly through with his preparation for the law; he showed him that the clerkship was, at best, a precarious position, the fees of which might be reduced, and that, even if they were not, he would be merely a clerk for the rest of his life. "Go on," said the wise counselor, "and finish your studies; you are poor enough, but there are greater evils than poverty; live on no man's favor; what bread you eat, let it be the bread of independence; pursue your profession; make yourself useful to your friends, and a little formidable to your enemies, and you have nothing to fear." [1]

This advice, though unexpected, was sane and convincing, and Daniel, after one or two sleepless nights, determined to follow it. He now had to confront the painful necessity of notifying his father of his decision. Borrowing several hundred dollars from Joseph Taylor, one of his Boston friends, he hired a seat in a country sleigh which had come down to Boston to

[1] Autobiography, National Edition, XVII, 21.

market, and reached The Elms just at sunset. There sat his father warming his hands before the fire, his face pale and his cheeks sunken, very feeble from illness and old age. He could not at first understand his son's refusal of the lucrative clerk-ship, and for a few seconds he looked angry. Then, as if resigned to the inevitable, he said, "Well, my son, your mother has always said you would come to something or nothing. She was not sure which; I think you are now about settling that doubt for her."

The subject was never brought up again. With the borrowed money, Daniel paid some family bills and made purchases for his parents and sisters. Within a week he was back again in Gore's office with his books in front of him. Before two years had passed, the fees of the clerkship were materially reduced.[1] If Webster had accepted it, he might never have become a figure of national importance. It may well be that Christopher Gore, intervening at the psychological crisis, rescued Daniel Webster from oblivion.

Because of some negligence on the part of Thomas W. Thompson, Webster's admission to the bar was unnecessarily delayed.[2] In March 1805, however, he was admitted to practice in the Court of Common Pleas of Suffolk County, being introduced formally to the judges by Mr. Gore, who made a short speech predicting the future success of his pupil. Having achieved his immediate goal, he proceeded at once to Amherst, New Hampshire, where his father was sitting on the bench, and accompanied him back home. He had now to select a place in which to hang out his shingle. Many of Captain Webster's neighbors were eager to have Daniel settle at the Center Road Village, in the town of Salisbury.[3] He himself had virtually resolved to go to Portsmouth, but, when he found his father very feeble and ill, he could not desert him.[4]

[1] In the summer of 1805, Daniel evidently tried to secure the same clerkship for his brother, Ezekiel, but the latter also decided not to accept it. See National Edition, XVII, 215–16.

[2] National Edition, XVII, 188, and XVI, 670.

[3] Ibid., XVII, 197–98.

[4] In telling Bingham of his decision, Webster said that it was made "partly through duty, partly through necessity, and partly through choice." (Ibid., p. 206.)

Accordingly he rented in early April an office in Boscawen, where he had studied not many years before under Dr. Wood. Webster knew it well. It was only six miles south of the Salisbury Lower Village, and from it he could reach his parents quickly in an emergency.

Boscawen — accented on the opening syllable, and pronounced locally *Bos-kwine* — was first settled in 1733, and incorporated in 1760, when it was named as a compliment to the famous British admiral. It is to-day a picturesque New England village, built along a wide and shaded street parallel with the west bank of the Merrimack, between that river and a low ridge of hills. The valley at this point is more than half a mile wide — an intervale of rich alluvial deposits, rising across the Merrimack in a steep sandy ascent to the town of Canterbury on the eastern shore. Houses are still standing which were there in Webster's time, and the general appearance of the spot has altered very little in a century and a quarter. It has always been a hospitable community, and the inhabitants are justly proud of its distinguished sons — among whom, besides Daniel and Ezekiel Webster, have been Charles Carleton Coffin and John A. Dix. The population by 1800 had increased to fourteen hundred, and there was a thrilling moment, just before Webster settled there, when Boscawen had a slender chance of being designated as the state capital. But Concord had more influential backers, and, after a little flurry, Boscawen relapsed into its customary calm.

Webster's first clients were received in a small building attached to a dwelling house on King Street — the home of Lieutenant Colonel Timothy Dix. In this residence John A. Dix was born in 1798, and he was a child playing with his toys when Webster began to practise law. The Webster office was torn down before 1880, but the site is marked by a bronze tablet fastened to a large boulder. There he remained until September 1807, a period of approximately two years and a half, lodging meanwhile with Mr. Joel French, in the one-story dwelling still standing north of the village parsonage.

In Boscawen, then, Webster opened what he cynically called

a shop "for the manufacture of justice writs," and a modest
business soon came his way.   Within a few weeks he wrote
Ezekiel that he had already drawn fourteen court writs and
that Mr. Dix had given him about forty demands of various
descriptions to collect; [1] but he added less optimistically on
July 29, "I pick up . . . but very little cash, hardly laying
my hand upon a dollar." [2]   He had originally set five hundred
dollars as the sum which he ought to earn for the first year,
and had determined not to remain in Boscawen if his receipts
fell short of that amount.   How far he achieved this modest
desire may be judged from a letter which he wrote on January
19, 1806, to Bingham : —

It is now eight months since I opened an office in this town, during
which time I have led a life which I know not how to describe better
than by calling it a life of writs and summonses.   Not that I have
dealt greatly in those articles, but that I have done little else.   My
business has been just about so-so; its quantity less objectionable
than its quality.   I shall be able at the end of the year to pay my bills,
and pay perhaps sixty pounds for my books.   I practice in Hillsborough, Rockingham, and Grafton.   Scattering business over so
much surface is like spilling water on the ground.   In point of profit
I should do better, much better, if it were convenient to attend the
courts in one county only. [3]

Webster confessed later that his legal business at Boscawen,
while tolerable, was not altogether to his mind, and that there
were in the village "no pleasures of a social sort."   He worked
very hard, often sleeping on a cot in his office, and seldom retiring before midnight.   Most of his cases involved the collection of bills, and the clientage which he was building up was
not the sort which, in his dreams, he had thought of himself
as securing.   He found, furthermore, that "an accursed thirst
for money vitiates everything," and after some experience
with shyster rivals he wrote Bingham : —

Our profession is good if practised in the spirit of it; it is dam-
nable fraud and iniquity, when its true spirit is supplied by a spirit of
mischief-making and money-catching. [4]

[1] National Edition, XVI, 6–7.   [2] Ibid., XVII, 214.   [3] Ibid., p. 220.
[4] Letter of January 19, 1806 (National Edition, XVII, 222).

Although disillusioned as to the law, he did not lower his own ideals He still maintained that study was "truly the grand requisite for a lawyer," and, when he felt "the burden of perpetual solitude and seclusion," he took down a volume on law or history and buried himself in its pages. After deploring the corruption and depravity of his country, he sought refuge in the Latin classics. He even wrote at least four articles for the *Monthly Anthology*, a literary magazine started in Boston in 1804. The first, published in 1806, was an intellectual review of Tunis Mortman's *Treatise on Political Economy*. This was followed, in 1807, by a criticism of Volume I of Johnson's *New York Reports*, and by an article on the French language. In 1808, appeared a review of Lawe's *Treatise on Pleading*. His attendance at the various courts obliged him to travel considerably, and we hear of him at Boston (December 1805), at Fryeburg (August 1806), and at Portsmouth, as well as at other places less distant. He wrote to "Zeke," September 24, 1805, "I have been absent a month on the tour of courts, or you would have heard from me before." He signalized his return to his own section of the state by delivering, in 1805, an Independence Day Oration before the Federalists of Salisbury.[1]

Tradition says that Webster's first argument after his admission to the bar was made before a justice of the peace — "Old Justice Jackman, who received his commission from George II." Webster himself once wrote that his first speech before a jury was made when his father was on the bench, and added, "He never heard me a second time." [2] Apparently this plea was made in September 1805, at the court house in Plymouth, the county seat of Grafton County, during a session of the Court of Common Pleas.[3] General Lyman, who visited

[1] Letter to Ezekiel Webster, July 28, 1805 (National Edition, XVII, 213).
[2] Letter to Blatchford, May 3, 1846 (*Ibid.*, XVIII, 228).
[3] Mr. Alfred Russell, writing in 1853, after some exhaustive researches, declared that Webster's first case was tried before the Superior Court, in Plymouth, with Chief Justice Jeremiah Smith presiding. In view of the fact that Webster was not admitted to practice before the Superior Court until May 1807, this version seems improbable. Furthermore, Captain Webster could not have sat on the bench of the Superior Court, being only a Justice of the Court of Common Pleas.

Plymouth in 1852, met several older people who remembered
the case and the part which Webster took in it; and Joel
Parker said that it was an action founded on a tavern bill,
amounting to twenty-four dollars, seventeen dollars of which
Webster recovered for his client.   In his Address at the Webster
Centennial at Dartmouth College, David Cross, a New Hampshire lawyer and judge, asserted that, according to the records,
Webster, at the September Term, in 1805, of the Superior
Court of Hillsborough County, entered at Hopkinton twenty-
two writs and argued two causes before a jury.[1]   One of these
was *Haddock* v. *Woodward*, which he won; the other was
Corson v. *Corson*, which he lost.   The opposing counsel in
both suits was Webster's friend, Parker Noyes, whom he had
known in Thompson's office at Salisbury.[2]   Jacob McGaw,
usually a trustworthy witness, described a case in Grafton
County involving the trial for murder of a man who had
once worked for Captain Webster.   Daniel Webster, then
attending the court, went to see the prisoner, who implored
him to lend what aid he could give to his counsel, Mr. Sprague.
The latter, convinced of the guilt of his client, declined to
represent him; and Webster, stepping forward, made "an
argument of such wonderful force and ingenuity, that all who
heard him were astonished," and Chief Justice Smith was
lavish in his encomiums.[3]   Another interesting trial was that
of "Old Man Hodgdon," of Northfield, who had been accused
of stealing a saddle.   Webster, for the defense, showed that his
client was the victim of a conspiracy, and that the real criminal
had hidden the saddle behind Hodgdon's chimney.

    Though it is difficult to prove the truth of some of these

---

    [1] *Webster Centennial Proceedings*, p. 248.   Cross also said that these cases were
argued " in the presence of his father, one of the judges upon the bench," but this is
obviously an error, for Captain Webster was never a Judge of the Superior Court.   The
original writs in these cases are on file in the Court House at Nashua, New Hampshire.

    [2] Parker Noyes (1776–1852), of South Hampton, New Hampshire, studied law with
Thomas W. Thompson and became his partner in 1804, after marrying Thompson's
daughter.   In 1810, when Thompson moved to Concord, Noyes bought out his business,
and later took one of his pupils, George W. Nesmith, as a partner.   He held a high rank
at the New Hampshire bar.

    [3] National Edition, XVII, 52.

tales, there can be no doubt of the lasting impression which Webster, at this early period of his career, made on competent critics. Chief Justice Joel Parker, of the New Hampshire Court of Common Pleas, told of a brilliant argument delivered by Webster in September 1806, which created a sensation among his colleagues at the bar, and was the subject of discussion for several days.[1] John H. Morison, in his *Life of Jeremiah Smith*, described a suit for trespass tried in Hopkinton at the May Term of the Superior Court in 1807.[2] Webster, although associated with a Mr. Wilson as counsel for the plaintiff, was not yet legally entitled to argue a case in the Superior Court; but, in view of the fact that he was soon to be admitted, the Chief Justice allowed him to present his cause. The scene which followed was depicted by Sheriff Israel W. Kelley, of Concord, later Webster's brother-in-law : —

When Mr. Webster began to speak, his voice was low, his head was sunk upon his breast, and his eyes were fixed upon the floor, and he moved his feet incessantly, backward and forward, as if trying to secure a firmer position. His voice soon increased in power and volume, till it filled the whole house. His attitude became erect, his eye dilated, and his whole countenance was radiant with emotion. The attention of all was at once arrested. Every eye in the crowded court-room was fixed on the speaker but my own; for I was obliged to watch the door that I might prevent confusion by the throng of spectators that were constantly crowding into the hall.[3]

In May 1806, at Plymouth, Webster was assigned by the court to defend one Josiah Burnham, charged with killing two of his companions in the cell of the Haverhill jail, by stabbing them with a weapon made from the point of a scythe. Webster's plea was an argument against capital punishment, but the jury brought in a verdict of "Guilty," and Burnham was hanged, August 12, 1806, on Powder House Hill, near Haverhill, before a throng of ten thousand people.[4]

[1] Harvey, pp. 44–45.
[2] Morison, *Life of Jeremiah Smith*, pp. 179–80.
[3] Harvey, pp. 46–47.
[4] *Granite State Monthly*, IV, 101.

It makes little difference whether these stories are regarded as truth or as fanciful legends. The fact underlying them all is that Daniel Webster, even as a young lawyer, made himself respected and feared. It was during this period that he first encountered the redoubtable Jeremiah Mason,[1] later his intimate friend and associate. Mason — who told the story to Webster's biographer, George Ticknor Curtis — was asked to defend a hitherto respectable citizen who had been indicted for forgery. The action was to be tried in one of the counties in which Webster practised, and he had been asked by the Attorney-General to prepare the argument for the prosecution. Mason had heard vague rumors of a wonderfully clever young country lawyer, said to be "as black as the ace of spades," but had never been brought into contact with him. On the day of the trial, the Attorney-General was ill, and the prosecutors, with Mason's consent, placed the case in Webster's hands. The unknown Boscawen lawyer con-

[1] Jeremiah Mason (1768–1848), born at Lebanon, Connecticut, was the sixth of nine children of Jeremiah Mason, all but one of whom lived to maturity. His father, like Webster's, was a farmer, a Revolutionary veteran, and a member of the state legislature. Mason graduated from Yale in 1788, studied law at New Haven under Simeon Baldwin for a year, and then at Westminster, Vermont, under General Stephen R. Bradley for eighteen months, and was admitted to the Vermont bar at New Fane in June 1791. He settled in Westmoreland, New Hampshire, in the following autumn, moving in 1794 to Walpole, six miles up the Connecticut, and in 1797 to Portsmouth, where he soon rose to the head of his profession. We are told that, from 1805 to 1808, the number of original entries made by him at any court session was usually more than those of all the other attorneys in Portsmouth together. He married, November 9, 1799, Mary Means, daughter of Robert Means, of Amherst, New Hampshire. He was six feet, seven inches, in height, and she was so short that she often tied her handkerchief to his wrist so that she could reach it. In 1802, Mason was made Attorney-General of New Hampshire, but held the office only three years. Elected to the United States Senate in June 1813, as a Federalist, he associated himself with colleagues of similar political principles, such as Rufus King and Christopher Gore; but he wearied of the office and resigned his seat in 1817. It was his only service in Congress. His stooped shoulders and rather awkward manner made him seem at first glance rather sluggish, and his face, except for his keen and vigilant eyes, looked heavy. But once stirred to action, he was transformed. He was, in the courtroom, simple and direct, using homely phrases and a provincial pronunciation and speaking without gestures; but he had Yankee shrewdness and common sense, and he was so lucid that nobody ever failed to understand him. Unlike Webster, he was not a wide general reader, but devoted himself entirely to his profession. As a lawyer, he compelled his opponents to do their best, for no one arguing against him could be negligent or superficial. Like Rufus Choate, he did not really care for politics, and was always glad to get back to his office desk. See the *Dictionary of American Biography*.

WEBSTER IN HIS FORTY-THIRD YEAR

From a portrait by Francis Alexander
(Courtesy of Dartmouth College)

WEBSTER AS A YOUNG MAN

From a portrait by an unknown artist
(Courtesy of Long Island Historical Society)

ducted the proceedings in a masterly manner. "He broke upon me like a thunder storm in July," confessed Mason, "sudden, portentous, sweeping all before it." Surprised by this "remarkable exhibition of unexpected power," Mason was barely able to save his client, and he had from that time forth a wholesome regard for Webster's prowess.[1] It was not to be long before the two were to meet as professional rivals in the same community; and Mason, with the generosity and lack of jealousy which were among his many admirable characteristics, never ceased to encourage his younger friend to enter a broader field. "I never lost sight of Mr. Webster," he said, "and never had but one opinion of his powers."

Some meagre traditions still remain of Webster's life in Boscawen. It is said that he organized a voluntary military company, recruited chiefly from a group of men employed in manufacturing barrel staves at a local coopering establishment, and that these soldiers, with hoop-poles for weapons, used to march up and down King Street to the music of fife and drum.[2] He took some interest in town affairs, enrolled himself as a member of the religious society, voted at town meeting, and served on the school committee. But he viewed his residence in Boscawen as only temporary, and, on his occasional trips to Boston and Portsmouth, he looked enviously and eagerly upon those larger communities, where there was more life and more scope for his talents. Scrupulously and uncomplainingly he was keeping his bargain with his father.

Ebenezer Webster, after several months of failing strength, died on April 22, 1806, and was buried in the little cemetery at The Elms, only a short distance from the Merrimack. In tribute to him, Webster wrote in 1846: —

[1] This story is told in Curtis, I, 77, and also in Hillard, *Life of Mason*, p. 41. Still another version is quoted in Lodge's *Daniel Webster*, pp. 39–40, in which the case is spoken of as a " murder trial." Additional details are preserved in Harvey, pp. 58–59, where the offense of the prisoner is described as " passing counterfeit money." I have been unable to find the case reported in any of the newspapers of the period.

[2] Coffin, *Boscawen and Webster*, pp. 446–47. If this story is authentic, it is almost the only indication throughout Webster's career of a relish for military distinction. He was later opposed on principle to the War of 1812 and to the Mexican War.

I neither left him nor forsook him. My opening an office in Boscawen was that I might be near him. I closed his eyes in this very house. He died at sixty-seven years of age, after a life of exertion, toil, and exposure : a private soldier, an officer, a legislator, a judge, everything that a man could be to whom learning never had disclosed her " ample page." [1]

Daniel, who had already paid out large sums for his father,[2] now assumed his debts,[3] and undertook to supply money also for the living expenses of his mother and sisters.[4] Meanwhile Ezekiel had been reading law in the office of James Sullivan, — later Governor of Massachusetts for two terms, — in Boston, and with Parker Noyes, in Salisbury. Admitted to the New Hampshire bar in September 1807, he took over almost immediately, by agreement with Daniel, the latter's office in Boscawen, and also became manager of the family farm at the Lower Village. The important facts about these arrangements were written from Portsmouth by Daniel to Bingham : —

The truth is, our family affairs at Salisbury rendered it necessary for one of us to reside in that neighborhood, and not very willing to take charge of the farm, I concluded to indorse over to my brother both farm and office, if he would take them both together. Being thus left to seek a new place of abode, I came to this town, a measure which I had in some degree contemplated for a length of time. I found myself here in the latter part of September. I knew few people here, and Mr. Adams was the only person who advised the measure.[5]

Thus suddenly precipitated by Fate into a new community, Ezekiel Webster, a man of exceptional ability, soon adjusted himself to his environment, made for himself a distinguished career as a lawyer, and became Boscawen's leading citizen.

[1] National Edition, XVIII, 229. [2] *Ibid.*, XVI, 8.

[3] According to George Ticknor, quoted in Curtis, I, 78, Webster did not entirely pay off his father's obligations until 1817.

[4] Webster's youngest sister, Sarah Jane, died of consumption on March 19, 1811. His older sister, Mehitable, died on July 4, 1814, thus leaving the mother absolutely alone on the farm. Mrs. Ebenezer Webster, after spending her last days with her son, Ezekiel, at Boscawen, finally died on April 25, 1816, almost exactly ten years after her husband, and was buried by his side.

[5] Letter to Bingham, February 27, 1808 (National Edition, XVII, 228).

He married and built for his family a beautiful home, with attractive gardens; and, when he died very suddenly, at the age of forty-nine, he was buried in the lovely old Boscawen Cemetery, on a slope above the Merrimack.

Daniel Webster was admitted in May 1807 as Counselor in the Superior Court of New Hampshire; and, with Ezekiel comfortably established in Boscawen, he transferred in September all his belongings to Portsmouth, where he hoped, against keener competition, to make a name for himself in the law.

IV

A WIDER HORIZON: WEBSTER IN PORTSMOUTH

I lived in Portsmouth nine years, wanting one month. They were very happy years.

— WEBSTER, Autobiography

Should we meet the flitting ghost of some old-time worthy, on a staircase or at a lonely street corner, the reader must be prepared for it.

— ALDRICH, An Old Town by the Sea

PORTSMOUTH, New Hampshire, on the south bank of the Piscataqua River, was, in 1807, a place of some consequence. Settled first in 1623, it had acquired by the close of the eighteenth century a population of more than five thousand and was twelfth among the cities of the United States. It had the only harbor and was the largest city in New Hampshire, surpassing both Exeter and Concord in wealth and number of people,[1] and it was quite able to hold its own in commerce with its Massachusetts rivals, Salem and Newburyport. There was an insignificant village called Hooksett, near what was to be the cosmopolitan industrial centre of Manchester, and there was a sparse settlement at Watanic, on the site of what to-day is Nashua. But manufacturing had not yet contaminated the valley of the Merrimack, and the sea was still the most important factor in New England's prosperity.

It was in Portsmouth that the earliest newspaper in the state — the *New Hampshire Gazette* — was started in 1756. Portsmouth had been the colonial capital of New Hampshire until patriots during the Revolution moved the seat of government inland to Exeter.[2] In Market Square — Portsmouth's

[1] Belknap's *History of New Hampshire* gives the population statistics for 1790 as follows: Portsmouth, 4720; Concord, 1747; Exeter, 1722.

[2] From 1775 to 1807, the Legislature adjourned from town to town, sometimes to Portsmouth, and often to Exeter and Concord. At the close of the first session in 1807, it adjourned to Concord, which has since been the capital.

Place de la Concorde — was the Old State House, the scene of many public demonstrations, on the eastern balcony of which President George Washington was welcomed in 1789. Towards the eastern end of the Square was the town pump, long used as a whipping post; and at the south was the broad plaza known as the "Parade," where processions were formed and the citizens promenaded on summer evenings. On Vaughan Street could be seen the Assembly House,[1] where Portsmouth's "four hundred" gathered for dancing parties and musicales, and where Washington, attending a ball, found "about seventy-five well-dressed and many very handsome ladies."

Everywhere, in the Portsmouth of 1807, there were evidences of prosperity. It boasted, in 1798, 626 dwelling houses, of which, however, only sixteen were of three stories. On nearly every street was some stately mansion, with the gambrel roof which dated it before the Revolution. At a later period had come the great, square three-storied residences, usually of wood, but giving the impression of substantiality and filled with furniture which now makes the antique hunter's heart ache with envy. These houses reflected the good taste of the shipowners and superannuated sea captains, who, retiring with a competence, had established them as a refuge for their old age. Such were many of the landmarks for which Portsmouth is famous: the Warner House, the brick for the eighteen-inch walls of which was imported from Holland; the Moffatt House, once the wonder of the town, and now the property of the New Hampshire Society of the Colonial Dames of America; and the truly noble Governor Langdon Mansion, where Washington dined and where such dignitaries as Louis Philippe and James Monroe were guests. All these, and many others almost as beautiful, were familiar sights to Daniel Webster as he strolled about the streets. Most of them stood some yards back from the flagstone sidewalks, and behind them were attractive gardens, colorful in the right season with lilacs and

[1] The Assembly House was altered in 1838, and now constitutes two separate buildings, one on either side of Raitt's Court.

roses and dahlias, and here and there a small orchard laden with blossoms or fruit. There was not a ramble along a side avenue which did not open some unexpected vista full of old-world charm.

The Portsmouth of the early nineteenth century, however, was a hustling community, more interested in its present than in its past. Along the wharves, there was abundant activity, as cargoes were unloaded or sailors wandered back and forth from vessels to taprooms. Aldrich, in sentimental reminiscence, has said : —

At the windows of these musty countingrooms which overlook the river near Spring Market used to stand portly merchants, in knee-breeches and silver shoe-buckles and plum-colored coats with ruffles at the wrists, waiting for their ships to come up the Narrows; the cries of the stevedores and the chants of sailors at the windlass used to echo along the shore where all is silent now.

The unmistakable aroma of the sea — a pleasing blend of brine and tar — permeated the atmosphere, and the ships returning from distant India or China gave it an exotic flavor, quite different from that of inland cities. There were taverns for the stranger, ready to cater to his needs: Mr. John Staver's Earl of Halifax, from which the first stage set out for Boston in 1761 and the name of which was discreetly changed by the proprietor during the Revolution to the William Pitt Tavern; the Bell, on a post in front of which hung a huge bell, painted a gaudy blue, and at which the patriots had once held their seditious meetings; and Stoodley's, on the north side of Daniel Street, which, in Webster's day, was the fashionable resort of bucks and "bloods."

Portsmouth was a comfortable town, — rather complacent and conservative, as befitted a community in which most of the citizens were well-to-do, — and very hospitable. Belknap, writing in 1792, said, "In Portsmouth, there is as much elegance and politeness of manners, as in any of the capital towns of New England." [1] Webster, arriving there not long after the

---

[1] The Marquis de Chastellux, a visitor in 1782, speaks of handsome women elegantly dressed, and of rich houses beautifully furnished.

days of wigs and cocked hats and flowered waistcoats, found a society quite self-sufficient and dependent on itself. It had its eccentric characters, its legends of ghosts and witches, and its mysterious tragedies, as any ancient place should have, and its citizens had no envy of Philadelphia or New York.

Certainly an ambitious young lawyer might have chosen many worse spots in which to seek his fortune. But, although the residents of Portsmouth were only faintly aware of the nemesis descending upon them, its "golden days" were almost over. For the moment it was flourishing, and Webster had selected it in the belief that its future was as promising as that of Boston. But the Embargo Act was soon to fall like a blight upon its foreign trade, and the War of 1812 was to bring with it an even greater decline in shipping. Webster reached there just as the old Portsmouth of the days "before the war" was to become a memory. To-day, the traveler is likely to think of it, in Aldrich's phrase, as "An Old Town by the Sea," where "the wormeaten wharves, some of them covered by a sparse, unhealthy beard of grass, and the weather-stained, unoccupied warehouses are sufficient to satisfy a moderate appetite for antiquity." Portsmouth's prosperity, such as it is, is now of another kind. There are factories, but they seem incongruous with their surroundings. Even automobiles are not altogether suited to the "Parade."

During the passage of a century or more, Portsmouth has greatly changed. The old houses are still alluring, but in some instances they resemble "the crumbling shells of things dead and gone." Once-fashionable avenues are now the slums of the city. Gracefully carved doorways have been damaged by the hands of ignorant vandals. The former haunts of fashion and luxury have been turned often to ignoble uses. There is, of course, on the part of some older residents, an interest in the past, but in the business quarter a new generation has grown up — or come in — which is indifferent to traditions. It is significant that there is no memorial to Webster in the city.

The Portsmouth of 1807 was so small that the arrival of a

stranger — especially a stranger like Daniel Webster — aroused
the curiosity of its inhabitants. We are told by Mrs. Eliza
Buckminster Lee [1] that, when he first was seated next to the
minister's family in the Old North Church, called the "three-
decker" because of its tiers of galleries, her eldest sister reported
"that there had been a remarkable person in the pew with
her, and that she was sure he had a most marked character for
good or for evil." Mrs. Lee, describing him as he then
appeared, wrote : —

Slender and apparently of delicate organization, his large eyes and
massive brow seemed very predominant above the other features,
which were sharply cut, refined, and delicate. The paleness of his
complexion was heightened by hair as black as the raven's wing.[2]

This vivid sketch corresponds well with a miniature of
Webster painted at about this period,[3] but Mrs. Lee's emphasis on his "paleness" is inexplicable when we recall that everybody else particularly mentions his swarthy hue. Mrs. Lee
added that her father, noticing that Webster's constitution
was not very robust, persuaded him to join him in sawing wood
for half an hour before breakfast each morning — an exercise
which had beneficial results upon his physique. Before he left
Portsmouth, the slim and frail-looking young lawyer was in
excellent health and gradually acquiring the portly proportions
of his prime.

Having rented bachelor quarters not far from the Buckminster home, Webster was soon the centre of an admiring circle.

[1] Eliza (Buckminster) Lee (1794–1864), one of Webster's best friends in Portsmouth
and in later life, was the sister of his former teacher at Exeter, the Reverend Joseph
Stevens Buckminster, and the daughter of Dr. Joseph Buckminster, pastor of the Old
North Church, in Portsmouth, for thirty-three years. She married Thomas Lee, of
Boston, and moved to that city, where she became well known as an author. In the
Old North Church, which stood on the west side of Market Square and has been replaced
by a more modern edifice on the same site, Webster had a pew, and he was a warden
there in 1815–16.

[2] From an interesting reminiscent letter to Fletcher Webster, dated January 23,
1856, and printed in the National Edition, XVII, 438 ff.

[3] A photograph of this miniature is reproduced in Fisher, p. 81, and shows Webster
with a face which was sharp and narrow, instead of broad and square, as it was in his
later days. The likeness between this and the pictures of his old age is, however,
unmistakable.

His clever imitations of peculiar people established his reputation as a mimic, and he had a charm of manner which was irresistible. Thrown for the first time into a society which was opulent and urbane, he was quick to adopt its tone. If he had been hitherto a little uncertain about rules of etiquette, he rapidly learned how to play the game, and, mingling with polished men and women, was accepted as one of them. His letters, not numerous during these years, tell us little of his experiences, but he did meet such Portsmouth personages as the stately Governor John Langdon;[1] Honorable Jonathan Warner, who had been a member of His Majesty's Council before the Revolution; Captain William Rice, the enterprising merchant who controlled a fleet of privateers in the War of 1812; Honorable John Goddard, who had refused a nomination to the United States Senate; and the astute Judge Samuel Sherburne, who had served two terms in Congress, had been appointed United States District Attorney, and had ended as a judge of the Circuit Court. Association with men of cultivation, who had traveled widely, gave him a broader outlook than had been his in provincial Boscawen. It was in Portsmouth that Webster gained poise and sophistication.

To the ladies of Portsmouth, Webster was not attracted, for he had already made his choice of a life companion. Writing to Merrill, March 8, 1807, he said: —

I rejoice that you have so comfortable a cage. A bird you cannot but find easily. Your friend Webster has neither bird nor cage. However, he lives in hopes.[2]

Within the next few months the hopes developed into realities, for he wrote, December 2, 1807: —

[1] John Langdon (1741–1819) was perhaps the most picturesque figure in New Hampshire politics at the opening of the nineteenth century. Born in Portsmouth, he fought in the Revolution at Bennington and Saratoga, and became a prosperous merchant. He was a member of the State Legislature and its Speaker; delegate to the Constitutional Convention of 1787: Governor of New Hampshire (1788); Senator from New Hampshire (1789–1801) and first President of the United States Senate; and again Governor for five terms between 1805 and 1812. He was a strong Democrat, and Jefferson offered him in 1801 a place in his cabinet as Secretary of the Navy, which he refused. He also declined the Democratic nomination for Vice President in 1812.

[2] National Edition, XVII, 226.

I have been a young dog long enough, and now think of joining myself, as soon as convenient, to that happy and honorable society of which you are one; the society of married men.[1]

The young lady on whom he had set his heart was Grace Fletcher, daughter of the Reverend Elijah Fletcher, the minister of Hopkinton, — about ten miles southwest of The Elms, — who had died, April 8, 1786, leaving four small children, of whom Grace was the youngest. Mrs. Fletcher — whose maiden name was Rebecca Chamberlain — had married again, her second husband being the Reverend Christopher Paige, also of Hopkinton, to whom she had borne three sons and one daughter.[2]   Grace Fletcher, after graduating at Atkinson Academy in 1800, had been intermittently a school teacher, for a time at Boscawen, and, in 1805, at Salisbury.   Her older sister, Rebecca, had married Judge Israel W. Kelley, of Salisbury, in whose home Grace lived when employed in that vicinity.   It is said that Webster saw her first at church in Salisbury, when she wore a tight-fitting dress and looked "like an angel." [3]   He did not find it difficult to carry on a courtship, for Judge Kelley lived at Salisbury Center Village, only a few miles from Boscawen.

Some sort of understanding must have been reached between Webster and Grace Fletcher before he moved to Portsmouth. In the late spring of 1808, he rode away from his bachelor's headquarters without notifying anyone of his destination, and,

[1] National Edition, XVII, p. 227.

[2] Mrs. Paige's third son, James W. Paige, Esquire, who first met Webster in 1807 at the Paige house, later became one of his close friends.   He was afterwards a prosperous merchant in Boston and was named as one of the trustees under Webster's will.   A considerable correspondence, chiefly on matters of business, was carried on between the two.   Paige died, May 19, 1868, in Boston.

[3] According to the story told by William T. Davis in an article, " Memories of Daniel Webster " (*New England Magazine*, April 1902), Rebecca Kelley on one Sunday morning told Grace not to dress up for church, as it was stormy, and no one would be there for whom she cared.   When she returned home, she said, " I did see some one, a man with a black head, who looked as if he might be somebody."   The stranger was Webster. The earliest reference to Grace Fletcher in Webster's correspondence is in a letter from Ezekiel to Daniel, from Boston, July 10, 1805, in which he asks, " Is Grace in Salisbury, and is B. attentive to her? "

THE ENTRY OF DANIEL WEBSTER'S MARRIAGE IN
THE SALISBURY CHURCH RECORDS

on Sunday, May 29,[1] he was married to her at Judge Kelley's house, — "in the middle west room," — by the Reverend Thomas Worcester.[2] Mrs. Webster was a year and two days older than her husband, having been born on January 16, 1781, in Hopkinton. Judging from her portrait by Chester Harding, she could not have been beautiful, but she was attractive in manner and habitually amiable.[3] Although she was physically not strong, she possessed a brilliant mind and was a congenial companion for her husband, who relied much upon her judgment. She seems to have been quite equal to the social demands made upon her, and she preserved a dignified composure, not only in Portsmouth, but also in the more exacting drawing-rooms of Boston and Washington. George Ticknor, who saw much of the Websters in Portsmouth, wrote, "Mrs. Webster was pleasing and animated, and her manner to the friends of her husband, and to us young men, was very kind and cordial." [4]

After his marriage, Webster rented a house on Vaughan Street, which had formerly been occupied by his friend, Jeremiah Mason.[5] This dwelling, which is still standing as "Number 137," was built in 1760 by George Meserve, and had been Mason's home from 1800 to 1808. It was a pleasant resi-

[1] The date given by Webster in his formal Autobiography is June 24, which is obviously incorrect. Dearborn's *History of Salisbury* says that the marriage took place on May 29, 1808, which fell on a Sunday. The Salisbury Church records give the date as May 29.

[2] Dr. Worcester came to Salisbury in 1791, as Parson Searle's successor in the church at Salisbury Center Village. To this church, Daniel Webster had been united while still a young man, but the date, September 13, 1807, given in Dearborn's *History*, is probably a misprint for September 13, 1797.

[3] Mrs. Lee, writing to Fletcher Webster regarding his mother, said, " Uniting with great sweetness of disposition, unaffected, frank and winning manners, you will readily believe that no one could approach your mother without wishing to know her, and no one could know her well, without loving her." (National Edition, XVII, 440.)

[4] Quoted by Curtis, I, 85.

[5] With his increased income, Mason had built, in 1808, a large three-storied house on the southeast corner of State and Summer Streets, in a location which was then thought to be very secluded, although it was not more than a third of a mile from Market Square. It was an imposing mansion, enclosed by a white fence, and with an orchard and extensive gardens, in which he took much pride. It is still standing to-day, very little altered, and occupied by a member of the Treadwell family, into whose possession it came after Mason left Portsmouth, in 1832.

dence, with a gambrel roof, and behind it was a garden extending south to School Street. Diagonally opposite, on the west side of Vaughan Street, was the Assembly House, where the beaux and belles of Portsmouth held their balls. The place was centrally located, only a short distance from the business centre, and in what was then considered to be a desirable locality.[1]

Exactly how long Webster remained in the Vaughan Street house it is impossible to say, but we do know that he soon purchased for six thousand dollars what George Ticknor called "a small, modest, wooden house," on the northwest corner of Court and Pleasant Streets, only two blocks from Market Square.[2] It was of the same size and arrangement as the Reverend Samuel Langdon House, only a short distance away on Pleasant Street, just north of the Universalist Church, and, like it, was two stories in height, with a gambrel roof and twin chimneys, and two windows on either side of the front door. Separating it from the street was a fence, with carved posts at the gateway leading to the entrance. It was to a room in this dwelling that Mrs. Lee referred when she wrote, "There certainly was never a more charming room than the low-roofed simple parlor, where, relieved from the cares of business, in the full gayety of his disposition, he gave himself up to relaxa-

[1] The changes in Portsmouth during the past century can be illustrated in no better way than by the story of the evolution of this once fine dwelling. It is difficult to trace all its various owners after the Websters left it; but it came, in 1839, into the hands of Robert Gray, by whom it was well kept up and in whose family it long remained. In the late nineteenth century it was purchased by two men who were indifferent to its beauty and who, after removing the charming interior stairway and much of the exquisite woodwork, had the ground floor remodeled for stores. One side is now occupied by a Food Shop and the other by a Pool Room; while the second story is rented for apartments. A giant sassafras tree, said to have been the oldest in New Hampshire, was ruthlessly cut down about 1918 in order to make room for a lunch cart. Not many people in Portsmouth have any idea that it was once Webster's home; but the Assembly House, across the street, is marked by a tablet commemorating Washington's appearance there at a ball in 1789.

[2] General Lyman, perhaps ignorant of the house in Vaughan Street, wrote: "When Mr. Webster went to Portsmouth to reside with his wife, they took lodgings at the house of a widow lady, where they resided some time, and were regarded as the proprietors of the establishment, he paying all the expenses. At last he bought the house, furniture and all pertaining to it, and had just paid for it, when it took fire and was burned to ashes." (Lyman, II, 38.)

tion." [1] Unfortunately, it was consumed in the great conflagration of December 1813,[2] while Webster was in Washington, and when he returned, in the following spring, he moved his family into a third house, on High Street, still in existence, although a large addition has since been constructed in the rear. The original portion, as Webster knew it, is in excellent condition.[3] The east room on the ground floor, opening on High Street, is about fourteen by eighteen feet in dimensions, with a ceiling approximately nine feet high, and four windows. The only other room on this floor must have been used as both dining-room and kitchen, although it is possible that there may have been a small wing at the back in which cooking was done. There were two large bedrooms on the second floor. This four-room dwelling was certainly no very pretentious habitation for a Congressman.

Webster's domestic affairs in Portsmouth were happy and untroubled. Two children were born to him there: Grace Fletcher Webster, born April 29, 1810, and described by Ticknor as "a child of uncommon intelligence, with a brilliant red and white complexion, and deep-set eyes, and hair as black as her father's"; [4] and Daniel Fletcher Webster, born July 23, 1813 The preference of both Webster and his wife was for simple pleasures, and, although they sometimes attended elaborate social functions, they did not entertain lavishly themselves. Instead, Webster would sit in the evening in his parlor, "a bright and cheerful room," and read the plays of Shakespeare to friends who chanced to drop in.

Webster's office, during the greater part of his residence in Portsmouth, was on the west side of Market Street, only two or three doors from the square, in the second story over what is to-day Peyser's clothing store. The rooms which he once

[1] National Edition, XVII, 441.

[2] The site of the Webster house is now occupied by an ugly three-story tenement, painted brown, and quite out of place in the vicinity of the beautiful residences near it.

[3] The building is still called "Webster House," and is used as a boarding house at 58 High Street.

[4] Quoted in Curtis, I, 85. This child was born while Webster was attending court at Hopkinton (National Edition, XIII, 549).

occupied are now utilized by the job-printing establishment
of Richard I. Walden, and have been somewhat remodeled;
but there are closets which look much as they did in Webster's
time. The only description which we have is from the pen of
George Ticknor, who wrote: —

His office was a common, ordinary-looking room, with less furniture
and more books than common. He had a small inner room, opening
from the larger, rather an unusual thing.[1]

This office was only a short distance from the houses in which
he lived. It was but slightly over one hundred yards, for instance, from his third residence, on High Street, to his place of
business. From its windows, Webster could look into Market
Square, and he could easily be reached by anyone in need of
legal counsel.

The practice upon which Daniel Webster now entered was,
after a few weeks, of a size to demand his careful attention.[2]
His reputation as a pleader had preceded him, and clients
flocked to his door. Like every attorney of that era, he spent
much time in the collection of small debts on a commission —
an occupation which was neither uplifting nor profitable. But
he was able to write Bingham: —

I have done as much business as I ought to expect. There are
eight or nine of us who fill writs, in town. Of course my share cannot
be large even if I should take my equal dividend. On the whole, however, I am satisfied that I did right to come, and suppose shall meet
with as much success as I deserve.[3]

It was not long before Webster was making almost two
thousand dollars a year — a considerable income for a young
man who did not know what it was to be free from debt and
who had been glad, at Boscawen, when he could count on five

[1] Curtis, I, 85.
[2] According to Harvey, p. 51, Webster wrote in the fall of 1807: " Thursday I tarried
in Concord; Friday I came to this place; Saturday I got my office swept and my books
put up, and this week I have been quite at leisure."
[3] Letter to Bingham, February 27, 1808 (National Edition, XVII, 228).

hundred dollars annually.[1] Much of his professional work was carried on by following the sessions of the Superior Court through the state, as Lincoln did thirty years later in Illinois. New Hampshire was then divided into six counties, five of which — Rockingham (in which Portsmouth was located), Strafford, Grafton, Hillsborough, and Cheshire — had been named by Governor John Wentworth for his friends among the English nobility. The sixth — Coos — had been split off from Grafton in 1803. Sessions of the court were held at the various "shire" towns, and brought about an intimate association of both lawyers and judges. By chaise in summer and by sleigh in winter, Webster traveled with his colleagues and rivals from one centre to another in Rockingham, Grafton, and Hillsborough Counties, coming back to Portsmouth whenever possible for week-ends, but often detained from home for long periods by bad weather or rush of business. He slept at uncomfortable inns, ate unpalatable food, and endured all the trying vicissitudes of the New England climate.

Meanwhile, he was being subjected to a discipline at which he may sometimes have revolted, but which tested his mettle and brought out all his latent powers. To the people in the vicinity, the court sessions were dramas, eagerly anticipated and largely attended. Every important trial was a tournament in which champions were matched against each other, and farmers drove in from all the surrounding country to hear a case argued by two famous advocates. Under these conditions, lawyers were always tense and eager, and the one who did well was sure of congratulations in the evening as he sat with his fellows around the dinner table. Novitiates, through this system, had the opportunity of listening day after day to masters of their art.[2] Facing each morning a new problem,

[1] By May 5, 1808, Webster could write Bingham: " I have nothing to charge against fortune, on the score of professional success, and yet have nothing to boast, beyond the ordinary success of young men. I am earning a small living, and have long been convinced that I shall never be rich." (National Edition, XVII, 230.) In 1813, he wrote that from 80 to 100 cases a term originated in his office. (*Ibid.*, XVI, 671.)

[2] Senator George F. Hoar, recollecting the circuit system, wrote, " I cannot but think that the listening to the trial and argument of cases by skillful advocates was a better law school than any we have now." (*Autobiography of Seventy Years*, II, 368.)

Webster had to acquire the faculty of adjusting himself quickly to changed conditions. It was obviously impracticable for a lawyer on the circuit to carry with him a large library, and books were seldom to be found in the towns where court was held. Under the circumstances, a skillful pleader found himself relying, not on precedents, but on his wits, and victory usually fell, not to him who knew the most, but to him who could reason best and think most rapidly on his feet. There was no opportunity for a lawyer to demur or delay.[1] He had to prepare his case for jury or court in a hurry, under a pressure which was unfavorable to calm scrutiny of the facts. In this never-ending competition month after month, a man's true ability was bound to be disclosed, for he had either to hold his own in the rough-and-tumble intellectual battle or drop out. Webster did not drop out. Indeed, it was not long before the popular judgment placed him on a parity with the great miracle-worker, Jeremiah Mason, whose "Titanic bulk and elephantine movement" made him conspicuous wherever members of the bar were assembled.

No one can study the legal career of Webster without concluding that his obligation to Jeremiah Mason was very great. In his earlier appearances in the courtroom, Webster, not yet cured of the sophomoric tendencies shown in his college orations, had been rhetorical and even bombastic.[2] He had formed the insidious habit of using words merely because of their sound, and his sentences were too heavily freighted with ornamentation. It was hard for him, as it was for so many of his contemporaries, to resist the lure of "fine writing." Now Jeremiah Mason, a shrewd Yankee, had evolved a style which had no "frills," but was above all plain and direct. He wasted no words, but aimed to become intimate with each member

---

[1] " In his earlier years in circuit practice, Lincoln and other travelling attorneys were employed by clients as soon as the Judge and his legal retinue arrived. . . . A bill in chancery, an answer, a demurrer, special pleas, and the like would have to be determined and prepared ' before the opening of the court the next morning.' " (Beveridge, *Abraham Lincoln*, I, 518.) Such was substantially the procedure in Webster's day.

[2] William Plumer, the elder, thought Webster, as a young man, to be " too excursive and declamatory," and this criticism is sustained by the recollections of other New Hampshire lawyers.

of the jury and to address them in a language which they could comprehend. He even assumed a provincial accent and a homeliness of phrasing in order to make rural jurymen feel at ease. Webster, who was his own severest critic, soon perceived the art behind Mason's apparent simplicity and began himself to experiment with those short, incisive sentences for which he was to become notable. As he watched and heard Mason, his respect for the latter's technique increased, and he left a permanent acknowledgment of his indebtedness in a passage frequently cited: "Mason's method of argument led me to study my own style and set about reforming it." In his Autobiography, furthermore, Webster recorded his mature estimate of Mason's ability: —

He has been of infinite advantage to me, not only by his unvarying friendship, but by the many good lessons he has taught, and the example he set me in the commencement of my career. If there be in the country a stronger intellect, if there be a mind of more native resources, if there be a vision that sees quicker, or sees deeper into whatever is intricate, or whatsoever is profound, I must confess I have not known it.[1]

It was not merely Mason's choice of words which had its influence upon Webster. Devoted whole-heartedly to his law practice and indifferent to social advancement or public honors, Mason prepared himself for each legal battle as a general girds himself for an attack. His round face and rather sleepy eye-lids did not seem to indicate persistence, but he had a resolute mouth. He was usually courteous to opponents, but, when stung, he could be almost savage, and Webster testified that his sarcasm was "not frothy or petulant, but cool and vitriolic." Pitted against such a foe, Webster was obliged to marshal all his resources. Once, in conversation with Rufus Choate, Webster said with unmistakable sincerity: —

I regard Jeremiah Mason as eminently superior to any other lawyer whom I have ever met. I would rather, with my own experience (and I have had some pretty tough experience with him), meet them all combined in a case than to meet him alone and single-handed. He

[1] National Edition, XVII, 24.

was about the keenest lawyer I ever met or read about. If a man had Jeremiah Mason and he did not get his case, no human ingenuity or learning could get it.[1]

Such unsought testimony as this, even allowing for Webster's expansive generosity of spirit, has a genuine ring to it. It is supplemented, moreover, by a paragraph in a letter from him to Mason, February 27, 1830, long after he had left Portsmouth : —

I have been written to, to go to New Hampshire to try a cause against you next August, brought by Mrs. Mellen *v.* Dover Company. Where is the August Court holden ? I suppose up at the Lakes. If it were an easy and plain case on our side, I might be willing to go ; but I have some of your pounding in my bones yet, and don't care about any more till that wears out.[2]

Mason, in his turn, repeatedly praised the genius of his younger rival. The truth is that each of these legal giants had a wholesome respect for the other. The story has often been told of the litigant who called on Webster to retain him in a case. Webster was already engaged on the other side, but recommended Mason. "What do you think of Mr. Mason?" was the query. "I think him second to no man in the country," was Webster's prompt reply. The man then went to Mason and asked him about Webster's ability. "He's the very devil in any case whatever," responded Mason, "and, if he's against you, I beg to be excused." [3]

The two were soon dividing most of the really desirable legal work in Portsmouth and vicinity, and were retained on opposite sides "pretty much as a matter of course" — to quote

[1] Quoted by David Cross at the Webster Centennial of Dartmouth College in 1901. See *Proceedings of the Webster Centennial*, p. 251. Towards the close of his life, Webster confessed to a friend, "If you were to ask me who was the greatest lawyer in the country, I should answer, John Marshall, but if you took me by the throat and pinned me to the wall and demanded my real opinion, I should be compelled to say it was Jeremiah Mason."

[2] National Edition, XVII, 489.

[3] The difference between Webster and Mason was once expressed with some accuracy in the sentence : " Mr. Mason was a great lawyer; but Mr. Webster was a great man practising law."

Webster's own words.[1] Thrown together on their travels around the circuit, they discovered congenial tastes and soon formed the practice of driving side by side in a chaise, with their luggage in a trunk strapped under the vehicle; and they shared the same room at taverns and boarding houses. Only once is any friction between them mentioned. Something having exasperated Mason in the courtroom, he turned upon Webster "with the ferocity of a tiger," and assailed him with the withering sarcasm of which, under provocation, he was capable. While Webster was telling his wife of the incident, Mason's servant was announced and said that his master would be glad to see Webster at his office. When they met, Mason greeted him cordially, saying, "I was irritated about something when my eye fell on you, and I vented my feelings in the way I did. Don't think of it, for I meant nothing of the sort." [2]

We have a contemporary judgment of Webster from the pen of William Plumer,[3] the younger, at that time a staunch Democrat and opposed to him in politics. In an entry in his Diary for August 1810, Plumer, then a law student in Portsmouth, wrote of Webster: —

As a speaker merely he is perhaps the best at the bar. His language is correct, his gestures good; and his delivery slow, articulate, and distinct. He excels in the statement of facts; but he is not thought to be a deep-read lawyer. His manners are not pleasing, being haughty, cold, and overbearing.[4]

Looking back from the perspective of forty years, Plumer could recall that Webster's demeanor was, like Cardinal

---

[1] National Edition, XVII, 24.

[2] Harvey, p. 60.

[3] William Plumer (1789–1854), — not to be confused with his father, Governor William Plumer, — after graduating from Harvard in 1809, studied law with his father and was admitted to the bar in 1812. He was elected to Congress in 1818 and served three terms. He became an ardent abolitionist, and vigorously opposed the admission of Missouri as a slave state. Later he sat in the New Hampshire Senate (1827–28), and was a member of the state Constitutional Convention of 1850. His letter to George Ticknor, written on April 2, 1853, and published in the National Edition, XVII, 546–47, is an important contribution to Websteriana, although Plumer was not altogether in sympathy with Webster and his views on current questions.

[4] National Edition, XVII, 546–47.

Wolsey's, "lofty and sour to those that loved him not," and
he quoted Dr. John Goddard, one of the most extreme of New
Hampshire Republicans, as having said, "Webster has talent
equal to any office; but he is as malignant as Robespierre, and
not less tyrannical." It was Plumer's father Governor
William Plumer,[1] who on one occasion triumphed over the
arrogance of young Webster. During a trial in which they
were engaged in opposite sides, Plumer quoted from Peake's
Law of Evidence; whereupon Webster criticized the passage
for its wretched logic, denounced the book as worthless, and
then, casting it to the floor in his lordly way, said contemptuously, "So much for Mr. Thomas Peake's compendium of
the Law of Evidence!" Then Plumer, who was too old a hand
to be disconcerted, produced a volume of *Reports,* from which
it appeared that the paragraph which Webster had rejected
with such disdain was taken word for word from a decision by
the great Lord Mansfield. Thus he secured his vindication.[2]
There are other stories to prove that Webster, in his early days
at Portsmouth, was sometimes unceremonious and even rude,
not having yet attained the solemn courtesy which was later
one of his distinctive mannerisms. It may be that the adulation of his admirers had temporarily turned his head.

Of the law cases with which Webster was concerned while
at Portsmouth, not much can be learned; but there were
situations in which he seemed to be inspired. One of these
was the dramatic trial of a wealthy resident of Portsmouth
named Matthew Bramble, who had attempted to swindle a
poor shoemaker named Brown out of an annuity of one hun-

---

[1] William Plumer (1759–1850), born in Newburyport, Massachusetts, was at the
age of eight taken by his family to Epping, New Hampshire, received there a public-
school education, and was admitted to the bar in 1787. He served in the Legislature
for eight terms, — during two of them as Speaker, — and he was President of the
State Senate in 1810–11. Elected United States Senator in 1802 to fill a vacancy, he
remained in that office until 1807. At first a Federalist, he changed his views under
the influence of Clay and John Quincy Adams, and was Republican Governor of New
Hampshire in 1812–13 and 1816–17. It was he who, as Governor, planned to transform
Dartmouth College into a state university. We shall hear of him later in this volume.

[2] This story, told first in Plumer's *Life of William Plumer,* pp. 214–15, is also related
in a vigorous way in Lodge's *Webster,* pp. 36–37.

dred dollars a year which, under contract, he had been paying to him. Bramble's attorney was Jeremiah Mason, and it looked as if the prisoner, who had some influence in the community, would escape the penalty of his fraud. By a fortunate accident, Webster ascertained during the proceedings that a worthless scoundrel named Lovejoy, slated to testify against Brown, had been seen furtively taking a paper from Bramble. After hearing Lovejoy's somewhat stilted testimony, Webster shrewdly concluded that the document had contained information which the latter had memorized; and finally, drawing himself up and marching out from behind the bar to the witness stand, he glared at Lovejoy and burst out, "Give me the paper from which you are testifying!" Terrified by this apparition, the witness pulled the sheet from his pocket, and Webster seized it. Mason quite naturally protested, but, when he was told of all the circumstances, warned his client, Bramble, that he would better settle as quickly as possible. Eventually Bramble was obliged to pay five hundred dollars to Brown, by way of indemnity, and to defray Webster's fees as well as Mason's. The case became a classic in New Hampshire legal history. Years afterwards, some old men, meeting Webster in Exeter, where the trial had been held, asked him the question, "How did you know that Lovejoy had that paper in his pocket?" [1]

It is of the Portsmouth period that another story is told which, although possibly apochryphal, deserves to be recorded. A certain John Greenough, living in Grafton County, being in litigation regarding the title to his farm, had engaged as counsel Moses P. Payson, of Bath, Maine, who had called upon Webster as a fellow Dartmouth man for assistance. When Greenough inquired about the associate counsel, Payson explained that he was to be Daniel Webster, son of old Ebenezer, of Salisbury. "What!" he cried, "That little black stable-boy who once brought me some horses! Then I think we might as well give up the case." At that late hour it was impossible

[1] Harvey, pp. 67–73.

to drop Webster, and Greenough attended court like the Knight of the Rueful Countenance, so disheartened that, when Webster rose to make the closing speech, his client sat dejected, paying little attention to what was being said. Gradually his attention was arrested by Webster's voice, and he could not help listening; and, as he listened, he was held spellbound by its witchery. When the lawyer had finished, Payson turned to Greenough and asked, "What do you think of him now?" "Think!" was the answer. "Why, I think he is an angel sent from Heaven to save me from ruin, and my wife and children from misery!"[1]

In the merciless give and take of this practice in the New Hampshire courts, Webster gained skill and confidence. He later told Plumer that he "had never found any place where the law was administered with so much precision and exactness as in the County of Rockingham." He no longer spent hours with the standard treatises on legal questions, and we do not find him commended by his colleagues for his extensive learning or familiarity with precedents. He tended to rely more and more upon what he called "knowledge of general principles," and his success encouraged him to believe that his policy was correct. "Clearness, force, and earnestness," he said, "are the qualities which produce conviction." For the drudgery involved in poring over the pages of *Reports* he had to count upon the assistance of his colleagues. "It so happened, and so has happened," he wrote in his Autobiography, "that, with the exception of instances in which I have been associated with the Attorney-General of the United States, for the time being, I have hardly ten times in my life acted as junior counsel."[2] He took pains to consult others as to the law, but he was more interested in what the law ought to be.

Webster once told to Thomas Jefferson a story illustrating the point that men sometimes get more credit for readiness and extent of knowledge than they really deserve. In his Ports-

[1] This story, often since repeated, was told originally by Harvey, pp. 76–78, in much greater detail.
[2] National Edition, XVII, 24.

mouth days a blacksmith brought him a case under a will concerning a trifling estate. After going through all his own books, as well as the libraries of Jeremiah Mason and Peyton R. Freeman, another Portsmouth attorney, he reached the conclusion that the bequest was either a *contingent remainder* or an *executory devise*. Still persistent, he sent to Boston for Fearne's *Essay* and other books, costing in all fifty dollars. After studying the subject for some weeks and preparing an elaborate brief, he went into court, argued the case, and secured a verdict for his client. Touched by the blacksmith's poverty, Webster charged him a fee of only fifteen dollars, and was thus considerably out of pocket as a result of taking the suit.

There was, however, a sequel to demonstrate that virtue has its reward. Some years later, while Webster was on his way to Washington, Aaron Burr consulted him in New York on a case which involved the same basic principle as that of the blacksmith's bequest. After listening attentively to Burr's statement of the facts, Webster began to reply, his amazing memory coming to his aid, and cited a series of precedents going back to the reign of Charles II. So astounded was Burr that he could not help asking Webster whether the latter had been consulted by the other side. Later Webster drafted a written opinion, for which he charged Burr enough to compensate himself for the expenses to which he had been originally subjected. In relating the episode, Webster said, "Mr. Burr, no doubt, thought me a much more learned lawyer than I was, and, under the circumstances of the case, I did not think it worth while to disabuse him of his good opinion of me." [1]

Incidents of this kind — and there are several others illustrating the same point — prove that Webster was not indolent and that, when necessity demanded, he would spare no exertion to establish his case. If he had been lazy or careless, he could not have held his own in the competition. He later told Choate that "he had never met anywhere else abler men than some of those who initiated him in the rugged discipline of the

[1] This story is related in Harvey, pp. 74-76, and Curtis, I, 224-25.

New Hampshire Courts." Among those from whom he learned most was Jeremiah Smith,[1] who had been Judge of the United States Circuit Court (1801–02) and Chief Justice of the Superior Court of New Hampshire (1802–09). After serving one term as Governor (1809–10), he had been defeated for reëlection by John Langdon, and had resumed his law practice, in which he was engaged during Webster's early years at Portsmouth. From 1813 to 1816, he was Chief Justice of the Supreme Court of New Hampshire, and, in that position, performed a valuable service in reorganizing the administration of law in the state, which, before that time, had been chaotic and unsystematic. After that Court was abolished in 1816, through a political intrigue, Judge Smith held no other public offices. He was defective as an orator, but he was an agreeable conversationalist, and probably superior in exact scholarship to either Mason or Webster. In writing to his widow, Webster once said, "For what I am in professional life I owe much to Judge Smith. I revere his character; I shall cherish his memory as long as I live." [2] Smith was so frequently on the bench or in political office that his professional career, until after 1816, was constantly interrupted, but he and Webster were frequently opposed in the courts between 1809 and 1813. There is a tradition that Chief Justice Smith, after hearing Webster argue a case in Hillsborough County, remarked that "he had never before met such a young man as that." [3]

[1] Jeremiah Smith (1759–1842), born in Peterborough, New Hampshire, enlisted in the Revolutionary Army and was wounded at Bennington. He spent two years at Harvard (1777–79), but transferred to Rutgers, where he graduated in 1780. After studying law, he was admitted to the bar at Dover, New Hampshire. A Federalist by conviction, he served in Congress from 1791 to 1797, and he was United States District Attorney from 1797 to 1800. He received the degree of Doctor of Laws from Harvard in 1807. Although he had his prejudices and preferences, he was said to have been, on the bench, the very "personification of justice." Webster wrote of him: "Jeremiah Smith was perhaps the best talker I have been acquainted with; he was full of knowledge of books and men, had a great deal of wit and humor, and abhorred silence as an intolerable state of existence." (National Edition, XVIII, 296.)

[2] In commending Judge Smith to Chancellor Kent in 1825, Webster wrote: "He knows everything about New England . . . and as to the law, he knows so much more of it than I do, or ever shall, that I forbear to speak on that point." (National Edition, XVII, 384.)

[3] Curtis, I, 76.

Certainly Smith became Webster's friend and patron, and the latter profited by coming into contact with Smith's quickness of perception, exemplary integrity, and dispassionate judgment. The highest praise ever accorded him on the bench was that "no one had anything to hope from his friendship, or to fear from his enmity." [1]

Another eminent advocate with whom Webster contended was the handsome and elegantly dressed George Sullivan,[2] of Exeter, whose flowing eloquence had power to stir the flinty hearts of jurymen, but who was inferior to Smith and Mason in logic and legal knowledge. Still younger, but destined to a brilliant career, was the "Little Giant," Ichabod Bartlett,[3] who had been born in Webster's native town of Salisbury, and who was to succeed him and Mason as the leader of the New Hampshire bar. William Plumer, Jr., who knew them all, described his father, Governor Plumer, as the Nestor or Ulysses of the group; Smith, as the Menelaus, "with a touch of the Thersites humor"; Mason, as the Ajax or Agamemnon; and Webster as the Achilles, "*impiger, iracundus, inexorabilis, acer.*"

From 1807 until 1813, Webster devoted himself unstintedly to his private law practice. Many years later, Robert Rantoul, Jr., alluding to the brilliancy of the New Hampshire bar in the

---

[1] Morison, *Life of Jeremiah Smith*, p. 208. The inscription on Judge Smith's tombstone, in the old cemetery at Exeter, was prepared by Webster and George Ticknor, and describes him as " equalled by few in original power, practical wisdom, and judicial learning and acuteness; surpassed in the love of honor, justice, and truth by none."

[2] George Sullivan (1771-1838), the son of General John Sullivan, was born in Durham, New Hampshire, graduated at Harvard in 1790, studied law, and began to practice in Exeter, where he resided during the remainder of his life. He was in the State Legislature in 1805, and was later Attorney-General, serving from 1815 to 1836. John M. Shirley said of him: " He relied too little on his preparation, and too much upon his oratory, his power of illustration and argument. But neither the court, the jury, nor the people ever grew tired of listening to the silver tones of his arguments, that fell like music on the ear." (McClintock, *New Hampshire*, pp. 514-15.)

[3] Ichabod Bartlett (1786-1853), after graduating at Dartmouth in 1808, studied law and was admitted to the bar in 1812. He was for three terms in Congress (1823-29), but had a disinclination for political life. He was ready of speech, tactful, and successful in gaining verdicts. Though small of stature, he was quite able to take care of himself by his wits. When the gigantic Mason once said to him that, if he did not cease his insolence, he would put him in his pocket, Bartlett replied, " Do it, and you will have more law in your pocket than you ever had in your head."

early nineteenth century, said, "The collision of such minds invigorated and sharpened the faculties whose native temper was competent to sustain the shock." [1]   It was a struggle which Webster enjoyed, and for six years he held his own single-handed against older and younger rivals.   After his election to Congress in 1812, however, he was no longer able to ride the circuit, and he acquired a partner, Timothy Farrar,[2] who kept his office open and carried on routine business during his long absences in Washington.   At about this time, according to Webster's explicit statement, he was nominated by Governor John Taylor Gilman [3] as Attorney-General of New Hampshire, but the Council rejected him by a vote of three to two.[4]

[1] Rantoul, *Eulogy on Justice Levi Woodbury*, October 16, 1851.

[2] Timothy Farrar (1788–1874), son of Chief Justice Timothy Farrar, of the New Hampshire Court of Common Pleas, was born in New Ipswich, New Hampshire, and was later, from 1824 to 1833, Judge of the State Court of Common Pleas.   He published in 1819 a *Report of the Dartmouth College Case* and in 1867 a *Manual of the Constitution of the United States*.   Webster wrote to Farrar, March 4, 1813, proposing a partnership, and it was actually formed on March 24, 1813.   (National Edition, XVI, 671.)

[3] John Taylor Gilman (1753–1828), of Exeter, a large landowner and popular New England Federalist, was Governor of the state for eleven consecutive terms, from 1794 to 1805, being finally displaced by the Republican, John Langdon, during Jefferson's administration.   Later the War of 1812 brought New Hampshire back into the Federalist ranks, and Gilman was again Governor for three years, from 1813 to 1815. He was a handsome, genial, and efficient man, who made few enemies and invariably ran ahead of his party ticket.   He and Captain Ebenezer Webster were political allies and personal friends, and the Governor did much to aid Daniel Webster in getting a footing in the law.

[4] Webster's own account of the incident was given in a speech at a dinner in Syracuse, New York, in May 1851 (National Edition, XIII, 422 ff.), and reads in part as follows: " At the age of thirty I was in New Hampshire, practising law, and had some clients. John Taylor Gilman, who, for fourteen years, was Governor of the State, thought that, a young man as I was, I might be fit to be an Attorney General of the State of New Hampshire, and he nominated me to the Council; and the Council taking it into their deep consideration, and not happening to be of the same politics of the Governor and myself, voted, three out of five, that I was not competent, and very likely they were right."   The facts are rather difficult to check up.   Governor Gilman was elected in March 1813, and took office in June, by which date Webster had been elected to Congress and obviously could not have held a position as Attorney-General.   The Governor in 1812, when Webster was " at the age of thirty," was William Plumer, who, recently converted to Republicanism and elected on that ticket, would hardly have appointed a Federalist to any state office.   The Governor in 1810 and 1811 was John Langdon, also a Republican.   I have been unable to find any record of Webster's nomination as Attorney-General, but the facts indicate that it must have taken place in December 1815, when Daniel French resigned the office.   Gilman was then Governor and three of the council were Republicans.   Thus conditions then would have been as Webster described them.   George Sullivan was eventually appointed to succeed French and

Although Webster's reputation was spreading from Portsmouth to the far corners of the state, he spoke very infrequently outside the courts. In the summer of 1809, however, when he was invited to deliver the Phi Beta Kappa Oration at Dartmouth College, he drove, with his wife and Mr. and Mrs. Mason, to Hanover, preparing his address at the various inns along the route. "Much was written on the road," he declared, "and many things were conned over and delivered which were never written at all." His subject was "The State of our Literature" — a theme rather difficult to handle at a moment when the United States had no literature of any consequence, and when Irving, Poe, Longfellow, Whittier, and Emerson, to say nothing of Hawthorne and Whitman, had yet to appear. Webster was obliged to confess that "this country or this age is not distinguished by uncommon literary zeal" and to add that there was "an apathy in the pursuit of literary and scientific objects." [1] This deplorable condition he attributed chiefly to two causes: "an inordinate ambition to accumulate wealth," and an exaggerated emphasis on politics. He was moved to recommend most earnestly the formation of an historical society in New Hampshire,[2] saying: —

A historical society is one of the most easy and useful associations of literary men. It is an object of primary consideration, in every country that is desirous of giving its history to posterity.

George Ticknor,[3] who had graduated from Dartmouth in 1807, was back for Commencement, and reported that the

served for twenty years. When Webster was consulted regarding the matter in 1814, he wrote to Moody Kent: "I cannot say whether I would or not accept the office if offered. I was once rather in a temper for it, but of late my opinion is somewhat altered. . . . My indifference to the office does not arise from any wish to be here [Washington]. I do not intend spending another winter in this Great Dismal." Van Tyne, p. 69.

[1] Webster had probably not read Wordsworth, Coleridge, or Scott — although later he became very fond of the *Waverley Novels* and used to recite long passages from *The Lady of the Lake* and *Marmion*.

[2] To-day, the New Hampshire Historical Society, in its beautiful stone building at Concord, has the finest collection of Websteriana in existence.

[3] George Ticknor (1791–1871), to whom all students of Webster are greatly indebted, was born in Boston, and, after graduating from Dartmouth, studied law, and was engaged in practice from 1813 to 1817 in Boston. A scholar by inclination, he then

Websters and Masons made "a very merry party" and were "objects of great interest in the village through the whole time they remained there." Ticknor's comment on the Phi Beta Kappa Oration was acute : —

Mr. Webster's manner in speaking was very fine, — fresh, earnest, and impressive (I was then eighteen years old) ; his oration was very much admired and praised ; but it seemed to me, at the time, that the excitement he created and the homage he received were due rather to their affection for the man, and their great admiration of him, than to the merit of that particular performance.[1]

Although Webster's income, during his Portsmouth period, would seem to have been adequate to his needs, and although he lived modestly, he accumulated debts which it took him some years to pay off. "Property was something," said Frank B. Sanborn, "which Webster could acquire, but never retain." [2] It has been plausibly suggested that he had become so much reconciled to debt in his father's household that he was very little disturbed at owing money. Of the frugality so often ascribed to the New England Yankee, neither he nor his father had the slightest trace. He went through Dartmouth on borrowed funds; he assumed his father's obligations, and paid them off; and, when cash came in easily, it was spent as if the source were inexhaustible. "He does not know the value of money, and never will," said Judge Jeremiah Smith. "No matter; he was born for something better than hoarding money-bags." [3]

---

accepted a position as Professor of the French and Spanish Languages at Harvard, remaining in that position until 1835. During the remainder of his life he wrote his *History of Spanish Literature* (1849), and other important books, including a *Life of William Hickling Prescott* (1864). His *Life, Letters, and Journals* (1876) is rich in references to Webster.

[1] Curtis, I, 96.

[2] Professor Edwin D. Sanborn, who married a niece of Daniel Webster, said, in his *History of New Hampshire* (1875), of Webster: "When he left Portsmouth in 1817, his debts there, unpaid, amounted to thousands, which his Boston friends cheerfully paid." On what authority this statement was based I have not been able to ascertain, but Sanborn doubtless had sources of information denied to those outside the immediate family, and his assertion is supported by traditions of long standing.

[3] National Edition, XVII, 547.

WARNER HOUSE, PORTSMOUTH, NEW HAMPSHIRE

GOVERNOR LANGDON'S HOUSE, PORTSMOUTH,
NEW HAMPSHIRE

William Plumer, the younger, once told a story illustrating the marked contrast between Webster and Mason in their attitude towards money. While in Congress, they kept a carriage between them; and, at the close of one session, their landlord asked Webster to remove a small shed which they had put up as a stable. "Why," said Webster, with one of his careless gestures, "remove it when you please. It is of no further use to us. If it is worth anything to you, you are welcome to it." As the landlord was thanking him for his generosity, it occurred to Webster that one-half the property belonged to Mason, and he told the man to consult the latter on the subject. Mason, when he was approached, said, "You may take down the shed and sell the materials either at auction or at private sale, and account to me for the proceeds. But this is no time to sell it to advantage when everybody is selling out, at the close of the session. Wait a while, till it will bring a fair price, and I will settle with you for it, next winter." This was true New England prudence and foresight, contrasted with Webster's careless indifference to a few dollars.[1] His temperamental lavishness of disposition would be less culpable if it had not led him to regard the borrowing of money as a matter of small importance, and to accept only too readily the sacrifices of others in his behalf. The maxim, "Easy come, easy go," never had a better demonstration than in Webster's career.

The calamity which finally wrecked Webster's finances was what is known even to-day as the "Great Fire." At seven-thirty, on the evening of December 22, 1813, while he was on his way to Washington,[2] a blaze was discovered in a barn belonging to Mrs. Woodward, on the corner of Church and Court Streets, just back of Webster's residence. Within half

[1] National Edition, I, 546–48.

[2] Brewster, in his *Rambles about Portsmouth*, Second Series, p. 210, is responsible for the frequently repeated story that Webster, at dinner at Jacob Sheafe's, not far away, heard the cry of "Fire!" and that Mr. Sheafe, pouring out a fresh supply of wine, insisted on taking a parting glass with his guest before he left. This tale is, of course, entirely fanciful, like certain other stories in Brewster's entertaining but frequently inaccurate volumes.

an hour it had spread to his house, which was speedily consumed, and it was soon raging over a considerable area almost
in the heart of the town. The flames, fanned by a light wind,
moved so rapidly that almost nothing could be rescued by the
victims. When the conflagration was checked, at about five
o'clock on the following morning, fifteen acres lay in smouldering ruins, and 272 buildings had been destroyed, including
108 dwelling houses and 64 stores and shops, with a total loss
of more than $300,000.[1]   It was a clear winter's night, and the
illumination could be seen as far away as Boston.

When Webster reached Washington, he found there a letter
telling him of the disaster, and he promptly wrote Ezekiel: —

I arrived here last evening, and here learned of the Portsmouth fire
and the consumption of my house.   I have only time to say, that the
safety of my family compensates the loss of the property. . . .   I have
not time to say more, but thought you would be glad to hear that I
am in possession of myself after the knowledge of such a loss.[2]

On January 6, 1814, he wrote to I. P. Davis, from Washington, saying: —

Our town has met with another conflagration.   I heard not a
syllable of it till I reached here.   I found a letter from my wife, but
so horrible was the general account which the people about me gave,
that it put my firmness to a severe test to open it.   When I found
nothing lost but house and property, you may well imagine how much
I felt relieved from distress.[3]

Mrs. Webster apparently spent the ensuing winter partly

[1] Waldron wrote Webster: "The real distress & consternation at Portsmouth
is beyond all discription & I hope something great and liberal will be done for them —
you will see how many widows & people in low & middling circumstances have lost all
& are unable even to put up a shelter." (Van Tyne, p. 48.)
[2] Letter of December 29, 1813, National Edition, XVII, 237. Webster's house,
which was uninsured, was worth $6,000, and his library also was very valuable. Mrs.
Webster, at a dinner at which Josiah Quincy was present, on February 17, 1826, said
jestingly that Webster regretted most the loss of a pipe of wine, adding, "It was the
first pipe of wine we ever had, and the getting it was a great event." To this sally
Webster replied that "it had been on tap for some time, and our table was not without
guests," and that it "could scarcely have been more than *half a pipe* at the time of the
fire." (Quincy, *Figures of the Past*, pp. 254–56.)
[3] National Edition, XVII, 238.

with the hospitable Masons and partly with Ezekiel Webster, who was comfortably settled in a large house in Boscawen. At this time, it must be remembered, Daniel's oldest child, Grace, was only four, and Daniel Fletcher Webster was a baby only a few months old. In sending a note to his wife in January, Daniel urged her "to do a great deal of visiting," especially in the neighborhood of Salisbury. When he returned in the spring, they at once rented the house on High Street, which they occupied until they moved to Boston.

Biographers of Webster have been disposed to pass over the Portsmouth period as of slight importance, and it has been overshadowed by the extensive investigations which have been made into his later life. But it is a mistake to dismiss it with a few casual sentences. It was a time when Webster, both in law and in politics, was unconsciously preparing himself for a broader career — a career which he hoped might be his, but of which he was never oversanguine. We have seen how rapidly he rose to a foremost position at the bar of New Hampshire. The early stages of his advancement in politics must now be considered.

V

FIRST ADVENTURES IN POLITICS

> Every boy and every gal
> That's born into the world alive
> Is either a little Liberal
> Or else a little Conservative.
>
> — GILBERT, *Iolanthe*

We are, sir, from principles and habit attached to the union of the states. But our attachment is to the substance, and not to the form.

— WEBSTER, *The Rockingham Memorial*

The voice of the whole mercantile interest is united, to an unprecedented degree, against the war, which is declared to be undertaken, at so much hazard of blood and treasure, for their benefit.

— WEBSTER, Address before the Washington Benevolent Society, Portsmouth, N. H.

OLD Ebenezer Webster was once taken suddenly ill in a village which had cast its vote for Jefferson. "Carry me back home," he cried. "I don't want to die in a Republican town!" [1] Such was the fierceness of the partisanship to which the Webster boys were accustomed in their youth. Captain Webster had been a stubborn and influential figure in the legislature at a period when New Hampshire people took their politics very seriously. He favored the new Constitution in 1789, and later, during Washington's administration, sided with Hamilton against Jefferson. An uncompromising Federalist, he was sure that the nation was on the brink of ruin in 1801, when John Adams was superseded in the White House by the restless statesman from Virginia.

Daniel Webster's political creed was codified before he was

[1] The party of Thomas Jefferson, to-day usually known as "Democratic," was, during the first two decades of the nineteenth century, more frequently called "Republican." Other terms, such as "Whig" or "Antifederalist," were also not infrequently used.

of voting age. The opinions quoted with approval about the hearthstone in the Webster tavern were those of his father's cronies, the Federalist leaders of New Hampshire, such as Governor Gilman or Judge Jeremiah Smith. Some lads, revolting against this parental dogmatism, might have become radicals out of sheer perversity. But Daniel was temperamentally a conservative, who preferred familiar objects and long-traveled roads. He could not understand Jefferson's passion for experimenting with science and society, and he had a distrust of all reformers, heretics, and rebels. He was no Percival, to follow "wandering fires," but an institutionalist, a supporter of family, church, and country; and he liked, indeed probably overvalued, tradition, law, and regularity. By individualists, such as William Lloyd Garrison, he was repelled, and he cherished no desire to be "free from heart-withering custom's cold control."

As he became more and more identified with the prosperous and established elements in the community, his innate convictions hardened, and his tendency was to resist changes. He was neither bigoted nor unprogressive, but he wished, if possible, to avoid innovations. Thus, to his admirers, he became a symbol of stability. Whenever waves of popular unrest threatened to inundate the republic, he remained firm, as immutable as that Mount Kearsarge under the shadow of which he had been born.

In his Hanover Oration, in 1811, Webster denounced the revolutionary ideas of Napoleon. Two years later, at Fryeburg, as we have seen, he asserted that any alteration of the Constitution was a serious business, "not to be undertaken without obvious necessity, nor conducted without caution, deliberation, and diffidence." *Caution, deliberation, and diffidence!* These are strange words on the lips of a young man just out of college. This is not the rashness which we condone in "flaming youth." Henry Clay, in his "salad days," flung prudence to the winds, and Andrew Jackson as a mature statesman was not precisely discreet. Even the sedate John Quincy Adams had his radical moments. But critics had no occasion to call Webster "reckless" or "impulsive." Governed by his reason, he saw the wisdom of a strong central government, under which a too ebullient individualism should be restrained. The border line between caution and cowardice is difficult to define, and Webster's enemies often accused him of being afraid. It was not timidity or inertia, however, which made him a conservative, but rather a carefully considered philosophy, inherited, and also confirmed by experience. When he was ready to cast his ballot, not even Governor Gilman was a fiercer Federalist than he.

It was inevitable that Webster, with his interest in public affairs and his facility in debate, should be drawn into politics. The first campaign in which he participated was that of 1804, while he was in the office of Christopher Gore. President Thomas Jefferson, detested by New England Federalists for what they regarded as his radicalism in economics, in government, and in religion, was a candidate for reëlection, with Charles C. Pinckney as his Federalist opponent. In August, New Hampshire Federalists enjoyed a brief moment of triumph through the success, by a small majority, of their Congressional ticket, and Webster was much encouraged.[1] Events soon showed, however, that he had been too sanguine. In November, electors were chosen for the first time in New Hampshire by a system of popular suffrage, and the Federalists were beaten.[2] Nor were the results in other sections of the country satisfactory to Webster. Only two states — Connecticut and Delaware — cast all their votes for Pinckney and King; and two more votes, secured from Maryland, gave the Federalists a miserable total of 14 as compared with 162 for Jefferson. It looked as if Federalism were moribund, if not defunct.

In the gubernatorial election of the following March, the Federalist, Gilman, was a candidate for the twelfth consecutive time, his opponent being John Langdon, a sagacious and popular Republican. During the bitterly contested campaign,

[1] Webster to Davis, October 20, 1804 (Van Tyne, p. 16).
[2] At this election, held on November 5, 1804, the seven Republican electors from New Hampshire received 6607 votes against 6336 for their opponents.

Webster, while on a visit to his father, wrote "at a single sitting of a winter's day and night" a pamphlet, published anonymously in February 1805, under the title, *An Appeal to the Old Whigs of New Hampshire*. Captain Webster was under financial obligation to both candidates. In the autumn of 1801, he had secured Governor Gilman's assistance in borrowing "a few hundreds"; [1] and some years before that, he had obtained the loan of a considerable sum from the wealthy and generous Langdon.[2] Neither debt had been paid, and the position was embarrassing to Daniel, who could understand all its complications.

Encouraged, perhaps, by his anonymity, Webster traced the historical origin of the Republican Party back to the Antifederalists of 1787 and the Jacobins of the French Revolutionary days, and then reviewed the record of Jefferson's first term, condemning especially that President's attack on the judiciary, his abolition of internal taxation, and his abandonment of the navy. Webster thought rather highly of his first contribution to campaign literature. "Not long ago," he wrote in 1829, "I found a copy of this sage production. Among other things of a similar kind it is certainly not despicable." [3]   But he could not hold back the tidal wave of Jeffersonian Democracy, then at its flood. At the election on March 12, 1805, New Hampshire rejected Gilman and chose a Republican Governor.[4] Prophets of gloom wailed that New England and the nation were about to suffer the fate of Nineveh

---

[1] Ebenezer Webster to his sons, December 21, 1804 (National Edition, XVII, 197).
[2] Sanborn, *New Hampshire*, pp. 286–87.
[3] The full text of this *Appeal* is reprinted in the National Edition, XV, 522 ff. Webster said that he had had the pleasure of seeing his pamphlet " kicked about under many tables."
[4] The State Senate had seven Republicans and four Federalists. The *New Hampshire Gazette*, on June 11, said gleefully, " At length the triumph of Republicanism is complete." William Plumer wrote to Josiah Quincy: " Democracy has obtained its long-expected triumph in New Hampshire. John Langdon is governor-elect. His success is not owing to snow, rain, hail, or bad roads, but to the incontrovertible fact that the Federalists of this state do not compose the majority. Many good men have grown weary of a system whose labors bear a close affinity to those of Sisyphus." (McClintock, *New Hampshire*, p. 474.) Governor Langdon took office on June 6, 1806, at Concord.

and Tyre. In his first political skirmish, Webster had been defeated.

While this local clash of factions was taking place, the mighty duel between Great Britain and Napoleon for European supremacy was moving towards a crisis, and the United States, as the most important neutral shipping power, was the unlucky victim of the punitive measures of the warring empires. With each of the belligerents hoping to coax or coerce America into an alliance, it was not easy for us to preserve that neutrality enjoined by Washington in his *Farewell Address*. There were, of course, open adherents of both England and France within our borders. The situation resembled that during the early months of the World War, when England and Germany, heading powerful confederations, were endeavoring to force us to choose between them. The diplomatic correspondence of Jefferson and Madison resembles in tone that of Wilson and Lansing more than a century later. In 1915 and 1916, however, the United States was relatively much stronger than in 1806 and 1807, and was consequently freer to adopt an independent course.

Commercial interests in New England were chafing under diminishing profits. Every time an American trader was seized or sunk by a foreign warship, some Yankee was out of pocket. Whenever a Salem merchantman was searched by a British frigate and our sailors were forcibly impressed into service under the Union Jack, new irritation developed. It was at the seaports that resentment was keenest; interior sections, although humiliated at our impotence, were not affected so directly by these outrages. Jefferson, although not a non-resistant, was a philosophical pacifist, who considered war as a last resort, justifiable only when all peaceable means of adjusting difficulties between nations had been exhausted. His apparent procrastination and his reluctance to adopt measures of "preparedness" were the logical outcome of his idealistic principles. As a result, the country, at the opening of his second term, was as nearly without naval and military protection as it has ever been in its history.

What many New Englanders were thinking may be gathered from Webster's oration on Independence Day, in 1806, before the "Federal gentlemen" of Concord. He did not discriminate between England and France, but, condemning them both for their affronts to the United States, demanded "a naval force sufficient to protect our harbors and convoy the great branches of our trade." He declared that the French Empire had "all the immorality, the licentiousness, the prodigality and corruption of declining Rome"; but he also referred to England's attitude on the matter of our maritime rights as "jealous, haughty, and arrogant." On the broad question of preparedness, he said: —

Nothing seems plainer than this: if we will have commerce, we must protect it. So long as we are rich and defenseless, rapacity will prey upon us. The government ought either to defend the merchant, or to repeal the laws which restrain him from defending himself. It ought to afford him the assistance of armed vessels, or to suffer him to arm his own vessels.[1]

He concluded with a striking sentence, the purport of which he had already employed in his *Fryeburg Address*, and which he was to use again forty-six years later at the conclusion of his last speech in Congress: —

A genuine patriot . . . feels that the last end, which can happen to any man, never comes too soon, if he fall in defense of the law and liberty of his country.[2]

The unusual feature of this oration was the impartiality with which Webster struck out at both warring nations, instead of confining himself, like most of the Federalists, to the castigation of Napoleon. The insults which so stirred his indignation at Concord were trifling, however, compared with those which were to come. England and France now resorted to a series of retaliatory measures, calculated to force neutrals into the fray, on one side or the other. Already, on May 16, 1806, Charles James Fox had issued an Order in Council placing the

[1] National Edition, XV, 537 ff.   [2] *Ibid.*, p. 521, and X, 170.

entire European coast from Brest to the Elbe under blockade, with the object of shutting off supplies from the armies of Napoleon. The French Emperor, choosing a moment when the victory of Jena had made him military master of Prussia, replied with the defiant Berlin Decree (November 21, 1806), isolating the British Isles and forbidding any ship which had touched at an English port to enter a harbor in France. Britain's response was another Order in Council, prohibiting all neutral vessels from trading with any French port from which British commerce was excluded. Napoleon then countered with the sweeping Milan Decree, declaring that any boat calling between British ports was lawful prize and that any craft which submitted to search by an English cruiser thereby relinquished its neutral character. Strict enforcement of all these measures was, of course, impossible. But, in spite of the fact that they were merely fierce gestures, our commerce suffered more and more, and protests to the Department of State became frequent. It has been estimated that, between 1803 and 1812, more than nine hundred of our vessels were captured by the British and more than five hundred by the French.

Although his equanimity was disturbed by these drastic edicts and by the ravages on our commerce, Jefferson was not ready for war. He preferred instead a policy of "peaceable coercion." Recalling the success of the Non-Importation Acts of 1756, he resolved to bring economic pressure to bear on Europe. As a preliminary warning, the administration issued a Non-Importation Act, prohibiting the admission of certain British commodities to the United States, the purpose being to deprive England of her American market and thus to persuade her to modify her hostile attitude towards neutral countries. Even when the British frigate *Leopard* bombarded our *Chesapeake*, killing three men, badly wounding fourteen, and compelling her to haul down her colors and give up four sailors, the President declined an opportunity to lead the country into war. Instead he issued a dignified Proclamation, called a special session of Congress, and, on December 22, 1807, signed an act declaring an Embargo, unlimited in duration, on all American shipping engaged in trade with any foreign port.

By the Embargo, Jefferson hoped to protect our merchant vessels, to secure time for the atmosphere to clear, and, through economic pressure to compel England and France to respect our maritime rights. If it had been heartily supported by the country, it might have succeeded. Instead it was greeted by merchants and shipowners with derision and disapproval. They did not want war, but they were even less favorably disposed to an embargo. The news was printed in the issue of the *New Hampshire Gazette* for December 29, 1807, by which date Daniel Webster had become a resident of Portsmouth, which, like most of the Atlantic coast towns, was dependent on its carrying trade. After a temporary decline during the Revolution, our commerce had undergone a marked revival. The tonnage of Portsmouth on December 31, 1806, was 22,798, and, during the preceding twelvemonth, 103 vessels had cleared from there for the West Indies alone. Its exports during the year 1807 aggregated $680,000, and its imports amounted to more than $800,000.[1] It needed no trained economist to predict what the effect of the Jeffersonian policy would be.

As if by the waving of a devil's wand, tons of shipping in Boston, Salem, Newburyport, and Portsmouth became worthless. The value of our exports dropped in a year from $110,000,000 to $20,000,000. The Embargo was, no doubt, frequently evaded, but, through its operation, thousands of industrious people were deprived of their means of livelihood. It was as if an army should turn its machine guns on its own troops in an effort to annihilate the enemy.[2] Republican newspapers in New England, loyal to their leader, tried to be cheerful, but it was a bitter draught for them to swallow.

To the shipowners of the coast towns, born and bred in

[1] These statistics are quoted from Barstow's *History of New Hampshire* (1842), p. 341 ff.

[2] An attempt has sometimes been made to prove that the Embargo had on New England commerce a less detrimental effect than has ordinarily been supposed. But it is difficult to find any other explanation for the extraordinary decline in shipping which immediately followed the promulgation of the Embargo measures.

Federalism, it seemed as if Jefferson, whose political strength
was drawn principally from the South and West and from the
agrarian classes, were wreaking vengeance on the Northeast
and its commerce.[1] The hatred formerly felt towards England and France was now transferred to the President. Soon,
by one of history's strange mutations, the Federalists of New
England were driven from their nationalist position into one
which was anti-national and sectional; and, in the privacy
of their homes, they began to whisper threats of disunion.
Self-interest transformed them into advocates of State rights,
and they used arguments similar to those which were later
advanced by South Carolina. While a storm of protest
rumbled along the Atlantic, the possibility of separation from
the Union was discussed in Market Square by men who were
Webster's clients and friends.

To the controversy thus precipitated, Webster made a contribution in a small pamphlet called *Considerations on the
Embargo Laws*, published as propaganda during the summer
preceding the elections of 1808. Gallatin, the Secretary of the
Treasury, had courageously sent a letter to Jefferson, insisting
that an unlimited embargo was unconstitutional; and Webster,
developing this point, treated the matter as a question of
constitutional law, comparing Jefferson's act unfavorably
with the sixty-day embargo laid by President Washington
in 1794. At the moment when Webster's argument appeared,
the Jeffersonian Embargo had been in operation for more than
seven months without affecting the attitude of England and
France towards us. A few captains, habituated to risks and
indifferent to punishment, had made money by escaping the
vigilance of patrols; but the average man noticed only that

---

[1] The Federalists were not placated by Jefferson's tactless letter to the Legislature
of New Hampshire, in August 1808, advising the citizens of that state to retire from
the seas and to provide for themselves " those comforts and conveniences of life for
which it would be unwise ever more to recur to distant countries." The condescension
of this counsel was peculiarly galling to merchants who were losing thousands of dollars
a month. Nor was their fury allayed when they read in the *New Hampshire Gazette*
for April 19, 1808, such cowardly doctrine as this: " The British have captured about
50, the French 10 or 15, American ships, under their respective blockading decrees!
What would have been the total if the Embargo had not kept our ships in port?"

the Embargo was limiting our trade, causing many bank-
ruptcies, and hastening the decay and ruin of our merchant
fleets.[1]

Webster specifically charged Jefferson with having instituted
the Embargo in order to favor France and encourage her in
her war against Great Britain.[2]   The New England Federalists
were attached to England by various ties — social, financial,
and sentimental.   Webster's patron, Christopher Gore, had
resided for several years in London, and, like Rufus King, had
returned sympathetic with the British people.   At times this
pro-British feeling, as in the case of Senator Timothy Pickering,
savored of Anglomania, and to this extreme Webster was not
disposed to go.   Like most of his Federalist associates, however, he reasoned that the success of England in the contest
with the "detestable tyrant," Napoleon, was essential to the
welfare of an Anglo-Saxon country like the United States;
and he was fearful that the Embargo might precipitate open
war with Great Britain, thus weakening that nation at the
crisis when all her resources were needed.   The policy of the
Federalists was dictated mainly by economic considerations.
It was because of our carrying trade that they wished to rid
themselves of the Embargo and to preserve peace with England.

The reaction in New England against Jefferson showed itself in the presidential election of 1808, when New Hampshire,
Massachusetts, and Rhode Island all went for Pinckney.[3]   In
the rest of the country, however, Republicanism was still
strong.   The Federalist candidates secured forty-seven electoral votes as compared with fourteen in 1804; but James
Madison was triumphantly carried into the White House,

---

[1] "When the Tenth Congress assembled for its winter session, on November 7, 1808,
no sensible man in the United States doubted that the embargo was a failure.   It had
destroyed the commerce and impoverished the sailors and ship-owners it was supposed
to protect; as an instrument of coercion it had proved futile." (Morison, *The Life
and Letters of Harrison Gray Otis*, II, 1.)

[2] Webster's pamphlet may be found in the National Edition, XV, 564 ff., reprinted
from a rare copy in the possession of the Massachusetts Historical Society.

[3] At this period, parties were very evenly divided in New Hampshire.   The Republican Legislature passed, June 14, 1808, an address to President Jefferson, compliment-
ing him upon his record.   In the following autumn, however, the state cast its electoral
vote for Pinckney and King.

there to continue the work of his predecessor, to whom he
was indebted for his office. The full vigor of the opposition
was not revealed until after the passage of the so-called "Force
Act," of January 9, 1809, which bestowed upon government
officials almost unlimited power to carry out the provisions
of the Embargo. . . . Then came the explosion. Never
had the Federalists, even in 1798, claimed or exercised such
autocratic authority as that now assumed by the Jeffersonians.
For the moment, the tactical advantage passed to the Federalists. The General Court of Massachusetts denounced both
the Embargo and the Force Act as unconstitutional. Town
meetings sent in their protests from all over New England.[1]
The grumbling at dinner tables, the threats of disunion, the
demands for repeal, became more emphatic.[2] Even Northern
Republicans were beginning to join with the Federalists against
the administration. At last, three days before the close of his
term, Jefferson yielded, and the Embargo was withdrawn.

He himself must have been aware that his plan had failed.
Our trade had not been absolutely indispensable to England
and France. Conceived with the best intentions, the Embargo had almost ruined our commerce. It had weakened
our national morale by its tacit assumption that it is better
to be safe than to fight; and it had insidiously led the Republican Party into a justification of despotism.[3] In retaliation,
the Federalists had taken refuge in a sectionalism which,
before another decade had passed, was to be their destruction.

As a resident of Portsmouth, Webster had identified himself
with the Federalists. He cast his first vote there on March
8, 1808, when the citizens met in town meeting and balloted
for Governor, as they did throughout the state. John Lang-

[1] In his reminiscences, Jefferson wrote, " I felt the foundation of the government
shaken under my feet by the New England townships."

[2] The *New Hampshire Gazette*, in Portsmouth, was hard put to it to meet the slashing
arguments of its Federalist rival, the Portsmouth *Oracle*. Jefferson, who was really
astonished at the whirlwind which he had raised, wrote, " I did not expect a crop of so
sudden and rank growth of fraud and open opposition by force could have grown up
in the United States."

[3] See Henry Adams, *United States*, IV, 413 ff., for a full and adequate review of the
disastrous consequences of the Embargo.

don, the popular Republican, had still enough prestige to win the election, in spite of the resentment against the Embargo. In the following spring, however, Webster and his friends induced Jeremiah Smith to resign as Chief Justice of the Superior Court and accept the Federalist nomination for Governor, and he defeated Langdon by a majority of two hundred.   A year later, after the abandonment of the Embargo, the Republicans regained their ascendancy, and Langdon had a small margin over Smith.   On July 3, 1810, Webster was appointed chairman of a committee to arouse Federalist enthusiasm in Portsmouth and its vicinity.

Having secured the repeal of the Embargo, the Federalists were disposed to be quiet.   Nor did the Madison Administration have any plan for positive action.   Uncertain what to do, Congress passed a new Non-Intercourse Act, forbidding American vessels to trade with either England or France until the offensive measures of those countries had been withdrawn, but allowing commerce with other nations.   Erskine, the British Minister at Washington, promised, on behalf of his government, that the Orders in Council would be abandoned if the United States would cease to enforce the Non-Intercourse Act against Great Britain.   Trade was resumed with England, and the spirits of the Portsmouth merchants were buoyant. And then Canning, declaring that Erskine had exceeded his instructions, repudiated the agreement, and the quarrel was revived.   Madison had shown himself willing to be on good terms with England.   Now that his overtures had been openly rejected, he was ready to try what France had to propose.

Still in a temporizing mood, Congress, on May 1, 1810, passed what was known as "Macon's Bill, No. 2," authorizing the President, if either France or England would revoke her restrictions against our commerce, to put the Non-Intercourse Act in operation against the rival belligerent.   This naïve experiment in international bribery induced the crafty Napoleon to notify our Minister, through his Foreign Secretary, that he would abandon the Berlin and Milan Decrees on November 1, 1810, if, during the interval, the British would repeal their Orders in Council or the United States should cause its rights to be respected by England. Although this promise was made merely in an informal note, Madison grasped it with relief and elation, and, reopening our relations with France, declared our trade with England closed after February 2, 1811.

The bickering, the recrimination, and the interchange of diplomatic notes still continued. Napoleon, on April 28, 1811, rather vaguely repealed the obnoxious edicts, but his fleet still continued to capture American vessels for violating them. He was playing his usual devious game, marked by evasions and falsehoods, and he must have smiled cynically as he watched the two Anglo-Saxon countries debating whether or not the Berlin and Milan Decrees had really been revoked. Meanwhile other incidents were exacerbating the bitterness between us and England. Our ships were still being forcibly searched; our seamen were being impressed from our decks by prowling British cruisers; and there were ominous clashes between British and American war vessels. People were raising the cry of "Free Trade and Sailors' Rights." But, even with such provocation, the New England Federalists preferred peace to the hazards of battle.

A new factor, however, was now to be reckoned with. Along our frontier appeared a group of aggressive young men, full of military ardor, resentful of insults, and eager for national expansion. They wanted to wrest Canada from England, Florida from Spain, and Texas from Mexico. With their anger stirred by our grievances, these adventurous spirits saw an opportunity to realize their ambitions. The uprising of Tecumseh, backed by British encouragement, followed by the Battle of Tippecanoe (November 7, 1811), offered another pretext for war. Why should not the American republic stretch from the Isthmus of Panama to the Arctic? By a paradox, it was not commercial New England which ultimately led us into conflict with Great Britain, but rather the West and the Southwest, alarmed by the alliance between the Indian tribes and the British, and craving some outlet for their energies.

The Twelfth Congress, meeting in the autumn of 1811, was controlled by audacious men, led by Henry Clay and John Caldwell Calhoun. They were disgusted with "peaceable coercion," which had been tried but had accomplished nothing. Of the members from New Hampshire, — all of them Republicans, — three were for war, and one of them, John Adams Harper,[1] was the author of the statement, "To me, sir, it appears that the Author of Nature has marked our limits in the south, by the Gulf of Mexico; and on the north, by the regions of eternal frost." President Madison sent a vigorous message to Congress, threatening a breach with England, and it was soon apparent that the expansionists were in the saddle.[2] John Randolph correctly analyzed the situation when he said, "Agrarian cupidity, not maritime right, urges the war." Through the winter the discussion continued, and finally, after another message from Madison, the House of Representatives voted, seventy-nine to forty-nine, for war. A study of the vote shows that the South, with Kentucky, Tennessee, and Ohio, was virtually solid for the administration; while the Eastern and Middle states were in opposition. Two weeks later the Senate concurred by a vote of nineteen to thirteen, and the formal declaration was made on June 18. Only five days later, the British Cabinet repealed all its Orders in Council, thus settling most of the American complaints. If there had been a transatlantic cable, much bloodshed might have been averted. Even a little more patience on the part of the "War Hawks" might have made a conflict unnecessary. As it was, fighting continued, both on land and sea, for many months.

[1] John Adams Harper (1779–1816), born in Derryfield, New Hampshire, attended the Phillips Exeter Academy, began to practice law in Sanbornton, and moved to Meredith Bridge (now Laconia) in 1806. He was Clerk of the State Senate, served in the New Hampshire Lower House, and was elected to the Twelfth Congress as a War Democrat. He was a leading figure during the first session, and his speeches did much to stimulate a war spirit. His defeat in 1812 removed him from political life, and he died disappointed four years later.

[2] For an excellent discussion of the causes of the War of 1812, see *Expansionists of 1812*, by Julius W. Pratt (Macmillan, 1925), which explains the rise of the doctrine of " Manifest Destiny " in the West and Southwest.

Webster's position throughout the debate in Congress was typical of that of the New Hampshire Federalists. They had demanded government aid for the protection of their commerce; they had objected to the Embargo because it destroyed their trade; but they did not want war. They saw clearly that it would be disastrous to importers and exporters, and that it would give political preponderance to the West and South. They were, furthermore, on general principles unwilling to break off friendly relations with England. The War of 1812 was precipitated, not by the section which had suffered most from British depredations, but by that which hoped for an increase of territory as part of the terms of peace.

It was easy to make a declaration of war, but the actual fighting was a different matter. The United States was pitiably unprepared for the emergency. Although a clash had been imminent for several years, there were only sixteen vessels in our navy, which, under Jefferson, had been allowed to disintegrate and rot at the wharves. Our army was badly organized and poorly officered. Our frontier was long and exposed to attack. We were in no condition for facing even a third-rate power. Hostilities had hardly begun before General William Hull made a disgraceful surrender of his troops at Detroit. The nation was certainly not a unit, and the Federalists, always opposed to the war, were now resolved to do nothing to win it. We might postpone disaster, but no one familiar with our vulnerability could doubt what the outcome would be, especially if England, freed from her long contention with Napoleon, should concentrate her veteran navy and army upon us.

The news of the declaration of war had hardly reached Portsmouth before Daniel Webster's opportunity arrived. His views on the subject were no secret. It was natural that the Washington Benevolent Society,[1] made up of Federalists,

[1] Organizations bearing this name had been formed in many sections of New England during Jefferson's administrations, the object being to unite the Federalists under the ægis of " The Father of His Country " and to give the impression that the Federalists, in opposing Jefferson and the Republicans, were carrying on the Washington tradition.

— or, as they chose to style themselves, the "Friends of Peace," — should invite him to deliver their Independence Day Address. On the Fourth of July, in 1812, there were two patriotic celebrations in Portsmouth. The Republicans held a "giant mass meeting," with William Claggett, Esquire, as the orator, and followed this with a jubilant dinner at Frost's Hotel.[1] On the same Saturday morning, the Washington Benevolent Society, escorted by the gorgeously uniformed "Gilman Blues," marched through the streets to "Rev. Mr. Ballou's meeting-house, in pleasant street," where, after an invocation by the Reverend Mr. Parker and the reading of *The Legacy of Washington* [2] by Major Samuel Larkin, Webster delivered his address.[3] The procession then reformed and paraded to "Underwood's Rope Walk," where more than four hundred citizens joined in a collation. It was one of Portsmouth's memorable days.

To those who lived through the World War and observed its psychology, it will seem incredible that Daniel Webster and the "Friends of Peace" could have opposed the War of 1812 without bringing upon themselves the charge of disloyalty and being persecuted as "pacifists" or "undesirable persons." We had probably even more direct provocation for challenging England in 1812 than for fighting Germany in 1917. Yet at a public gathering, on the anniversary of our national independence, Webster expressed himself as out of sympathy with Madison's foreign policy — a policy which three out of New Hampshire's five Congressmen had approved. His earlier

[1] The Republican *New Hampshire Gazette* said on July 7, 1812, of this celebration: " It was the spontaneous effusion of honest zeal, of patriotic ardor, of disinterested feeling for their grossly insulted and much injured country, towards whose altar the old and young were eagerly pressing, there to renew the oath TO LIVE FREE OR DIE!" The *Gazette* ostentatiously refrained from mentioning the Federalist ceremonies on the same day. Claggett graduated from Dartmouth in 1808 and had only recently been admitted to the bar.

[2] This was evidently Washington's *Farewell Address*, a favorite document with the Federalists.

[3] The Portsmouth *Oracle*, decidedly Federalist in point of view, reported on July 11: " An address was delivered before the Society by Daniel Webster, Esq., in a more impressive and eloquent manner than we ever witnessed on a similar occasion." The *Oracle* made no reference in its columns to the Republican celebration of the same date.

occasional addresses had been largely conventional, safe, and platitudinous, and only rarely partisan in temper. Now he burst out in a strongly Federal utterance, in which he condemned the government for leading us into an unjustifiable war.[1]

After some characteristic paragraphs praising Washington as a statesman "whose conduct was the result of well-considered and settled principles," Webster went on to show that the Federal Constitution was originally adopted "for no single reason so much as for the protection of commerce," which, under the ineffective Articles of Confederation, had been in distress; that, because of the aid offered by the Constitution, a large and lucrative shipping trade had been built up, to the immense advantage of "every interest and every class of the community"; that the subsequent "total abandonment of all provision for our naval defense" under Jefferson[2] was a colossal blunder in that it left our fleet exposed to an enemy; that Washington, facing crises far more ominous, had managed, "by able and impartial negotiations," to avoid armed conflicts with European countries; that it was unjust to single out England and not to proceed with equal vigor against France, with whom there was "still abundant cause of war"; and that the War of 1812 was "premature and inexpedient," undertaken ostensibly for the benefit of merchants, but likely to bring about their ruin.[3] Webster's aversion to Napoleonic France was like the horror felt by many respectable Americans for "Red Russia" during the aftermath of the World War; and he closed his address with the fervent declaration that he and the "Friends of Peace" would never allow the "unhallowed hosts" of France to land on our shores

[1] This Address is printed in the National Edition, XV, 583 ff., from a version published by the Oracle Press, in Portsmouth.

[2] The Federalists were accustomed to pass quietly over the fact that the bill allowing the President, at his discretion, to reduce our naval force to thirteen vessels was signed by the Federalist President, John Adams, on March 3, 1801, as one of the last acts of his administration.

[3] At that moment, Webster did not realize the significance of the expansionist movement along the frontier, but he saw clearly that New England would be the section to suffer most through the war.

without resisting to the death. . . . His voice was not the only one raised that day in protest against the war. All over New England the opposition was becoming articulate. At the Independence Day Banquet of the Boston Federalists one of the toasts drunk with the most enthusiasm was: *"The Existing War — the Child of Prostitution. May No American Acknowledge It Legitimate!"*

There were uncompromising Federalists who believed that New England, in view of the unsympathetic attitude of the administration, had sufficient justification for leaving the Union; and the possibility of secession was frequently hinted at in the correspondence of Northern statesmen. The economic situation was precisely the reverse of that which existed in the "1830's," when South Carolina was convinced that the North was conspiring to ruin her. So strong is the instinct of self-preservation that any section of the Union is likely to contemplate separation when it finds its welfare threatened by the central government. Those who, in 1812, held to the "compact theory" of the Union had good precedents to quote and plausible arguments to advance. On several occasions since Washington took the oath of office, individual states had claimed the right to nullify Congresssional enactments and had asserted their authority as superior, under certain conditions, to that of Congress.[1] The Virginia and Kentucky Resolutions — the first drawn up by Madison, the second mainly by Jefferson — had, in 1798, declared the Alien and Sedition Bills unconstitutional and had defiantly announced that those two states would resist their operation. Indeed, the Virginia Resolutions had set forth the doctrine that, whenever the Federal Government assumes powers not delegated to it by the states, "its acts are unauthoritative, void, and are of no force."

But suggestions of separation had not arisen entirely from

---

[1] At a later date, William Rawle's *A View of the Constitution of the United States* (1825), used at the United States Military Academy at West Point when Grant and Lee were students there, taught the doctrine that a state has a right to withdraw from the Union without being in rebellion. Rawle was a leader of the Philadelphia bar and long an attorney for the Bank of the United States.

Republican sources. With the triumph of Jefferson in 1800, the disgruntled Federalists, now for the first time in a minority, had meditated the creation of a Northern Confederacy; and members of the notorious "Essex Junto" had seriously talked over such a project.[1] These individualists maintained that each state, having of its own free will entered the Federal compact, had the privilege of withdrawing from it, just as the member of a corporation, dissatisfied with its management, resigns after due notice. That they never pushed through their scheme was owing to their inability to secure the support of certain influential leaders without whose approval they dared not go on.

In 1808, during the turmoil occasioned by the Embargo Act, separatist sentiment in the Northeast again flared up, and might have been dangerous if the repeal of the offensive measure had not come when it did. The acquisition of Louisiana had been regarded by the New England Federalists as a despotic act; and when it was proposed to admit the Territory of Orleans to the Union as the State of Louisiana, Josiah Quincy announced on the floor of the House of Representatives (January 14, 1811) that, if the bill were passed, "the bonds of this Union are virtually dissolved," and declared that it would then be the duty of some of the states "to prepare definitely for a separation; amicably if they can, violently if they must."

Proud and sensitive minorities usually try every device for escaping from the tyranny of immovable majorities. If Daniel Webster, as a faithful Federalist, had lent an ear to those who were dallying with the project of a Northern Confederacy, it would not have been unexpected. Nevertheless he claimed to be an adherent of the Union. In his Portsmouth Address, he lamented the commencement and continuation

---

[1] The Essex Junto — so named because it comprised a small group of statesmen from Essex County, Massachusetts — included Timothy Pickering, Fisher Ames, Theophilus Parsons, George Cabot, and others, representing the " upper classes." Most of them were rich, well-educated, and socially prominent, and they were aristocratic in all their political theories. The democracy which Jefferson represented and advocated was to them peculiarly abhorrent.

of the strife with the mother country. He felt that it would endanger rather than secure our rights upon the sea. He shuddered at the prospect of being thrown into an alliance with the detested Bonaparte. And yet, when he came to suggest a possible course of action, he said : —

With respect to the war, in which we are now involved, the course which our principles require us to pursue cannot be doubtful. It is now the law of the land, and as such we are bound to regard it. Resistance and insurrection form no parts of our creed. The disciples of Washington are neither tyrants *in* power, nor rebels *out*. If we are taxed, to carry on this war, we shall disregard certain distinguished examples, and shall pay. If our personal services are required, we shall yield them to the precise extent of our Constitutional liability. At the same time, the world may be assured that we know our rights, and shall exercise them. We shall express our opinions on this, as on every other measure of government, I trust without passion, — I am certain without fear. We have yet to learn that the extravagant progress of pernicious measures abrogates the duty of opposition, or that the interest of our native land is to be abandoned, by us, in the hour of her thickest dangers, and sorest necessity. By the exercise of our Constitutional right of suffrage, by the peaceable remedy of election, we shall seek to restore wisdom to our councils, and peace to our country.[1]

This was a statesmanlike utterance. Seldom had the duty of a loyal but disapproving citizen, in an hour of national peril, been asserted more frankly. The right of the individual American to disagree with a governmental policy and to criticize it openly was courageously maintained. There were, of course, sections of the United States in which Webster's doctrines were not altogether palatable. In Portsmouth itself, he was probably in a minority. But among the "Friends of Peace," his words were accepted as gospel, and they applauded and concurred. It must be reiterated, however, that Webster never refused to aid the government when called upon to fulfill his obligations as a citizen.

Because of this Independence Day Address, Webster was

[1] National Edition, XV, 594.

conceded the supremacy among the younger Federalists in Rockingham County, no one of whom had his eloquence or his skill in argument. His speech, printed by the *Oracle* in a diminutive broadside, went quickly through two editions; newspapers throughout New England commented on its vigor and courage; and puzzled voters seeking guidance turned to him, as they always do when a leader appears. Although he was only thirty years old and without political experience, his success at the bar had given him assurance, and he did not disappoint those who relied upon him.

While the inadequate but plucky American navy was preparing to face heavy odds and General Hull was waiting vainly at Sandwich for the Canadian yeomen to enroll under his standard, a meeting of the Federalists of Rockingham County was called for August 5, 1812, at Brentwood, about five miles west of Exeter.[1] Brentwood is to-day hardly more than a hamlet, away from the main thoroughfare, and looking as if the world had passed it by. It was, however, situated near the geographical centre of the county, and easily reached by coach or carriage from every point. The gathering was to have been held in the meetinghouse, but, as party after party drove up, it was apparent that they could not all be accommodated indoors, and arrangements were hastily improvised for seating them under what the Portsmouth *Oracle* called "the great canopy of Heaven." A platform was nailed together under the shade of a tall pine, and there, before an audience of more than two thousand, the Honorable Samuel Tenney, of Exeter, took the chair. An Epping clergyman pronounced the invocation, after which the Honorable George Sullivan, then a member of Congress and one of Webster's rivals in the law, delivered an address, said by enthusiastic

---

[1] The notice printed in the Portsmouth *Oracle*, July 25, 1812, reads: "A Meeting of the *Friends of Peace*, of the County of Rockingham, without regard to former Political Distinctions, will be holden at Brentwood, on Wednesday, the 5th day of August next, at ten o'clock A.M. Every lover of *Honorable Peace* is requested to attend. It is expected the meeting will be numerous and respectable." It was hoped that such a call might appeal to certain Republicans who, because of business interests, were opposed to the war, and might, consequently, be willing to join with the Federalists in denouncing it.

partisans to contain "great political truths, conclusive and convincing arguments, enforced in language, elegant, impressive, and energetic." Sullivan was then a better-known figure than Webster, and his speech was printed in full in all the Federalist papers in New Hampshire. The assembly then adjourned until the afternoon in order to allow the committees to prepare their reports and the guests to enjoy their basket luncheons on the village common.[1]

Webster had been appointed chairman of a committee instructed to prepare a memorial, among the other members being Nathaniel Gilman and George Sullivan, — both of Exeter, — Colonel Bradbury Cilley, of Nottingham, and Thomas W. Thompson, his first tutor in the law, who had since moved to Concord. Notified in advance what his duties would be, Webster had drafted a suitable document, which was formally approved by the committee. On that still and sultry afternoon, he read to the throng what has since been known as the "Rockingham Memorial," addressed to "James Madison, Esquire, President of the United States." It was adopted unanimously, amid lusty cheers from Federalist throats.

In language sonorous but restrained, Webster recapitulated the familiar grievances and reviewed the events of the preceding five years. He perceived in the General Government "a disposition to embarrass and enthrall commerce by repeated restrictions," and to make war "by shutting up our own ports." He and the "Friends of Peace" were quite ready to shoulder arms if their rights and liberties required the sacrifice, but they could not see that the breach with England was warranted by "justice, necessity, and expediency." The number of cases of impressment by British ships had been "extravagantly exaggerated." Those sections of the country which were maritime and which, therefore, might be

---

[1] The Portsmouth *Oracle* described the gathering editorially as " indeed the solemn assembly of the people," and proudly reported: " The greatest harmony and order prevailed throughout the day. Not the slightest disturbance or irregularity took place."

supposed to be most seriously disturbed by impressments were those unalterably opposed to the war. The army and navy were unprepared for emergencies, and the Republican administration, although long aware of the imminence of hostilities, had done nothing for our protection. The reasons for going to war with Napoleon were even more cogent than those for fighting Great Britain. Certainly the Federalists of Rockingham County would in no event "assist in uniting the Republic of America with the military despotism of France." This, however, was the only ultimatum in the appeal, and Webster closed with a statement which was dignified and temperate: —

It only remains for us, to express our conscientious convictions, that the present course of measures will prove most prejudicial and ruinous to the country, and to supplicate the government to adopt such a system as shall restore to us the blessings of peace and commerce.[1]

One or two paragraphs in the Rockingham Memorial have sometimes been cited by historians to prove that Daniel Webster at this period was not unwilling to see New England separated from the Union. In view of charges later made by his political foes, it is important to know precisely what his language was. Fortunately it was neither ambiguous or evasive: —

We shrink from the separation of the states, as an event fraught with incalculable evils, and it is among our strongest objections to the present course of measures, that they have, in our opinion, a very dangerous and alarming bearing on such an event. If a separation of the states ever should take place, it will be, on some such occasion, when one portion of the country undertakes to control, to regulate, and to sacrifice, the interest of another; when a small and heated majority in the Government, taking counsel of their passions, and not of their reason, contemptuously disregarding the interests, and perhaps stopping the mouths, of a large and respectable minority, shall by hasty, rash, and ruinous measures threaten to destroy essential rights; and lay waste the most important interests.[2]

[1] National Edition, XV, 610.   [2] *Ibid.*, p. 609.

This was but a simple statement of fact, accompanied by a warning. It indicated no desire on the part of Webster, or of those whom he represented, to withdraw from the Union. On the contrary, as if suspecting that he might be misconstrued, he took pains in the next paragraph to clarify his position so that there could be no doubt of his loyalty : —

It shall be our most fervent supplication to Heaven to avert both the event and the occasion; and the Government may be assured, that the tie which binds us to the Union, will never be broken, by us.[1]

Webster was unmistakably incensed at the repeated blows to Portsmouth's prosperity; he despised the administration then in power; and he was fearful that its policies might endanger the Union. When the Governors of three states — Connecticut, Massachusetts, and Rhode Island — refused, even at the formal request of the Secretary of War, to call out their militia, and when Federalists everywhere were declining to subscribe to war loans, Webster's gloomy forecasts had some justification. But, although apprehensive of such a cleavage, Webster also deplored it.

The Rockingham Memorial was extensively quoted in the press, and was hailed with enthusiasm by Federalist papers.[2] By the Republicans, it was greeted with the sneers and indifference customarily bestowed by partisans upon the argument of a political enemy.[3] President Madison made no acknowledgment or reply.

[1] National Edition, XV, 609–10.

[2] The New York *Evening Post,* in printing the full text of the Memorial, remarked that other important material had been omitted in order to satisfy the popular demand. The Philadelphia *Freeman's Journal* said of it, " It is one of the most interesting, eloquent, and powerful appeals to the judgment and justice of our Administration we have ever read." Webster himself thought that it was " of a tone and strain less vulgar than such things are prone to be."

[3] A long letter appeared in two installments of the *New Hampshire Gazette* for August 18 and September 1, 1812, accusing Webster of inconsistency in his attitude towards England, and quoting passages from his Concord Oration of July 4, 1806, and the Portsmouth Oration of July 4, 1812, to prove the point. It ended: " Perhaps even the orator may improve by experience; and be more cautious in the future of vain boasting. ' This is a consummation devoutly to be wished.' Such an event would add to his fame and happiness, and promote the prosperity of his country. American patriots, who are his best friends, would hail him welcome to their fraternity and real Americans will join in the exclamation of AMEN."

Before the Brentwood gathering broke up, Daniel Webster was nominated, on a so-called "Peace Ticket," as a Representative in Congress from New Hampshire. His Independence Day Address had made him the outstanding Federalist candidate in Rockingham County for office in the state or the nation;[1] but, according to William Plumer, when it was first suggested that he go actively into politics, Webster rejected the idea on the ground that he was poor and must attend to his business as a lawyer. Within a few hours, however, he had reconsidered his impulsive decision and had written to Jeremiah Smith, confessing that he should not decline a seat in Congress if elected. "As to the law," he said, "I must attend to that too, — but honor after all is worth more than money."[2]

The delegation from New Hampshire in the House of Representatives, hitherto numbering five, had been increased in 1812 to six, and the candidates of both parties were placed on a general ticket to be voted for throughout the state. The slate prepared at Brentwood included, besides Webster, Colonel Bradbury Cilley, of Nottingham, Honorable William Hale, of Dover, Samuel Smith, Esquire, of Peterborough, Honorable Roger Vose, of Walpole, and Jeduthun Wilcox, Esquire, of Orford. Somewhat later, on September 10, the Republicans held their convention at Kingston Plains, the only one of their Congressmen to be renominated being the "War Hawk," John A. Harper. During this summer, the caustic Isaac Hill, editor of the *New Hampshire Patriot*, first recognized the dangerous qualities in Daniel Webster and began a virulent attack which hardly ceased until 1850. Hill referred to the Portsmouth *Oracle* as "Daniel Webster's paper," and dwelt on its "stupidity and malevolence." It was not, however, an administration year, and, at the November election, the entire Federalist ticket was elected, Webster, with 18,597

[1] The Keene *Sentinel* for August 29, 1812, said, " We rejoice to find the list headed with the name of Daniel Webster, Esq., of Portsmouth, a gentleman of commanding talents and undoubted patriotism."

[2] Letter of William Plumer to George Ticknor, April 2, 1853, in National Edition, XVII, 547.

votes, running second only to Vose. It was long since the New Hampshire Federalists had won such an overwhelming victory. Thus, in his thirty-first year, Webster was chosen to that office which his father had coveted long and vainly.

Webster must now have felt that he had at last reached an arena where his talents would have sufficient scope. His success is remarkable because he had hitherto held no office in town, county, or state. Without having served any apprenticeship, he had, by a single speech, become conspicuous even among those who had long been active in politics. Rarely indeed does so young a man, with no discipline whatever in legislative affairs, step from a law office into the National Capitol. Webster may possibly, as Lodge asserted, have matured late, but he had accomplished much at an age when many a prospective statesman is toiling obscurely.

VI

A CONGRESSMAN IN OPPOSITION

Thou
Whom the rich heavens did so endow
With eyes of power and Jove's own brow,
With all the massive strength that fills
Thy home-horizon's granite hills.
— WHITTIER, "The Lost Occasion"

Wholly inexperienced in public affairs, my first object is to comprehend the objects, understand the maxims, and imbibe the spirit of the first administration, persuaded as I am that the principles which prevailed in the Cabinet and Councils of that period, form the only anchorage in which our political prosperity and safety can find any hold in this dangerous and stormy time.
— WEBSTER, Letter to Pickering, December 11, 1812

ON a Tuesday morning in June, 1813, there was a quaint scene at the White House, then referred to in Washington as the "Palace." President Madison, weakened by several days of fever, lay propped up on pillows, a nightcap on his head and his pretty wife, Dolly, as a nurse by his side. To the sick chamber were admitted young Congressman Webster, of New Hampshire, and John Rhea, — "old Rhea," — of Tennessee, who had been designated by Mr. Speaker Clay to transmit certain resolutions passed by the House, and asking questions which, it was hoped, might embarrass the Executive. The invalid received the papers and replied, with his habitual quiet courtesy, "They will be attended to." Two days later, Webster, with inconsiderate glee, wrote to a friend, mentioning Madison's illness and adding, "I think he will find no relief from my prescription." Webster had already addressed Madison in the Rockingham Memorial, but this was his first experience in bearding a President in his home. The incident, though trivial, is symbolical of Webster's attitude throughout the War of 1812. Whenever the administration was in straits, he was on hand to annoy those responsible for its actions.

During the months just before he took the Congressional oath of office, Webster was much in the public eye. Portsmouth politics were seething during the winter of 1813. While the *New Hampshire Gazette* was printing the bulletins of Napoleon's Grand Army on its retreat from Moscow, the Federalists and Republicans, whose antagonism the French Emperor had indirectly done so much to promote, were engaged in one of their periodical clashes. Early in January, it was announced that the veteran Federalist, John Taylor Gilman, would accept a nomination for Governor by the "Friends of Peace." Governor William Plumer [1] was once more the Republican candidate — and the perennial rivals fought a closely contested battle. During the campaign Webster dwelt effectively on the damage done to New Hampshire commerce by the war,[2] and assailed Plumer for calling out the militia. The March election reversed the situation, and the Federalists were once more in the saddle, winning both branches of the Legislature and swinging Gilman into office.[3] On Saturday, June 5, the Governor took the oath at Concord, and the state was again in what Webster believed to be safe hands.

Before that day arrived, however, Daniel Webster had set out on his first great political adventure. By an act of the preceding session, the Thirteenth Congress was to assemble

[1] No majority having been secured by either candidate in the popular vote of 1812, Plumer had been elected by the Legislature (June 4, 1812), by a vote of 104 against 82 for Gilman.

[2] General Lyman (*Memorials of Daniel Webster*, II, 42–44) described dramatically one of the Federalist meetings during this campaign, when the crowd refused to listen to any orator but Webster and responded to his remarks with " thunders of applause."

[3] The vote for Governor was 18,107 for Gilman against 17,410 for Plumer. The Portsmouth *Oracle* announced on March 20, 1813, " We feel much pleasure in announcing the restoration of New Hampshire to the true principles of the Washington school." Webster's friend, Thomas W. Thompson, was chosen Speaker of the House by a vote of 106 to 75, and the Senate was Federalist, 9 to 3. After Dr. John Goddard had declined an election as United States Senator, the Legislature agreed on Jeremiah Mason as a successor to Charles Cutts.

on May 24, 1813; and he was at his desk, in Washington, filled with curiosity and expectation, when the House of Representatives was called to order. He had gone to the capital alone, for Mrs. Webster had little Grace to care for, and was also expecting another child in midsummer. He made most of the journey by mail coach, following a route through Boston, Hartford, New Haven, New York, Princeton, and Baltimore,[1] and he was ten days on the road. The trip from Portsmouth to Washington in those days was much more hazardous than a voyage to Europe in the twentieth century.

The national capital was then a city of fewer than ten thousand people,[2] which Webster, not without justification, called "this dismal place." The original plan of Major L'Enfant was magnificent, but, because of inertia and lack of funds, it had not been carried out. The corner stone of the Capitol had been laid as early as 1794, and the north and south wings were in use in 1813; but the space between them, intended for the dome, was merely an improvised passageway roofed over with rough boards, and no additional appropriation had been passed by Congresss since 1810.[3] The "President's House" had been completed in 1809, but Pennsylvania Avenue, although boasting a few unhealthy trees planted under Jefferson's administration, was lined with ugly shanties and made a poor impression upon visitors; and in winter its mud seemed bottomless. Three hotels in the vicinity of Capitol Hill did all the business, the best being the Indian Queen, on The Avenue, in front of which hung "a large swinging sign upon which figured Pocahontas, painted in glaring colors."[4]

---

[1] Lyman, II, 45. Plumer, *Life of William Plumer*, p. 41, says that the journey from New Hampshire to Washington in 1801 was not usually performed in less than ten or twelve days. Jeremiah Mason, in 1814, consumed six days between Hartford and Baltimore, his course being by stage from Hartford to Mount Pleasant (on the Hudson River), by packet boat to New York, by boat to New Brunswick, by stage to Philadelphia, and by mail stage to Baltimore. Writing on November 24, 1814, from Washington, Mason said: "Yesterday Gerry died very suddenly. He had travelled from Boston to this place in five days, which was enough to kill a younger and stouter man."

[2] A census gave the population of Washington in 1807 as 5652.

[3] Hazelton's *The National Capitol*, p. 34, has an excellent drawing of the building, as it appeared in 1814, before its destruction by the British.

[4] Poore, *Reminiscences of Sixty Years*, I, 42.

Most members of Congress lived in boarding houses,[1] paying approximately fifteen dollars a week for attendance, wood, candles, food, and plenty of brandy and whiskey, which was placed on the table in decanters without extra charge. There were no homes in Washington as luxurious as some of those which Webster had known in Portsmouth. It was probably his fastidiousness which led him to take up his quarters in Georgetown,[2] three miles away, driving back and forth to the Congressional sessions in a rickety coach. Women of culture were not numerous, and Webster complained of the "unvarying masculinity" of the society.[3] There was a good deal of whist playing and faro gambling. The one theatre was occasionally opened by a company from Philadelphia, but other recreations were few.

Webster, of course, was seeing the city in war time, when gayeties would naturally be curtailed. Indeed there was always the fear that it would be besieged by the enterprising British, who, just before Webster's arrival, had ascended Chesapeake Bay under Admiral Cockburn, burning and pillaging Havre de Grace and other villages, and coming uncomfortably close to Washington. Mrs. Madison wrote, May 12, 1813, "For the last week all the city and Georgetown

[1] It was estimated in 1816 that only 20 per cent of the Senators and Congressmen lived in hotels.

[2] On a drive with Peter Harvey, Webster once ordered the coachman to stop and, pointing to an old and decaying mansion, said: "That large white house, with dilapidated walls and broken fences, was the hotel where I boarded when I first entered Congress from New Hampshire. It was then the Federalist Headquarters. Governor Gore, Rufus King, and John Marshall were fellow-boarders. Governor Gore used to drive out of that gate in a coach drawn by four horses, and attended by servants in livery." Harvey names the location as Alexandria, but this is obviously a misprint for Georgetown. (Harvey, p. 176.) William Lowndes wrote from Washington in December 1811, "The comforts of a city are such in winter that I think I shall spend the next (if I come here at all) in Georgetown." (Meigs, *Calhoun*, I, 113.)

[3] There was another side to the social life. Mrs. Samuel Harrison Smith, writing on March 13, 1814, said: "Washington possesses a peculiar interest, and to an active, reflective, and ambitious mind, has more attractions than any other place in America. . . . There are here peculiar facilities for forming acquaintances, for a stranger cannot be long here, before it is generally known. The house of representatives is the lounging place of both sexes, where acquaintance is as easily made as at public amusements." (*The First Forty Years of Washington Society*, p. 94.) Doubtless Webster, in his bachelor quarters, received quite a different impression.

(except the cabinet) have expected a visit from the enemy, and were not lacking in their expressions of terror and reproach." [1]

Washington presented the appearance of a capital "made to order," and its unlighted streets, disfigured with mud holes in wet weather, were felt to be discreditable to the young nation. Gazing at the unused planks and stones which surrounded the unsightly and unfinished Capitol, the editor of the *National Intelligencer* was reminded of the ruins of Rome as described by Volney.[2] Webster did not enjoy the climate, and he wrote to Ezekiel on Independence Day, "The weather is already very hot; more so than ever I experienced." [3]

But uncomfortable though he may have been, Webster's mind was intent on other matters besides architecture, society, and climate. The Hall of Representatives, with its twenty-four Corinthian columns and its semicircular galleries, had been completed in 1807, and provided on the floor sufficiently commodious quarters for the membership of 182. Here he found that one of his friends had marked a seat for him, "in good company" — with Joseph Lewis, Jr., and Daniel Sheffey, both of Virginia, on his left, and Joseph Pearson and William Gaston, both of North Carolina, and Timothy Pitkin, of Connecticut, on his right.[4] He made at once a formal call upon President Madison, but wrote, "I did not like his looks, any better than I like his Administration. I think LaVater could find clearly eno in his features, Embargo, Non-Intercourse, & War." [5]

The House had little difficulty in organizing, for the administration had a substantial working majority, — 114 Republicans to 68 Federalists, — and promptly elected Henry Clay,[6] of Kentucky, as Speaker. Bold and autocratic, ready in debate, fiery in manner, and magnetic in personality, he was more susceptible to emotion than to reason. He was

---

[1] *Memoirs and Letters of Dolly Madison*, p. 90.
[2] Bryan, *National Capital*, I, 618.   [3] National Edition, XVII, 237.
[4] *Ibid.*, XVI, 14. Pitkin was Clay's opponent for Speaker, and received 54 votes to the latter's 89.   [5] *Ibid.*, p. 15.
[6] Henry Clay (1777–1852), five years older than Webster, was born in Virginia, the son of a poor white preacher. His father died when the boy was four, and, his mother

tall and thin, with gray eyes and petulant mouth, and his rich voice and captivating smile were irresistible. With his breezy cordiality and superficial cleverness, he combined a talent for managing men, and he exercised over his admirers an influence almost hypnotic. He was often politician and demagogue as well as statesman; but in 1812 he held proudly aloft the banner of "Young America," and was himself principally responsible for our aggressive policy towards Great Britain. To his adoring followers, he was gallant "Harry of the West," aflame with patriotic ardor, the hero of newly settled territories and pioneer peoples. They pictured him as a plumed knight in shining armor, riding to overthrow the cherished idols of an old and perhaps decadent civilization — the civilization of comfort and degenerate ease in which they suspected Webster of living. In Clay were centred all the vague aspirations and suppressed desires of that virile and hard-won land beyond the Alleghanies.

If Clay was all feeling, another "war hawk" — John Caldwell Calhoun,[1] of South Carolina — was all logic. With his

---

having married again, his stepfather secured a place for him in the office of the Clerk of the High Court of Chancery in Richmond. Licensed to practise law, he moved west to Lexington, Kentucky, where he quickly rose to distinction. After sitting in the State Legislature, he was elected in 1806 to fill an unexpired term in the United States Senate, although still under the legal age for that position. At the close of his term, he became Speaker of the Kentucky Assembly, but, in 1809, again went to the United States Senate to complete an unexpired period. Elected to the Twelfth Congress, he was immediately chosen Speaker and assumed the leadership of the war party. In a great speech on January 8 and 9, 1813, he had defended Jefferson and accused New England of having fomented a plot " that aims at the dismemberment of the Union." His audacity and nationalism at this period are strongly contrasted with Webster's conservatism and sectionalism.

[1] John Caldwell Calhoun (1782–1850), two months younger than Webster, was born in Abbeville, South Carolina, and graduated from Yale College in 1804. He studied law in Litchfield, Connecticut, was admitted to the bar in 1807, and opened an office at Abbeville. He served for two sessions in the South Carolina Legislature, and, at the age of twenty-eight, was elected to the House of Representatives, where, despite his youth, he attracted attention and was recognized as a leader of the administration on the floor of that body. At the first meeting of the Committee on Foreign Relations, to which he had been appointed, Calhoun was unanimously made Chairman, and it was he who, in his report on a section of the President's Message, sounded the first authentic note of war, in 1811, saying, " The period has now arrived when, in the opinion of your committee, it is the sacred duty of Congress to call forth the patriotism and the resources of the country." When Webster took his seat, Clay and Calhoun were the outstanding figures in the House.

gaunt frame and long black locks, his bushy eyebrows above
sunken sockets, he gave the impression of dynamic intensity.
He was then and later the spokesman of the aristocratic South,
the dispassionate interpreter of its troubles and its needs.
Although some people found him reserved, he made friends
readily, and there was but one opinion as to his genius for
leadership.   A gentleman by birth and breeding, he could argue
fiercely without indulging in personalities; and even when
Webster opposed Calhoun's tenuous theories, he could not help
liking the man and respecting the sincerity of his motives.

The temptation to draw sharp contrasts is one which few
historians can resist, and the differences between Clay and
Calhoun are bound to impress any student of the two statesmen.   Clay was impulsive; Calhoun was cool and calculating.
Clay was sociable; Calhoun was solitary.   The Kentuckian
was gay and shallow; the South Carolinian was serious and
profound.   One was full of humor; the other was so lacking in
it that he seldom smiled.   Clay was flexible, quickly susceptible
to external influences, and easily moved; Calhoun was rigid and
introspective.   Finally, Clay, with all his brilliancy, was at
heart an opportunist; while Calhoun was made of martyr stuff.

Thus, in 1813, the members of the Great Triumvirate, —
Clay, Calhoun, and Webster, — who were later so long to dominate the Senate, came together in the Lower House.   At that
moment, Clay and Calhoun were nationalists, uttering the
sentiments of the country as a whole.   As time went on, however, Calhoun was to express the peculiar doctrines of the
South just as Clay those of the West and Webster those of New
England.   To read the speeches of these three is to cover
American history for forty years.

Among other conspicuous members of the House were
John McLean, of Ohio, who was later to sit on the Supreme
Court Bench as the nominee of President Jackson; Charles
J. Ingersoll, of Pennsylvania, who, under Tyler and Polk, was
to be an influential Chairman of the House Committee on
Foreign Affairs; George M. Troup and John Forsyth, both
from Georgia, the latter afterwards Jackson's Secretary of

State; and, from South Carolina, the brilliant William Lowndes, who died prematurely at the age of forty, and the versatile Langdon Cheves, Clay's successor as Speaker when the latter resigned early in 1814 to accept a place on the Peace Commission.   These men were Republicans and supporters of Madison. Josiah Quincy, the Massachusetts Federalist who had stirred up such a turmoil during the previous session, had declined a reëlection; and the erratic John Randolph, half genius and half madman, had, to the relief of Calhoun and his coterie, been defeated by Jefferson's son-in-law, John W. Eppes. Among Webster's allies were Colonel Timothy Pickering, of Massachusetts, the most intolerant of the Essex Junto;[1] Alexander C. Hanson, the brilliant and caustic editor of the Baltimore *Federal Republican;* and William Gaston, of North Carolina, a new member who was to become Judge of the Supreme Court of North Carolina.   The Federalists were relatively weak in numbers, but they included some men of marked ability, and their quality was high.   In the Senate, which was then the less important body, were Christopher Gore, Rufus King, and, within a few weeks, Jeremiah Mason, whom Webster was proud to call his friends.

Webster reached Washington with a course of action carefully prepared.   Sustained by the knowledge that his constituents were back of him, he proposed to denounce the war and to withhold his support when measures for its prosecution were introduced.   Always before him was the possibility of embarrassing the Republican administration.   It was not a very noble ambition, and there was nothing constructive in Webster's plan.   Although his views must have been familiar to Clay, the latter gave him an assignment on the Committee on Foreign Relations, under Calhoun as Chairman.[2]   It was a

[1] Webster wrote Pickering, December 11, 1812: "Among the consequences which may grow out of recent events, I look forward to none with more pleasure than the opportunity which may be afforded of cultivating the acquaintance of one of the masters of the Washington school of politics."   (National Edition, XVI, 12.)

[2] March wrote Webster, from New York, May 31, 1813: "I am glad to see by the *Intelligencer* you are on the Foreign Committee; and wish you had a majority on your side. . . .   Calhoun I don't know personally but have a high respect for his talent. He is young and if honest may yet be open to conviction."   (Cong. Lib. Misc. I.)

distinction for a new member to be placed on a committee of such importance.

There was no tradition in the House to restrain a new member from asserting himself too soon. Clay had been chosen Speaker at the opening of his first term in that body, and Webster, at what he felt to be a moment of national crisis, was in no mood to postpone the attack. He quickly seized upon what he thought to be the best available issue and made the most of it.[1] It had been asserted by the Duke of Bassano, the French Minister of Foreign Affairs, that the revocation by Napoleon of the Berlin and Milan Decrees had been transmitted to the French Minister at Washington for delivery to our Secretary of State. As nothing had been divulged by the administration regarding this alleged repeal until after Congress had passed its declaration of war, the Federalists suspected that President Madison had received but had suppressed this very important information. The Republicans naturally doubted the veracity of the French nobleman, but Webster, with strategical skill, saw an opportunity for putting Madison on the defensive.

When routine preliminary matters had been disposed of, Webster was ready for action, and wrote to his friend, Charles March,[2] in New York, on Monday, June 7 : —

"Tomorrow I intend to bring forward a motion, calling for information relative to the famous Trent Decree, repealing the Berlin & Milan Decrees. Lest some accident should prevent, you will say nothing of this, till you see or hear more of it. If they choose to oppose it & to bring on a general battle, we are ready."[3]

[1] In a speech delivered at Madison, Indiana, June 1, 1837, Webster said: " Among the luminaries in the sky of New England, the burning lights which throw intelligence and happiness on her people, the first and most brilliant is her system of common schools. I congratulate myself that my first speech on entering public life was in their behalf." (National Edition, II, 253.) Where and when this speech was delivered, I have not been able to ascertain, and there is no record of it in the Proceedings of this Congress.

[2] Charles March was a New York merchant, a son of Dr. Clement March, of Greenland, New Hampshire, a small village about eight miles south of Portsmouth. Webster kept him carefully informed as to everything which occurred during this session, sending him brief letters almost every day.

[3] National Edition, XVI, 19.

Webster's début was unavoidably postponed until Thursday, June 10, on which date he rose and made his first speech in the House of Representatives, submitting five resolutions for its consideration.[1] In his remarks, he focused attention on the fact that, if the decree of April 1811, said to have been transmitted to the President, had been published at the time when it was received, the war with England would probably not have taken place, for its appearance would have "produced the repeal of the British orders in council" — and it was upon this issue mainly that the question of peace or war was decided. He declared, therefore, that the honor of the nation demanded "a full and free inquiry into a subject of so much importance." [2]

It was said by one who was present that no member "ever riveted the attention of the House so completely in his first speech," [3] and this may well be true, for Webster was very much in earnest and the Representatives were not accustomed to his sonorous style of oratory. In the earliest edition of his collected works — the *Speeches and Forensic Arguments*, published in 1831 — it was not included, perhaps because Webster did not wish then to revive recollections of the days when he had been strongly sectional in his views. Chief Justice John Marshall, at the time when the volume appeared, expressed his disappointment at not finding this argument among the contents and said to Justice Story: "I read these speeches with very great pleasure at the time. At the time when the first was delivered, I did not know Mr. Webster; but I was so much struck with it, that I did not hesitate to state that

[1] Webster wrote March, on the afternoon of June 10: "The *resolutions* were offered today — they lie until tomorrow for consideration. What the House will do with them, I cannot say. The question to consider them was carried 138 to 28. I have done what I tho't my duty & am easy about the result." (National Edition, XVI, 20.)

[2] A report of this speech, evidently an abstract, is printed in National Edition, XIV, 3 ff. taken from the Boston *Messenger*. Webster himself arranged to have the Resolutions forwarded to the New York *Commercial Advertiser* and asked March to send copies to Thomas W. Thompson, Ezekiel Webster, and Isaac P. Davis, of Boston, as well as to William Garland, of Portsmouth.

[3] The same observer said: "Members left their seats when they could not see the speaker face to face, and sat down or stood on the floor fronting him. All listened attentively and silently during the whole speech; and when it was over, many went up and warmly congratulated the orator." (Lyman, II, 51.)

Mr. Webster was a very able man, and would become one of the very first statesmen in America, and perhaps the very first." [1] Webster's constituents were given an abstract of it in the Portsmouth *Oracle*, and its effect on other sections of the country may be surmised from an editorial in the *New York Herald*, which referred to Webster as "second to none on the floor of the House." At a dinner in Keene, New Hampshire, on July 5, one of the toasts offered was "Mr. Webster's Resolutions, — the Northern Emetic, skillfully administered. May it operate to restore health and vigor to the body politic!" There is probably no instance in Congressional history where a Representative of so little legislative training produced such a striking impression on his colleagues. From that day it was admitted that Clay and Calhoun had a foeman worthy of their best efforts.

Webster's resolutions precipitated a sharp debate, in the course of which Calhoun rushed to the defense of the Administration. It was the first of the numerous verbal duels in which the two leaders were to take part. But the opposition had the better of the encounter. "Poor Madison!" wrote Webster to March on June 14. "I doubt whether he has had a night's sleep these three weeks." [2] Again, five days later, he said: "The fact is, the Administration are, for the moment, confounded. They are hard pushed in our house — much harder in the Senate. . . . They are in a sad pickle. Who cares?" [3] Soon the Republicans realized the inadvisability of stifling the inquiry. Objections were removed, and the resolutions were duly passed on June 21. [4] Webster, as we have seen,

---

[1] Quoted in Curtis, I, 110.
[2] National Edition, XVI, 21.
[3] *Ibid.*
[4] Webster sent his version of the matter to March, June 21, 1813: " The Resolutions have passed unaltered, except putting in the usual saving in the last Resolution, which was left out by accident. The last Resolution passed 93 to 68. I made no speech. When I came to the House this morning, Calhoun told me, the motion for indefinite postponement would be withdrawn — his motion to amend withdrawn — & he & some of his friends should vote for the Resolutions as they are. I, of course, could not object & considering the thing given up on their part, I forebore to speak. They have acted very strangely. A dozen motions, made & withdrawn — some pulling one way — some another. They do not manage like so many Solomons." (*Ibid.*, p. 22.)

was appointed, with John Rhea, to deliver them to the Chief Executive.

The sequel was unexciting after such a tempest. A reply was submitted on July 12, showing that the earliest official intimation of the French repealing decree had been received by our government from Barlow, our Minister to France, on July 13, 1812, some weeks after war had been declared. Calhoun, as Chairman of the Committee on Foreign Relations, — to which this answer was referred, — reported a resolution approving the conduct of the President, but the House declined to act upon it, there being too much urgent business to attend to, and nothing more had been done at the date when Congress adjourned on August 2, 1813.

Even before Madison's answer had been scrutinized by Congress, Daniel Webster, convinced that he was needed more urgently in Portsmouth than in Washington, was on his way home. He wrote on July 6: "For four or five days I have found myself getting out of sorts, & have determined to stay here not much longer. So late is the period of the Session, so hot the season, so languid is every body, that I incline to think we shall have no general battle about the War."[1] On Saturday, July 10, he said to March: "I expected to leave this place Tomorrow, & to be with you by the middle of next week. But understanding that we are to hear from the President either to-day or Monday, I shall wait a few days longer."[2]

Early in the following week, he started on his long journey north, arriving in Portsmouth in season for the birth of his oldest son, Daniel Fletcher Webster, on July 23. He had been away for only a brief period. He had modestly refrained from talking too much or too long, but he was the only member of the New Hampshire delegation who had had anything to say. The Federalists, sadly in need of leadership, had

[1] Letter to March, National Edition, XVI, 24. On July 9, he was given leave of absence from Sunday, July 11, for the remainder of the session. Webster's last vote was cast on Saturday, July 10, and Madison's Report was presented on the following Monday.
[2] National Edition, XVI, 25.

welcomed him and had accorded him a position usually conceded only to veteran statesmen.[1] The fear with which he was regarded by Clay and Calhoun was evidenced by his removal from the Committee on Foreign Relations, of which he had been far from a tractable member.

The second Thursday of September, 1813, had been set apart by the President as a solemn fast day. And indeed it did seem as if an appeal to divine Providence were our only recourse. A series of shameful disasters, beginning with the Battle of Queenston (October 13, 1812), had disclosed the incompetency of our commanders and the pusillanimity of our militia. American soldiers had not only run away from bullets; they had stolidly refused to serve outside their own states. Never have our armies met with such reverses as when Hull, Van Rennsselaer, Smyth, and Dearborn were defeated in succession; and Eustis, the Secretary of War, resigned on December 3, 1812. The only real victory of the year was won by the navy at Lake Erie, on July 10, under Commander Oliver Hazard Perry. In the autumn of 1813, with the crushing of Napoleon at Leipzig and the British successes in the Spanish peninsula, it looked as if England might soon be free to turn all her guns on us.

Webster returned to Washington somewhat late for the second session of the Thirteenth Congress,[2] only to be greeted with the disconcerting news of the Portsmouth fire. While he was hesitating whether his duty was not with his homeless family, a letter from his dauntless wife reassured him, and,

[1] The *New Hampshire Patriot*, ably edited by Isaac Hill, a strong Democrat, continued during this summer its virulent attacks on Webster. In its issue for July 27, Webster could have read that " the great Mr. Webster, who is so extremely flippant in arguing petty suits in our courts of law, cuts but a sorry figure at Washington; his overweening confidence and zeal cannot *there* supply the place of knowledge. We think he will not be anxious again to appear in the Capitol." It spoke on August 17 of his " imprudent and abortive attack on the administration."

[2] News items in the Portsmouth *Oracle* indicate that Webster left for Washington on December 11, five days after the session opened. He stopped for a few days in New York and did not reach the capital until the evening of December 28. He reported on Wednesday, December 29. He voted with the majority on the following day for a resolution asking the President to give up any information explaining the failure " of the arms of the United States on the Northern frontier."

with his fears removed, he turned from domestic to national calamities. With premeditated malice, he became a gadfly to the Madison administration, prepared to sting whenever a vulnerable spot was exposed. Although his country was obviously in peril from a foreign foe, he preferred to hamper rather than to help those who were entrusted with its defense.

The policy which he followed can best be illustrated by a consideration of his stand on specific measures. When the House, by a vote almost unanimous, approved of an inquiry into "the causes of the failure of our arms," Webster declared that the war had been "ill-judged and ill-timed in the beginning." With annoying pertinacity, he continued: —

If its advocates can show satisfactorily that this war was undertaken on grounds plainly and manifestly just; if they can show that it was necessary and unavoidable; that it is strictly an American war; that it rests solely on American grounds; and that it grew out of a policy just and impartial as it related to the belligerents of Europe, — if they ever make all this manifest, the war will change its character. It will then grow as energetic as it is now feeble. It will then become the cause of the people, and not the cause of a party.

Webster's sarcastic reference in this speech to our two "drivelling campaigns" could not have mollified Clay and the other "war hawks." But the member from New Hampshire was to make himself even more disagreeable. When a resolution was introduced for inquiring into the expediency of placing the trial of citizens for treason under military jurisdiction, Webster was at once on his feet, and, in a brief speech only imperfectly reported, described the proposed measure as "an enormous stride of usurpation," which took away the orderly processes of "indictment, arraignment, and trial," substituting in their stead a military tribunal.[1] By a strange shifting in point of view, the party of Thomas Jefferson now sponsored an act no less subversive of individual liberty than the Federalist Alien and Sedition Bills of 1798; while the Federalist Party appeared in the unfamiliar guise of defender of the rights of

---

[1] Speech on January 10, 1814 (National Edition, XIV, 11 ff.).

citizens. Largely because of Webster s timely protest, this measure, although referred by a majority of eleven votes, was never again brought up.

The first of Webster's Congressional speeches to be fully reported was delivered on January 14, 1814, in the course of the debate on a proposal for filling the ranks of the regular army by offering each recruit a bounty in money and land.[1] He reminded the House that the Federalists had not brought on the conflict; that they had, on the contrary, resorted to every legitimate device to delay a declaration of hostilities; and that they had predicted with some accuracy the misfortunes which would result. With exasperating irony, he compared the administration of James Madison with that of Lord North in respect to incapacity and persistence in keeping up a foolish and wasteful war. He was quite willing, he averred, to approve measures for defense only; and he recommended that the government abandon "futile projects of invasion," take up fortified positions on land, and rely on the navy for victory. Above all, with the welfare of New England shipping in mind, he urged that the system of commercial restrictions be abandoned, saying: —

Unclinch the iron grasp of your Embargo. Take measures for that end before another sun sets upon you. With all the war of the enemy upon your commerce, if you would cease to war upon it yourselves, you would still have some commerce. That commerce would give you some revenue. Apply that revenue to the augmentation of your navy. That navy will, in turn, protect your commerce.

---

[1] Webster wrote to Ezekiel, January 30, 1814, in a letter enclosing some printed copies of this speech: "The speech is not exactly what it ought to be. I had not time. I had no intention of speaking till nine o'clock in the morning, and delivered the thing about two. I could make it better, but I dare say you think it would be easier to make a new one, than to mend it. It was well enough received at the time, and our side of the House said they would have it in this form. So much for speeches." (National Edition, XVII, 239.) As soon as a version reached Keene, New Hampshire, the *Sentinel* advertised that a pamphlet edition, containing sixteen pages, was in press and would be on sale " at the very low price of 6 cents single and 4 cents by the 100, 50, or even 25 copies, for distribution." Comparatively unknown two years before outside of Rockingham, Grafton, and Hillsborough counties, Webster was now recognized as the chief spokesman of the Peace Party.

These terse and pregnant sentences show a marked improve-ment over his earlier somewhat grandiloquent style. There is more weight in these crisp, incisive words than in the longer balanced periods, modeled on Cicero, to which he had been so much addicted. In this oration, Webster attained a maturity of expression which proved that he had profited by his court-room and legislative experience. He was not done experi-menting, but he had acquired a manner and a method peculiarly his own.

Calhoun had charged that the Federalists, through their factious opposition, were to blame for the failure of the war. In reply, Webster declared that this opposition was not only conscientious, but "constitutional and legal," and rested "upon settled and sober conviction." "The more I perceive a disposition to check the freedom of inquiry by extravagant and unconstitutional pretences," he said, in ringing words, "the firmer shall be the tone in which I shall assert, and the freer the manner in which I shall exercise it." [1]

The opening act of the session, passed before Webster's arrival, had been a new Embargo, requested by the President, covering the coastwise and foreign trade of the country and forbidding commerce by water, not only between different states, but between ports in the same state. As a result of this ill-considered measure, which Webster believed to be unconstitu-tional and his constituents thought to be iniquitous,[2] the residents of the island of Nantucket found themselves cut off from all intercourse with the "Continent." When a bill was introduced granting them relief, Webster opposed it on the somewhat perverse ground that he would not vote to restore a privilege of which they could not legally be divested.[3] Even with this necessary modification, the Embargo was far from

[1] National Edition, XIV, 25.
[2] The Portsmouth *Oracle*, on Saturday, January 1, 1814, complained, " In addition to those ministers of vengeance with which it has pleased God to visit us, the Sword, Fire, and Famine, we have again stalking amongst us, like a pestilence, the mammoth EMBARGO."
[3] The bill relieving Nantucket of these commercial restrictions was eventually passed, Webster and seven others voting in the negative.

being a success, and in the following March, only three months after it had been passed, Madison called for its repeal.   Calhoun, in explaining the motives for this sudden reversal of policy, showed himself very adroit, but he opened himself to some ironic observations by Webster, who said : —

Sir, a government which cannot administer the affairs of a nation without producing so frequent and such violent alterations in the ordinary occupations and pursuits of private life has, in my opinion, little claim to the regard of this community.[1]

With Republicans and Federalists united against it, it was not remarkable that the Embargo was repealed by a decisive majority.   A few days later the stormy and unproductive session was brought to a close.

There is some evidence to indicate that Webster's loyalty to the mercantile interests of the Northeast was not unrewarded.   Writing to March on June 14, 1813, he said, in a sentence the importance of which he brought out by underlining, "You must contrive some way for me to get rich as soon as there is a peace." [2]   March, who was an importer and therefore very anxious to see all commercial restrictions removed, was kept informed by Webster of everything contemplated by Congress.   On June 29, 1813, the latter wrote March, "Shall draw on you today or tomorrow,"[3] and on November 20 he drew on the New York merchant, with the latter's consent, for nine hundred dollars.   With only these meagre facts as a basis, it is impossible to ascertain the precise relationship between Webster and March; but it would not be astonishing if the former had accepted remuneration for his services in behalf of his friends in business.   Such a practice would have been considered less reprehensible then than now.   Today similar conduct, if discovered, might subject a Representative to congressional investigation.

Webster returned to discover that his course in Congress

---

[1] Webster's speech "On the Repeal of the Embargo" was delivered in the House on April 6, 1814.   It is printed in National Edition, XIV, 35 ff.

[2] National Edition, XVI, 21.

[3] Ibid., p. 24.

was approved by most of his fellow citizens.[1] His speeches had been printed in the local newspapers, and even those who disagreed with his views, with few exceptions, acknowledged his ability.[2] At the state election in March 1814, the Federalist, John Taylor Gilman, again defeated Plumer for the Governorship. In June, Webster received the unanimous endorsement of his party for a second term. The Republicans, inspired by the *Patriot*, fought hard against him, declaring that "the self-importance and gross egotism" which he had displayed were disgusting and that he had "by his own extravagance and folly involved himself in pecuniary difficulties at home."[3] At the election on August 29, however, he and the other nominees on the "Peace Ticket" had a comfortable margin over their opponents, who attributed their failure to the absence from the state of so many soldiers.

Meanwhile, during the summer and autumn of 1814, disaster was piling up on disaster. Napoleon's abdication in April enabled England to release veteran troops and fresh ships against America. It is true that our forces did well at Lundy's Lane (July 25, 1814) and that Commodore Macdonough's victory on Lake Champlain lightened the gloom. But most of our seaports were blockaded, and part of the coast of Maine was held by the enemy. The currency was disordered, and the President issued a pathetic appeal for

[1] The Keene *Sentinel*, March 26, 1814, asking the question, "Who is the greatest man in the House of Representatives, party influence aside?" said, "Mr. Webster is a young Ajax in political disquisition, and gives every promise of a towering politician."

[2] The Portsmouth *Oracle*, Federalist in sentiment, said, July 23, 1814: "Even the opposition must feel their pride secretly gratified unless party spleen has banished every vestige of native pride from their hearts, at the lustre, shed on New Hampshire by the pre-eminent talents of a Mason and a Webster." Even Webster's implacable foes were compelled to concede his ability, and the New Hampshire *Patriot* confessed, August 27, "He is the only one of the members from New Hampshire that has opened his mouth." The editor of the *Patriot*, Isaac Hill, had gradually gained for his paper a circulation of more than three thousand subscribers, and, recognizing that Webster was dangerous, assailed him bitterly.

[3] *New Hampshire Patriot*, August 2 and August 9, 1814. In the midst of the campaign, Isaac Hill wrote: "As to the talents of Webster, if we may take his speeches which have from time to time appeared before the public as a specimen, they afford evidence, indeed of what? Not that he is a statesman, not that he ever could originate a single idea that would be of any service either to his own party or to his country, — but that, like the moon-struck maniac, he can tire the ear with much speaking."

men and money. The culminating misfortune came in August, when British regulars, landing in Maryland, routed our militia at Bladensburg (August 24, 1814), and, marching into Washington with practically no resistance, burned the Capitol and some other public buildings, including the "President's Palace." Portsmouth, threatened in May, was in real danger in September,[1] and its citizens, directed by Webster, prepared to resist a possible British landing at Rye Beach or Hampton, south of the city. Because of the crisis, Webster was late in returning to Congress, and the *Patriot* accused him of delaying in order to obtain legal fees in Portsmouth.

President Madison, having called Congress into an emergency session, confessed that the treasury was on the verge of bankruptcy, and Senator Mason wrote: "The Government is in utter confusion and distress. Without a cabinet, without credit or money, the nation is in a most deplorable condition." [2] When Webster arrived, on October 14, he found Congress occupying temporary quarters in a ramshackle building on 7th Street, formerly allotted to the Patent Office and the General Post Office, and, before that, in succession a theater, a tavern, and a boarding house. The room assigned to the Lower House was so small that not all the members could have desks, and every spot, even on the window ledges and in

[1] At a Town Meeting, called on September 3, to arrange for the defense of Portsmouth, Jeremiah Mason was Moderator, and Webster offered some patriotic resolutions, which were adopted. A nonpartisan Committee of Twelve was appointed, with Webster as Chairman. On September 10, the *Oracle* printed a letter from Belfast, Maine, predicting that the enemy would soon attack Portland and Portsmouth, and Governor Gilman, as Commander-in-Chief, issued instructions for the militia to be in readiness. But the expected landing never was attempted. Webster was always proud of his share in these proceedings and, in 1835, wrote Caleb Cushing asking him to include the following paragraph in an article which the latter was preparing on Webster: "In the recess of Congress, in the summer of 1814, when the whole seaboard was threatened by invasion, Mr. W. gave the principal part of his time in coöperating with others for preparing for defense, in case of an attack by the enemy in the neighborhood. By the citizens of Portsmouth, & on the nomination of that venerable republican, John Langdon, he was placed at the head of the principal committee raised to concert means of defense, & he offered his personal services to the Governor of the State to be commanded in any mode in which they might be thought useful." (Fuess, *Caleb Cushing*, I, 172–73.)

[2] Hillard, *Jeremiah Mason*, p. 93.

the fireplaces, was filled. Certain spiteful Federalists, acting on their usual determination

> To rule the nation if they could,
> But see it damned if others should,

improved the opportunity presented to them of causing trouble for the administration and proposed removing the capital to another city. Webster arrived just in time to cast his vote in favor of removal. Fortunately the bill was negatived in the House, and the seat of government remained on the Potomac.

Webster, joining the assault on the administration, rose to speak on October 24, during the debate on a plan to raise money for carrying on the war by doubling the land tax. With his wrath aroused by the threatened British attack on Portsmouth and by the evidences of enemy destructiveness all around him in Washington, Webster might have cried loudly for revenge. Not at all! He seemed to be more incensed against Madison than against the Prince Regent. He attributed the "fearful wreck and ruin" of the public credit to "an incompetent management of the powers of government." In a spirit partisan rather than patriotic, he denounced the Republicans for their failures. He ended by expressing his intention of voting against the tax bill, justifying himself by the fact that it was certain to pass and that, by opposing it, he could voice his disapproval without holding up the prosecution of the war.[1]

Conditions did not improve as the year drew to a close. Writing to Ezekiel on November 29, Webster said: —

We are on the Eve of great events — I expect a blow up soon. My opinion is, that within sixty days Govt. will cease to pay even Secretaries, Clerks & Members of Congress. This I expect & when it comes

---

[1] Webster had some difficulty in deciding what course to adopt. He wrote Ezekiel, October 20, 1814: "My present inclination is, not to deny all sorts of supplies, in the present crisis, but to hold myself quite at liberty to vote for or agst. any particular tax. . . . As to increase of the land tax, I have not decided." (National Edition, XVI, 30.)

we are wound up. . . .   In short, if Peace does not come this winter, the Govt. will die in its own weakness.[1]

He had one more opportunity on December 9, when a measure for a compulsory draft of all the free male population between the ages of eighteen and forty-five was up for debate. A plan of much the same kind was introduced in Congress in 1917 and quickly passed, as a necessary step in our participation in the World War.   But Daniel Webster, in 1814, was its uncompromising critic.

In what turned out to be his last speech on the war, Webster declared that the principles of the bill were "not warranted by any provision of the Constitution."   The question at issue was "nothing less than whether the most essential rights of personal liberty shall be surrendered, and despotism embraced in its worst form."   He reviewed the disasters of the preceding months, during which people had seen "the public credit destroyed, and the national faith violated and disgraced."   Referring specifically to the Conscription Bill, he painted a vivid but much exaggerated picture of the plan in operation, "when the class shall assemble to stand its draft, and to throw the dice for blood."   Conscription to him was "an abominable doctrine," an "infamous expedient," and a "horrible lottery."   "The nation," he continued, "is not in a temper to submit to conscription."   And then, carrying his anti-administration theories to the farthest extreme which he ever reached, he added, with regard to the military draft: —

In my opinion it ought not to be carried into effect.   The operation of measures thus unconstitutional and illegal ought to be prevented by a resort to other measures which are both constitutional and legal.   It will be the solemn duty of the State Governments to protect their own authority over their own militia, and to interpose between their citizens and arbitrary power.   These are among the objects for which the State Governments exist; and their highest obligations bind them to the preservation of their own rights and the liberties of their people.[2]

It is impossible to avoid the conclusion that Webster was

[1] National Edition, XVI, 31.   [2] Ibid., XIV, 68.

here threatening, and even justifying, state nullification of a Federal law — an astounding doctrine to be advanced by a disciple of Washington and Hamilton.   To such an extreme position had he been forced through his opposition to the war and his abhorrence of Jeffersonian principles!   His influence was exerted successfully.   Although an act to much the same effect had passed the Senate by a majority of seven, the bill was indefinitely postponed in the House, and the announcement of peace a few weeks later made any further discussion futile.

For some reason this speech was not published at the time in the Portsmouth newspapers,[1] and it was not included in the earlier editions of Webster's works.   Indeed, George Ticknor Curtis said that it had not been preserved.[2]   Webster, however, had written it out after delivering it, and his manuscript found its way into the archives of the New Hampshire Historical Society, where it was discovered by Van Tyne, who included it as an "unpublished speech" in his edition of the *Letters of Daniel Webster*, in 1902.   As the utterance in which Webster showed himself most concerned regarding the rights of states, this speech deserves careful study.   It was fortunate for him that, when he was later condemning the nullifiers of South Carolina, there was no one to revive against him the words which he had used in 1814.   Even Calhoun, who must have been on the floor when Webster's remarks were being made, never saw fit to resurrect them.   In fairness to Webster, however, it must be added that, although he did defend nullification, he devoted his closing paragraph to the repudiation of disunionism : —

Allusions have been made, sir, to the state of things in New England, and, as usual, she has been charged with an intention to dissolve the Union.   The charge is unfounded.   She is much too wise to entertain such purposes.   She has had too much experience, and has too strong a recollection of the blessings which the Union is ca-

[1] Senator Jeremiah Mason's speech on the same question, delivered in the Upper House in November, was printed in the Portsmouth *Oracle* for December 3, 1814.

[2] Curtis, I, 138.   Referring to this speech in 1831, Webster said, " I had a hand, with Mr. Eppes and others, in overthrowing Mr. Monroe's conscription in 1814."

pable of producing under a just administration of government. It is her greatest fear, that the course at present pursued will destroy it, by destroying every principle, every interest, every sentiment, and every feeling which have hitherto contributed to uphold it. Those who cry out that the Union is in danger are themselves the authors of that danger. They put its existence to hazard by measures of violence, which it is not capable of enduring. They talk of dangerous designs against government, when they are overthrowing the fabric from its foundations. They alone, sir, are friends to the union of the States, who endeavor to maintain the principles of civil liberty in the country, and to preserve the spirit in which the Union was framed.[1]

Webster's absence from New England during this Special Session covered the period of the "New England Convention," which sat from December 15, 1814, to January 5, 1815, in Hartford, Connecticut. Such a gathering had been suggested at least as early as December 15, 1808, by Harrison Gray Otis to Josiah Quincy, but action was delayed, and it was not called until Massachusetts issued a formal invitation to the other New England states. Twenty-three delegates were present, including representatives from Rhode Island, Connecticut, and Massachusetts, as well as one from Vermont and two from New Hampshire. When the notification from Massachusetts was received in New Hampshire, the Legislature was not in session. Governor Gilman, a thoroughgoing Federalist, was quite ready to name delegates, but was apparently blocked in his design by the opposition of his Counselors, three out of five of whom were Republicans.[2] The people of

[1] National Edition, XIV, 69.

[2] In June 1814, the Legislature elected Elijah Hall, of Portsmouth, as a member of the Governor's Council. Hall was a Republican, and Webster, in a letter to Moses P. Payson (National Edition, XVI, 28), expressed indignation that a legislature supposedly Federal should have chosen him. Later an alleged illegality was discovered in Hall's election as Representative at the Portsmouth Town Meeting, and Webster appeared before the Legislature to demand a rejection of the votes. He carried his point, but, when the election was again held, the Legislature chose Hall once more, by a majority of two votes. This gave the Republicans a majority in the Council, and, according to Cyrus P. Bradley, prevented Governor Gilman from arbitrarily naming delegates from New Hampshire to the Hartford Convention. (*Biography of Isaac Hill*, pp. 38–39, published in Concord, in 1835.) The *New Hampshire Patriot* for November 29, 1814, asserted that, at a secret Federalist meeting at Exeter, Webster had opposed the proposed Hartford Convention and had blocked a plan to send delegates to it.

Cheshire and Grafton Counties, along the Connecticut River, did, however, hold assemblies and elect two men to represent them.

About the Hartford Convention and its deliberations there has always been an atmosphere of mystery. The call for the Convention, sent out by the Massachusetts General Court, spoke of a conference of the New England states upon "the subjects of their public grievances and concerns," and there were undoubtedly some among the delegates who, like Harrison Gray Otis, favored a new national convention for the radical revision of the Federal Constitution. That even bolder measures, including the formation of a Northern Confederacy, were suggested, cannot be denied. Among those who took an active part in the discussions held in the council chamber of the old Hartford State House were bold spirits who advocated secession as a drastic but effectual remedy for their ills.[1] But the majority seem to have been moderate Federalists, not unlike Webster in their point of view, and the report of the proceedings did not seem incendiary.[2] Briefly, it confessed that the hour for open resistance had not arrived, and made four innocuous recommendations: that state armies be raised; that seven specified amendments to the Constitution be passed; and that, if Congress failed to act, a second Convention be called in June, in Boston. If the war had continued much longer, it is conceivable that the restless agitators behind the Hartford Convention might have caused trouble. But the news of Jackson's victory at New Orleans, followed closely by the tidings of the Treaty of Ghent, — welcomed by New England more warmly than by any other section of the country, — removed all the motives for separation and left Harrison Gray Otis and his followers without an argument.[3]

[1] John Quincy Adams, with his usual lack of moderation, called the Convention "unconstitutional and treasonable . . . wholly abnormal, hideous, and wicked."

[2] A full account of the Convention was published in the Portsmouth *Oracle* for January 14, 1815, only nine days after it had dissolved.

[3] Senator Mason wrote of the Hartford Convention, November 24, 1814: "I do not expect much from it at present, whatever may be the wishes or intentions of those gentlemen, & expect it will end in a strong declaration of principles & a recommendation of moderate measures." (Hillard, p. 103.)

Some years later, when Webster had become the outstanding advocate of the inviolability of the Federal Union, efforts were made by his political foes to implicate him with the Hartford Convention. The plot was a complete failure. There were witnesses to prove that he had advised Governor Gilman not to appoint delegates from New Hampshire, and that he was fearful lest it might be led into treasonable utterances. George Ticknor, in his *Recollections*, speaks of a visit which he made to Washington in January and February, 1815, just after he had left Hartford, and makes the following statement: "Mr. Gore, and more especially Mr. Mason and Mr. Webster, expressed their dissatisfaction with the meeting of the convention; and more particularly that they received no information by correspondence from its members." [1] On August 24, 1835, in reply to a letter of inquiry from James H. Bingham, Webster put himself on record as follows: —

If it would gratify yourself and friends, I would give you sundry facts and dates, which show, what is strictly true, that I had no hand or part whatever in the Hartford Convention, and it is true that I expressed an opinion to Governor Gilman, that it would not be wise in him to appoint delegates. Further than this I have no recollection of interfering in the matter. At the same time, it is true that I did not regard the proposed convention as seditious or treasonable. I did not suppose that Mr. Cabot, Mr. West, Judge Prescott, and their associates, were a knot of traitors. [2]

At a date even later, Webster prepared for Hiram Ketchum a formal statement of the facts, emphasizing the point that he had nothing whatever to do with the meeting at Hartford, and concluding: —

It is certain that, after ten years of painstaking of all kinds (beginning in Mr. Adams's administration), not a scrap or syllable has been found, fixing upon me any approbation of, or concurrence in the objects or the results of that convention. The truth is, I kept aloof from all concern with it, and, as I had duties to perform here, confined myself to their performance. [3]

[1] Curtis, I, 136.   [2] National Edition, XVIII, 11.
[3] *Ibid.*, pp. 184–85. This letter is sufficiently explicit to meet every charge raised by Webster's opponents.

As winter set in, Webster and the Federalists redoubled their attacks on the administration. On December 22, 1814, he wrote Moody Kent: "The Govt. *cannot* execute a Conscription Law, if it should try, — It cannot enlist soldiers — It cannot borrow money — what can it do?" [1] Meanwhile the rumors of peace which had been in the air developed into something more than gossip. The British and American Commissioners, who had convened at Ghent in the preceding August, were, in spite of vacillations and delays, bringing their negotiations through to a satisfactory conclusion, and a treaty was signed on December 24, 1814. It conceded virtually nothing to the United States, but conditions were such in this country that the American envoys were glad to give their assent to the agreement. The news of Jackson's defeat of Pakenham on January 8, 1815, was a solace to the despondent Republicans, and was followed in the middle of February by the announcement of peace.[2] Webster had returned to Portsmouth, reaching there on February 22, and heard the church bells ringing joyfully to proclaim the end of the war. Although he probably did not realize it at the moment, the Federalists were left without an issue.

When Daniel Webster had reached such prominence that his political record was being searched for inconsistencies, his utterances before and during the War of 1812 were revived, like ghosts, to testify against him. In the autumn of 1828, the *Jackson Republican*, a semi-weekly journal established in Boston by some former Federalists who had espoused the cause of Andrew Jackson, published an article asserting that John Quincy Adams, conversing with Thomas Jefferson, had declared that Webster and other well-known Federalists had, in 1807 and 1808, been "engaged in a plot to dissolve the Union and reannex New England to Great Britain." Webster, who was in 1828 a Senator of the United States, was naturally

[1] National Edition, XVI, 32.

[2] The Portsmouth *Oracle* for February 25, 1815, which printed the full text of the Treaty, said, " The Treaty of Peace reached Portsmouth in 76 hours from the City of Washington, a distance of 550 miles." Ratifications of the Treaty were exchanged on February 18, 1815.

aroused by this accusation, and brought a suit for criminal libel in the Supreme Judicial Court against Theodore Lyman, Jr., one of the proprietors of the newspaper. The trial was held on December 16, 1828, before a jury, with the distinguished Chief Justice Isaac Parker presiding.[1] As Lyman belonged by birth to that inner circle of Boston society, to which Webster had been admitted through his talents, the case became a kind of *cause célèbre*, the outcome of which was awaited eagerly.

The evidence showed that Adams, in mentioning the "leaders of the Federal party in New England," had never named Webster specifically, and that the perpetrator of the alleged libel had included Webster only because of his later important position in the Federalist councils. Samuel Hubbard, in defending Lyman, made the point that it could not be libelous to assert that a man had plotted to dissolve the Union, for "every State has a right to secede from the Union without committing treason" — a declaration particularly interesting because of the fact that Webster's *Reply to Hayne* was made only a little more than a year later.

It was, of course, preposterous to suppose that Webster, who, in 1808, was a struggling attorney in Portsmouth with only a limited political influence, had then anything to do with the plans of the Essex Junto. The jury were unable to reach a verdict, although it was reported on good authority that they stood ten to two for conviction. That Webster failed to obtain the vindication he desired was due to a doubt on the part of the jury as to whether the charge were ever really made. Mr. Benton, who studied the details carefully, reached the conclusion that Lyman never intended to accuse Webster of complicity in a treasonable plot to break up the Union and that, therefore, no ground for libel ever existed. Lyman and Webster were later reconciled, but echoes of the trial were heard long after at dinners on Beacon Hill.

[1] The story of this famous suit has been vigorously and entertainingly told by Josiah H. Benton, in *A Notable Libel Case*, a booklet published in 1904, by Charles E. Goodspeed, of Boston. Most of Webster's biographers have neglected to mention the episode, and it has seldom been accorded the attention which it deserves.

Webster, during the period covered by this chapter, was guided in his political conduct mainly by two factors — his own instinctive antagonism to Republican principles and his regard for the financial interests of his own section of the country. Jefferson's commercial restrictions and the war with England were prejudicial to the merchants and shipowners of Portsmouth, whom Webster represented.[1] In opposing the Embargo and the war, Webster was thinking in terms, not of the nation from the Atlantic to the Mississippi, but of New England. Professor Van Tyne was not far wrong in styling him a "local politician," for there was indisputably a provincial feeling in all that he had to say on the fateful issues of that period. It was not until later that he was to boast, as he did on March 7, 1850, "I wish to speak to-day, not as a Massachusetts man, nor as a Northern man, but as an American."

[1] It is noteworthy that, throughout this period, the town of Portsmouth regularly gave a small majority for the Republican candidates, both for Governor and for Congress. Undoubtedly the wealthier citizens of that seaport were strongly Federalist, but the middle and lower classes — so-called — were usually Jeffersonian in their principles and votes.

VII

LIFE BECOMES MORE COMPLEX

> Sweet with persuasion, eloquent
> In passion, cool in argument,
> Or, ponderous, falling on thy foes
> As fell the Norse god's hammer blows.
> — WHITTIER, "The Lost Occasion"

My efforts in regard to the banks, at different times suggested, and in regard to the currency of the country, I think were of some small degree of utility to the public.

> — WEBSTER, Autobiography

DANIEL WEBSTER was a thoroughly healthy human being, with keen senses, sound digestive organs, and a mind free from those complexes and repressions which so fascinate the pathologist. Once it was reported that Webster had said that he wished that he had never been born; but Rufus Choate, when he heard of it, declared that this must have been a momentary fit of gloom, occasioned by disaster, for "Webster was rather a constitutionally happy man." His personality was neither subtle nor inexplicable. His attention was fixed, not in his own reactions, but on externalities; on lawsuits and politics, not on the elusive mysteries of life or the hidden wonders of the universe. Busy with practical matters, he refused to yield to moods. He escaped both despondency and exaltations, and was in this respect quite different from the neurotic and introspective Abraham Lincoln.

Webster seldom unlocked his heart. His letters tell us what he is doing, not what he is thinking. His so-called "private correspondence" is as public as a newspaper. It was not that he was secretive. He simply attached no importance to those caprices and mad desires which make the confessions of Cellini and Rousseau so charming. Nor was it that he was dull. He was almost as uncommunicative about himself as Grant or Cleveland, but there are countless stories of him, told by others, which divulge the essential man, undraped and off guard — a very human person, with frailties which make us love him.   What we miss are those intimate and indiscreet disclosures in which writers like John Quincy Adams and Roosevelt so completely reveal themselves.   If we are searching for the real Webster, we find him in Harvey's *Reminiscences* and in the hundreds of anecdotes, verifiable or legendary, which indicate how superbly vital he was.

Of his daily life in Washington during his early terms in Congress we know very little aside from some meagre items culled from his letters.   His salary of six dollars a day and mileage did not permit of luxurious quarters, but he had lodgings at Crawford's Hotel, in Georgetown, with Senator Mason,[1] as well as with such wealthy men as Christopher Gore and Rufus King, both of whom brought their wives with them and maintained considerable style.   Webster for some time had a room next to Mason's, and the two ate at a congenial table in the hotel, often, however, dining with Gore and King.[2]   "In the mess," said Ticknor of Webster, "he was very amusing, talking gayly, and as if no care rested upon him.   Everywhere he was liked as a social companion."

Into the formal society of the capital Webster seems not to have entered, except in a casual way.   After a little experience, he wrote to Bingham : —

A few ladies, indeed, are to be seen by going to the weekly rout at the palace ; but they are there only as so many curiosities — *raræ aves* — fit for all the purposes of social life, save only the unimportant

[1] Mason wrote, November 2, 1814, that he had " an excellent chamber, consisting of two apartments," at Crawford's Hotel. On December 27, he added, " The mess (as it is here called) with which I dine, consists of eight or ten gentlemen, mostly well-informed, pleasant, and agreeable."

[2] In speaking of Webster, Ticknor wrote: " His society was much sought. His relations with Mr. Gore, dating from the period of his studying the law, and his intimate friendship with Mr. Mason, never at any moment interrupted or disturbed, made him a most welcome member of that brilliant circle, which generally met in the evening in the private parlor belonging to Mrs. King and Mrs. Gore, which was rather an elegant drawing-room, for the time." (Curtis, I, 135.)

particulars of speaking and being spoken to. . . . I have been to the
levee or drawing room but once. It is a mere matter of form. . . .
You stay from five minutes to an hour, as you please; eat and drink
what you can catch, without danger of surfeit, and if you can luckily
find your hat and stick, then take your French leave; and that's going
to the "levee." [1]

He once dined with "Col. Pickering, Mr. Stockton, and a
few others" at Mount Vernon, as the guest of Judge Bushrod
Washington, and had "a very pleasant time." But he tells
us nothing of the food, the clothes, or the conversation.

His colleagues, however, were talking about him and learning
to respect him. New member though he was, he was appointed
in July 1813 on a Federalist "steering committee," with Timothy
Pickering as Chairman, to control party matters in the House.[2]
Ticknor, writing of a period in the early months of 1815,
declared that Webster, although he had then been in Congress
less than two years, "was already among its foremost men,
and stood with Gaston and Hanson to lead the opposition in
debate, on the floor of the Lower House."[3] He had taken pains
to familiarize himself in a practical way with the technique of
legislation, and his spare time was devoted to reading in history
and economics.[4] He was well aware that, in Congress, the man
whose mind is stored with information is certain to acquire
influence.

[1] National Edition, XVII, 234.

[2] *Ibid.*, p. 237.

[3] Regarding Webster's power as a speaker, Ticknor wrote: " I heard Mr. Webster
several times in the House, not in formal speeches, but in that very deliberate con-
versational manner, and with the peculiar exactness of phraseology, which marked him
as a public debater to the end of his life. He did not fail then, any more than afterward,
to command the attention of the House. The subjects on which he spoke related to the
common course of business, and were not exciting or particularly interesting."

[4] The best witness as to Webster's reading at this time is again George Ticknor,
who said: " He was at this time much occupied with the study of British politics.
Volumes of the 'Annual Register' and the 'Parliamentary Debates' covered his table;
and while I was in Washington he read through Brougham's 'Colonial Policy of the
European Powers,' parts of which he praised to me, while with other portions he was
much dissatisfied. When conversing with the other members with whom I constantly
saw him, he seemed to me to know more about the details of business before the House
than any of them. I mean that he appeared to know more what was to come up next,
or soon, facts which I was anxious to know." (Curtis, I, 136.)

In his physical appearance, Webster, although only a little over thirty, had become a commanding figure, who moved among others as if conscious of his superiority. Visitors perceived that he was no ordinary man. Some thought that he was too theatrical, and indeed he did have the dramatic instinct which makes the orator and the actor akin. But it was his sincerity, backed by that broad forehead and those lustrous eyes, which endowed him with power. Massive and leonine, he dominated others even before his lips were open; and, when the rich tones rolled forth, his hearers were enchanted, like the mariners listening to the Sirens. His easy flow of language and his calm self-possession, even in the fury of debate, were noticeable. He never stammered or groped for an idea, and he had a clearness of expression which was refreshing when issues were confused and timid men were hesitating which way to turn.

To the first session of the Fourteenth Congress, which opened in December 1815, Webster returned late. He reached Washington with Mrs. Webster in early January 1816, but they were almost at once called north by the serious illness of their daughter, who had been left with friends in Cambridge. When he was finally able to resume his seat, on February 7, 1816, he was aware that the divergencies between parties were no longer as obvious as they had been. The Treaty of Ghent had deprived the Federalists of their cherished grievance, and the party was slowly dying of inanition. The Hartford Convention, so menacing to the Administration a year before, now seemed a fiasco, and Harrison Gray Otis's mission to Washington had made him the laughingstock of the Republicans. There were, of course, nominal divisions in the House, with Clay and Calhoun still heading one group and Webster exercising a large influence over the other. But the " Era of Good Feeling" was at hand. Questions of the currency and the tariff, with which this session was mostly concerned, were not discussed primarily as problems of party policy, but rather on their merits as economic measures.

Congress reassembled in a plain brick structure, which had

been erected during the preceding summer by John Law and leased to the government as temporary headquarters.[1] Looking around him in the crowded hall assigned to the House, Webster could see, besides Clay in the Speaker's Chair and Calhoun on the floor, William Pinkney, — then the undisputed leader of the American bar, — the eccentric John Randolph, once more in his place after two years out of office, and, among the new faces, these of Joseph Hopkinson, of Pennsylvania, and Samuel R. Betts, of New York. Webster declared in 1831 that he had seen no such Congress for talents as the Fourteenth.[2] In such a galaxy, the most conspicuous figures were undoubtedly Calhoun and Webster, although we are told that Randolph talked more than either.

The important topic in Congress was that of the reëstablishment of a National Bank, on which Webster's utterance was eagerly awaited, for he had already discussed the matter in the preceding session. When the original Bank of the United States, organized in 1791 through the foresight of Alexander Hamilton, expired at the end of twenty years, an effort to recharter it was defeated, chiefly because Republicans were suspicious of its Federalist origin. Meanwhile a mania for state banks had resulted in an era of paper money, over which the Federal Government had no jurisdiction; and the doubtful state of the currency was a constant menace to legitimate business. In the autumn of 1814, with the treasury facing an enormous deficit, the party of Thomas Jefferson became through necessity the advocate of the very institution which it had condemned less than a quarter of a century before. Webster himself, as a loyal follower of Hamilton, favored a National Bank; but, being a "hard money" man, he stipulated that it should be compelled to redeem its notes in specie, that it should not be overcapitalized, and that it should be free to determine for itself whether or not it should make loans to the government. The principles on which Webster insisted are entirely sound,

---

[1] Hazelton, *The National Capitol*, p. 39. This "Brick Capitol," as it was called, stood on the corner of A and First Streets, N. E.

[2] From a manuscript letter quoted by Curtis, I, 146.

and, in the opinion of the best authorities, are at the basis of any wise system of banking. It would have amazed Ebenezer Webster, who was always in debt, to hear his son, also not unaccustomed to borrowing, discoursing on theories of banking. But Daniel Webster could arrange the financial affairs of a nation far better than he could his own monetary perplexities.

The bill as proposed by the administration in December 1814 had established a "paper money" bank, with a capital of fifty million dollars, of which only four million dollars was to be specie. Furthermore the government was to have not only the power to borrow up to thirty millions of dollars, but also the right to frame regulations regarding specie payments. In plain terms, the bank was to be merely the creature of the government, with almost no authority of its own, and existing mainly that its funds might be available for government demands. The effect of this plan would have been to put into circulation an irredeemable paper currency, founded upon forty-six millions in government stocks, then much depreciated because of the war. In commenting on this phase of the project, Webster said, in a memorandum written in 1831 : —

Throughout all the debates on the bank question, I kept steadily in view the object of restoring the currency, as a matter of the very first importance, without which it would be impossible to establish any efficient system of revenue and finance. The very first step toward such a system is to provide a safe medium of payment. I opposed, therefore, to the full extent of my power, every project for a bank so constituted that it might issue irredeemable paper, and thus drown and overwhelm us still more completely in the miseries and calamities of paper money. I would agree to nothing but a specie-paying bank.[1]

The Secretary of the Treasury, Alexander J. Dallas, who sponsored the measure, resorted to every possible device in order to drive it through Congress. It had originally been rejected by the House in late November; but Dallas, undaunted, had it introduced in the Senate and was able to

[1] Curtis, I, 140.

secure its passage there.   On the day before Christmas it was
reported, with some unimportant amendments, by the Committee of the Whole in the House.   Alarmed, the Federalists
sent for Webster, who was spending the holiday in Baltimore,
and he rode the forty miles to Washington on horseback, in
season to appear in his seat on the morning of Tuesday, December 27.   Owing to the death of a Senator, the bill was laid
upon the table until Monday, January 2, 1815, when Webster
made a powerful speech in criticism of it.   His remarks, which
displayed a thorough acquaintance with the basic principles as
well as the history of banking, stressed the desirability of a
specie-paying bank, free to transact business without outside
interference.   The essence of his argument is compressed in a
single paragraph : —

Excessive issues of paper, and a close connection with government,
are the circumstances which of all others are the most certain to destroy the credit of bank paper.   If there were no excessive issues, or,
in other words, if the bank paid its notes in specie on demand, its
connection with government and its interest in the funds would not,
perhaps, materially affect the circulation of its paper, although they
would naturally diminish the value of its stock.   But when these two
circumstances exist in the condition of any bank, that it does not pay
its notes, and that its funds are in public stocks, and all its operations
intimately blended with the operations of government, nothing further need be known, to be quite sure that its paper will not answer the
purpose of a creditable circulating medium.[1]

Unanswerable objections such as these had their effect even
on prejudiced minds.[2]   After the House had refused to recom-
mit the measure, it was brought to a direct vote, the roll call
showing 81 "yeas" and 80 "nays."   Speaker Langdon Cheves,
of South Carolina, then rose, and, after giving reasons for his

[1] National Edition, V, 44–45.   This speech was the earliest of Webster's Congressional speeches to be included in the official edition of his works.   The New York
Evening Post said of this speech that it presented its readers " with more sound sense,
more practical knowledge of the subject in a style plain and unadorned, yet precise and
chaste, than we have yet seen from any other man."
[2] For a good summary of Webster's criticisms of the bank bill, see Robert L. Carey's
Daniel Webster As an Economist (1929), pp. 101–04.

action, cast his vote in the negative.[1]   The bill was thus lost
by a tie.   Calhoun, who felt keenly the humiliation of the
administration, then strode dramatically across the floor to
Webster's desk and, holding out his hands in appeal, begged for
his assistance in framing an act which would have the latter's
support.   When Webster pledged himself to help, the South
Carolinian burst into tears.[2]

Webster kept his promise.   A revised plan, meeting most of
his objections, was drafted, and, after undergoing some modifications in the Senate, was passed by both Houses.   But
President Madison now became a factor in the controversy and,
on January 30, returned it without his signature, advancing
various reasons for his veto.   Writing to Ezekiel, Webster said,
"The President has negatived the bank bill.   So all our labor
is lost.   I hope this will satisfy our friends, that it was not a
bank likely to favor the administration.   What is to be done
next nobody can tell."[3]   Although another project, intended
to meet the criticisms of the Chief Executive, was now introduced, the news of the Treaty of Ghent interrupted the debate,
and, when the end of the session came on March 3, 1815, nothing had been accomplished.

By resisting these attempts to organize a bank which would
have only an insubstantial basis of credit, Webster performed a
genuine service to the nation.   Against untried panaceas and
delusive remedies for the ills of the body politic, he stood firm,
convinced that it was better to be safe than to run the risk of
insecurity.   What Hamilton started, Webster continued, and
no theorist could dislodge him from his position.

Such was the history of the preliminary stages of the measure

---

[1] Langdon Cheves (1776–1857), one of the most brilliant of South Carolina lawyers,
entered Congress in 1811 and was a strong supporter of the war with England.   He
succeeded Henry Clay as Speaker of the House, receiving the support of the Federalists
against Felix Grundy, who was the candidate of the administration.   In 1819, Cheves,
who had been a judge of the Superior Court of South Carolina since 1816, was made
President of the Bank of the United States and was largely responsible for establishing
its credit.   When he resigned in 1822, he had transformed it into a strong and reputable
institution.

[2] Quoted in Curtis, I, 143, from Ticknor, who heard the story from Webster himself.

[3] National Edition, XVII, 251.

which Webster found under discussion when he resumed his seat in February 1816. At the first convenient opportunity, on February 28, he reiterated his convictions in a speech which was undoubtedly the most important contribution to the debate.[1] Because of his incontrovertible arguments, the proposed large capitalization ($35,000,000) was considerably reduced and the power of the President to authorize the suspension of specie payments was stricken out. Webster was also opposed to the subscription of stock on the part of the government and to the appointment of government directors, but was unable to bring about any alteration in these features of the plan. When this bill, as modified by the Senate, came once more before the House, Webster, in reply to Grosvenor, of New York, spoke in an amiable and tolerant way, pointing out again the fact that it placed in the hands of the government altogether too much control over the proposed National Bank. With perfect consistency, he cast his vote against the measure, but it was passed by Congress, April 10, 1816, and signed by the President. Although he had been defeated, Webster could comfort himself with the knowledge that the Bank was sure to be a better one because of his inflexible opposition to some of the dangerous features which had been proposed.[2]

In connection with another important measure of this session, Webster showed his skillful leadership. Calhoun, as Chairman of the Committee on the National Currency, presented a plan, suggested by the Treasury Department, requiring all government revenues to be paid in nothing but gold, silver, copper, such foreign coins as were legal tender, and treasury notes, thus excluding the notes of banks which were not specie-paying. The opposition from the friends of state banks was very determined, and the bill was eventually lost by a margin of one vote.

[1] A condensed and inadequate version of this speech is printed in National Edition, XIV, 70 ff.
[2] Calhoun always contended that, as Chairman of the Committee on the National Currency, he was the one responsible for the Second Bank of the United States. " I might say with truth," he said in the Senate, January 13, 1834, " that the bank owes as much to me as to any other individual in the country; and I might even add that, had it not been for my efforts, it would not have been chartered." (Meigs, *Calhoun*, I, 194.)

Then Webster gave an amazing display of his power.   On the
following morning, he introduced a joint resolution covering
precisely the same principle, supporting it in a speech so clear
and so persuasive that it actually converted some of his
opponents to his side.   He pointed out that the situation of the
country "in regard to its finances and the collection of its
revenues" was "most deplorable"; he asserted that, because
of the lack of a uniform system of collection, the whole revenue
was thrown into "derangement and endless confusion"; he
exposed what he called "the plausible and insidious mischiefs
of a paper-money system"; and he reiterated his conviction
that these evils required the immediate attention of Congress.
He made no attempt to be rhetorical.   He endeavored, by his
earnestness, to carry conviction.   Seldom has a complicated
matter been more lucidly explained.

Webster's sheer audacity enabled him to succeed where
Calhoun had failed.   The resolution went through all the
stages of legislation on the same morning, was ultimately passed
by a large majority, and was signed by the President four days
later.   It provided that, after February 20, 1817, all monies due
the government must be paid in coin, treasury notes, notes of
the Bank of the United States, or of other banks redeeming
their bills in legal currency.   Thus the policy of specie payments was formally adopted.   The Second Bank of the United
States, under William Jones, once Secretary of the Navy and
Acting Secretary of the Treasury, as president, was opened for
business in 1817, and, after some vicissitudes, the country was
on a sound money basis.   The achievement of this happy result
was due largely to Webster's personal intervention.   In commenting on what had been accomplished, he wrote proudly in
1831 : —

The resolutions had all the desired effect.   They brought about
an entire change in the currency of the country.   Duties and taxes,
debts for lands, etc., were then equally borne and equally paid.   After
some years of unfortunate management, the national bank took a
good direction; and from that time to this the United States have
had a currency perfectly sound and safe, and more convenient, and

producing local exchanges at less expense, than any other nation is
or ever was blessed with.

No small part of Webster's constructive work as a legislator
was carried on in the unromantic but exceedingly useful guise of
an economist.   The average citizen does not become ecstatic
over columns of figures and prefers tales of battles and sieges to
pages of statistics.   Yet the statesmen who provide revenue for
the machinery of government often perform more lasting services than those who revel in picturesque adventures.   Too little
attention has been paid to Webster's share in stabilizing our
finances and keeping the ship of State off the rocks of insolvency.

The tariff, too, is a prosaic subject, but one with which
Webster was much concerned during certain periods of his
career; and the criticism to which he was subjected because of
his change of attitude makes it necessary to explain his position
in 1816.   As a representative from a district in which shipping
was the chief industry, he was in theory an advocate of free
trade, looking upon import duties as justifiable only as a means
of paying government expenses.   At the time of the proposed
repeal of the Embargo Act in 1814, Webster, replying to a
speech by Calhoun favoring the retention of certain duties as a
protective measure, said forcibly that he doubted the wisdom
of retaining double duties "as a more effectual safeguard and
encouragement to our growing manufactures." [1]   His exact
words are important in view of the *volte-face* which he later
made:

In respect to manufactures, it is necessary to speak with some precision.   I am not, generally speaking, their enemy.   I am their
friend, but I am not for rearing them, or any other interest, in hot-
beds.   I would not legislate precipitately, even in favor of them;
above all, I would not profess intentions in relation to them which
I did not purpose to execute.   I feel no desire to push the capital into
extensive manufactures faster than the general progress of our wealth
and population propels it.

---

[1] This speech was delivered on April 6, 1814, called forth by Calhoun's proposal,
on April 4, to repeal the Embargo Act.   It is printed in National Edition, XIV, 35 ff.

This is very good *laissez faire* doctrine, actuated, in Webster's case, by the fact that Portsmouth was a seaport town and that New England was relying for its continued prosperity mainly upon its carrying trade. His opinions on economic matters were formed by the needs and demands of his section. Born and brought up on a farm, he was not eager to stimulate manufacturing at the expense of agriculture; and it was this feeling which was responsible for one of his eloquent paragraphs still quoted in legislative halls: —

I am not anxious to accelerate the approach of the period when the great mass of American labor shall not find its employment in the field; when the young men of the country shall be obliged to shut their eyes upon external nature, upon the heavens and the earth, and immerse themselves in close and unwholesome workshops; when they shall be obliged to shut their ears to the bleating of their own flocks upon their own hills, and to the voice of the lark that cheers them at the plough, that they may open them in dust, and smoke, and steam, to the perpetual whirl of spools and spindles, and the grating of rasps and saws.[1]

Before many years had passed, great manufacturing centres were to rise along the Merrimack: Hooksett was to become Manchester, Watanic was to be transformed into Nashua, and Lowell, Haverhill, and Lawrence were to develop into teeming hives of industry. Even at Franklin, only a short distance from Webster's hitherto isolated birthplace, textile mills were to bring prosperity to thousands of employees. The wharves along the coast, as if in reaction, were slowly to fall into abandonment and decay, and the farms along the ridges were to be deserted. With this change were to arise novel and puzzling problems: the difficulties of foreign immigration, the social and hygienic questions presented by crowded tenements, the inevitable adjustments between capital and labor. When this complex era dawned, Webster's views had to be modified; but in 1814 he said with fervor: —

It is the true policy of government to suffer the different pursuits of society to take their own course, and not to give excessive boun-

[1] National Edition, XIV, 45.

ties or encouragements to one over another. This also is the true
spirit of the Constitution. It has not, in my opinion, conferred on
the government the power of changing the occupations of the
people of different states and sections, and of forcing them into other
employments. It cannot prohibit commerce any more than agriculture, nor manufacture more than commerce. It owes protection to
all.[1]

With the War of 1812 over, Congress was free to turn its
attention to matters of internal policy, among which the tariff
was foremost. An act, framed principally by the Secretary of
the Treasury, and intended to protect "infant industry," was
introduced in the spring of 1816, and, strangely enough in the
light of future events, received the support of Calhoun and
Lowndes, of South Carolina.[2] Webster, although he did not
enter into any discussion of the broad issues involved, devoted
his efforts, not unsuccessfully, to reducing the duties on textiles,
and especially on iron and hemp, which New Englanders
employed extensively in ship construction. He did not attempt
to fight a policy which obviously had a considerable majority in
its favor, contenting himself with guarding the interests of his
constituents. Then, as always, the attitude of different sections of the country towards the tariff was determined mainly
by selfish motives.

During this session, Webster voted in favor of a measure for
raising the pay of Congressmen from six dollars a day, and
mileage, to $1500 a year. At the passing of this bill, there was
an outcry throughout the country, and many of the members
who had sanctioned the increase failed to secure a renomination.
Webster himself had nothing to lose, for he had moved to
Massachusetts, and was no longer eligible to office from New
Hampshire.

Even in the heat engendered by controversy, Webster did not

[1] National Edition, XIV, 45.
[2] Calhoun was not the author of the Tariff of 1816, but he approved of it and declared
his belief that " a certain encouragement should be extended, at least, to our woolen
and cotton manufacturers." There was then a strong sentiment in South Carolina
favoring protection. (Meigs, I, 191.)

indulge in personalities,[1] and was invariably courteous and tactful towards those who disagreed with him. It was not in his nature to allow differences on public matters to degenerate into private grudges. He kept on polite terms with President Madison, whose policies he was so vigorously opposing; and he and Calhoun, meeting at dinner, showed no disposition to quarrel. But, in the spring of 1816, he incurred the wrath of the fiery John Randolph, of Roanoke, by objecting to a tax on sugar which the latter wished to incorporate in the tariff bill; and Randolph, following his customary practice, challenged Webster to meet him on the "field of honor." Under similar conditions, Alexander Hamilton had felt obliged to meet the requirements of the "code." But Webster, who disapproved of dueling, had the temerity to decline a meeting, and replied to Randolph refusing to concede the latter's right to call him to account for "words of a general nature used in debate." He concluded : —

It is enough that I do not feel myself bound, at all times and under any circumstances, to accept from any man, who shall choose to risk his own life, an invitation of this sort ; although I shall always be prepared to repel in a suitable manner the aggression of any man who may presume upon such a refusal.[2]

Friends of the two men, well aware that Randolph had only the flimsiest excuse for his conduct, now intervened and arranged an amicable adjustment, and Webster emerged from the affair without loss of prestige, even with hot-headed Southern Congressmen. Indeed, Randolph, when his blood had cooled, was so far pacified as to send Webster, at the latter's request, a copy of the correspondence between them. Thus was "honor" satisfied a century ago.

Webster's high expectations of a Congressional career had not

---

[1] The New Hampshire Republicans still hated him, and Hill's *Patriot* published, on January 16, 1816, a poem, which included the lines : —

> What though a Thompson or a Webster plume
> Their powder'd skull-caps, with prodigious bloom;
> And, high in office, loud in voice, proclaim
> Each other's title to respectful fame?

[2] Letter to Randolph, April, 1816, published in National Edition, XVII, 259.

been altogether realized. The House, until its novelty had worn off, had been interesting, but he had found there the same incompetency, the same intolerance, the same selfishness, which were to be encountered in Portsmouth — or in any other city. Withdrawn for weeks at a time from his law practice, he had revived his legal ambitions.[1] In February 1814 he had been admitted to practice before the Supreme Court of the United States, and, at that term, was employed in at least two cases involving prizes of war. His first appearance as counsel before the Supreme Bench was in the matter of the *St. Lawrence* (8 Cranch, 210 ff.), in which certain claimants had appealed from the Circuit Court of the United States for the District of New Hampshire. A United States vessel, going to England after the war had started, had brought back a cargo belonging principally to British subjects, and had been captured and condemned. Webster, who appeared for two of the many claimants, — some New York merchants, McGregor and Penniman, — was able to convince the Court that his clients had some recognizable rights, although the decision, rendered by Judge Henry B. Livingston, declared that the Circuit Court was bound to confiscate the cargo of the *St. Lawrence* as a legitimate prize of war.[2] At the same term, Webster was an associate of the distinguished Samuel Dexter [3] in the case of the *Grotius* (8 Cranch, 219 ff.), another prize appeal, of no great importance. This sitting of the Supreme Court was dominated by

[1] Webster's first case in the United States Circuit Court was *United States* v. *McNeal* (1 Gallison, 387), tried at the May term in 1813, before Joseph Story, Circuit Judge, and Sherburne, the District Judge. A question of perjury was involved, and, when Webster proved that the indictment gave the wrong date, his client was acquitted. Mason and Webster were joint counsel for the defendant, and Humphreys appeared for the plaintiff.

[2] The other attorney for the claimants was Irving, and the lawyer for the defendants was Pitman. In this case, Webster charged one of his clients three hundred dollars — the largest single fee which he had received up to that time.

[3] Samuel Dexter (1761–1816) was, in 1816, nearing the close of a brilliant legal career. He had been United States Senator (1799–1800), Secretary of War (1801), and Secretary of the Treasury (1801), and had then resumed the practice of law, appearing every winter before the United States Supreme Court. Once a Federalist, he had turned Republican in 1812 on the issue of the war with England. In court, he was a clear reasoner and shrewd thinker, but lacked the eloquence of Pinkney.

Dexter, Robert G. Harper, and William Pinkney, the last named of whom was employed in nearly all the suits. Webster, as a young attorney, was glad to have an opportunity of learning how business was conducted before the highest legal tribunal in the land.

The first appeal of any significance in which Webster was engaged was that of *The Town of Pawlet* v. *Daniel Clark, et al.* (9 Cranch, 292 ff.), which came up from the Vermont Circuit Court at the February term in 1815. It involved, in the first place, the question of the jurisdiction of the Supreme Court in controversies arising between citizens of the same state claiming land under grants of different states, when one of the states involved had been admitted after the adoption of the Constitution. Taking a liberal interpretation of the Constitution, Webster persuaded the Court that the clause in question covered not only the thirteen original parties to the compact, but also all those which had been, or might be, legally admitted to the Union at a later date. Arguing with Pitkin for the plaintiffs, Webster also secured a decision sustaining the validity of a Vermont statute affecting Pawlet. A colonial grant had divided the land set apart for the town into sixty-eight shares, one of which had been designated as "a glebe for the Church of England as by law established." There being no Church of England in Vermont before the Revolution, the town had administered that share as Trustee, and the income from it had later been appropriated to the use of the public schools. The right of the town to do this was asserted by the Supreme Court. The chief significance of the case lay in Webster's plea for the enlargement of the jurisdiction of that tribunal.

The modest successes which Webster had enjoyed in these cases before the Supreme Court undoubtedly stirred his dormant ambition to build up a larger practice in his profession. To do this, it was essential that he should escape from Portsmouth to a more important city, where opportunities would be more numerous. On March 26, 1816, he wrote frankly about his plans to Ezekiel: —

I have settled my purpose to remove from New Hampshire in the course of the summer. I have thought of Boston, New York, and Albany. On the whole, I shall, probably, go to Boston; although I am not without some inducements to go into the State of New York. Our New England prosperity and importance are passing away. This is fact. The events of the times, the policy of England, the consequences of our war, and the Ghent Treaty, have bereft us of our commerce, the great source of our wealth. If any great scenes are to be acted in this country within the next twenty years, New York is the place in which those scenes are to be viewed.[1]

This jeremiad, occasioned partly by the news which he received regarding the decline of shipping in Portsmouth, showed no vision of the prosperity which was shortly to come to New England from her mills and manufactures. But Webster doubtless displayed good judgment in seizing upon that moment as opportune for moving to a wealthier and more populous city. He could hope for very little enlargement of his professional income if he stayed in Portsmouth. He had gone as far as he could go in that community, and it was time to seek a broader field.

While he was still occupied with Congressional business, his aged mother, after some months of declining health, died in Boscawen, at the home of Ezekiel, on April 10, 1816. On the following day, unaware of her death, Daniel wrote to his brother, "I pray for her everlasting peace and happiness, and would give her a son's blessing for all her parental goodness."[2] Congress rose on April 30, and Webster was back in Portsmouth in early May. In June, he and his wife went to Boston to inspect houses, and he moved with his family to that city in August. Only eleven years had passed since he had left Boston, an obscure and untried law student; now he returned, with a reputation as one of the foremost advocates in New Hampshire and a fame almost national as a leader in Congress. There was no danger that clients would not flock to his door.

Webster, through his change of residence, was, of course,

---

[1] National Edition, XVI, 256.
[2] Letter to Ezekiel, April 11, 1816 (National Edition, XVII, 257).

ineligible for a renomination to Congress. His place at the head of the Federalist ticket was taken by Jeremiah Smith; but, despite the latter's popularity, the Republicans won in November by a vote of 8309 to 7231.[1] Had Webster been a candidate, he would undoubtedly have met the same fate, so strong was the reaction towards Republicanism after the war.

One more session still remained of the Fourteenth Congress, and Webster had arranged with Senator Mason to take their wives to Washington for the winter. If the schedule as outlined was carried out,[2] the Websters left Boston on Monday, November 11, driving by "hack or gig" to Hartford, by way of Worcester and Stafford, taking one more day to New Haven and two days from there to New York. They spent a week seeing the sights of New York and Philadelphia, finally reaching the capital on November 31. On the following day, Mrs. Webster sent to her brother, James W. Paige, a letter so rich in details that we cannot help regretting that so little of her correspondence has been preserved. In describing their quarters, she said: —

We reached this place, called a city, yesterday. Our journey was pleasant and much less fatiguing than I expected. We have not yet taken permanent lodgings, but shall in a day or two. We shall be, and indeed are now, on the hilly Capitol, I should say very near the house where Congress sits, which is a pleasant circumstance. Mr. and Mrs. Mason, my husband and myself, make what is here termed a *mess;* indeed there are to be no other lodgers in the house.[3]

On December 14, after she had had time to look around, she wrote: —

I have twice been to see the ruins of the Capitol. It was more splendid than I had imagined. The external, which is of stone, is entire except the windows. There is considerable remains yet of the architecturing, tho broken and defaced. . . . The Capitol is

[1] The *Patriot* said exultingly on September 24, 1816, " Mr. Webster, the great gun, has left the ticket." Webster wrote to Bingham, October 9, 1816, " From the symptoms exhibited in Rockingham, I thought nothing but exertion necessary to carry the Fed. Ticket in Nov." But he was too optimistic.

[2] Letter to Mason, October 29, 1816 (National Edition, XVI, 35).

[3] Van Tyne, p. 72.

directly in front of our lodgings, and if Congress sat there, it would add much to our amusement to see them pass and repass.[1]

While Mrs. Webster and Mrs. Mason made themselves acquainted with the city, Webster himself was once more in Congress, listlessly fulfilling his duty. He wrote to William Sullivan, January 2, 1817: —

We are doing nothing now but quarrel with one of our laws of the last session, called the horse law (not because horses made it, for it was made by asses), its object being to pay the Kentucky men for all the horses which died in that country during the war. So far very well; but there was a section put in to pay for all houses and buildings burned by the enemy on account of having been a military deposite. This played the very d——. All the Niagara frontier, the city of Washington, &c., wherever the enemy destroyed anything, was proved to have been a military deposite; one tavern, twenty-seven thousand dollars, because some officers or soldiers lodged in the house a day or two before the burning; one great rope-walk, because a rope had been sent there to mend from the navy yard, &c. &c. Some say the fault is in the law, some say it is in the commissioner who executed the law; others say there is no error in either, and others insist that there are great errors in both. I agree with the last, as the most probable proposition.[2]

What promised to be a happy winter spent in a less rigorous climate was rudely interrupted by the critical illness of little Grace Fletcher Webster, who had been left with Mrs. Samuel Webber, widow of the former President of Harvard College, in Cambridge. Before her parents started for Washington, she had developed what seemed to be a tumor on the neck, but which later was diagnosed as a manifestation of an acute form of tuberculosis. Hastily summoned, the father and mother returned to Cambridge to find her critically ill, and within little more than a week she was dead.[3] She had been a precocious

[1] Van Tyne, p. 73.

[2] This letter is published in the National Edition, XVII, 254–56, under the date of January 2, 1816, but internal evidence makes it certain that the date should be January 2, 1817.

[3] Webster wrote to Ezekiel, January 26, 1817, regarding Grace: "Her death, though I thought it inevitable, was rather sudden when it happened. Her disease, the consumption, had not apparently attained its last stages. The day of her death, she was

and delicate child, whose unselfishness had endeared her to all the friends of the family. Mrs. Lee, who was present when Grace died, remembered that, as Webster turned away from the bed, "great tears coursed down his cheeks."[1]

Sorrowful and alone, Webster returned to Washington and busied himself with his appointments in the Supreme Court. After the destruction of the Capitol in 1814, the Court had been obliged to seek temporary quarters, and, in 1817 and 1818, it occupied "a mean apartment of moderate size" which had been hastily fitted up in the midst of the charred ruins of the North Wing. This was, however, an arena where momentous issues were being discussed, and Webster, meeting as opponents or associates Hoffman, John Sergeant, Samuel Dexter, and William Pinkney, found that he had to keep his wits sharpened or fail in the competition. Pressure of Congressional business prevented him from accepting any retainers in 1816, but he was engaged at the February term in 1817 in several prize cases, and he appeared for the defendant in *United States* v. *Bevans* (3 Wheat., 336), which defined the power of the Supreme Court over harbors in the different states. It was a period when, as we shall see later, Chief Justice Marshall and his fellow judges were to promulgate a series of far-reaching decisions, greatly extending the authority of the Federal Government.

Absorbed in legal work, Webster, although still a member of Congress, attended its sessions in a perfunctory manner. No issue was raised which called him out of his melancholy, and he was bored with politics. When Calhoun introduced a project for setting aside the bonus and dividends of the Bank of the United States to carry out a comprehensive scheme of "internal improvements," Webster sustained him by his vote, thus voicing his belief that Congress had full authority to devote money to such purposes. After Madison vetoed the bill on the

---

pretty bright in the forenoon, though weak. In the afternoon, she grew languid and drowsy. She, however, desired her friends to read and talk with her until a few minutes before eleven, when her countenance suddenly altered, and in five or six minutes she expired." (National Edition, XVII, 263-64.) Ezekiel's daughter, Mary, had died only a short time before.

[1] Curtis, I, 158.

pretext that it was unconstitutional, Webster was among those who tried unsuccessfully to pass the measure over the Executive's disapproval. The significant fact is his coming out openly for a liberal interpretation of the Constitution and for the doctrine of "implied powers."

The Federalist Party, to which Webster still nominally adhered, was now disrupted as a national organization. At the election of 1816, James Monroe had received 183 votes against 34 for Rufus King, the Federalists getting the support of only three states — Massachusetts, Connecticut, and New York. Republicanism, to Webster's disgust, was everywhere triumphant. He remained in Washington until after March 4, seeing for the first time the ceremonies ushering a new President into office. When his cases before the Supreme Court had been argued, he went back to Boston and resumed the practice of his profession. Although he always regarded Portsmouth with affection, he seldom returned there, and his life, almost exactly half over, was now to be lived in Massachusetts and Washington. In a sense his preparation, both as lawyer and statesman, was completed. The remainder of his career was to show how his promise was to be fulfilled.

VIII

THE ATHENS OF AMERICA

What care though rival cities soar
   Along the stormy coast,
Penn's town, New York and Baltimore,
   If Boston knew the most!
               — EMERSON, "Boston"

I'll tell you, though, if you want to know it, what is the real offence of Boston. It drains a large water-shed of its intellect, and will not of itself be drained.
               — HOLMES, *The Autocrat of the Breakfast-Table*

I shall enter upon no encomium of Massachusetts; she needs none. There she is. Behold her, and judge for yourselves. There is her history; the world knows it by heart. The past, at least, is secure. There is Boston and Concord and Lexington and Bunker Hill; and there they will remain forever.
               — WEBSTER, *Reply to Hayne*

WHEN Daniel Webster moved from Portsmouth to Boston, he became a resident of a place which, although still under the town form of government, was actually the third city in the United States in population and importance. It was a homogeneous community of not far from forty thousand persons, largely of the same race, habits, and religious faith.[1] Although the official directory had a separate list of "people of color," most of the inhabitants were descendants of the original British settlers, and there was no "foreign quarter." The great immigration of Irish to Boston did not begin until 1848. Nor were there any "slums," for even unskilled laborers were in fairly comfortable circumstances. The atmosphere was that of a large village. Clerks stopped to chat on the street corners

---

[1] William Tudor, writing in 1819, said, " A more peculiar and unmixed character, arising from its homogeneous population, will be found here than in any other city in the United States." (*Letters on the Eastern States*, p. 319.)

as they walked to their offices, and ladies, from behind their window curtains, stared curiously at strangers.[1]

Although enterprising financiers were investing in mill securities, Boston was still second only to New York in her maritime commerce, and her extensive docks — the marvel of visitors — were teeming with activity. There could be seen every sort of vessel, from the tiny fishing smack to the towering brig, and the harbor seemed a "forest of masts." India Wharf and Central Wharf were lined with rows of warehouses, at which cargoes from all corners of the globe were unloaded — bags of ginger, cases of nutmeg and cinnamon, bales of palm leaf, and hogsheads of molasses. In Boston drawing-rooms were carved ebony elephants, teakwood tables, silk draperies from the Orient, and porcelain vases in colors which seemed the product of witchery.   Along the water front, Boston was exotic, and one could learn there something of

> The beauty and mystery of the ships
> And the magic of the sea.

The Boston of the first half of the nineteenth century was both primitive and romantic.   The standardizing process which has made American cities so much alike had not yet done its deadly work.   The downtown streets, many of them so narrow that two vehicles could barely pass, were paved in the middle with cobblestones from the neighboring beaches; and the overhanging second stories of the houses and shops made the town look as mediæval as York or Nürnberg. A foreigner spoke of the streets as "scarcely more than lanes, which at noontime are choked with good-natured strollers."   The oysterman and the lobsterman still plaintively called their wares, and the lamplighter, with his ladder and torch, was a picturesque figure on his rounds just before sunset.   Pipes for lighting the city by gas were first laid in 1826, and, before that, candles and whale oil were the only sources of illumination.   Pound-

---

[1] Describing the Boston of his boyhood, Henry Cabot Lodge said, " It was possible to grasp one's little world, and to know and be known by everybody in one's own fragment of society."   (Lodge, *Early Memories*, p. 18.)

keepers and fence-viewers were chosen annually at the Town Meeting, held in the Old State House, at the head of State Street. The Town Crier rang his bell from the steps of the Exchange Coffee House to announce a missing child or a lost pocketbook. There too was the headquarters for importers and brokers, who gathered for final informal conferences at "Change Hour" before strolling to their homes for a three o'clock dinner. Some wealthy Bostonians still went personally to market in Faneuil Hall before breakfast and brought home the food for luncheon in a basket. The town was governed, as a rule, by intelligent, well-educated, public-spirited leaders. For many years Charles Bulfinch, the eminent architect, was Chairman of the Board of Selectmen and Superintendent of Police. The first Mayor, who took office on May 1, 1822, was the aristocratic John Phillips, and his successor was Josiah Quincy, in whose veins flowed the bluest blood of Boston.

No one can comprehend the operations of Webster's mind without understanding the community of which he was a part. He was, at times, a very independent thinker, but he was also peculiarly susceptible to his surroundings, and he was profoundly affected by Massachusetts traditions. Webster helped to mould public opinion in Boston, but he was also moulded by it. He carried into the Senate a message to the nation from State Street and Beacon Hill.

In extent, the Boston of 1820 was much smaller than that of a century later.[1] Retail business was confined to a limited section on Washington Street, Scollay Square, Hanover, Court, and State Streets, and, — inevitably, — the harbor front. Much of the district known as Back Bay was then mud flats and salt marsh, and the land in that locality now adorned with massive structures of steel and brick was once submerged. During Bulfinch's active administration, the Mill Pond at the foot of Beacon Hill was filled with earth scraped from the peak

---

[1] Edward Everett Hale's *A New England Boyhood* offers a charming picture of Boston in the early nineteenth century. See also the *Life, Letters, and Journals of George Ticknor*, and Morison's *Harrison Gray Otis* and *Maritime History of Massachusetts*. Josiah Quincy's *Figures of the Past* has some interesting material, as does Mark A. DeW. Howe's *Boston*.

behind the State House, thus adding seventy acres to the north
end of the town; and Charles Street was laid out over a swamp.
The Mill Dam, available for travelers in 1821, connected Beacon
Street with Brookline and gave Boston an important outlet
to the main land. Webster's Boston included the territory
around Beacon Hill and extending south and east to the
wharves. Emerson wrote of it,

> " Each street leads downward to the sea,
>   Or landward to the west."

The Bulfinch State House, with the dignified façade, naturally dominated the landscape and was one of the sights to
which visitors were first taken. Park Street, recently opened
up as an approach to the Capitol, was lined with new and attractive residences.[1] At its foot was the Park Street Church
on what came to be known as Brimstone Corner because of
the incendiary nature of the Calvinistic theology there ex-
pounded. King's Chapel and the Granary Burying Ground
have been little changed by the passage of years, and St. Paul's
was dedicated in 1820. Webster himself usually attended
the Old Brattle Street Church, where what John Adams styled
"the politest congregation in Boston" gathered on Sundays,
both morning and afternoon, to listen to Dr. Palfrey.[2] Faneuil Hall, remodeled and enlarged by the indefatigable Bulfinch, looked then much as it does to-day, except for the motor
traffic which encircles it. Quincy Market was not completed
until 1827. The Court House, built on School Street in 1810,
has long since been superseded by the more imposing edifice
which overshadows Pemberton Square.

The historic Common, then ornamented by only a few scattered elms, was "a piece of pasture land with a small pond in
the middle, and surrounded by low wooden posts with one or

---

[1] Several of these houses are still standing, somewhat altered, most of them being
occupied by business concerns. Their outline, silhouetted against the sky, is picturesque when viewed from the Common.

[2] John G. Palfrey, who succeeded " young Mr. Everett " in 1818, was pastor of the
Brattle Street Church until 1824. Three of Webster's children — Julia, Edward, and
Charles — were baptized in that church.

two rails between them." Cows still grazed there, and the children of "the solid men of Boston" played marbles or flew their kites unmolested by the police, or even fished in the muddy Frog Pond. As late as 1847, an indignant citizen wrote to the *Journal* objecting to "the pestiferous dusting of dirty carpets" on the Common. Along Beacon Street — "the sunny street that holds the sifted few" — were some noble mansions, including that of John Hancock, next to the State House, and that of John Phillips, of brick, still standing on the corner of Walnut Street. On Chestnut and Mount Vernon Streets, and their tributary avenues, were many houses bearing the Bulfinch stamp, and the neighborhood was becoming fashionable. After 1829, Webster's friend, George Ticknor, occupied the stately residence at the corner of Park and Beacon Streets, — "the best location in Boston," — where he could overlook the Common and in which he welcomed many noted people, exerting such an influence that one of his friends proposed that the name of Boston be changed to Ticknorville. On the Tremont Street side of the Common, there rose, in 1830, the splendid Masonic Temple;[1] and not far away, on the corner of Tremont and West Streets, were the Washington Gardens, a favorite resort of the pleasure-loving, which delighted their habitués in May 1817 by installing gas lights for illumination. The distinctive feature of Tremont Street, however, was Colonnade Row, a line of nineteen four-story brick buildings constructed by Bulfinch, in which at various times dwelt many of Webster's closest friends, including Jeremiah Mason, Benjamin Rich, Peleg Sprague, and Benjamin Gorham.

Taverns, like the Indian Queen and The Bunch of Grapes, still allured travelers with large swinging signs. The Exchange Coffee House, in Congress Square near State Street, was reputed to be "the most capacious building and the most extensive establishment of its kind in the United States."[2] In

[1] The site is now occupied by the department store of the R. H. Stearns Company.
[2] The famous Exchange Coffee House was built in 1808, from designs by Bulfinch, of stone, marble, and brick, and was seven stories high. Here President Monroe was entertained during his visit to Boston in 1817. It was almost totally destroyed by fire on November 3, 1818.

winter, the small boys used to coast down Beacon and School Streets, past the Latin School, where the present Parker House has its entrance.

Poring over the yellow and brittle newspapers of that period, we are in touch with a world far removed from ours. We read that, on June 15, 1820, three pirates were hanged in public at ten in the morning; that the Plymouth Beach Lottery was in operation and prizes would soon be awarded; and that old Madeira was for sale openly by the cask. But human nature was the same then as now. Dr. Rolfe's Botanical Drops and Dr. Meade's Antidyspeptic Pills are no longer sold, but they have their substitutes to-day. The Extract of Roses, "for cleaning, preserving, and beautifying the hair," sounds very modern. And for amusements, Bostonians could choose, in December 1820, between a performance on the "musical glasses" or *Barnwell, or the London Apprentice*, advertised to begin "at 6 precisely." The only holidays were Washington's Birthday, Fast Day, Independence Day, and Thanksgiving. No one had thought of a Saturday half-holiday.

The circle to which the Websters were admitted was perhaps as exclusive and as cultured as any to be found on this side of the Atlantic. The members were near neighbors, meeting constantly on the streets or at social gatherings.[1] Many of them had amassed fortunes in foreign trade and had accumulated heirlooms through several generations. They owned houses in which the furniture, according to Edward Everett Hale, was "stately, solid, and expensive," and the table linen and silver exquisite. Dinner parties were commonly held in the afternoon, with suppers of a less formal character at nine in the evening. Decanters of wine ornamented every sideboard, including that of Daniel Webster, and, after the ladies had retired, the bottle was passed freely. Nothing about the entertaining was ostentatious, but there was a great deal of "cheerful, frank hospitality, and easy social inter-

[1] Russell Sturgis spoke of Boston society as "like a large family party," and added, "There were many who could announce the precise degree of relationship between any two people in any assembly."

course." There being no great discrepancies in wealth, few tried to outdo the others in extravagance. Among the chief families were the Derbys, Otises, Lawrences, Cabots, Amorys, Lymans, Lowells, Minots, Boylstons, Langdons, Adamses, and Blakes, the descendants of many of whom may be found in Boston's Social Register.

Like all those who have acquired possessions, these Bostonians were distrustful of changes, fearing that they might lose if the established order were overturned. They wished to keep their own world stable and unaltered. They were not interested in those who wanted to undertake reforms. The day had not come when a craze for organization was to produce the countless societies for the relief of the poor and suffering which now flourish in Boston. Webster's friends were generous, but in an unscientific fashion, and they lived their lives quite untroubled by the ills and wants of any "submerged tenth." As for pacifists, and feminists, and abolitionists, and communists, and prohibitionists, they did not yet exist. Not for a decade or more was Boston to become, in the words of Dr. Frothingham, "remarkable for explosions of mind."

Into such a group Daniel Webster was welcomed by congenial spirits who recognized his intellectual and social kinship with themselves. It was a far cry from the simple fare and crude furnishings of The Elms to the brilliance of Captain Israel Thorndike's dinners, but Webster was entirely at ease in his luxurious environment. The awkward rustic had been transformed, almost without realizing it, into an aristocrat on the British model, who loved comfort and longed for an estate where he could move like a lord among his retainers. In certain obvious respects, Boston society was enervating, creating and fostering prejudices and producing a narrow point of view among those long subjected to its influence. But Webster had the stamina to resist its provincialism, although he was unable entirely to stand out against the temptation to easy living.[1]

[1] Josiah P. Quincy, writing in 1881 of Boston in the early part of that century, said: " Many of the peculiarities of Puritanism had been softened, and so much of the old severity as remained supported the moral standards which the God-fearing founders

Webster was soon thoroughly Bostonian in his tendencies and habits. The Athenæum Library, established in 1807, had a list of distinguished proprietors, to which his name was added as early as 1822, when it moved from Tremont Street to Pearl Street. He was soon elected to that institution which called itself proudly "*the* Historical Society," [1] and he belonged to a famous dinner club, which met every Saturday. He was on the Committee of Thirteen, appointed in 1821 to frame a municipal charter, some of his associates being Josiah Quincy, William Tudor, William Prescott, and Lemuel Shaw, with John Phillips as Chairman. Beginning with his much-discussed Speech on the Tariff, on October 2, 1821, he spoke again and again in Faneuil Hall, until it seemed as if that auditorium were incomplete without his bodily presence on the platform.

Boston was not yet the literary and cultural centre which it was to become in the days when Emerson and Longfellow and Holmes and Lowell walked the streets. It did, however, enjoy a reputation as an intellectual oasis where the liberal arts were respected. Harvard College and its faculty gave a certain tone to society, and Commencement at Cambridge was one of the notable events of the year. Visiting foreigners were entertained at Harvard, and, from there, found their way to Beacon Hill. The sons of Webster's associates were enrolled almost automatically under Presidents Kirkland and Quincy, and Fletcher Webster graduated there in 1833.

It is essential to keep in mind that Daniel Webster became the authentic and trusted representative of the merchants, the bankers, and the professional men who were clustered in offices around State Street. They were his clients, and his daily associates when he was in the city. Through them he made

---

of the State had raised. A few men were accepted as the leaders of the community and lived under a wholesome conviction of responsibility for its good behavior. If the representatives of good society were in no sense cosmopolitan, their provincialism was honest, manly, and intelligent."

[1] The Massachusetts Historical Society, the oldest organization of the kind in the United States, was founded in January 1791. On its rolls are most of the most distinguished men of Boston.

his living, and from them, in some degree, he derived his opinions. Webster was identified with the so-called "upper classes." While he was in no sense a "snob," he lacked the democratic spirit of such leaders as Jefferson, Jackson, and Lincoln. Like many patricians, he was popular with servants, but he was out of touch with the great bulk of humanity — those who patiently carry on the dull routine and bear the burdens of the world. More and more he was thrown, through his profession, with the rich, the cultured, and the well-born, and his attitude towards current problems was thereby profoundly affected.

According to Webster's own evidence, he and Mrs. Webster came to Boston to live on August 14, 1816, bringing with them their two children, Grace and Daniel Fletcher. For two or three weeks they boarded with a Mrs. Delano, but Webster soon rented from ex-Senator Jonathan Mason a house on the north side of Mount Vernon Street, only a few rods from the State House.[1] In December 1819 he bought a home at 37 Somerset Street,[2] on a site now covered by the City Prison, a part of the Boston Court House which was constructed in 1886. It was then a select residence district, but conditions in the vicinity make it now seem quite different. Webster sold his place in 1822, and, on May 10, went with his family to spend the summer at the house of a Mr. Welles, in Dorchester, one of the suburbs. On their return to the city in November, they took lodgings with a Mrs. Le Kains, in Pearl Street, nearer the harbor.[3] During the summer season of

[1] This house is still standing at No. 57 Mount Vernon Street and is probably little changed since Webster's day. It has four stories, with a very handsome grilled iron balcony opening from the second-story window at the left, over the front door. It sits some fifty feet back from the street, and the lawn in front is surrounded by an iron fence. For interesting details regarding this house, which was built in 1804, see Chamberlain's *Beacon Hill* (1925), pp. 95–96. The first story is stone, the others brick. Webster was succeeded as a tenant by Reverend Sereno Dwight, of the Park Street Church. It was later the residence of Charles Francis Adams.

[2] It was an immense square, three-storied house, with the stone steps of the front porch rising directly from the street, and a narrow alley on the south side. It was later the home of Abbott Lawrence.

[3] Pearl Street, even as late as the " 40's," was a charming residence quarter, in which were fine old houses.

1823 they were again in Dorchester; but Mrs. Webster, with Julia and Edward, accompanied him to Washington in the autumn, remaining until the following June.[1] After another summer in Dorchester, Webster moved in November 1824 into a house belonging to Israel Thorndike on the corner of High and Summer Streets,[2] an imposing brick dwelling, set somewhat back from the road, with a garden surrounding it. Lined as it was with superb horse-chestnut trees, Summer Street was a shaded avenue with an eighteenth-century atmosphere. The first shop is said to have invaded it in 1847, and it is now devoted entirely to business. Daniel Webster Square — as the junction of Summer, High, and South Streets is called to-day — is a very crowded spot, through which most of the commuters from the near-by South Station walk to their offices. There is nothing to remind one of the more leisurely days when Daniel Webster had his home there.

He had agreeable neighbors. Next to him, to the north, lived the hospitable Captain Israel Thorndike,[3] with whom he became so intimate that the latter built a passageway between the two houses so that they could be used together for large receptions.[4] On Summer Street also lived John Lowell, Jonathan Callender, Charles P. Curtis, and Chief Justice Isaac Parker, as well as many retired shipowners, who liked to be within easy walking distance of the wharves.

[1] Webster preserved these details in an interesting manuscript called "Autobiographical Notes," owned by the New Hampshire Historical Society and printed in National Edition, XIII, 549-51.

[2] This house was torn down about 1860 and replaced by "a splendid block of stores called Webster's buildings." These were destroyed in the Great Fire of 1872, and a modern block was erected on the same site, at Nos. 136 and 138. This structure, called the Webster Building, is occupied now by mercantile establishments, and the ground floor is used by the Waldorf Lunch Company. It is five stories high and bears a large carved stone inscription, "The Home of Daniel Webster."

[3] Israel Thorndike (1755-1832), born in Beverly, accumulated a large fortune in shipping and moved about 1800 to Boston, where he increased his wealth by judicious investments, chiefly in real estate. He was said at this period to be the richest man in Boston, and he left at his death an estate appraised at nearly $1,200,000.

[4] It was through this device that Webster secured sufficient space for his reception to General Lafayette on June 17, 1825, after the Bunker Hill Oration. On February 2, 1826, Ticknor wrote Webster, "We went the other night to a great ball at Colonel Thorndike's, a part of which extended into your house, which it was not altogether agreeable to enter without finding its owner there to welcome us." (Ticknor, I, 371.)

In his serene and comfortable family life, Webster found solace from the tribulations of his profession. The loss of his daughter, Grace, in 1817, had been hard to bear, but a year later, on January 16, 1818, in the house on Mount Vernon Street, a second daughter was born. His eldest son, Daniel Fletcher Webster, — usually known as Fletcher, — was by that date a boy of nearly five years. He had two more children — Edward, born on July 20, 1820, and Charles, born on December 31, 1822, both in the Somerset Street house. The latter, however, died on December 18, 1824, in the Summer Street house, leaving only Fletcher and Edward as Webster's male heirs. During the early years in Boston, Mrs. Webster's time was so filled with domestic duties that she had little leisure for attending dinners and balls. One servant, Hannah, who had been with them since their Portsmouth days, was sufficient for their normal needs. Mrs. Webster, who had no ambition to be a society matron, certainly did not maintain the style of some of her husband's clients; but she was a popular member of a select circle of ladies and did her share of informal entertaining.

All contemporary descriptions of Webster agree in portraying him as a handsome and impressive man. Physically he was much more robust and was gradually putting on weight. He was slightly above five feet, ten inches tall, with a head which seemed abnormally large even for his muscular shoulders. His dark eyes were conspicuous for their rich glow, and his abundant hair was still a deep black. Mrs. Lee wrote, "The majestic beauty of his countenance was never more striking than at this period." [1] Although there were months when he had little rest, the effects of good eating were beginning to be manifest. With the passing of youth he acquired the stern and portentous dignity which made him such an imposing figure. Soon the slender schoolmaster of Fryeburg had been metamorphosed into a stalwart man who tipped the scales at nearly two hundred pounds and who had exchanged his earlier vivacity for a slow stateliness which was awesome to strangers.

[1] National Edition, XVII, 442.

He was usually up with the sun, waking the other members of the household by singing his favorite hymns. The family breakfasted together in unhurried, patriarchal fashion, and the father was very attentive to his children and their unceasing prattle. He then walked to the office,[1] and did not return until two or three o'clock in the afternoon, unmistakably fatigued and hungry. After a heavy dinner, he would throw himself upon the sofa, where his children would gather, eager to be as near him as possible. Mrs. Lee noted that, if visitors called in the evening, "Mr. Webster was too much exhausted to take a very active part in the conversation."[2] He constantly taxed his glorious physique and his steady nerves to the utmost, requiring many hours for recuperation. At this period he did not, apparently, use tobacco, either for smoking or for snuff, and, while he enjoyed his Madeira, we do not hear that he drank to excess.

With most people Webster seems to have been rather grave, if not solemn, in his manner, but he had his moments of relaxation, and even of frivolity. Ticknor, writing on August 17, 1826, regarding Webster's Oration on Adams and Jefferson, said, "He was at our house the evening before, entirely disencumbered and careless; and dined with us unceremoniously after it was over, as playful as a kitten."[3] He was not, however, a quick or clever conversationalist, and nobody has recorded any remarkable specimen of wit or repartee. In serious discussions he was always ready to do his part. Ticknor mentions a dinner at the home of Isaac P. Davis, when Webster "talked a good deal about Europe," having been reading up on that subject.

[1] Fletcher Webster could remember his father when they lived on Mount Vernon Street, " dressed in a frock coat, with tight pantaloons, a pair of long blucher boots reaching to the knee and adorned with a tassel, a bell-crowned beaver hat set a little on the side of his head, and a riding whip in his hand, as he proceeded to mount his horse for his morning ride." (Harvey, p. 318.)

[2] Webster belonged to the type of worker who, to quote Dr. William Osler, " loves to see the sun rise " and " comes to breakfast with a cheerful morning face, never so fit as at 6 A.M.," as contrasted with the man who is saturnine in the morning and then slowly gains in good humor as the day draws on, until he is at his best by midnight. (Osler, *The Student Life*.)

[3] Ticknor, I, 379.

Webster's first office in Boston was on the northern corner of Franklin Avenue, a narrow alley running from Cornhill to Court Street, which it entered at a point near the present Old Colony Trust Company. Later he rented more commodious quarters on the second floor of a building on the northern corner of Court and Tremont Streets, only a short distance from the Court House and the banking and commercial section. He was often away from home, sometimes in Washington at sessions of the Supreme Court,[1] and frequently in various New England cities.

He seems to have entered almost at once upon a lucrative practice, and his retainers, especially after the publicity which he derived from the Dartmouth College Case, show a substantial advance. For the year extending from August 14, 1818, to August 12, 1819, he received in fees the sum of $15,181, excluding "several small affairs and sums under ten dollars." [2] He charged $2000 for appearing for the Bank of the United States in *McCullough* v. *Maryland*. During the years immediately following, however, his fees seem to have diminished, and Curtis's estimate that his professional income from 1818 to 1823, when he entered Congress for the second time, was not far from $20,000 is probably much exaggerated.[3] For a young man who, in Portsmouth, had never taken in more than $2000 annually, he was, however, doing very well. Certainly his courage in declining the Clerkship of the Hillsborough County Court had been amply rewarded.

Even if this book were devoted exclusively to Webster's

[1] In a letter to Justice Story, January 2, 1821, Webster gives an interesting account of one such trip to Washington, which occupied from Saturday noon to Wednesday afternoon. Webster said, "Our journey was safe and expeditious." (National Edition, XVII, 314.)

[2] See *Ibid.*, p. 291 ff., for a full statement of Webster's professional receipts during this year.

[3] According to Webster's own manuscript record (printed in National Edition, XVII, 545), his fees for the five years from 1818 to 1823 were as follows: August 14, 1818–August 12, 1819, $15,181; 1819–20, $8393; 1820–21, $10,240; 1821–22, $12,805; 1822–23, $5095. The total is $51,714, an average of approximately $10,342 a year. For the year extending from September 1827 to September 1828, he took in (including his pay as Senator) about $16,000. On the basis of Webster's own books, there was no year up to 1832 when his legal income was above $17,000.

legal career, it would be impossible to treat in any detail the multitudinous cases in which he participated. Although he was primarily what we call to-day a "corporation lawyer," he was engaged in suits of every conceivable kind, criminal as well as civil, and involving a variety of principles. Among his clients were many of Boston's foremost citizens, including Harrison Gray Otis, George Crowninshield, James Otis, Samuel Hubbard, George Blake, John Brooks, and others. He was retained in 1819 by John Jacob Astor, and he made a note of having received, on January 2 of that year, $400 "Of *Casus Extraordinarius*" — a mysterious reference which will probably never be elucidated.

It was not long before Webster, by the common consent of those familiar with his practice, both in Boston and in Washington, was placed at the head of the American bar. "That Mr. Webster was the foremost American lawyer of his time," declared Senator George F. Hoar, "as well in the capacity to conduct jury trials as to argue questions of law before the full court, will not, I think, be seriously questioned by anybody who has read the reports of his legal arguments or who has studied the history of his encounters before juries with antagonists like Choate or Pinkney." This high estimate of Webster's genius is corroborated by the unsolicited testimony of such eminent advocates as Rufus Choate, Charles O'Conor, Isaac Parker, and William H. Seward.[1]

Of many of Webster's *nisi prius* cases hardly a mention can be found, even in contemporary newspapers, and we have to rely on gossip and tradition for the details of what must have been interesting litigation. A trial which greatly appealed to the public at the time was that of the Kenniston brothers, at Ipswich, in April 1817, for the alleged robbery of Major

[1] Choate perceived in Webster " a whole class of qualities which made him, for any description of trial by jury whatever, criminal or civil, by even a more universal assent, foremost." Seward, speaking in the Senate, declared of Webster that " the fifty thousand lawyers in the United States conceded to him an unapproachable supremacy at the bar." Justice Sprague, of the Supreme Court of Massachusetts, said of him, " In consultation no man was ever more weighty; in trials at the bar no man was his equal."

Elijah P. Goodridge.[1] According to a tale related by Good-ridge, — and substantiated in part by facts, — he had been assaulted about nine o'clock on a December evening while riding on the highway between Newburyport and Exeter, and had been dragged from his horse, relieved of a considerable sum in cash and notes, and beaten until he was unconscious. Afterwards, apparently in a state of delirium, he crawled to the nearest tavern, where, to prove his fantastic story, he displayed a small bullet wound in the palm of his left hand, between the third and fourth fingers. He later recovered sufficiently to guide some persons to the scene of the attack, where many of his possessions were scattered on the ground. He accused the Kennistons of the crime, identified as his own a piece of gold which he claimed to have unearthed under a pork barrel in their cellar, and had them brought to trial. The circumstantial evidence was very strong, and the Kennistons, in spite of their guileless simplicity and previous good reputation, were in some danger of being convicted.

Webster, on his way home from the Congressional session, heard the details from a Mr. Perkins, of Newburyport, who rode with him in the stage from Providence to Boston and offered as a theory the startling suggestion that Major Good-ridge, in order to avoid paying some of his debts, had concocted the whole tale, and, for the sake of realism, had shot himself deliberately through the inside of the left hand. On the following morning, after breakfast in Boston, Webster was called upon by two gentlemen from Newburyport, who told him that a fund had been subscribed for the defense of the Kennistons and urged him to take the case. Weary from his long trip, he at first refused, but finally yielded to their appeals and, with only a few days of preparation, appeared in court. It was his first case in Essex County, and a great throng packed the courtroom to hear him.[2]

---

[1] The name is also spelled Goodrich. Both forms seem to have been used in the newspapers of the period.

[2] The story as related by Harvey (*Reminiscences*, pp. 97–102) contains some discrepancies and a few misstatements, but tells the gist of the trial.

At the trial itself, Webster's genius was demonstrated in his cross-examination of Goodridge, who, embarrassed when called upon to explain how the wound happened to be on the inside of his hand, was cleverly drawn into some palpable contradictions in his evidence. To account to the jury for Goodridge's peculiar conduct, Webster argued that the latter, originally actuated merely by a desire to avoid his obligations or perhaps also by a passion for notoriety, had been forced, by the course of events, into the necessity of casting the blame on somebody; and he built up the plausible theory that Goodridge, intending only to shoot himself through the coat sleeve, had by accident perforated his hand. Webster's earnest and impressive manner had a moving effect on the jury, who promptly acquitted the Kennistons. Later Webster successfully defended one Jackson, another victim of Goodridge's malicious charges; and when still another, Ebenezer Pearson, brought an action for damages against Goodridge, Webster recovered a verdict for the plaintiff to the amount of $2000.[1] Eventually Goodridge, completely discredited, left New England for parts unknown. Some years later, when Webster, on a trip to Niagara Falls, was spending the night at an inn near Geneva, New York, he noticed that the barkeeper seemed very much agitated at his appearance. Later he ascertained that the unfortunate Goodridge had sought in the obscurity of that country tavern a refuge from the indiscretions of his past.[2]

Cases of this kind, fascinating though they are to the layman, were not reported in the court records. If we turn the pages of the Reports of the Supreme Judicial Court of Massachusetts and of the Circuit Court of the United States for the First Circuit, we find Webster's name mentioned in connection with many decisions, some of them of the highest importance to lawyers. His first appearance in the Supreme Judicial

[1] The *Boston Advertiser*, on January 8, 1819, speaking of Webster's argument in this case, said, " On this occasion we witnessed a degree in ingenuity, a chain of close logical reasoning, and a force of eloquence seldom exhibited in this or any other court."

[2] This sequel appears in two slightly different versions, one in Harvey, pp. 101–2, and the other in Curtis, I, 175.

Court of Massachusetts was to have been for the defendant
in *Wightman* v. *Coates* (15 Mass., 1), a suit for breach of promise,
but it was called for the March term in 1818, when he was in
Washington very much occupied with the Dartmouth College
Case, and he was obliged to be absent. At the October term
in 1818, he was associated with Phinney for the plaintiff in
Thomas Cochran v. *The Inhabitants of Camden* (15 Mass., 296).
The earliest instance of his appearing in that court as sole
counsel was in *Welsh* v. *Barrett* (15 Mass., 380), called at the
March term in 1819, in which he argued unsuccessfully for the
plaintiff in a matter involving a promissory note, the real point
at issue being whether the memorandum book of a bank messenger, deceased, could be admitted as evidence.

Biographers have expressed some astonishment at the rapidity with which Webster climbed to a leading position at the
Massachusetts bar. As a matter of fact, he was well known
in legal circles long before he took the decisive step of settling
in Boston. Stories of his effectiveness in the courtroom had
drifted down from New Hampshire, and many Boston attorneys, retained in cases which were tried in that state, had
reason to remember his prowess. Furthermore his Congressional experience had brought him into rather intimate relationship with such distinguished Bostonians as Francis Cabot
Lowell and George Cabot, and he was already acquainted with
Christopher Gore. He came to Boston under the best of
auspices, with his character and capability guaranteed.

Boston was a city in which rivalry among lawyers was keen
and merciless. Two of the greatest — Theophilus Parsons
and Samuel Dexter — died not long before Webster's arrival.
But there were others who had made their reputations and,
in their prime, were formidable competitors. Among them
were William Prescott, twenty years Webster's senior, who had
moved to Boston from Salem in 1808 and was unequaled as a
maritime and insurance specialist; Samuel Hubbard, who had
come to Boston in 1810 after a successful career in Biddeford,
Maine, and who was to end as a Judge of the Supreme Judicial
Court of Massachusetts; Charles Jackson, who had left New-

buryport in 1802 to open an office in Boston, and had been appointed to the Supreme Judicial Court only ten years later; Benjamin Gorham, the brilliant son of a brilliant father; William Sullivan, a masterly orator, who was long the President of the Suffolk Bar Association; Lemuel Shaw, who, in 1830, succeeded Isaac Parker as Chief Justice of the Supreme Judicial Court, serving in that office for almost thirty years; and a group of promising younger men, like Samuel Hoar, Marcus Morton, Franklin Dexter, Peleg Sprague, and Charles G. Loring, each of whom was to make his mark in state and national affairs. Not one of them was a Dartmouth man. All but two of them — Hubbard and Morton — were graduates of Harvard, but they gave to him the right hand of fellowship as if he were akin to themselves in antecedents and spirit.

It was not long before Webster's transcendent talents made him as supreme among these gifted lawyers as he had been at the bar of Portsmouth. His practice extended outside the county of Suffolk, into Essex, Middlesex, and Plymouth, and to sections even more distant. Whenever an important case arose, the first impulse of each litigant was to secure the aid of Daniel Webster. But it was his work before the Supreme Court of the United States which won for him a truly national reputation.

IX

THE DARTMOUTH COLLEGE CASE

Our college cause will be known to our children's children.
— WEBSTER, Letter to Hopkinson, March 22, 1819

It is the legitimate business of government to see that contracts are fulfilled, that charters are kept inviolate, and the foundations of human confidence not rudely or wantonly disturbed.
— JOHN FISKE

To many people, especially lawyers, but most of all to Dartmouth graduates, the name of Daniel Webster brings up the picture of a small crowded courtroom in Washington. Chief Justice John Marshall, his robes draped carelessly about him and his hands tightly clasped on his desk, presides with dignity. He and his associates, as well as the audience, have been sitting for three hours enthralled by the persuasive tones of the orator — a heavy, broad-chested man, firm as a pyramid of granite, with a domed forehead and gloomy eyes that pierce the soul. The speaker pauses, as if in sorrowful meditation. No one stirs. Then, under the influence of an emotion which even to-day, after all these years, sets our pulses throbbing, he begins again, with quivering lips and tremulous voice, "It is, sir, as I have said, a small college — and yet there are those who love it. . . ." Daniel Webster is finishing his argument in the Dartmouth College Case.

Dartmouth College v. *Woodward* (4 Wheat., 518) was argued by Webster for the plaintiff before the Supreme Court of the United States in 1818 and decided in his client's favor in February 1819. The complicated issues involved have been frequently analyzed, and the history and significance of the case have been exhaustively treated by competent legal authorities.[1] Here it will be examined mainly with regard to the conspicuous part taken by Daniel Webster in its permanent settlement. Around the Dartmouth College Case, — as it is commonly called, — as around few others in the annals of the Supreme Court, a romantic tradition has developed. There is, furthermore, the fact that it has been cited more than a thousand times in subsequent litigations, and that, to quote Henry Cabot Lodge, "it extended the jurisdiction of the highest federal court more than any other judgment ever rendered by them." [2]

Stripped of technicalities and nonessentials, the immediate issue decided by the Dartmouth College Case was the inviolability of the charter of incorporation of an institution of learning. It settled the question as to whether the charter was a contract at all, within the meaning of the Constitution, and answered the query, "Does the legislature of a state have the power, under the Constitution of the United States, to modify or abrogate a charter legally granted in all good faith to a college?" By implication it involved the whole subject of the stability of contracts, and thus affected other institutions founded and endowed in the same manner as Dartmouth. In another sense, it was a phase of the historic conflict during the formative days of the Republic between conservatives and liberals, Federalists and Democrats, John Marshall and Thomas Jefferson. It need hardly be said that Daniel Webster was on the side of established order.

The original charter of Dartmouth College, granted in 1769, was signed in the name of George III by John Wentworth, "Governor and Commander in Chief in and over the Province

---

[1] The fullest account is contained in John M. Shirley's *The Dartmouth College Causes and the Supreme Court of the United States* (1879), a badly arranged but indispensable book. Charles Warren discusses the case in his *The Supreme Court in United States History* (1922), I, 474 ff., and Albert J. Beveridge in his *John Marshall* (1919), IV, 220–81. See also "Historical Note on the Dartmouth College Case," by Charles Warren, in *American Law Review* for 1912, Vol. XLVI. There are some sane comments on the case in Tucker's *My Generation* (1919), pp. 271–96.

[2] Lodge, *Webster*, p. 96. This book, although often grossly unjust to Webster, contains a very intelligent account of the Dartmouth College Case.

of New Hampshire." [1]   The project was the outgrowth of what had been a charity school for Indians, founded at Lebanon, Connecticut, by a philanthropic clergyman, Eleazar Wheelock, who had raised in England funds amounting to more than eleven thousand pounds from various persons of benevolent tendencies, headed by William, Earl of Dartmouth, Secretary for the Colonies. This royal charter created the institution since known as Dartmouth College; appointed Wheelock as President, with the privilege of designating his successor — who was, however, subject to removal by the trustees; and established "one body corporate and politick in deed, action, and name," made up of twelve members, to be called the Trustees of Dartmouth College, with ample authority to buy, receive, and hold lands, to fill vacancies on the Board, and to make all necessary laws, rules, and regulations for the institution. Under this charter forming a perpetual and self-perpetuating corporation, Dartmouth College was opened in the town of Hanover, on the east bank of the Connecticut, and had endured, through various vicissitudes, for nearly half a century. It was the ninth and last of the colonial colleges.

Even the American Revolution had not broken the continuity of Dartmouth College. Eleazar Wheelock, dying in 1779, bequeathed the presidency to his son, John, and when the latter took over his father's duties at Hanover a majority of the trustees were in sympathy with him and the Wheelock family tradition. As age crept upon him, however, John Wheelock grew obstinate and tenacious of authority, and lost the respect of most of the undergraduates. The membership of the Board, meanwhile, had gradually changed, and several of the new men were less subservient to Wheelock's wishes.

For diverse reasons, political, economic, and religious, a controversy arose between the President and the majority of the trustees, resulting in a bewildering series of charges and counter-charges. The grave question as to who should preach in the

---

[1] This charter is printed in full in Chase's *A History of Dartmouth College and the Town of Hanover*, Vol. I, Appendix A.

village church kept the townspeople, the faculty, and the trustees in a turmoil. Wheelock, a Presbyterian, succeeded in arraying other religious denominations against his opponents, who were, for the most part, Congregationalists. Although he had originally been a Federalist, Wheelock managed to rally around him most of the Antifederalists and Republicans; while the trustees had the support of the Federalists and conservatives. The President angered the trustees by requesting the New Hampshire Legislature to appoint a committee for investigating the conduct of the college; and in May 1815 he published an anonymous pamphlet, *Sketches of the History of Dartmouth College and Moor's Charity School*, in which he assailed the trustees and perpetrated what was later described by them as a "gross and unprovoked libel." The dispute culminated on August 26, 1815, when the trustees removed Wheelock from office and elected the Reverend Francis Brown, of Yarmouth, Maine, as his successor. By this time the controversy had attracted widespread attention, and the *Patriot* was filled with the details. Its Republican editor, Isaac Hill, of course, took Wheelock's part.

For the moment, the trustees, by their prompt and vigorous action, had the better of the quarrel; but it was now to be carried into the realm of state politics. In March 1816, the Federalists, after holding control in New Hampshire throughout the war, were turned out, and William Plumer, a convert to Republicanism, was elected Governor, with a party majority in both branches of the Legislature. Dartmouth College had now become the innocent victim of partisan disputes. The trustees, warned of danger, did their utmost to avert trouble; but Governor Plumer, in his inaugural speech, announced that the college charter contained principles "hostile to the spirit and genius of a free government," and demanded action.[1]

[1] Governor Plumer's Message was read on June 6, 1816. Later he sent a copy to Thomas Jefferson, who replied, July 21, 1816, saying that it was "replete with sound principles, and truly Republican." Commenting on what Plumer had said with regard to Dartmouth College, Jefferson declared it to be most absurd "that institutions, established for the use of the nation, cannot be touched or modified," and ridiculed the idea "that the earth belongs to the dead, and not to the living." For the complete

With enthusiastic alacrity, the Legislature passed, on June 27, 1816, a bill changing the name of the institution to Dartmouth University, increasing the number of trustees from twelve to twenty-one, and providing for a board of twenty-five overseers, appointed by the Governor and Council and entrusted with the power of veto over any measures of the trustees. Thus, for all practical purposes, the college was placed under the thumb of the Legislature, and the Board of Trustees was to be packed with Wheelock's friends. The bill was actuated mainly by political motives, and it excited much bitterness among the old trustees, who rightly declared that, if it were carried into effect, every collegiate institution in the state would "hereafter hold its rights, privileges, and property, not according to the settled established principles of law, but according to the arbitrary will and pleasure of each successive legislature."

With little delay, the Governor named the trustees and overseers of the newborn university, and these officials took formal possession of the college property; but a majority of the old trustees refused to yield, and Dartmouth College continued to function, though the President and faculty were ousted from their quarters. The University, of which John Wheelock had been designated as President, was but a skeleton organization; it was difficult to obtain a quorum of either the trustees or the overseers, and almost no undergraduates registered. The college students — among whom was Rufus Choate — calmly went to lectures and recitations in Rowley Hall, not far from the campus.

But the college trustees had no intention of submitting without a fight. After consulting counsel, they brought an action of trover,[1] on February 8, 1817, in the Court of Common Pleas

---

text of Jefferson's letter, see *The Life of William Plumer*, by William Plumer, Jr., pp. 440–41.

[1] For the benefit of laymen, it may be explained that an action in trover is a proceeding under common law for recovering the value of personal chattels wrongfully converted by another to his own use. The plaintiff in such an action seeks damages, not possession, and cannot recover the specific chattel involved. In this case, it was agreed that the return of the college seal and record books would satisfy the demands of the verdict.

of Grafton County, against William H. Woodward, the former
treasurer of the trustees, for the recovery of the charter, the
records, and the seal, all of which he had refused to surrender.
By consent of both parties, the case was taken directly to the
Superior Court of Appeals of New Hampshire, for adjudication.
The trustees, as Samuel W. McCall once said, "were making
a struggle for self-preservation against great odds."

Daniel Webster, even more than most Dartmouth graduates,
had kept in touch with the situation. As a Federalist Congressman from New Hampshire, he was alive to its political significance. He had been in college under President Wheelock, and
he knew personally nearly everybody involved. As early as the
winter of 1815, Wheelock had intimated to Webster his desire
to have the latter act as his counsel; and in June, at Concord,
he had talked with him and obtained his conditional promise
of professional assistance. When the Legislature appointed
a Special Committee to investigate the concerns of the college,
the President wrote to Webster, enclosing twenty dollars
as a retainer and requesting him to come without delay to
Hanover and appear before this Committee as his personal
representative.

During the interval, Webster had been discussing the affair
with his former patron, Thomas W. Thompson,[1] — who had
been a trustee of Dartmouth since 1801, — and had decided
not only that Wheelock was in the wrong but also that certain
political aspects of the controversy made it inadvisable for himself to appear as the champion of the President. He therefore
discreetly declined to reply, and Wheelock was obliged to rely
on Judge Jonathan Hubbard and Josiah Dunham. When a
confidential letter from Senator Thompson to Professor Ebenezer Adams came into Dunham's possession, indicating that
Webster was about to take sides with Wheelock's critics,
Dunham at once wrote to Webster, enclosing a copy of the

[1] Thompson had been Speaker of the House of Representatives in 1813–14, and had
been chosen United States Senator in 1814 to fill the vacancy occasioned by the resignation of Nicholas Gilman. At this period, Senator Thompson was a man of considerable
importance in New Hampshire politics.

document, and accusing him of treachery. To this outburst, Webster replied with dignity, pointing out that he had not regarded the request to appear before a Legislative Committee as a professional matter, and saying, "I am not so fully convinced as you are, that the president is altogether right, and the trustees altogether wrong." As to how far Webster was ethically bound, there may be some question and there is no record of what he did with Wheelock's twenty dollars. Practically, however, it would have been both injudicious and inconsistent for him to let himself be the tool of the Wheelock faction, which was drawing its support from the Republicans, his political foes. Furthermore, Thompson, Jeremiah Mason, and Jeremiah Smith, all of whom were Federalists, were involved, and Webster was inclined to follow where they led.

As the day approached for the meeting of the Legislature in 1816, Webster's alarm increased. He wrote, June 4, 1816, from Portsmouth, to President Brown : —

You do not feel a stronger wish than I do, that nothing may take place at this session detrimental to the college, and I am willing to do anything in my power to soften the irritated feelings of democracy towards it.

As a strategic measure, he suggested that the General Court be encouraged to form a new college, possibly at Concord, in the hope that such a proposal would induce that body to keep its hands off Dartmouth. After the Legislature had passed the obnoxious act of June 27, Senator Thompson conferred with Webster, who joined with Senator Mason, Judge Peabody, and Timothy Farrar in the opinion that it was the duty of the trustees to make a legal resistance; and he concurred in the action of trover which they brought early in the following year. By that date he had moved to Boston and was a resident of Massachusetts.

It seems to have been taken for granted that Webster would be among the counsel for the college trustees; but, when *Dartmouth College* v. *Woodward* came up for a hearing in May 1817, at Haverhill, New Hampshire, the college was represented only by Jeremiah Mason and Jeremiah Smith.[1] Webster may, perhaps, have held back, feeling that it was important to have Mason and Smith, both older and more influential than he, actively enlisted in the case. At this preliminary clash, the university attorneys were George Sullivan, then Attorney-General of New Hampshire, and Ichabod Bartlett — advocates whose skill Webster had frequently tested. The Superior Court, only recently established, comprised Chief Justice William M. Richardson, Samuel Bell, and Levi Woodbury, all appointees of Governor Plumer, all Republicans, and all high-minded jurists.[2] The hearings at Haverhill were incomplete, and, to allow further argument, the case was continued at the September term, called at Exeter. During the summer, Webster, at their urgent request, had joined Smith and Mason.[3]

When the case was called on September 19, Mason opened the argument for the plaintiffs, in a plea which was a model of condensed logic, maintaining that the recent acts of the Legislature forming the university were not binding because (1) they were not within the scope of legislative power; (2) they violated the Constitution of New Hampshire; and (3) they

[1] Smith had only recently, through the repeal of the Judiciary Acts of 1813, been removed from his position as Chief Justice of the Supreme Court of New Hampshire, and had returned to private practice.

[2] Mason, a none too tolerant Federalist, confessed that " three more men so well qualified as the present Judges, and who would accept the office, could not be found in the state." Levi Woodbury (1789–1851), later Governor of New Hampshire (1823–24), United States Senator (1825–31), Secretary of the Navy (1831–34), Secretary of the Treasury (1834–41), United States Senator (1841–45), and Justice of the United States Supreme Court (1846–51), was a statesman with whom Webster was frequently to be embroiled. But for his sudden death in 1851, he would probably have been nominated for President instead of Franklin Pierce by the Democratic Party, and would, of course, have been elected.

[3] On September 4, 1817, Webster wrote Mason from Boston: "Judge Smith has written to me, that I must take some part in the argument of this college question. I have not thought of the subject, nor made the least preparation; I am sure I can do no good, and must, therefore, beg that you and he will follow up in your own manner, the blows which have already been so well struck. I am willing to be considered as belonging to the cause and to talk about it, and consult about it, but should do no good by undertaking an argument. If it is not too troublesome, please let Mr. Fales give me a naked list of the authorities cited by you, and I will look at them before court. I do this that I may be able to understand you and Judge Smith." (National Edition, XVII, 265–66.)

violated the Constitution of the United States. His speech occupied two hours, and that of Smith, who followed him, took four. Bartlett and Sullivan, responding for the defendant, filled three hours between them. Then Webster closed for the plaintiffs in a plea two hours long, which no one took the trouble to preserve.[1] Those who heard him, however, remembered later that he was very emotional and even had tears in his eyes. But neither reasoning nor pathos were of any avail to the supporters of Dartmouth. The case was continued for further advisement to the next session of the Court, at Plymouth. There, on November 6, the Chief Justice rendered a decision adverse to the plaintiffs. The university had drawn first blood.

Chief Justice Richardson's opinion — which Webster later admitted to be "able, ingenious, and plausible"[2] — was thoroughly Jeffersonian in doctrine. Asserting that the college trustees formed a public corporation, it denied that they were as a body sheltered under that provision of the New Hampshire Bill of Rights declaring that no person should be deprived of his property, immunity, or privileges except by judgment of his peers or by the law of the land. Even if the charter were a contract, the Legislature, as the supreme authority, had a right to modify it at its discretion; and the "law of the land" meant any statute which the Legislature might choose to enact. In plain language, the Legislature, being a popular assembly, could do exactly what it pleased. Furthermore, the Court definitely ruled that the legislation under discussion was "not repugnant to the Constitution of the United States."

It had been assumed by the college trustees that, if they failed in the Superior Court, they would carry their case to the Supreme Court of the United States and that Daniel Webster should take charge of it there. The latter was quite willing to go, but he could not afford to give his services; and he wrote

---

[1] Farrar, *Report of the Case of the Trustees of Dartmouth College against William H. Woodward*, omitted Webster's argument, merely stating that the latter's views were more fully disclosed before the Supreme Court.

[2] National Edition, XVII, 287.

President Brown suggesting that, for the sum of a thousand dollars, he would undertake not only to appear in Washington but also to engage Joseph Hopkinson, of Philadelphia, as associate counsel.[1] The trustees, delighted at Webster's acquiescence, undertook to raise the money, and he set to work assembling material.[2] An acceptance from Hopkinson[3] assured Webster of competent support.

For the next few weeks, Webster, before going south, was in correspondence with both Mason and Smith, and must have met them in conference.[4] It was possible, on a writ of error to the New Hampshire Superior Court, to bring the case before the Supreme Court of the United States, under that provision of the Federal Constitution giving the Supreme Court appellate jurisdiction in matters involving the interpretation of that document. The section covering the Dartmouth situation was the famous clause declaring that "no State . . . shall pass any bill of attainder, ex post facto law, or law impairing the obligation of contracts."[5] The only basis on which the case, as it stood, could be brought to the Supreme Court was that the legislative act modifying the Dartmouth charter did impair the

[1] For the full text of this letter, dated November 15, 1817, see Chase's *History of Dartmouth College*. It does not appear in the collected correspondence.

[2] Webster wrote to Mason, November 27: " I should like to know something of the court's opinion; I wish you or Mr. Farrar could get a copy for me. If I go to Washington, and have this cause on my shoulders, I must have your brief, which I should get of course without difficulty, and Judge Smith's. . . . Will you inform me whether a copy of Judge Richardson's opinion can be had, and whether you can devise a mode in which I can get Judge Smith's minutes if I should go to Washington?" (National Edition, XVII, 266–67.)

[3] Joseph Hopkinson (1770–1842), after graduating from the University of Pennsylvania in 1786, studied law and began practice in Easton, but later opened an office in Philadelphia, where he became a leader of the bar. Webster had met him as a Federalist member of Congress in 1815–17. He was known as the author of the patriotic song, " Hail, Columbia!" written in 1798.

[4] Webster wrote to Mason, from Boston, December 8, 1817: "Judge Smith has written for a form of citation in the College cause, which I shall send him & write to him for his minutes. My wish is to see both him & you, before I go to Washington. If I should not be kept in town by the Court, as I do not expect to, I intend seeing you about Christmas or New Year. Everybody will expect me at Washington to deliver the Exeter argument. Therefore the Exeter argument must be drawn out before I go. I will spend a day or two on this subject at Portsmouth or Exeter, if you incline that I should do so." (National Edition, XVI, 39.)

[5] *Constitution of the United States*, Article I, Section 10, Clause 1.

obligation of a contract, thus violating the Federal Constitution. As this point had been touched upon only briefly by the attorneys for the plaintiff at Exeter, Webster was disturbed at the narrow range of inquiry involved, and suggested bringing another action in the United States Circuit Court,[1] such as suing for the Wheelock lands,[2] which would allow the college counsel to present all their arguments to the attention of the highest tribunal in the country. After a conference between Webster and the trustees in January 1818, three such actions were entered in the Circuit Court, at Plymouth, but they could not be advanced enough to reach Washington in season. The hearing on the Writ of Error was called for March 10, 1818, before the Supreme Court. Meanwhile, Webster had resolved that he would argue his case upon not only the Constitutional issue, but all the other points concerned. This he shrewdly managed to do, with such success that it was unnecessary to resort to further litigation.

The university trustees were not altogether happy in their choice of counsel. There was a feeling that it would be a needless expense to send to Washington either Sullivan or Bartlett, the two New Hampshire lawyers who had hitherto conducted the case. Accordingly John Holmes,[3] a Congressman from Maine, was engaged, with a recommendation from Woodward that he was "extremely ready, of sound mind and a good lawyer, inferior to D. W. only in point of oratory." Later

[1] Webster wrote Judge Smith, December 8, 1817: "It is our misfortune that our cause goes to Washington on a single point. I wish we had it in such shape as to raise all the other objections, as well as the repugnancy of these acts to the Constitution of the United States. I have been thinking whether it would not be advisable to bring suit, if we can get such parties as will give jurisdiction in the circuit court of New Hampshire. I have thought of this the more, from hearing of sundry sayings of a great personage." (National Edition, XVII, 267.)

[2] For purposes of the action, land owned by Wheelock in Hanover was leased or sold to citizens of Vermont, thus making it an interstate litigation.

[3] John Holmes (1773–1843), a graduate of Brown in 1794, studied law, was admitted to the bar in 1799, and settled in Alfred, Maine. A strong Jeffersonian, he served in the Massachusetts General Court, and in Congress from 1817 to 1820, when, on the admission of Maine to the Union, he was elected United States Senator. In 1818, Holmes was forty-five years old, a keen politician, but bombastic in his oratorical style and not very refined in his tastes. He was a good " stump speaker," but lacked dignity and poise.

William Wirt,[1] Attorney-General of the United States, was also retained. These two attorneys presented the argument for the defendants.

The case was argued before a full bench in a "mean apartment of moderate size" in the North Wing of the Capitol, assigned to the Court while its regular quarters were being rebuilt after the fire of 1814. In the centre, dominating his associates, was the great Chief Justice, John Marshall,[2] whose luminous intellect and sane judgment did so much to determine the course of our national history — a lovable personality, tall, ungainly, careless in dress and awkward in gesture, combining simplicity of manner with dignity of bearing. Long after Federalism had perished as a political force, he resolutely upheld its doctrines from his throne of power. The other members included Bushrod Washington, — "a little, sharp-faced gentleman, with only one eye, and a profusion of snuff distributed over his face," — who had been appointed in 1798 and was the favorite nephew of President Washington; William Johnson, of South Carolina, who had taken his seat on the bench in 1804, when he was only thirty-three years old — "a large, athletic, well-built man . . . with a full, ruddy, and fair countenance, with thin white hair, and partially bald"; Henry Brockholst Livingston, of an old New York family, with his "fine Roman face, aquiline nose, high forehead, bald head, and

---

[1] William Wirt (1772–1834), although not a college graduate, became one of the most brilliant lawyers in Virginia. He did not care for political office, but served for twelve years as Attorney-General. Wirt in 1818 had just entered the cabinet and was worn out with the task of putting his papers in order. He described himself on January 21 as " extremely fatigued," and he complained that he had no time to get ready for Webster and Hopkinson.

[2] John Marshall (1755–1835) was then in his sixty-third year and had been Chief Justice since January 20, 1801. He had spent nearly six years in active military service during the Revolution, and had then moved rapidly to the front in the law. An admirer of Washington, he was also profoundly suspicious of Jefferson, and he became one of the stalwart adherents of the Federalist Party. As Chief Justice, he asserted vigorously the authority of the Supreme Court, and his opinions were almost as important as the Constitution itself. For him, Webster had the highest respect, and the two men agreed in their views on nearly every constitutional question. As early as March 28, 1814, Webster wrote: " There is no man in the court that strikes me like Marshall . . . I have never seen a man of whose intellect I had a higher opinion." (National Edition, XVII, 244.)

projecting chin," who was pronounced by Story to be "a very able and independent judge"; Thomas Todd, of Kentucky, "a dark-complexioned, good-looking, substantial man"; Gabriel Duval, of Maryland, "his head as white as a snowbank, with a long white cue hanging down to his waist"; and Joseph Story,[1] of Massachusetts, appointed w th Duval in 1811 — "below middle-size, of light, airy form, rapid and sprightly in his motions, and polished and courtly in his manners." Two only were avowed Federalists — Marshall and Washington. Of the remaining five, three had been selected by Jefferson and two by Madison. To convince such a court, even though the members were endeavoring to be completely impartial, was not an easy task for a New Hampshire Federalist.

At eleven o'clock on the morning of March 10, Webster opened the argument for the plaintiff, speaking from notes which he had carefully prepared. Webster himself felt that his audience was "small and unsympathetic."[2] Nevertheless, he occupied most of the session of the Supreme Court for that day, the length of time which he filled being variously estimated as from three to five hours. He necessarily covered much of the ground already traversed in New Hampshire by Mason and Smith and undoubtedly made good use of material which they had laboriously accumulated; but he made frank acknowledgment, both in private and in public, of his indebtedness to them, and, in view of the fact that neither one was present, it is difficult to see how he could have escaped reiterating what they had said at previous hearings.[3] In fairness to Webster, moreover,

[1] Joseph Story (1779–1845), a lawyer in Salem, Massachusetts, had been a leader of the Jeffersonian party in the Massachusetts Legislature, and had been named by Madison to the Supreme Court on his record as a sound Republican. He soon, however, showed himself to be Marshall's staunch supporter on most critical questions. Story was an alert and persevering scholar, of broad education and winning personality, with whom Webster was soon on the most intimate terms.

[2] *Congressional Reminiscences*, by John Wentworth, pp. 42–46.

[3] Webster wrote to Judge Smith, December 8, 1817: "If I argue this case at Washington, every one knows that I can only be the reciter of the argument made by you at Exeter. You are, therefore, principally interested, as to the matter of reputation, in the figure I make at Washington." On January 9, 1818, he wrote again to Judge Smith: "I must beg the favor of all your notes. I have not assurance enough, although not entirely destitute, to think of arguing this cause on my own strength. To

it should be added that he did rearrange the available material
and did not merely repeat the briefs of his associates.   His
argument was later carefully revised by him for publication and
fills less than thirty-nine pages in the standard edition of his
works.

After reviewing briefly the history of the case, Webster
declared that the legislative acts establishing Dartmouth University were not binding on the trustees of Dartmouth College :
first, because they were against common right and the Constitution of New Hampshire; second, because they were repugnant to the Constitution of the United States.   It was,
strictly speaking, only the latter point which it was permissible
to discuss before the Supreme Court.   But Webster, who apparently looked upon the Constitutional argument as the less
vital of the two, succeeded in introducing without the reproba-
tion of the Bench an analysis of the situation as it was affected
by the common law and also a passage showing that the legislative acts were in violation of the New Hampshire Bill of
Rights.   He summed up this portion of his plea in the following
paragraph : —

If the view which has been taken of this question be at all correct,
this was an eleemosynary corporation, a private charity.   The property was private property.   The trustees were visitors, and the right
to hold the charter, administer the funds, and visit and govern the
college, was a franchise and a privilege, solemnly granted to them.
The use being public in no way diminishes their legal estate in the
property, or their title to the franchise.   There is no principle, nor
any case, which declares that a gift to such a corporation is a gift to
the public.   The acts in question violate property.   They take away
privileges, immunities, and franchises.   They deny to the trustees
the protection of the law; and they are retrospective in their opera-

argue it as you did would be more than I shall ever be able to do."   (National Edition,
XVII, 269.)   On April 23, 1818, he wrote to Mason : " As to the college cause, I cannot
argue it any more, I believe.   I have told you very often that you and Judge Smith
argued it very greatly.   If it was well argued at Washington, it is a proof that I was
right, because all that I said at Washington was but those two arguments, clumsily
put together by me."   (*Ibid.*, pp. 280–81.)   Webster was doubtless overgenerous in
ascribing all the credit to Smith and Mason, but it is certain that their scholarly
researches made his own task much easier.

tion. In all which respects they are against the constitution of New Hampshire.[1]

Up to this point, Webster had devoted nearly three fourths of the space later assigned to his printed argument to a plea for abstract justice, supported by various precedents; he now proceeded to use the last nine pages in demonstrating that the acts in question directly violated that section of the Federal Constitution already quoted.[2] In dealing with this topic, — which was that upon which the case was eventually decided, — Webster alleged that the charter of Dartmouth College possessed "all the essential parts of a contract"; that the college was "a private, eleemosynary corporation"; and that, in this instance, the sanctity of all similar institutions in this country was at stake.   With an assurance which increased as he drew to a close, Webster said : —

It will be a dangerous, a most dangerous experiment, to hold these institutions subject to the rise and fall of popular parties, and the fluctuations of political opinions.   If the franchise may be at any time taken away, or impaired, the property also may be taken away, or its use perverted.   Benefactors will have no certainty of effecting the object of their bounty ; and learned men will be deterred from devoting themselves to the service of such institutions, from the precarious title of their offices.   Colleges and halls will be deserted by all better spirits, and become a theatre for the contentions of politics.   Party and faction will be cherished in the places consecrated to piety and learning.   These consequences are neither remote nor possible only. They are certain and immediate.[3]

The printed argument ended with a long quotation from Cicero,[4] which must have been impressive as Webster rolled it

[1] National Edition, X, 224.   This speech, in the revised form approved by Webster, is well worth reading as a specimen of his best legal style.   So clear and straightforward is the argument that even a layman can read it with pleasure and understanding.

[2] At the present day, Webster would probably not have been allowed by the Court to argue anything except the point of conflict with the United States Constitution.

[3] National Edition, X, 232.

[4] The quotation was taken from the early part of Cicero's *Pro L. Flacco*, but Webster omitted several phrases from the original passage in order to fit it to the situation.   It is the longest single passage of Latin used by Webster in any of his speeches.   I am indebted to Professor Charles H. Forbes, of Andover, for checking this quotation.

out in his deep and sonorous voice, but which probably not even the Chief Justice understood.

This argument is a model of lucidity.   We are told that it was carried on, for the most part, "in the calm tone of easy conversation," with a chain of reasoning so beautifully constructed that the audience unconsciously were drawn along with him; and even Justice Story, who had prepared himself, pen in hand, to take notes, sat fixed in the same posture, absorbed in what was being said.   Ticknor underrated it when he said that those who heard Webster wondered, as they read the printed version, "how such dry bones could ever have lived with the power they there witnessed and felt."   But Webster's native eloquence must have added weight to his words.

Webster's plea on that March afternoon was not all logic. In his *Memorial Oration* delivered on Webster in 1853, at Hanover, Rufus Choate, that eccentric but silver-tongued genius, quoted a version of Webster's peroration in his Dartmouth College Argument, sent to him by Professor Chauncey A. Goodrich, of Yale, who went to Washington in 1818 as the representative of his institution, the interests of which were likely to be affected.   Between 1818 and 1853, thirty-five years had gone by.   Goodrich was a professor of oratory and a brilliant speaker.   Choate had a vivid and romantic imagination. It is highly improbable that either could have quoted Webster's exact words.   But the famous passage, as repeated by Choate in the College Church on Hanover Green, is what Webster might have said, even if he did not employ the precise phrasing which Choate puts into his mouth.   The story, moreover, has become so bound up with Websterian tradition that it is almost irreverent to cast doubt on its verbal authenticity.

According to the account which Goodrich, at the age of sixty-three, gave of an incident which happened when he was twenty-eight, Webster, after his main argument was completed, stood for a time — Goodrich said, "for a few moments" — in silence, as if wondering whether to cease.   Then impulsively he turned to the Chief Justice and addressed him in language which seemed to flow spontaneously from his overburdened soul : —

This, sir, is my case. It is the case, not merely of that humble institution, it is the case of every college in our land. It is more. It is the case of every eleemosynary institution throughout our country, of all those great charities founded by the piety of our ancestors to alleviate human misery, and scatter blessings along the pathway of human life. It is more. It is, in some sense, the case of every man who has property of which he may be stripped, — for the question is simply this: Shall our state legislature be allowed to take that which is not their own, to turn it from its original use, and apply it to such ends or purposes as they, in their discretion, shall see fit? Sir, you may destroy this little institution; it is weak; it is in your hands! You may put it out; but if you do, you must carry on your work! You must extinguish, one after another, all those great lights of science, which, for more than a century, have thrown their radiance over the land! It is, sir, as I have said, a small college, — and yet there are those who love it. . . .

Pathos in oratory has never been more intense than in these lines. Even to write the words is to be stirred by their poignancy. But we are told that Webster, his body rigid and his outstretched hands shaking, as if striving to regain control of his feelings, went on to refer to his own attachment to the college. Very simply, he told of what his parents and his brother had done to assure him an education. "Every one," said Goodrich, "saw that it was wholly unpremeditated, — a pressure on his heart which sought relief in words and tears." . . . This may be true. But there is a well-authenticated story that Webster had said something of this kind to the Superior Court of New Hampshire, at Exeter. It is no reflection on his sincerity to say that he was too consummate an artist not to make the most of the situation. The orators of that period — Everett and Choate and Sumner, as well as Webster — often strove as consciously for an effect as Edwin Booth or Henry Irving ever did in *Hamlet*.

As Goodrich described the scene, Chief Justice Marshall was visibly stirred, and many persons in the room were weeping, quite unashamed. Finally the speaker drew himself up to his full height, and, after a scornful glance at the opponents of his college, turned to the Chief Justice and concluded: —

Sir, I know not how others may feel, but, for myself, when I see my alma mater surrounded, like Cæsar in the senate house, by those who are reiterating stab upon stab, I would not, for this right hand, have her turn to me and say, — *et tu quoque, mi fili!*, — "*and thou too, my son!*"

He sat down.   It was a dramatic termination to what must have been an amazing performance.   Stranger still, however, is the fact that, but for Goodrich's letter to Choate, the words would have been lost to the world.[1]   In the contemporary accounts of the case, Webster's remarks are not referred to except in very general terms.[2]   Holmes, of the opposing counsel, confessed that Webster's argument was "very able"; and a representative of the university trustees wrote back to President Allen,[3] "Mr. Webster has delivered his speech, which made no little impression."   But the full significance of the occasion did not appear until days and weeks had gone by.

[1] In Wheeler's *Daniel Webster, The Expounder of the Constitution*, published in 1905, was printed for the first time a manuscript in the Congressional Library, apparently prepared by Justice Story as a review of Webster's first volume of speeches, which appeared in 1830.   Describing Webster's argument, Story said: "There was an earnestness of manner, and a depth of research, and a potency of phrase, which at once convinced you that his whole soul was in the cause; and that he had meditated over it in the deep silence of the night and studied it in the broad sunshine of the day. . . . And when he came to his peroration, there was in his whole air and manner, in the fiery flashings of his eye, the darkness of his contracted brow, the sudden and flying flushes of his cheeks, the quivering and scarcely manageable movements of his lips, in the deep guttural tones of his voice, in the struggle to suppress his emotions, in the almost convulsive clenchings of his hands without a seeming consciousness of the act, there was in these things what gave to his oratory an almost superhuman influence. . . .   There was a painful anxiety towards the close.   The whole audience had been wrought up to the highest excitement; many were dissolved in tears; many betrayed the most agitating mental struggles; many were sinking under exhausting efforts to conceal their own emotion.   When Mr. Webster ceased to speak, it was some minutes before anyone seemed inclined to break the silence.   The whole seemed but an agonizing dream, from which the audience was slowly and almost unconsciously awakening."   (Wheeler, pp. 30–31.)

[2] The Washington correspondent of the *Columbian Centinel* wrote: "Our friend Webster never made a happier effort.   To a most elaborate and lucid argument he united a dignified and pathetic peroration which charmed and melted his hearers." The *Boston Daily Advertiser* said, March 23, 1818: "Mr. Webster opened the cause in that clear, perspicuous, forcible, and impressive manner for which he is so much distinguished; and for two or three hours enchained the Court and the audience with an argument which, for weight of authority, force of reasoning, and power of eloquence, has seldom been equalled in this or any court."

[3] President John Wheelock had died, April 4, 1817, and had been succeeded as president of the phantom university by Allen.

In April 1818, Webster prepared and printed several copies of his argument, but he declared, in explaining his action to Mason, "All the nonsense is left out." [1]   Shirley, in his account of the case, seized upon this phrase and surmised that Webster, during his speech, had digressed for an hour in an attempt to arouse Marshall's Federalist prejudices, and that this political passage was the "nonsense" which Webster had in mind. Lodge, in his biography of Webster, accepted this myth without investigation and drew a picturesque but wholly fanciful sketch of Webster as he stirred "the old war-horse" to action.   There is no evidence whatever to support Shirley's conjectures.   The "nonsense" which Webster left out in his printed version was the peroration afterwards reported by Professor Goodrich.   If Webster had done what Shirley and Lodge suggested, it would have been a gross breach of judicial decorum, which would rightly have been resented by the Republican members on the bench.[2]   Such an appeal, furthermore, might very well have been detrimental to his case, for a majority of the Court were Republicans, and opposed to the Federalists.

Holmes, opening for the defendants, occupied an hour on the first day, after Webster had finished, and also the following morning.   He was not in an enviable position, for Webster's eloquence had dazzled both the Court and the audience, and whatever he said was bound to seem inadequate.   But the Maine Congressman fell below the expectations of his friends. He employed cheap rhetorical devices which might have been well received in a stump speech but were inappropriate to an argument before that exalted tribunal.   Inwardly delighted with Holmes's failure, Webster wrote Mason, "Upon the whole, he gave us three hours of the merest stuff that was ever uttered in a county court." [3]

William Wirt then concluded for the defendants.   He opened on the afternoon of the second day, but, breaking down in the middle of his presentation, requested an adjournment until the

[1] Webster to Mason, April 23, 1818 (National Edition, XVII, 281).
[2] Beveridge, *John Marshall*, IV, 259.
[3] National Edition, XVII, 275.

next morning. Wirt was a very able man, who shares with
Caleb Cushing the distinction of being among the greatest of
our Attorney-Generals. But he was at the time much exhausted, and he admitted that he had not really examined the
facts. Webster was not impressed with Wirt's contribution
to the case; [1] but later, when it was reported that he had said,
"The weaknesses in my argument were supplied by Wirt's
speech," Webster repudiated this charge and wrote Wirt saying
that the latter's plea was a "a *full*, *able*, and most *eloquent*
exposition of the rights of the Defendant." [2]   It is indisputable,
however, that Wirt did not greatly strengthen the cause of his
clients.

The case for the plaintiffs was closed by Hopkinson, a
scholarly and experienced advocate, who "showed breeding
in every look, movement, word and intonation." [3]   His speech,
which adhered closely to points of law, was delivered in a quiet
manner, very favorably contrasted with the noisy declamation
of Holmes and Wirt. [4] The argument of the case ended on
March 12, having occupied only three days.

The judgment of contemporary witnesses was that the
plaintiff's counsel were much superior to their opponents.
Holmes and Wirt obviously did not work in harmony, and their
reasoning had some striking discrepancies and inconsistencies.
William Sullivan, writing to Mrs. Webster, said: "In a letter

[1] Writing to Mason, March 13, 1818, Webster said: " Wirt followed. He is a good
deal of a lawyer, and has very quick perceptions, and handsome power of argument;
but he seemed to treat this case as if his side could furnish nothing but declamation."
(National Edition, XVII, 275.) On March 14, Webster wrote Smith: " Wirt has
talents, is a competent lawyer, and argues a good cause well.   In this case he said more
nonsensical things than became him." (*Ibid.*, p. 277.) Wirt himself wrote, April 28,
1819, to Webster: " My argument was framed under great disadvantage, having to
prepare it very hastily and under the pressure of a load of official business which was
wholly new to me."

[2] This letter to Wirt, April 5, 1818, was first printed by Wheeler in his *Daniel Webster,
The Expounder of the Constitution*, pp. 32–33.

[3] Beveridge, *Marshall*, IV, 254.

[4] Webster wrote President Brown, March 13, 1818: " Mr. Hopkinson understood
every part of the cause, and in his argument did it great justice." (National Edition,
XVII, 274.) He wrote to Mason on the same day: " Mr. Hopkinson made a most
satisfactory reply, keeping to the law, and not following Holmes and Wirt into the
fields of declamation and fine speaking." (*Ibid.*, p. 276.)

which I have seen, it is said, 'In the College cause, Webster shone like the sun, and Holmes like a sun fish.'" David Daggett wrote to Mason: "Holmes went up like a rocket and down like a stick. The opinion was universal that Webster rose superior even to Wirt (though it is said that he appeared very well) and infinitely so to Holmes." Rufus King — who was, of course, strongly prejudiced — wrote to Gore, "Webster acquitted himself with the highest credit and produced the strongest sentiments of respect and admiration. Mr. Holmes fell below mediocrity." Webster's own attitude after the completion of the argument was optimistic, but not complacent.[1]

On March 13, the Chief Justice announced a continuance, and on the next day the Supreme Court adjourned for that term. No decision, therefore, could be expected for many months. During the ensuing summer and autumn both sides did their utmost to bring their views to the notice of the proper people. The university trustees circulated widely the *Opinion* delivered by Chief Justice Richardson in the New Hampshire Superior Court. On the other hand, Webster's argument, carefully revised by him, was privately printed and distributed judiciously, copies being sent even to some of the Supreme Court Judges.[2] Chancellor James Kent, of New York, whose influence with a few of them was known to be strong, seemed at first to be for the university. But President Brown visited him at Albany, conversed with him on various phases of the question, and ascertained that a perusal of Webster's argument had converted him. At least two members of the Supreme Court

[1] Webster wrote to President Brown, March 13, "You may say, however, to your friends, and give the students to understand, as far as useful, that the cause looks well here"; and he wrote to Mason on the same day, "In my opinion, the argument upon the law of the case on our side is not answered." More explicitly, he wrote to Smith, March 14: "The chief and Washington, I have no doubt are with us. Duval and Todd perhaps against us; the other three holding up. I cannot much doubt but that Story will be with us in the end, and I think that we have much more than an even chance for one of the others. I think we shall finally succeed." (National Edition, XVII, 276.)

[2] Webster wrote to Justice Story, September 9: "I send you five copies of our argument. If you send one of them to each of such of the judges as you think proper, you will of course do it in the manner least likely to lead to a feeling that any indecorum has been committed by the plaintiffs." (National Edition, XVII, 287.)

— Johnson and Livingston — consulted Kent and were somewhat guided by his verdict. Although nothing unethical was probably done by either disputant, every legitimate device was employed to affect the decision, and the issues were even debated in a few newspapers. President Brown, who was indefatigable, wrote to Webster in September regarding the latter's argument : —

It has already been, or shortly will be, read by all the commanding men of New England and New York ; and so far as it has gone, it has united them all, without a single exception within my knowledge, in one broad and impenetrable phalanx for our defense and support. New England and New York *are gained*. Will not this be sufficient for our present purposes ?

Doubtless the reference to "New England" and "New York" was a hint that Story and Livingston were felt to be supporters of the college.

Commencement, in August 1818, was observed at Hanover by both the college and the university, the exercises being held a week apart. On August 9, Judge Woodward, against whom the original suit in trover had been brought, died at the age of forty-three. Meanwhile the supplementary cases brought in the Circuit Court were carried along from one stage to another in preparation for a possible emergency.[1] The university trustees, dissatisfied with the presentation of their cause by Holmes and Wirt, sought to gain an advantage by retaining William Pinkney ; and he had familiarized himself with the facts in the hope that the Supreme Court would allow him to speak.[2] Webster informed Mason that Pinkney was planning to base his argument on the ground that all the power belonging

---

[1] Webster still retained his confidence in the argument based on the common law. He wrote Mason, April 28, 1818 : " The question which we must raise in one of these actions, is, 'whether, by the general principles of our governments, the State legislatures be not restrained from divesting vested rights ? ' This, of course, independent of the constitutional provision respecting contracts. On this question I have great confidence in a decision on the right side. This is the proposition with which you began your argument at Exeter, and which I endeavored to state from your minutes at Washington." (National Edition, XVII, 283.)

[2] Hopkinson wrote Webster, November 17, 1818 : " In my passage through Baltimore, I fell in with Pinkney, who told me he was engaged in the cause by the present

to Parliament belonged to the New Hampshire Legislature. Although he was not worried, Webster was by no means certain what would happen, and he was philosophically prepared for any eventuality.[1]

Whatever doubts he had were soon to be dissipated. At the February term, in 1819, the Supreme Court took possession of its former quarters, which had been undergoing renovation since the fire of 1814. This historic room, now used for the Law Library of the Supreme Court, is to-day packed with books, and seems much smaller than the present Supreme Court Chamber directly above it; but the dimensions are exactly the same. In 1819, it was fresh and newly finished, and each justice had his own mahogany desk and chair on the raised dais along the straight eastern side of the semi-circular room; but they complained that, in lieu of a retiring closet, they had to don their silk robes in the presence of the spectators. It was described by Senator Oliver Hampton Smith, of Indiana, as "the Judgment hall, with its low-browed roof and short columns modelled after the prison of Constance in *Marmion*." [2] Here most of Webster's great legal arguments were delivered, and the shadowy alcoves are haunted by the ghosts of Clay and Pinkney and Choate, as well as of the famous jurists, Marshall and Story and Taney.[3]

University, and that he is desirous to argue it, if the court will let him. I suppose he expects to do something very extraordinary in it, as he says Mr. Wirt 'was not strong enough for it, has not back enough.'" (*Ibid.*, p. 289.) Hopkinson and Webster were agreed that they would not consent to let Pinkney reargue the case, but that, if the Court did allow this, they would claim their right to reply.

[1] On the day when the Supreme Court met, February 1, 1819, Webster wrote to Mason: "Wirt and Pinkney still talk of arguing one of the college causes. On our side, we smile at this, not being able to suppose them serious. I hope they will not attempt it, as it would only lead to embarrassment about the facts. I should have no fears for the result." On the same day, he wrote Timothy Farrar: "Not a word has yet fallen from any Judge on the cause. They keep their own counsel. All that I have seen, however, looks rather favorable. I hope to be relieved of further anxiety by a decision for or against us in five or six days."

[2] Quoted by Warren, *The Supreme Court in United States History*, I, 460 from *Early Indiana Trials and Sketches* (1858).

[3] The room is on the ground floor, facing the east, and may be entered from the paved court directly off the street. The fluted pillars, with capitals, the crude bas-relief, by Franzoni, showing Justice awkwardly holding the scales, and the recessed windows are still there, as they were in Webster's time.

Here, on the morning of Tuesday, February 2, as soon as his colleagues had taken their seats, the Chief Justice, ignoring the eager Pinkney,[1] announced that the Court, during its recess, had reached a decision in *Dartmouth College* v. *Woodward*. He then proceeded to read the momentous opinion giving a verdict for the plaintiffs.

The Opinion promulgated by Marshall had been prepared by him during some weeks of leisure while he was in the mountains in the summer of 1818. Carefully reasoned and compactly written, it is one of the ablest of his papers.[2] Opening with a statement of the seriousness of the point at issue, — "the validity of a legislative act," — he declared that in no doubtful case would the Supreme Court "pronounce a legislative act to be contrary to the constitution." After quoting the language of the Federal Constitution regarding contracts, he held that a private corporate charter was a contract within the meaning of that clause. The real matter to be considered, then, was whether the Dartmouth College Charter created a public institution or a "private eleemosynary corporation." On this question he had no doubt, after examining the evidence, that the college was "incorporated for the purpose of perpetuating . . . the bounty of the donors to the specified objects of that bounty." It was this which led to his conclusion that the Dartmouth Charter was a contract, "the obligation of which cannot be impaired without violating the Constitution of the United States." It was conceded that the legislative acts under consideration did materially alter the Charter of Dartmouth College; hence they "are repugnant to the Constitution of the United States."

[1] Pinkney had prepared himself with zeal and thoroughness, and was ready to make " the supreme effort of his brilliant career." (Beveridge, *Marshall*, IV, 260.) Everybody in the Court was aware of his intention, and Marshall's failure to recognize him was deliberate.

[2] Beveridge, in his *John Marshall*, IV, 261 ff., gives an admirable summary of this Opinion, but it is worth reading in full. Writing to Mason on February 4, 1819, Webster said: " The Chief Justice's opinion was in his own peculiar way. He reasoned along from step to step; and, not referring to the cases, adopted the principles of them, and worked the whole into a close, connected, and very able argument." (National Edition, XVI, 44.)

Webster, as has been pointed out, had expected the decision to rest upon the theory that the legislative acts were in violation of the fundamental principles of government. Justice Story, who also read an Opinion (4 Wheat., 666–713), concurred with Marshall, but based his judgment on the assumption that legislation destructive of contracts was against "natural rights." If the Supreme Court had passed upon the case with this in mind, its decision would unquestionably have been the same. But the Chief Justice, for reasons readily understood, preferred to exalt the written Constitution of the United States.

That political affiliations had nothing to do with the decision is shown by the fact that it was concurred in by five of the seven justices, two of them Federalists and three Republicans. Todd, a Republican, was absent, and Duval, also a Republican, was the only dissenter. With remarkable independence, a Court, the membership of which leaned towards Republicanism, had agreed on an opinion which greatly strengthened the authority and prestige of the Federal Government, had set aside the legislative act of a sovereign state, and had undertaken, in the words of Marshall, to protect, "from even Legislative violence, those contracts which the Constitution of the country has placed beyond Legislative control." The integrity and fairmindedness of the Supreme Court were unmistakably demonstrated.

As soon as the Opinion was read, Webster withdrew and wrote to Ezekiel : —

All is safe. Judgment was rendered this morning, reversing the judgment in New Hampshire. . . . The opinion was delivered by the Chief Justice. It was very able and very elaborate; it goes the whole length, and leaves not an inch of ground for the University to stand on.[1]

By the same mail, Webster sent short notes to Mason and President Brown, saying to the latter, in conclusion, "I feel a load removed from my shoulders much heavier than they have been accustomed to bear."[2] Never in all his career was

[1] National Edition, XVII, 300.   [2] *Ibid.*, p. 300.

Webster more boisterously exuberant than at winning the Dartmouth College Case. His personal reputation was, of course, immensely enhanced, but even more important was the rescue of Dartmouth College from annihilation. On that morning, Joseph Hopkinson also sent to President Brown a letter which Dartmouth men have quoted again and again : —

Our triumph in the college cause has been complete. Five judges, only six attending, concur not only in a decision in our favor, but in placing it upon principles broad and deep, and which secure corporations of this description from legislative despotism and party violence for the future. The Court goes all lengths with us, and whatever trouble these gentlemen may give us in future, in their great and pious zeal for the interests of learning, they cannot shake those principles which must and will restore Dartmouth College to its true and original owners. I would have an inscription over the door of your building, "Founded by Eleazar Wheelock, Refounded by Daniel Webster."[1]

The death of Woodward, the defendant in the original suit, presented a few technical difficulties, but Webster promptly moved for judgment *nunc pro tunc*, which was entered at once for the sum of twenty thousand dollars. On the last day of February, he wrote Jeremiah Smith, "I have in my bag a mandate to the Superior Court of Judicature of the State of New Hampshire to carry this judgment into Execution."[2] The victory was indeed complete and unalterable. There was, it is true, some question as to the disposition of the auxiliary cases instituted by the college trustees for an emergency. It was whispered during the spring that new facts were available which might wreck the college. It was even hinted that Governor Wentworth had had no authority to grant the original charter. But such rumors had no foundation. In their first disappointment, Wirt and Pinkney evidently wished to carry on the fight still farther.[3] But nothing of this kind was ever

---

[1] National Edition, XVII, 301.   [2] *Ibid.*, XVI, 45.

[3] See Webster's letters to Jeremiah Mason, February 15 and February 23, 1818, published in National Edition, XVI, 49–52. On February 28, however, Webster wrote to Judge Smith, " *Inter nos*, I do not believe anybody expects the College Question ever to come here again." (*Ibid.*, p. 45.)

seriously undertaken. In the end, the decision had to be accepted, and the auxiliary cases were dismissed at the Spring Term of the Circuit Court.

The settlement of the Dartmouth College Case did not arouse much attention in the contemporary press. The *New Hampshire Gazette,* Portsmouth's Republican newspaper, asserted that the facts had not been adequately presented to the Court;[1] while the Portsmouth *Oracle,* Federalist in its principles, supported the decision as wise and sound. The only New England newspaper to appreciate its full significance was the *Columbian Centinel,* in Boston, which, on February 10, 1819, referred to Marshall's decision as "the most able and elaborate opinion which, perhaps, has ever been pronounced in a Court of Judicature." The *North American Review,* in 1820, said that "perhaps no judicial proceeding in this country ever involved more important consequences or excited a deeper interest in the public mind."[2] But it was not until several years had gone by that the profound significance of the case began to be understood.

Justice Story, however, was not inclined to belittle what had been done, and, in writing to Chancellor Kent, spoke "of the vital importance, to the well-being of society and the security of private rights, of the principles upon which that decision rested." With the spread of business corporations during the second quarter of the nineteenth century, it was perceived that the doctrine laid down by Marshall had actually done more than any other opinion to broaden the jurisdiction of the Supreme Court. Chancellor Kent himself, speaking in his *Commentaries,* of the Dartmouth College Opinion, said : —

It . . . did more than any other single act proceeding from the authority of the United States to throw an impregnable barrier around all rights and franchises derived from the grant of government, and to give solidity and inviolability to the literary, charitable, religious, and commercial institutions of our country.[3]

[1] The exact words were: "Had the case been fairly laid before the Court, no man, without impeaching their integrity or their common sense, can doubt but their decision would have confirmed that of the Superior Court in this State."

[2] *North American Review,* X, 83.

[3] Kent, *Commentaries,* I, 392.

It has been quoted again and again as a precedent and has been upheld by the Supreme Court repeatedly from decade to decade. Indeed, Chief Justice Waite, pronouncing an Opinion in *Stone* v. *Mississippi*, in October 1879, stated that the principles established in the Dartmouth College Case were "so imbedded in the jurisprudence of the United States as to make them to all intents and purposes a part of the Constitution itself."

From an economic point of view the decision stabilized business by guaranteeing to corporations and legitimate investors immunity from partisan legislation. Sir Henry Maine perceived very clearly that, because of it, the Constitutional clause forbidding the impairment of contracts became "the bulwark of American individualism against democratic impatience and socialistic fantasy." [1] Industry, relieved from the fear of whimsical legislation or persecution, could proceed with more orderly development, and, under the conditions which then existed, the opinion was very salutary. Property owners are bound to feel safer when they know that contracts cannot be broken by irresponsible politicians.

There is, of course, another side to the matter. Corporations in the more than a century since the opinion was rendered have sometimes become dangerous to the public. Practical considerations have necessitated certain modifications in the legislative attitude towards charters: first by forbidding any charter to grant rights which might be employed as a menace to the community; and second, by allowing any legislature to alter or repeal a charter when such action is obviously contributory to the protection of life, health, or morality.[2] Thus certain states have exacted measures reserving to the legislature the power, under certain circumstances, to modify corporate charters. But the basic principle of good faith underlying Webster's argument and Marshall's Opinion is just as vital today as it was in 1819.

When the news reached Hanover, cannon were shot off by

---

[1] Maine, *Popular Government*, pp. 247–48, quoted by Warren, *Supreme Court*, I, 491.
[2] Warren, *Supreme Court*, I, 490 ff. See also Beveridge, *Marshall*, IV, 276 ff.

the students and townspeople, and the functions of the university were at once suspended. Reoccupying the buildings from which it had been ejected, the college was soon running as if its continuity had never been interrupted. Under the direction of Webster's former law partner, Timothy Farrar, a full report of the proceedings was prepared and printed in a volume of over four hundred pages.[1] At Commencement, in August, Webster was present to receive the congratulations of his friends, and was extended a formal vote of thanks at the Phi Beta Kappa Dinner in the Dartmouth Hotel. The annual Exhibition was rendered memorable by the dramatic Valedictory Address of Rufus Choate, of the Senior Class, at which Webster was one of the audience.[2] Thus in the College Church, for the first time, were brought together perhaps the two most eloquent of American statesmen.

Webster was paid fifty dollars for his plea before the State Court and a thousand dollars for his appearance before the Supreme Court. Hopkinson received five hundred dollars for his services. The college trustees, conscious of the inadequacy of the fees given to their counsel, voted to request them all — Mason, Smith, Hopkinson, and Webster — to sit for their portraits to Gilbert Stuart.[3] These were completed within a year and are now in the possession of Dartmouth College. They hang — very appropriately — in Webster Hall.

But these are sordid details. Daniel Webster gained from the Dartmouth College Case something far more important than money. His argument "established forever his

[1] The title was *A Report of the Case of the Trustees of Dartmouth College against William H. Woodward*. Webster was much interested in this publication. He wrote Mason, April 10, 1819: " But I am still inclined to have the Book. One reason is, that you & Judge Smith may have the credit which belongs to you. Another is, I believe, Judge Story is strongly of opinion it would be a useful work, that Wheaton's Reports go only into the hands of Professional men, but that this Book might be read by other Classes, &c. &c." (National Edition, XVI, 48.)

[2] Fuess, *Rufus Choate*, pp. 36–38.

[3] Gilbert Stuart (1755–1828), after long experience in Europe and in New York, Philadelphia, and Washington, had come to Boston to reside in 1805, and lived there during the remainder of his life. Webster wrote Mason, November 15, 1819: " I have seen Stuart. He says the pictures shall be completed this week. I think they may be, perhaps, next." (National Edition, XVI, 55.)

reputation as a great jurist." [1]   Justice Story, perhaps the best
authority, said: "This argument was decisive of the future
professional reputation of Mr. Webster. It elevated him at
once to the first rank, and to the foremost competitors in that
rank. . . . It would not be too much to say, that it gave a new
direction to his own hopes and wishes." [2]   From that moment,
his legal ability was in constant demand by important clients,
and, whenever he desired, he could secure a lucrative practice in
the courts.

Cynical lawyers have sometimes declared that a speech such
as Webster delivered in the Dartmouth College Case, highly
charged with feeling and intensely dramatic, would not now be
tolerated by the Supreme Court, and that his sentimental
reference to his Alma Mater would be met with smiles rather
than tears. It is doubtless true that the Court to-day would
confine counsel more closely to the points at issue. But the
kind of eloquence which Webster displayed is always potent if
it seems sincere; and no one could doubt that he was in deadly
earnest. It was no mere florid rhetoric which Webster used.
He meant what he said. Furthermore, he was too sensitive an
orator not to make sure that his audience were in a receptive
mood. No one was better aware of the slender margin which
separates the sublime from the ridiculous. Finally, we must
not forget that the greater part of Webster's argument was
strictly logical, unified in its structure, and supported by a
wealth of precedent. The Dartmouth College Case was won,
not by Webster's famous plea for Dartmouth, but by the irrefutable reasoning which had preceded that pathetic outburst.

Daniel Webster became at once a hero at Dartmouth, and
has remained one to this day. President William J. Tucker
rightly said: "Before the country had grasped the scope of his

[1] Warren, *Supreme Court*, I, 480.
[2] Quoted in Wheeler, *Daniel Webster, The Expounder of the Constitution*, p. 31.
Samuel W. McCall said: "Although this was not the first cause argued by Webster
before the national high court, it especially marked the beginning of a career which
continued for more than a third of a century and stamps him on the whole as the greatest
figure who ever appeared at that august bar." (*Proceedings of the Webster Centennial
at Dartmouth College*, p. 118.)

argument, it was caught by the splendor of his courage.   Something of this high distinction of courage fell upon the college."
At Hanover, the beautiful Webster Hall perpetuates his name
in brick and granite.   But even more enduring are the reverence with which he is regarded by Dartmouth alumni and the
respect paid to his name wherever they are assembled.   They
know that his argument "served to nationalize the college."

More than thirty years later, in September 1850, Daniel
Webster, then an old man and Secretary of State for the second
time, gave a grand dinner in Washington to alumni of Dartmouth College.[1]   A discussion arose as to which one of his
arguments had been the most remarkable; and, with that
childlike naïveté which was one of his distinctive qualities, he
turned to his guests and asked: "What do you all say here,
to-day?   I ask the question of each and every one of you.
What has been my greatest effort?"   Various judgments were
expressed, and finally, after the dessert was removed, he was
called upon for his opinion.   Then, rising and pushing back his
chair, Webster talked for a full hour, familiarly reviewing the
notable achievements of his life.   "That is a man's greatest
effort," he began, "which brings to him the most opportunities
for other efforts and does the most towards securing to him
a permanent support for himself and family."   It was, he
declared, his Alma Mater, which gave him his real opportunity;
and ever afterwards he felt that his professional sign was
"Daniel Webster and the Dartmouth College Case."   His
heart was in that cause, and his victory secured for him a
practice equal to that of any of his rivals in the law.   "I am
poor," he concluded.   "I have done for Dartmouth College all
that I can.   Yet I feel indebted to her, — indebted for my
early education, indebted for her early confidence, indebted for
an opportunity to show to men, whose support I was to need
for myself and family, that I was equal to the defense of vested
rights against state courts and sovereignties."

[1] The story of this dinner is told by John Wentworth in his *Congressional Reminiscences*, an address delivered in Chicago, March 16, 1882, and published in the same year.

X

THE CONSTITUTIONAL LAWYER

Side by side with the great name of Marshall should be placed that of Webster. The arguments of the one were as necessary as the decisions of the other.

— EVERETT P. WHEELER, *Daniel Webster, the Expounder of the Constitution*

The great function of Daniel Webster's mind and of Daniel Webster's tongue was to make the Constitution clear, applicable, and enduring.

— GAMALIEL BRADFORD, *Daniel Webster*

LAWYERS, like actors, suffer in their fame because of the fleeting nature of the spoken word. The most eloquent appeal to a jury dies quickly upon the air. Even though the actual phrases may be preserved in type, nothing can bring back the subtle intonation, the unconscious gesture, which at the moment seemed so significant. Every attorney, moreover, in the course of his routine business, disposes of litigation which leaves no trace behind it. Thus in half a century the reputation of such a master as Rufus Choate is obscured, and his genius is preserved only in those anecdotes, many of them apocryphal, handed down by one legal generation to another. Few but trials before the highest courts are fully reported. The others may secure an evanescent publicity in the newspapers, but they are soon forgotten. There are dozens of cases into which Webster threw himself with ardor but which will remain hidden until some curious and persistent scholar brushes the cobwebs away.

Nevertheless, Webster was blessed beyond most of his rivals in that a large proportion of his professional work was highly constructive. It has been plausibly maintained that his talents were never more marked than in his arguments on Constitutional problems before the Supreme Court of the United States.[1] His reasoning in the Dartmouth College case won for him the title of Expounder of the Constitution. It was his fortune, during the years which followed, to be engaged in similar disputes which affected the whole future development of this country.

What were his qualifications as a Constitutional lawyer? He had long been a student of American history, especially of the formative period between the close of the Revolution and the inauguration of Washington. Extensive reading had acquainted him with political and economic problems both in ancient and modern times. He had supplemented this by practical experience in Congress during debates on important questions. He was not a profound scholar in legal precedents,[2] but he possessed, a mind which ignored trivialities, and could distinguish wheat from chaff. He had also the gift of clear reasoning and straightforward speech, animated by a faith derived from conviction. His intellectual and spiritual weaknesses, such as they were, were less evident in his work as a lawyer than in his career as a statesman.

Thus admirably equipped, Webster came forward at a period when vital issues had to be settled — whether our written Constitution was to be construed liberally or narrowly, whether the individual state or the Federal Government was to be the ultimate authority, whether a decision of the Supreme Court was to be really *supreme*. The framers of the Constitution had used language which was clear, but broadly general in its mean-

---

[1] Webster was always proud of his achievements as a lawyer. Speaking in 1847, before the Charleston bar, he said: "If I am anything, it is the law, — that noble profession, that sublime science which we all pursue, — that has made me what I am. . . . The law has been my chief stimulus, my controlling and abiding hope, nay, I might almost say, my presiding genius and guardian angel." (National Edition, IV, 88.)

[2] Rufus Choate said to Parker in 1852: "Webster has never since he was thirty, given himself to a scientific study of the law. He has been occupied in politics and general reading a great deal. His mind is far richer than Story's — more ideas; though Story is great." (Parker, *Reminiscences*, p. 263.)

ing; and when its clauses had to be applied to specific situations, an interpreter was required. As such an interpreter, Webster exerted the full force of his eloquence, his reasoning, and his personality on the side of a strong central government and of a wise freedom in elucidating the provisions of the Constitution. Before a Supreme Court the majority of whom had originally been Republicans and "strict constructionists" he argued so convincingly that they adopted his position. Backed always by Chief Justice Marshall, he never wavered at a period when a concession to Jeffersonian doctrine might have left us a loosely organized confederacy, the unity of which could have been destroyed by any aggressive state which chose to run wild. Majestic and oracular, Webster spoke like one of the prophets. With a sound conservatism he enunciated and reiterated certain fundamental principles. Our nation has profited, both politically and economically, because Webster said what he did when he did.

Within less than three weeks after the decision in *Dartmouth College* v. *Woodward*, Webster was facing the Supreme Court in another epoch-making case, — *McCulloch* v. *Maryland* (4 Wheat., 316), — in which, with Wirt and Pinkney, he was retained by the Bank of the United States. That he should be sought out by such a powerful client was a flattering recognition of the distinction which he had acquired through the Dartmouth College case. It had been almost inevitable that he, a leading New Hampshire lawyer and a Dartmouth graduate, should be employed by his own Alma Mater. Sentimental reasons alone might have dictated the choice. But only practical considerations could have brought about his selection as counsel for the Bank of the United States. There were other able lawyers resident in Washington and vicinity; yet the Bank turned to Daniel Webster, formerly of Portsmouth and now of Boston. It is true that he was a junior counsel, but Webster was pleased to be a lieutenant under William Pinkney as captain. Eighteen years older than Webster, Pinkney was nearing the close of his colorful career, and his argument in *McCulloch* v. *Maryland* was to be "the greatest effort of his life." [1] It was an interesting coincidence which brought together in this case the leader of the American bar and his no less brilliant successor to that title.[2]

McCulloch v. *Maryland* was called before the Supreme Court at a time of widespread financial distress. Following the refusal of Congress in 1812 to recharter the Bank of the United States, a large number of small and under-capitalized banking institutions had sprung up under the protection of the states, and a period of unjustifiable expansion and credit extension ensued. When the Second Bank of the United States was created in 1816, some of its policies, particularly a drastic curtailment of credits, made it unpopular, especially in the South and West; and the public was inclined to blame the Bank for poor business conditions, wherever they developed. Several states, under pressure from their local financial institutions, had undertaken, by penalizing the Bank of the United States, to drive it outside their borders. In Baltimore, where a branch of the United States Bank was soon established, the state banks, not relishing the prospect of a vigorous competitor, induced the Maryland Legislature to pass, in February 1818, an act taxing all banks not chartered by the state but doing business within its confines. It was a measure aimed at the Bank of the United States, the directors of which were not slow to realize the danger which was confronting them.

The suit had originally been brought to determine whether a sovereign state had the power to levy taxes on the Federal Bank. A decision in favor of Maryland had been rendered in the state courts, including the Maryland Court of Appeals, and the case, by agreement between the parties concerned, had been brought to the Supreme Court of the United States on a writ of error for final adjudication. The course which it had taken was in several respects similar to that pursued in *Dartmouth College* v. *Woodward*.

[1] Warren, *Supreme Court*, I, 507.

[2] Rufus Choate, a great admirer of Pinkney, often spoke of the latter's " splendid stream of words and arguments, the rapid torrent of his overwhelming enthusiasm, the grasp of his mind, and the glorious arrogance with which he carried all before him." (Parker, p. 31.)

It was the immediate function of the Supreme Court to decide whether the Maryland law, requiring all banks established "without authority from the state" to issue notes only on stamped paper and of specified denominations, was constitutional; but the broader issue, as Beveridge points out, was "the supremacy of the National Government as against the dominance of State Government." The case was simply another skirmish in the bitter war between the theories of Hamilton and those of Jefferson. Webster had taken part in the Congressional debate over the establishment of the Bank. The entire situation was familiar to him, and he had heard all phases of it discussed, both on the floor of the House and at private dinner tables. He was aware that the dispute between Nationalism and Localism had never been more lucidly delimited. If any sovereign state could do what Maryland had already done, the Federal Union was certain to be disrupted. All this seems plain to us to-day. It was made clear by Daniel Webster and John Marshall in 1819.

The argument in *McCulloch* v. *Maryland* covered nine full days, during which the renovated Supreme Court Chamber was "full almost to suffocation." [1] On Washington's Birthday, Daniel Webster, picturesquely attired in a blue dress coat with large brass buttons, tight breeches, and a broad expanse of starched shirt bosom and high soft collar, rose to open for the plaintiff in error. Of his speech we have only an abstract — sufficient, however, to show that he spent approximately one-half his time in demonstrating the right of Congress to charter a National Bank and the other half in showing that, since "an unlimited power to tax involves, necessarily, the power to destroy," no bank established by Congress can exist if the authority to tax it inheres in the state governments. "It is essential to the existence and preservation of the government," said Webster, in words which contain the

[1] Story, *Life and Letters of Joseph Story*, I, 325. The audience consisted of ladies as well as gentlemen. The argument was carried on from February 22 to 27, and then, after a short interim, from March 1 to 3. The Court during this session sat for the first time since 1814 in its quarters in the basement of the Capitol, in the room now devoted to the Library of the Supreme Court.

gist of his argument, "that Congress should be able to exercise its constitutional powers, at its own discretion, without being subject to the control of State legislation."

Webster's speech, which filled only part of one day, was followed by that of Joseph Hopkinson, his former associate in the Dartmouth College case, who, despite the fact that he was opposing his own convictions, presented a powerful summary of the cause of the State of Maryland. William Wirt continued for the Bank and Walter Jones, of Washington, for the State. The aged Luther Martin, one of the most versatile as well as one of the most dissipated members of the American bar,[1] concluded for the defendant; and, on Monday, March 1, Pinkney began his greatest effort, occupying three full days and enchanting his listeners by his brilliancy.[2]

Regarding the decision, Webster seems to have had no anxiety.[3] On the day after the proceedings were over, he set out for Boston, virtually certain of victory. Chief Justice Marshall had probably made a preliminary draft of his opinion, in Richmond, during the preceding autumn and winter.[4] Only on some such supposition can the speed with which the verdict was ready be explained, for it was given out on March 6, only three days after Pinkney had finished his pleading.

Marshall's Opinion — one of the longest which he ever rendered — has received the praise of the most eminent critics.[5] Beveridge has styled it "this epochal state paper — among the

[1] Luther Martin (1748–1826) was, in 1819, Attorney-General of Maryland. He had been a delegate to the Constitutional Convention of 1787, but had opposed its actions and had refused to sign the instrument. *McCulloch* v. *Maryland* was his last important case. A year later he had a stroke of paralysis and was an invalid for the rest of his life.

[2] The best description of Pinkney's argument was written by Story in a letter, saying: "I never, in my whole life, heard a greater speech; it was worth a journey from Salem to hear it; his elocution was excessively vehement, but his eloquence was overwhelming. . . . All the cobwebs of sophistry and metaphysics about State rights and State sovereignty he brushed away with a mighty besom." (Story, *Story*, I, 324–25.)

[3] Writing to Mason, February 15, 1819, before the case was called, Webster said, "I have no doubt of the result," and on February 23, after his argument had been completed, he again wrote Mason, "Of the decision I have no doubt."

[4] Beveridge, *Marshall*, IV, 290.

[5] Todd was absent, but the other five justices concurred with Marshall.

very first of the greatest judicial utterances of all time."[1] Lewis has called it "perhaps the most celebrated judicial utterance in the annals of the English speaking world."[2] Justice Story declared on the day when it was read that it established the Constitution "upon its great original principles." From the Federalist point of view, it was irrefutable.

The decision was indeed a splendid exposition of Hamiltonian principles. It condemned in vigorous language the tendency to construe too narrowly the broad phrases of the Constitution; it asserted that the Constitution was adopted by the people and not by the "sovereign and independent states." "The people," it contended, "were at perfect liberty to accept or reject it; and their act was final." It laid down the sweeping doctrine "that the government of the Union, though limited in its powers, is supreme within its sphere of action." Carrying this theory to its logical conclusion, it said : —

Let the end be legitimate, let it be within the scope of the Constitution, and all means which are appropriate, which are plainly adapted to that end, which are not prohibited, but consist with the letter and spirit of the Constitution, are constitutional.

Borrowing Webster's phraseology, Marshall repeated that a state, if it can tax a Federal Bank, can also destroy it. It is all "a question of supremacy." If an individual state can tax the instrumentalities of the National Government, then the statement that the Constitution and the acts made under it shall be the supreme law of the land is "empty and unmeaning declamation." He announced, therefore, that the Maryland law taxing the Baltimore Branch of the United States Bank was "contrary to the Constitution . . . and void," and that the judgment of the Supreme Court of Maryland was reversed.

It was fortunate that this Opinion came when it did. If Maryland had won, it is probable, as Wheeler has said, "that the whole character of the general government would have

[1] Beveridge, *Marshall*, IV, 289. [2] Lewis, *Great American Lawyers*, II, 263.

been altered." [1] Beveridge was right in describing it as "that opinion of John Marshall which has done more for the American Nation than any single utterance of any other one man, excepting only the Farewell Address of Washington." [2]

By his decision, John Marshall brought upon himself the denunciation of all exponents of State rights. John Tayloe, of Carolina, wrote his *Construction Construed and Constitutions Vindicated* to refute Marshall's reasoning; and the venerable Jefferson was roused into a condemnation of the Federal Judiciary as "a subtle corps of sappers and miners constantly working underground to undermine the foundations of our confederated fabric." It must have been galling to the Sage of Monticello to realize that the success of his party in the Legislative and Executive branches of the government was being neutralized by the presence of the Federalist, John Marshall, on the Supreme Bench.

It would be interesting if it could be shown that Marshall relied upon Webster's argument for the logic of his own matchless Opinion; but, while the Chief Justice occasionally employed phrasing which recalls the language of Webster's speech, there is no evidence that he borrowed from the attorney for the plaintiff. The two men thought along the same lines, and it would have been strange if there had not been similarities in what they had to say about a problem which had been so carefully debated.

The four cases which Webster argued before the Supreme Court in 1820 were of no special significance in constitutional law.[3] In 1812, however, he was engaged in the epochal suit of *Cohens* v. *Virginia* (6 Wheat., 264), appearing for the state against David B. Ogden and William Wirt for the plaintiffs.

---

[1] Wheeler, p. 39.

[2] Beveridge, *Marshall*, IV, 327. The discussion of this famous case in Beveridge's *Marshall*, IV, 6, is worth reading with much care.

[3] The four cases were *The London Packet* (5 Wheat., 132), a prize suit in which Webster appeared, with Pitman, for the captors; *United States* v. *Smith* (5 Wheat., 153), in which Webster, for the defendant, was opposed to Attorney-General William Wirt; *United States* v. *Pirates* (5 Wheat., 184), in which Webster, with Winder, was again against the Attorney-General; and *United States* v. *Holmes, et al.* (5 Wheat., 412), in which Webster represented the defendant against Wirt, as Attorney-General.

The matter immediately at issue was the authority of the State of Virginia to prosecute in its courts a man who had sold within its borders tickets in a District of Columbia lottery, contrary to the statutes of that state. Having been convicted in Virginia, Cohens appealed to the Supreme Court of the United States on a writ of error. The matter in itself was trivial, but the Virginia Legislature took the ground that the Supreme Court had no appellate jurisdiction in the case, and Senator James Barbour made an impassioned appeal that the writ of error be dismissed. Ogden and Pinkney, representing the plaintiff in error, maintained that the authority of the Supreme Court extended legally over "all cases arising under the constitution, laws, and treaties of the United States." This view was sustained by the Chief Justice in one of the most vigorous of his opinions, in which he held that the jurisdiction of the Supreme Court "in all criminal cases arising in State Courts in which a Federal question was involved, was undeniable and supreme." [1] He thus, according to Beveridge, "stamped upon the brow of Localism the brand of illegality." [2]

In this argument on jurisdiction — which was the kernel of *Cohens* v. *Virginia* — Webster did not participate. When, however, the Supreme Court, having asserted its authority, proceeded to examine the merits of the original decision, Webster took Barbour's place as attorney for Virginia. In spite of the best efforts of Ogden and Wirt, his opponents, Webster won for his client, the Court holding, in an Opinion delivered on March 5, 1821, that the judgment of the State Court must be affirmed. But Webster had nothing to do with the settlement of the point which has made this case one of the landmarks in our legal history.

In 1822, Webster had only three cases on the Supreme Court docket. One was *Ricard* v. *Williams* (7 Wheat., 59), in which, for the last time, he was pitted against William Pinkney, who

---

[1] Warren, *Supreme Court*, II, 10. Warren calls this opinion "one of the chief bulwarks of American unity."

[2] Beveridge, *Marshall*, IV, 353. Beveridge goes on to say that, while the practical result of this appeal was nothing, " it afforded John Marshall the opportunity to tell the Nation its duty in a crowning National emergency."

died suddenly only a few days after making his argument.[1] Another was that of *The Santissima Trinidad* (7 Wheat., 283), the most important of several prize cases settled at that session, in which it was decided that a public ship, engaged in privateering and, in violation of our neutrality, augmenting its crew in our ports, was bound to restore to their original owners any ships or goods captured and brought into our harbors. As a result, the captured vessel was ordered to be restored to its Spanish owners, Webster's clients. Littleton Waller Tazewell,[2] of Virginia, who was associated with Webster as counsel for the defendants, is reported to have said to him, after the argument was over, that "he was excessively clever but a lazy dog." William Wirt, a competent judge, declared that, as a result of this case, Webster was called superior by people who dwelt north of the Potomac, but that Tazewell was the favorite of the South.

Any list of noteworthy cases in which Webster participated must include that of *Le Jeune Eugénie* (2 Mason, 409), brought before the First Circuit Court, in Boston, at the May term of 1822, after his busy weeks in Washington. A slave ship, flying the French flag, had been captured by an American frigate and taken to the port of Boston. The slave trade was forbidden by the laws of France. It had also been prohibited after June 1, 1808, by act of Congress and had been made, in 1820, a capital offense. Webster, retained with George Blake for the United States and the captors, declared that the slave trade was simply piracy, "contrary to the conventional law of nations," and that "it instigated and encouraged the most atrocious crimes and barbarities."[3] Justice Story gave an

[1] Rufus Choate, describing this case, said: "I heard Pinkney in his last great argument, when, by his overwork, he snapped the cord of life. His diction was splendidly rich, copious, and flowing. Webster followed him, but I could not help thinking that he was infinitely dry, barren, and *jejune*."

[2] Littleton Waller Tazewell (1774–1860), of Norfolk, Virginia, was later United States Senator (1824–33) and Governor of the state (1834–35). John Randolph said, "Tazewell is second to no other man that ever breathed; but he has taken almost as much pains to hide his light under a bushel as Pinkney did to set his upon a hill."

[3] An abstract of Webster's argument is given in National Edition, XV, 278–81. Three years later, in the case of *The Antelope* (10 Wheat., 66), the Supreme Court ruled

opinion in Webster's favor, but the vessel, by arrangement, was surrendered to the French authorities.[1]

Before the Supreme Court in 1823, Webster was retained in eight suits — the largest number in which he had yet appeared in any single session. The death of Pinkney had placed Webster, when he was only a little over forty, at the head of the American bar. Charles J. Ingersoll recorded in his Diary for February 6, 1823, that Webster was "the most eminent practitioner in this court"; and William Lowndes, who had known him ever since they had been in Congress together, said, "We in the South have not his superior and you in the North have not his equal."

Few actions before the Supreme Court have stirred the country more deeply than *Gibbons* v. *Ogden* (9 Wheat., 1), commonly called the Steamboat Case, which determined the extent of the control of the Federal Government over internal commerce. The New York Legislature had granted in 1798 to the influential Chancellor Robert R. Livingston the exclusive right to navigate steamboats in New York waters. This privilege had been renewed from time to time, the consequence being that, after the spectacular success of Fulton's *Clermont* in August 1807, Fulton and Livingston enjoyed a monopoly so complete that no suit brought in the state courts had been able to disturb it. Finally ex-Governor Aaron Ogden, of New Jersey, having purchased from the monopoly the right to operate a steamship line between New York and Elizabethtown, brought a test case against his former partner, Thomas Gibbons, who had refused to work under the Livingston license and had started an opposition line of his own. It would not be profitable to review here the various trials which ensued. The matter reached the Supreme Court in January 1822, with Webster and Pinkney as opposing counsel, but it was not argued until 1824, after Pinkney's death.

---

that, as international law was then defined, the slave trade was not piracy. The viewpoint of Webster and Story was, however, upheld by public opinion. See Warren, *Supreme Court*, II, 45, and Wheeler, pp. 63–66.

[1] Webster's opponent in this case was William Sullivan, and Justice Story characterized the arguments of the counsel on both sides as "very able, eloquent, and learned."

From its inception, the Steamboat Case had attracted attention, and several eminent lawyers had been employed in connection with it. Associated with Webster, as attorneys for Gibbons, were Wirt and Ogden, whose abilities were outstanding. For the monopoly, two distinguished New Yorkers — Thomas A. Emmet and Thomas J. Oakley — had been retained. Laymen as well as lawyers recognized that the whole matter of the control of transportation was involved, for the question, freed from legal technical ties, was perfectly clear: "Did the New York laws granting a monopoly violate that section of the Federal Constitution which leaves to Congress the power 'to regulate commerce among the several states'?" It is not surprising that the Chamber was "excessively crowded" on the morning of Wednesday, February 4, 1824, when Webster rose to make that one of his legal arguments which Beveridge has pronounced "incontestably supreme." [1]

Several of Webster's biographers have repeated a dramatic story, originally vouched for by George Ticknor, to the effect that, on February 3, while Webster was speaking on a tariff measure in the House of Representatives, he was unexpectedly notified that *Gibbons* v. *Ogden* was to be called for the next morning; that, caught unawares and not having looked at his notes for more than a year, he at once concluded his speech, hurried to his lodgings, swallowed some medicine, and went to sleep until ten o'clock that evening; that he was then awakened and worked continuously until nine o'clock on the following day, when he took a light breakfast of tea and crackers, was shaved, looked once more over his brief, read the newspapers, and then went into court, where, in a speech two hours and a half long, he made the brilliant argument which, according to Justice Wayne released "every creek and river, lake, bay,

[1] The excitement which the case aroused may be judged from a letter written on February 1, 1824, by Wirt to his brother-in-law, in which he said: "To-morrow week will come on the great steamboat question from New York. . . . Come on and hear it. Emmet's whole soul is in the case and he will stretch all his powers. Oakley is said to be one of the finest logicians of the age, as much a Phocion as Emmet is a Themistocles, and Webster is as ambitious as Cæsar. He will not be outdone by any man, if it be within the compass of his power to avoid it."

and harbor, in our country, from the interference of monopolies." [1]

This is an anecdote which, for the sake of the picturesque, one could wish were verifiable. But Mr. Beveridge, with that thoroughness which was perhaps the chief of his many virtues as a biographer, investigated the facts, only to discover that the story must be rejected. The debate on the tariff in the House did not open until three days after the argument in *Gibbons* v. *Ogden* was over; Webster's own speech on the tariff was not delivered until a full month after the decision in that case had been rendered; and for at least a week before the Steamboat Case began, Webster, if the House Records may be trusted, took no part whatever in its proceedings. [2] It may be added that Webster's position at the bar was such that every care would have been used to notify him as far as possible in advance of the day when he was slated to appear. The fanciful tale of Ticknor must be discarded for lack of evidence to corroborate it.

No skeptic, however, can deny that Webster did open the argument for the plaintiff in error. [3] Starting with the frank admission that he must make out a "clear case" in order to succeed, he showed the extraordinary situation which would be produced if each state made its own commercial restrictions. Asserting that the acts granting a monopoly exceeded the authority of the Legislature, he added that "the power of Congress to regulate commerce is complete and entire, and, to a certain extent, necessarily exclusive." "The people intended," he said, "in establishing the Constitution, to transfer from the several States to a general government those high and important powers over commerce, which, in their exercise, were to maintain a uniform and general system." Any other doctrine, he declared, would end in chaos. In presenting

---

[1] See Wayne's "Address of Welcome," May 26, 1847, at Savannah (National Edition, IV, 97). The story is quoted in Curtis, I, 216–17.

[2] Beveridge, *Marshall*, IV, 424–25, note.

[3] " The argument was opened by Webster; and never in Congress or court had that surprising man prepared so carefully, — and never so successfully." (Beveridge, *Marshall*, IV, 424.)

this broad principle, Webster was at his best, and he said later, in commenting on the attention with which the Chief Justice listened to him : —

I think I never experienced more intellectual pleasure than in arguing that novel question to a great man who could appreciate it, and take it in; and he did take it in, as a baby takes in his mother's milk.[1]

Having reached the conclusion that Congressional regulation of commerce must be "exclusive," and that individual states cannot legislate upon the subject "without manifest encroachment and confusion," Webster ended by pointing out that the license which Gibbons had received under the laws of the United States was inconsistent with the statutes of the State of New York, and that the authority of Congress, being supreme, necessarily overruled "all inconsistent or repugnant state legislation."

Regarded as a whole, Webster's argument was probably the most effective ever made by him before the Supreme Court. He himself felt that he never did better than on that occasion,[2] and his view was sustained by Justice Story, who thought Webster's speech to be a perfect illustration of the working of his mind at its best and described it as equally remarkable "for profoundness and sagacity, for the choice, and comprehensiveness of the topics, and for the delicacy and tact with which they are handled."[3]

The speech of Oakley, who followed Webster, was said by the Washington correspondent of the New York *Statesman* to be "one of the most ingenious and able arguments ever

[1] Harvey, p. 142.

[2] Webster said to Harvey: "My forensic efforts have been those which pleased me most. The two arguments that have given me the most satisfaction were the arguments in the 'steamboat case' and the Dartmouth College argument." (Harvey, pp. 140–44.)

[3] Justice Story, in an unpublished manuscript quoted by Wheeler, pp. 59–60, said of Webster's argument: "We have here in as favorable a light as we could desire, his clearness and downright simplicity of statement, his vast comprehensiveness of topics, his fertility in illustrations drawn from practical sources; his keen analysis, and suggestion of difficulties; his power of disentangling a complicated proposition, and resolving it into elements so plain as to reach the most common minds."

made in this Court"; and the ardently Republican Emmet outdid himself in an oration which was heard by so many ladies that many of them had to be seated within the bar itself. Wirt, speaking for two hours on February 7 and for four hours on February 9, then closed the hearing in an argument which, by one newspaper correspondent, was effusively called "the finest effort of human genius ever exhibited in a Court of Justice," [1] and which seems to have impressed some of the audience as being even more convincing than Webster's. There had been a friendly disagreement between Webster and Wirt as to the line of reasoning to be followed, and Wirt, the older and more experienced man, had finally said, "Very well, let us each argue it in his own way, and we will find out which, if either, is right." [2] But it was not Wirt's speech — though he himself thought it "entirely conclusive" — which won the case for the plaintiff.

Webster had confidence that his side would be victorious,[3] and his optimism was justified by Marshall's decision, rendered on March 2, after a short postponement on account of an accident to the Chief Justice's shoulder. In this Opinion, — which, to quote Senator Beveridge again, "has done more to knit the American people into an indivisible Nation than any other one force in our history, excepting only war," [4]— Marshall, with a logic which strikes us now as axiomatic, declared that "the acts of New York must yield to the laws of Congress." Fearlessly taking up the question of the relationship of the several states to the Federal authority, he announced that,

[1] Quoted in Warren's *Supreme Court*, II, p. 65 from the *Richmond Enquirer*, for March 2, 1824.

[2] Harvey, p. 142. Many of the details in Harvey's account of the case are inaccurate, as, for instance, the statement that Webster followed Wirt.

[3] On February 15, Webster wrote Ezekiel, " Our Steam Boat case is not yet decided, but it *can go but one way*." (Van Tyne, p. 102.) On the same date, he wrote Mason: " We have no opinion yet in the Steamboat Cause; but I presume there can be no question how it will go. The case of collision, is, I think, unquestionably made out; and I have no doubt the Court will decide, that so far as respects commerce between different States (which is this case), the law of New York is inoperative." (National Edition, XVI, 81.)

[4] Beveridge, *Marshall*, IV, 429. Beveridge referred to it also as " the last but one of those decisive opinions which vitalized the American Constitution."

when they "converted their league into a government," their whole character underwent a change, the nature of which could be determined only by "a fair consideration of the instrument by which that change was effected." In vigorous language, the Chief Justice asserted the supremacy, not only of the Constitution, but of acts of Congress. He ended with a passage which undermined all the theorizing of the "strict constructionists": —

Powerful and ingenious minds, taking as postulates that the powers expressly granted to the government of the Union are to be contracted by construction into the narrowest possible compass, and that the original powers of the States are retained, if any possible construction will retain them, may, by a course of well-digested but refined and metaphysical reasoning founded on these premises, explain away the Constitution of our country, and leave it a magnificent structure, indeed, to look at, but totally unfit for use. They may so entangle and perplex the understanding, as to obscure principles which were before thought quite plain, and induce doubts where, if the mind were to pursue its own course, none would be perceived. In such a case, it is peculiarly necessary to recur to safe and fundamental principles to sustain these principles, and, when sustained, to make them the tests of the arguments to be examined.

Webster's satisfaction in this exposition of Federalistic principles was heightened by the knowledge that Marshall had based his Opinion almost exclusively on Webster's argument, ignoring Wirt's elaborate dialectics.[1] The decision of the Chief Justice adhered closely to the reasoning in which Webster had demonstrated that the laws passed by the Legislature of New York were inconsistent with certain statutes of Congress.

The Opinion in *Gibbons* v. *Ogden* was, as Charles Warren

[1] Webster is reported by Harvey to have said: "The result of the case was just this: the opinion of the court, as rendered by the chief justice was little else than a recital of my argument. The chief justice told me that he had little to do but to repeat that argument, as that covered the whole ground. And, which was a little curious, he never referred to the fact that Mr. Wirt had made an argument." (Harvey, p. 142.) Webster wrote Everett, October 30, 1851: "The argument is a pretty good one, and was on a new question. . . . It has often been observed that the Opinion of the Court, delivered by Chief Justice Marshall, follows closely the track of the argument." (National Edition, XVIII, 482.)

has pointed out, the first great "trust" decision in our history, and made the Chief Justice momentarily a popular figure. It must have astonished the sturdy old Federalist to be hailed as the champion of the rights of the common people. The results of his ruling were discernible almost immediately in an increased number of steamboats licensed to ply the New York waters and also the more remote Mississippi River. More important still was the encouragement offered, because of Marshall's courageous insistence on a broad interpretation of the Constitution, to those statesmen who believed in the policy of "internal improvements" and the centralization of power. Jefferson, in seclusion at Monticello, viewed with alarm "the rapid strides with which the Federal branch of our Government is advancing towards the usurpation of all the rights reserved to the States." We may be sure that Daniel Webster felt no regret at the reassertion of what to him had always been sound doctrine — a doctrine which he had helped in no small degree to expound and defend.

At this same crowded winter term of 1824, Webster was associated with Henry Clay and John Sergeant for the defendant in *Osborn* v. *Bank of the United States* (9 Wheat., 738), which, like *McCulloch* v. *Maryland*, had arisen from the attempt of a sovereign state to drive the United States Bank outside its borders. The Ohio Legislature, after levying a tax of fifty thousand dollars on the branches of the United States Bank in Cincinnati and Chillicothe, had followed this drastic action with punitive measures indicating a contempt for both the Bank and the Federal Government. Finally, by an order of the State Auditor, Ralph Osborn, the vaults of the Bank at Chillicothe were opened and the money, securities, and bank notes seized and carried off. The resulting action at law, begun in 1821, had been carried along for three years and had come before the Supreme Court in 1823.

In 1824, the Court wished to have it reargued in conjunction with *Bank of the United States* v. *Planter's Bank of Georgia* (9 Wheat., 904), another suit involving similar issues. The same attorneys argued both cases, the counsel for the individual states being Robert Goodloe Harper, of Maryland, ex-Governor Ethan Allen Brown, of Ohio, and the facetious Congressman John C. Wright, also of Ohio. No full report of Webster's argument was ever edited, but his reasoning could not have differed materially from that in *McCulloch* v. *Maryland*. The Opinion delivered by the Chief Justice on March 19, 1824, insisted that the vital question to be settled was "whether the Constitution of the United States has provided a tribunal which can peacefully and rightfully protect those who are employed in carrying into execution the laws of the Union, from the attempts of a particular state to resist the execution of those laws." After an analysis of the arguments, Marshall held that the act of the Ohio Legislature taxing the Bank of the United States was unconstitutional, and that the money thus confiscated must be returned to the Bank; and he also ruled that Ohio was unjustified in her claim that the suit against Osborn was a case in which that state was a party.

Still another case of an unusual nature made the winter term of 1824 a memorable one for Webster. *Ogden* v. *Saunders* (12 Wheat., 213), the hearing for which was opened on March 3, introduced the question as to the validity of bankrupt laws passed by various states, there being then no national bankruptcy act. Webster and Wheaton were retained for the defendant, opposed to a strong trio — Charles G. Haines, David B. Ogden, and Henry Clay. Webster, who strongly advocated the passage of a national bankruptcy act by Congress, contended that the Constitution did not permit individual states to legislate upon this subject. The Supreme Court, divided in its views, adjourned without reaching a decision; nor was it possible for it to come to an agreement in 1825 and 1826. In January 1827, however, it was reargued, with Webster and Wheaton against the validity of the state law and William Wirt, Edward Livingston, David B. Ogden, Walter Jones, and William Sampson — a formidable array of talent — representing the plaintiff. The Court, on February 18, 1827, rendered an opinion adverse to Webster's client, by vote of four to three, with the Chief Justice dissenting.

It was the first time in twenty-seven years that a majority of the Supreme Court differed from Marshall on a question of constitutional law.[1] Although defeated, Webster had the consolation that Marshall was in agreement with him; and the passage some years later of a national bankruptcy act was for him a form of vindication.

The attention which Webster devoted to his Supreme Court practice can be shown by cold statistics. He appeared in fifteen cases in 1826; in sixteen in 1827; in eight in 1828; in five in 1829; and in thirteen in 1830. Up to the year 1831, he had argued before that bench in 103 separate suits, many of them of the highest importance; and it has been computed that, during his lifetime, he was retained there in 170 cases — a record probably unequaled by any other lawyer in our history. While he was doing this, he was frequently busy in Congress, and often withdrew from the floor of the House or the Senate in order to meet an engagement downstairs in the Supreme Court Chamber. He usually finished the winter term much debilitated. In the spring of 1824, after a strenuous session, he wrote to Justice Story: "We have had a busy time of it since you left us. For myself, I am exhausted. When I look in a glass, I think of our old New England saying, 'As thin as a shad.' I have not vigor enough left, either mental or physical, to try an action for assault and battery."[2] The correspondent of the Boston *Courier* wrote, on March 3, 1827: "Mr. Webster, since I have been here, has been occupied almost every day in the Supreme Court. He is engaged in nearly all the important cases on the opposite side to Mr. Wirt. . . . Mr. Webster is, therefore, very little in the House and has not made any speech there of much importance since my arrival."[3] At the January term of the Supreme Court in 1830, while he was preparing and delivering his great speeches on Foot's Resolution in the Senate, Webster appeared in thirteen cases, involving a variety of complicated questions.[4]

[1] Beveridge, *Marshall*, IV, 481.
[2] National Edition, XVII, 348.
[3] Quoted in Warren, *Supreme Court*, II, 157, note.
[4] Two of the most interesting cases were those of the *Marianna Flora* (11 Wheat., 1),

The tradition as to Webster's invulnerability as a lawyer is one not easily overthrown. Mr. Charles Warren, however, after a thorough examination of the records, discovered that, between 1814 and 1851, Webster won 81 and lost 87 of his cases before the Supreme Court of the United States, there being two in which no decision was rendered. Between 1818 and 1823, Webster was retained in 37 cases before the Supreme Judicial Court of Massachusetts, winning 15 and losing 22. Mr. Warren makes the interesting point that a really great attorney is likely to fail more often than he wins before a final appellate court. In the first place, he is frequently called into a litigation in a last desperate struggle for victory. In the second place, he often appears only in the ultimate stages of the controversy, and, not "growing up" with it, is manifestly under a handicap.[1] The statistics prove beyond question that Webster was not only occasionally but frequently on the defeated side. It is true, however, that he was successful in the questions which were of the most importance. Probably it took a really momentous issue to draw forth all his powers. Rufus Choate once declared that Webster was not very formidable in a weak case. "But if it was strong," added Choate, "he was invincible; no man could take his verdict from him."

Webster's ability as a constitutional lawyer was due to an exceptional combination of qualities — or, rather, to ordinary qualities highly developed and skillfully blended. First of all, he thought clearly, discerning what was essential and ignoring what was trivial. He had the rare gift of being able, in his reasoning, to seize upon the vital issue and to cling to it. Once he had found the main road, he was not to be lured into any bypath. In the second place, he was simple in his language, avoiding the ambiguities and circumlocutions and technical jargon which so mar the style of otherwise good lawyers. He had learned from Jeremiah Mason that judges and juries turn a deaf ear to a vocabulary which they do not

in 1826, described by Quincy in his *Figures of the Past*, p. 246 ff., and *Bank of the United States* v. *Dandridge* (12 Wheat., 64), in 1827, analyzed by Warren in his *Supreme Court in United States History*, II, 156 ff.

[1] Letter to the author, November 26, 1929, from Charles Warren.

understand. In the third place, he had the utmost confidence
in the power of common sense. Before his ruthless practicality,
sophistry and evasion vanished, like dead leaves before a November wind. To him, precedents, no matter how numerous,
were not as convincing as logic. He was seeking the wise and
just solution, whether there was any past decision to sustain
it or not. Then there was his personality — his voice, his
gestures, his fascinating manner. By sheer magnetism, he
secured men's attention, and, as they listened, they were persuaded. His method seemed unstudied, but it was the product
of a consummate art. Finally, of course, there was his genius,
always inexplicable, but always unmistakable. There were
moments when he seemed inspired, when he seemed the mouth-
piece of some mysterious force. Those who heard him on
such occasions never forgot the experience.

A crowd of competent witnesses have testified to the impression which Webster made upon his contemporaries. Salmon
P. Chase, a student in the office of William Wirt, wrote in his
Diary for February 14, 1829, describing Webster's procedure
in *Wilkinson* v. *Leland* (2 Pet., 627): "He states his case with
great clearness and draws his inferences with exceeding sagacity.
His language is rich and copious; his manner, dignified and
impressive; his voice, deep and sonorous; and his sentiments high and often sublime. He argues generally from
general principles, seldom descending into minute analysis
where intricacy is apt to embarrass and analogy to mislead. . . .
If I could carry my faith in the possibility of all things to labor
so far as to suppose that any degree of industry would enable
me to reach his height, how day and night should testify to
my toils!" [1] Now and then we get a vivid sketch of him in
court, like the one given by Harriet Martineau, in her *Retro-
spect of Western Travel*, in which she refers to "Webster standing firm as a rock, his large, deep-set eyes wide-awake, his lips
compressed, and his whole countenance in that intense still-
ness which easily fixes the eye of the stranger." It amused
her to see how the Supreme Court Chamber would fill after

[1] Warden, *Private Life and Public Services of Salmon Portland Chase* (1847), p. 166.

Webster's entrance, and empty as soon as he returned to the Senate. It was Webster, and only Webster, whom visitors wished to hear. Young men, like Caleb Cushing and Rufus Choate, were strongly drawn to him, and even tried to model their methods on his. Charles Warren does not exaggerate when he says that Webster, after the death of Pinkney in 1822, "overshadowed all others in the importance of cases argued, and in the mastery of the great principles of constitutional law." [1]

Professor Channing has referred to seven leading cases in which, from 1803 to 1824, Marshall and his colleagues "announced the supremacy of the federal government over the States of the Union so far as powers had been delegated to it by the sovereign people through the medium of the Constitution." [2] The first three of these — *Marbury* v. *Madison* (1803), *Fletcher* v. *Peck* (1810), and *Martin* v. *Hunter's Lessee* (1816) — came up before Webster had entered upon his career before the Supreme Court. In each of the remaining four — *McCulloch* v. *Maryland*, *Cohens* v. *Virginia*, *Osborn* v. *Bank of the United States*, and *Gibbons* v. *Ogden* — Webster had an important part, to say nothing of *Dartmouth College* v. *Woodward*, which Channing does not mention. The stand which Webster, in these and other cases, took in favor of a liberal construction of Constitutional phraseology and a strong central government made him the legitimate successor to those men who, during the Federal Convention and afterwards, had insisted that the individual states must yield many of their earlier privileges to a higher authority. Webster's function as interpreter of the Constitution is, from the point of view of the historian, of hardly less importance than that of its framers. If he had done nothing more than this, he would have earned the eternal gratitude of his country.

[1] Warren, *History of the American Bar*, pp. 267–68.
[2] Channing, *History of the United States*, V, 309.

XI

IN THE PUBLIC EYE

Deep in the man sits fast his fate
To mould his fortunes, mean or great.
— EMERSON, "Fate"

We have a strong feeling of the injustice of any toleration of slavery.
— WEBSTER, *Memorial on Slavery* (1819)

A system of artificial government protection leads the people to too much reliance on government.
— WEBSTER, Speech on the Tariff (1820)

THE youthful Ralph Waldo Emerson once set down in his *Journal* an estimate of Daniel Webster given to him by a Boston lawyer.[1] "Webster," said Emerson's informant, a mysterious "Mr. K.," "has a long head, very large black eyes, bushy eyebrows, a commanding expression, — and his hair is coal-black, and coarse as a crow's nest. His voice is sepulchral — there is not the least variety or the least harmony of tone — it commands, it fills, it echoes, but is harsh and discordant." Speaking more specifically of Webster's character, he continued: "He possesses an admirable readiness, a fine memory and a faculty of perfect abstraction, an unparalleled impudence and a tremendous power of concentration. . . . He knows his own strength, has a perfect confidence in his own powers, and is distinguished by a spirit of fixed determination; he marks his path out, and will cut off fifty heads rather than turn out of it; but is generous and free from malice, and will never move a step to make a severe remark." Such was Daniel Webster in 1820 to a none too sympathetic observer, who must have watched him striding across the Common or chatted with him at "Change Hour" — a Webster who was

[1] Emerson's *Journal*, I, 16–17, entry for February 7, 1820.

dynamic, ambitious, and determined, a personality to seize and hold the imagination. Already he was as much a part of Boston as if he had been cradled within sight of Faneuil Hall.

So interwoven were Webster's many activities at this stage of his career that it is difficult to trace his progress. As a lawyer, he soon made his name known in sections remote from New England. But during years when his legal engagements might well have been engrossing, he had energy left for various avocations. He was, for instance, an occasional contributor to the *North American Review*, and one of his articles, "The Battle of Bunker Hill and General Putnam," printed in the issue for July 1818,[1] required an immense amount of research. It did, however, furnish him with much of the material for his Bunker Hill Oration in 1826.[2]

In the spring of 1817, at the close of the Congressional session, Webster called upon President James Monroe and urged him, in the interests of political harmony, to make a tour of the North. Partly as a result of this conversation, Monroe set out on May 31, reaching Boston in early July.[3] There he was received cordially, even by such irreconcilable Federalists as Harrison Gray Otis; and, as he dined with prominent citizens in the Exchange Coffee House or visited Harvard College, he was satisfied that the majority of people in the Northeast were attached to republican government.

Webster was not a member of the committee appointed to welcome Monroe in Boston, nor did he take any official part in his reception. He wrote Mason, on June 28, "We think

[1] National Edition, XV, 14 ff.

[2] Among Webster's other contributions to the *North American Review* were a criticism, in December 1816, of the *Extraordinary Red Book*, a volume giving statistics regarding the disbursements of the British Government for pensions, sinecures, and other unnecessary expenses; a review, in December 1818, of Vol. III of Wheaton's *Reports*, which he praised very highly; and a discussion, in July 1820, on "The Law of Creditor and Debtor," in which he took as his text some observations made on laws of creditor and debtor in the United States by British travelers. These three articles are reprinted in the National Edition, Vol. XV.

[3] For a description of this journey, see *The Tour of James Monroe, President of the United States, through the Northern and Eastern States in 1817*, by S. Putnam Waldo (1820). Monroe spent six days in Boston, receiving the degree of Doctor of Laws from Harvard and attending many parties at the homes of Webster's friends. At Portsmouth, on July 10, Mason delivered the address of welcome.

of nothing but the President's visit," but there is no other mention of it in his correspondence. Possibly he had so recently become a citizen of Boston that it was not deemed proper to include him among the hosts of the occasion. Then, too, he was as yet only a lesser luminary. . . . But when John C. Calhoun, the Secretary of War, came to the city in 1820, he was Webster's guest and dined with him at his house in Summer Street. It was Webster who accompanied him to the Charlestown Arsenal and drove with him through the suburbs; and the town fathers were willing to concede that Webster was perhaps the one best qualified by experience to entertain a member of the cabinet. By 1820, it had become a matter of importance in State Street that Webster was supporting Calhoun for the Presidency.

During the years between the visits of Monroe and Calhoun, Webster's reputation had grown locally through his participation in town affairs. In December 1819, a meeting of citizens was called at the State House to protest against the admission of Missouri to the Union as a slave state. Most of Boston's aristocracy attended, and "the galleries were adorned with circles of ladies, who appeared to take a lively interest in a subject in which the Rights of Humanity were so deeply involved." [1] In this gathering, Webster was recognized as a leader. At his motion, James Prince, United States Marshall for the District, was named as Chairman. Placed on a large committee to consider what measures the assemblage should take,[2] Webster joined in reporting a resolve that Congress possessed the constitutional power to prohibit negro servitude in a territory. Finally, he was appointed Chairman of a Committee of Five to draft a Memorial to Congress expresssing the views of Massachusetts regarding the exclusion of slavery from the states about to be formed across the Mississippi. During the discussion, Webster spoke at some length, emphasizing his conviction that Congress was called upon by

[1] *Columbian Centinel*, December 4, 1819.

[2] Among the other members of this committee were William Gray, Josiah Quincy, John Phillips, William Prescott, Thomas Handasyd Perkins, and William Eustis — a distinguished group, representing all shades of political belief.

all the principles of humanity and morality to keep slavery out of Missouri.

This speech — which was unfortunately not preserved — was Webster's earliest public utterance on slavery. That he also wrote most of the Memorial is probable from its style and content, although its authorship cannot be positively proved.[1] Even though the language may not have been his, the sentiments which were expressed were those which he favored. It presented a carefully developed argument to show that, under the terms of the Constitution, Congress could make the prohibition of slavery a condition of the admission of any new state. That such a policy was fair and wise was unquestionable: first, because it was unjust to existing states to admit a new state which would be entitled to the basis of representation in Congress already established by the Constitution for slaveholding states; second, because Congress ought "to prevent the further progress of a great and serious evil." The concluding words of the Memorial had a noble ring: —

We have a strong feeling of the injustice of any toleration of slavery. Circumstances have entailed it on a portion of our community which cannot be immediately relieved from it without consequences more injurious than the suffering of the evil. But to permit it in a new country, where yet no habits are formed which render it indispensable, what is it but to encourage that rapacity, fraud, and violence against which we have so long pointed the denunciations of our penal code?

Other protests of a similar tenor were sent to Congress from different sections of New England, and it looked as if the Northeast might be united on this question as it had been on the

[1] See National Edition, XV, 72–73, and Pierce's *Sumner*, III, 215, for the authorship of the Memorial. The other members of the committee were George Blake, Josiah Quincy, James T. Austin, and John Gallison, but Webster, doubtless because of his reputation as a constitutional lawyer, was designated as Chairman. A pamphlet copy of the Memorial in the Library of the Massachusetts Historical Society has a note in George Ticknor's handwriting stating that it was prepared by Gallison; but, if this is true, it must have been revised by Webster. The tone and argument of the Memorial correspond closely to the summary of Webster's speech printed in the Boston newspapers; and Sumner felt that the closing paragraph was " marked by his clear and cogent statement."

Embargo. But practical considerations mollified the *sæva indignatio* of the Boston moralists. Massachusetts wanted Maine to be a separate state, and this plan could be accomplished only by concessions to the South. Thus, after spirited debates in Congress and frequent threats of secession from Southern members, the Missouri Compromise providing that slavery should be prohibited in the territory of the Louisiana Purchase, — except in Missouri, — north of the line of 36 degrees and 30 minutes, was passed. The protests of Webster and his friends had been neutralized by the zeal and political strategy of Henry Clay, who at this time won the title of the "Great Pacificator." Maine was soon admitted to the Union by a separate act, and the crisis passed, as a threatening cloud sometimes blows by without a storm.

On one other matter which, to Massachusetts shipowners and importers, seemed then more important than the controversy over slavery, Webster also spoke his mind. It seemed likely in the autumn of 1820 that Congress, for the purpose of encouraging domestic manufactures, would raise certain tariff duties. Naturally the importers of New England saw in such a procedure a menace to their prosperity. In accordance with tradition, a meeting was called in Faneuil Hall, with "Billy" Gray, a wealthy merchant and retired shipowner, as Chairman; and Daniel Webster, whose economic ideas were well known, was invited to deliver the "keynote" address. It was his first appearance on that platform where, before many years had gone by, he was to feel very much at home.[1]

When the tariff measure of 1816 was under discussion in Congress, Webster had neither advocated nor opposed a protective policy, but had devoted himself chiefly to guarding the interests of his constituents in Rockingham County. Since then, manufacturing, especially in textiles, had been spreading, and mill-owners were calling for higher duties. Then, as to-day, the tariff was a selfish scramble for governmental

[1] *Boston Daily Advertiser*, October 11, 1820. The speech was delivered on Monday evening, October 2.

assistance, in which "logrolling" and lobbying were important factors.

Webster, in 1820, was, in theory and practice, a free trader.[1] While disclaiming any unfriendliness towards manufacturers, he questioned whether Congress had the right to enact revenue laws "with the avowed object of giving preference to particular manufactures." In his speech, he doubted whether it was wise or expedient for any government to grant special privileges, adding that all modes "of giving great preferences to some occupations and some modes of invested capital over others" had usually stirred up jealousies and animosities. The consequences of pampering certain industries have never been better brought out than in the following sentences: —

A system of artificial government protection leads the people to too much reliance on government. If left to their own choice of pursuits, they depend on their own skill and their own industry. But if government essentially affects their occupations by its systems of bounties and preferences, it is natural, when in distress, that they should call on government for relief.

This is an excellent exposition of the familiar doctrine of *laissez faire*. "To leave men to their own discretion, to conduct their own concerns by their own skill and prudence, and to employ their capital and labor in such occupations as they themselves found most expedient," he said, "has been found the wisest, as it is the simplest, course of political legislation." In 1820, the pressure from manufacturers was not sufficiently strong to compel Congress to raise the duties. Webster's views were those of the orthodox Federalism of that period. He and his merchant friends had their way, and nothing was done to change the system until the passage of the tariff of 1824.

The autumn of 1820 was a busy period for Webster. The setting off of Maine as a separate state during the preceding spring had led thoughtful citizens to propose the holding of a convention for the revision of the Constitution, under which

[1] For a discussion of Webster's free trade ideas, see Carey, *Daniel Webster as an Economist*, pp. 127–34.

the Commonwealth had been administered since 1780.[1] It was a time when the old divisions between Federalists and Republicans were rapidly being blotted out,[2] and it was possible to debate principles rather than party policies. The convention was called to order on Wednesday, November 15, at the State House, in the Hall of Representatives, by Lieutenant-Governor William Phillips. Among the five hundred delegates were included leaders from various sections of the Commonwealth, representing all classes and interests.[3]

At the opening of the convention, the patriarchal John Adams, who had drafted the original State Constitution in 1780, was complimented by an election as Presiding Officer, but he pleaded his eighty-five years, and Chief Justice Parker was made Permanent Chairman. From the beginning, Webster took a conspicuous part in the proceedings. His acquaintance with parliamentary procedure was a valuable asset, and he was frequently called upon to preside over the Committee of the Whole. His personality dominated the assembly, and he was constantly on the alert to see that business was properly conducted. On the floor, he acted with the moderate conservatives, keeping a critical eye on any radical changes in an instrument which, on the whole, had not worked badly.[4]

[1] The people voted, 11,756 to 6593, on August 21, 1820, in favor of holding a convention. Delegates were chosen at a special election on October 16. The highest vote in Boston was cast for William Phillips, who received 1694, as compared with 1689 for John Phillips and 1682 for William Gray. Webster was chosen, but received only 1223 votes.

[2] Federalism persisted in Massachusetts longer than in any other state. A Federalist Governor, the popular John Brooks, was elected for seven successive years, from 1816 to 1822. In 1823, however, Governor Brooks, then over seventy, refused to run, and the Federalist candidate, Harrison Gray Otis, bearing the burden of the Hartford Convention, was beaten by the Republican, Dr. William Eustis. After 1824, the Federalists nominated no candidate for Governor, and the party was virtually dead. A ticket of presidential electors, headed by Otis, received 156 votes in 1828, and was the last Federalist ticket ever voted for in the United States. See Morison's *Harrison Gray Otis*, pp. 246–48.

[3] The list of delegates included Isaac Parker, Joseph Story, John Phillips, Josiah Quincy, John Davis, Artemas Ward, Israel Thorndike, William Sullivan, George Blake, Lemuel Shaw, Samuel Hubbard, Leverett Saltonstall, John C. Warren, Levi Lincoln, the two Samuel Hoars, Peter C. Brooks, Joseph B. Varnum, and John Adams.

[4] Webster wrote Mason, January 12, 1821: "It was a great body in numbers, and though I think it generally was well disposed, there was a good deal of inflammable matter, and some radicalism in it. We were extremely fortunate in finding a con-

When anybody tried to rock the Ship of State, his was the voice to cry, "Steady! Steady!" Among those who wished to hold fast to that which was good, Webster was conceded the post of commander, and the course of the Convention was directed largely by a small group of experienced parliamentarians, of whom he was one.

In expediting routine business, Webster's assistance was indispensable to the Chairman. He was invariably ready with the correct motion, and even his opponents came to trust him on technical details. His first important speech was in favor of the system of proceeding by committees; and, when he had won a victory on that point, he argued very sensibly for having the committees named by the Chair instead of by ballot. He himself was Chairman of the committee instructed to consider alterations in the section relating to oaths of office. The sessions of the Convention were long, and often two were held in a day; but Webster showed no fatigue, and his enthusiasm was inspiring to others.

Webster's breadth of mind was shown in his successful effort to remove from the Constitution that clause specifying the necessity of a declaration of a belief in Christianity as a part of the oath of office. He himself had an orthodox religious faith, which he did not hesitate to confess whenever such a declaration seemed called for. His disapproval of a religious test was based on expediency, but it was a demonstration of tolerance. Most of the citizens of Massachusetts being, at least nominally, Christians, it was unlikely that anyone not a Christian would be elected to public office; furthermore, there were some respectable persons who had been offended by being required to make a declaration of faith.

In presenting the resolutions to his committee, — which recommended a simple oath of allegiance to the Commonwealth in lieu of the religious oaths and subscriptions formerly demanded, — Webster spoke very cogently in its behalf.[1]

---

siderable number of gentlemen well disposed, who might otherwise have occasioned much trouble." (National Edition, XVI, 60.) Joseph Story was much alarmed by the extreme views of some of the delegates who sat near him.

[1] Webster's remarks appear in National Edition, V, 4–7.

He was followed by the United States Marshal, James Prince, who read a long argument upholding the report. John Phillips and the Reverend Joseph Tuckerman espoused the cause of orthodoxy, and a prolonged and rather pointless debate ensued, in which many delegates participated and some temper was shown. Indeed this apparently minor matter aroused as much acrimony as any question raised in the Convention. Eventually, however, liberalism prevailed, and the recommendation was accepted by a good-sized majority.

Webster's tolerance was also shown in his work as Chairman of a Select Committee to inquire into and report upon the constitution, rights, and privileges of the Corporation of Harvard College. As a graduate of another college, Webster was not likely to be prejudiced in his investigation. In a carefully prepared report, the Committee suggested no important changes in the administration of Harvard except that the overseers, in electing clergymen to their board, should not confine themselves, as in the past, to only one denomination — the Congregational. The report was accepted after a discussion in which Webster, holding his own against the criticism of illiberal clerics, brought their bigotry into the open.

The restraining influence exerted by Webster was especially noticeable in connection with an amendment proposed by James T. Austin requiring the General Court to arrange for the choice of presidential electors by direct vote of the people. This was, of course, a measure favored by the Jeffersonian, or Republican, element among the delegates. To us it seems innocuous and logical. But Webster made a powerful extemporaneous argument against the plan, and was upheld on the floor by Justice Joseph Story. The opposition of these two conservatives was sufficient to persuade the more cautious members, who rejected the suggested innovation; and it was not for nearly a century that it was put into operation in Massachusetts.

Webster's resistance to change was even more apparent during the prolonged discussion regarding the basis of representation in the Senate — the upper house of the General

Court. There was no question about the House of Representatives, the members of which were chosen in proportion to the population of the towns represented, as they are to-day. The Constitution of 1780, however, had given to each district a number of Senators proportioned to the amount of its public taxes,[1] and Webster felt that this plan should stand unaltered. No one questioned the desirability of keeping the qualifications for voters the same for both branches. But men of progressive tendencies maintained that the practice of basing senatorial representation on the taxable property in a district was undemocratic and urged that the Senate be formed like the House, the only distinction being that a Senator should have a larger constituency than a Representative.

Like most of the New England Federalists, Webster had been educated in the conviction that the British parliamentary organization furnished the best working model, in many respects, for our own government. He had in mind always the different theories of representation in the House of Lords and the House of Commons, which afforded a check by one upon the other. Obviously it was neither practical nor expedient to adopt in the United States the system of hereditary and appointive rank upon which membership in the House of Lords depends. Nor was it advisable to revive property qualifications either for voters or for officeholders. But Webster did feel that property, as such, should be conceded some influence and power in government. Accordingly, he disliked to abandon a plan which had survived for forty years, and which, in operation, had not been injurious or inconvenient.

The debate on this question — which Webster considered to be the most important before the Convention — was opened on December 13, by Chief Justice Parker, and was continued by other leading citizens, including Levi Lincoln, William Sullivan, and Samuel S. Wilde. On the following day, contention was ably kept up by George Blake, Leverett Saltonstall, and

---

[1] On this basis, a section small in population but with a heavy property valuation might have more Senators than one with a large population but small property assessment. In theory, it gave an advantage to the rich over the poor.

the venerable John Adams, who, for the first time since 1780, participated in a public debate. Justice Story then read a long and carefully prepared address; and Webster, on December 15, made his most elaborate speech from the floor — an argument which virtually concluded the discussion.[1]

Throughout his life, Webster attached perhaps an undue importance to material possessions. As Carey has well said, he made "private property and the self interest incentive the foundation of his program of economic thought and action." His association with wealthy people undoubtedly had its effect on his attitude towards governmental problems. With astonishing courage, he asserted that "in the absence of military force, political power naturally and necessarily goes into the hands which hold the property" — a doctrine which very few statesmen would care to sponsor to-day. "If the nature of our institutions be to found government on property," he went on, "and that it should look to those who hold property for its protection, it is entirely just that property should have its due weight and consideration in political arrangements." Taking it for granted that a system of "checks and balances" is desirable, he pointed out that the plan which had long been in use was a simple and harmless device for bringing it about. His reasoning was adroit and plausible rather than sound, but it carried the day, in spite of the fact that General Henry Dearborn had reported from his committee an amendment apportioning Senators to each district in proportion to population.

In this case, it was the force of Webster's personality rather than the strength of his cause which won the victory. It was not long before both branches of the General Court were placed on the same basis, the only difference being that the Senators were fewer in number, each one representing a larger district. From a practical point of view to-day, the two chambers have much the same viewpoint and are actuated by similar motives, although traditionally the Senate, probably because of its smaller size, is rather more conservative. The whole ques-

[1] National Edition, V, 8 ff.

tion stirred up in 1820 no inconsiderable excitement, and provided an issue upon which two types of mind could clash.

In the disputes so far mentioned, Webster was able to swing the Convention in his direction. He was less successful in a matter which was really of more importance than any other brought up for consideration — that of the independence of the judiciary. In its original form, the Constitution permitted the removal of a judge by the Governor, with the consent of the Council, on the address of the two branches of the Legislature. Webster wished to introduce certain bars against hasty or ill-considered action by requiring a two-thirds vote in the Legislature, by insisting on adequate reasons for any proposal of removal, and by allowing the accused judge to claim a hearing. His remarks on this subject were listened to with attention and seem to be unanswerable.[1] But the vote was against him, probably because the delegates hesitated to entrust too much authority to judges.

The Constitutional Convention adjourned on January 9, 1821, after having made fewer alterations than had been prognosticated.[2] The net results were, in the end, rather disappointing. Fourteen amendments in all were recommended, but, when the referendum was taken on April 9, 1821, only nine were approved by the people and incorporated in the Constitution. The removal from the oath of office of a declaration of a belief in Christianity was carried by a substantial majority; but Webster's plan for liberalizing the Board of Overseers at Harvard was rejected. The voters also refused to sanction an amendment reducing the number of Senators and making changes in the method of their election, and another providing that no judicial officer should be removed until the alleged charges were stated on the Legislative Records and the accused man had had an opportunity to be heard. Much of Web-

[1] Webster's speech, made on December 30, 1820, appears in National Edition, V, 26–32.

[2] The action of the assembly was fully reported in the *Journal of Debates and Proceedings in the Convention of Delegates Chosen to Revise the Constitution of Massachusetts* (New Edition, 1853), which, in 670 closely printed pages, gives the discussions in detail. The debates, generally speaking, were intelligent and can still be read with interest.

ster's good work on the Convention floor was futile. The fact that he and his coadjutors accomplished so little is seldom brought out by historians of that period.

It was Webster's feeling, as the Convention drew to a close, that enough had been achieved to justify the hard labor which he had devoted to it.[1] It is probable that no abler body of men has ever gathered within the boundaries of the Commonwealth, and they were very much in earnest. There was a feeling among Webster's friends that he had added greatly to his fame by the useful service which he had rendered.[2] Aside from the tangible results of the Convention, it was good that leaders of diverging opinions should become acquainted.

Webster's finest contribution to the Convention had been as a preserver, not as a creator. He had been audacious — but always in assailing those who criticized the established order. He had been bold — but it was the boldness of the captain who holds the fort gallantly against a charge of the enemy. A more original mind would have seized the opportunity to put theories of government into operation. But Webster's function was to resist dangerous innovations and to retain as much of the old Constitution as had been tested and found good. He succeeded, and the conservatives were happy.

Not long after the adjournment of the Convention, Web-

[1] Webster summed up the results in a letter to Jeremiah Mason, January 12, 1821: "We think three good things are done: the Judiciary, the College, and the future amendment articles. As to the rest, there may be different opinions. The House of Representatives is not enough reduced; but we could go no further without departing altogether from town representation. The Senate stands pretty well. Whether the Religious Article is helped or hurt, its friends hardly know; so I suppose no great injury has probably been done it. Some smaller amendments about the militia, etc., have passed, which it would have been better to have omitted." (National Edition, XVI, 61.)

[2] Justice Story, who had sat on the floor with him, wrote, January 21, 1821, to Mason: "Our friend Webster has gained a noble reputation. He was before known as a lawyer; but he has now secured the title of an eminent and enlightened statesman. It was a glorious field for him, and he has had an ample harvest. The whole force of his great mind was brought out, and in several speeches he commanded universal admiration. He always led the van, and was most skilful and instantaneous in attack and retreat. . . . On the whole, I never was more proud of any display than his in my life, and I am much deceived, if the well-earned popularity so justly and so boldly acquired by him on this occasion, does not carry him, if he lives, to the Presidency." (Story, I, 395–96.)

ster was a principal figure in a trial which, at the time, was compared to that of Warren Hastings. James Prescott, Judge of Probate for the County of Middlesex, had been impeached on the charge of holding courts at other times than those authorized by law, of receiving illegal fees, and of acting as counsel in cases pending in his own court, before himself as judge. In accordance with the prescribed procedure, Judge Prescott was duly accused by the House of Representatives of "misconduct and maladministration in office," and the Senate was ordered to take measures for his impeachment. Seven men were then designated as Managers, to prosecute the case before the Senate.

The trial took place in April 1821, in the Senate Chamber, with Samuel Hoar, William Prescott, Samuel Hubbard, George Blake, Augustus Peabody, and Daniel Webster — six of Boston's leading attorneys — representing the respondent. The case had aroused such interest that the House of Representatives adjourned, and no legislative business was transacted until a verdict was rendered. The twenty-six Senators constituting the court took their responsibility very solemnly, and the scene was most impressive. After the witnesses for both sides had been called, Hoar and Blake each occupied parts of two days for the defense. Webster, who, because of the reputation which he had acquired by his pleas before the Supreme Court, was the central figure, opened for an hour on the afternoon of April 24. On the following afternoon, when he was to continue, the hall was jammed with curious people, and the galleries were filled with ladies from Summer Street and Beacon Hill. "It might almost be said," wrote Josiah Quincy, "that the pulse of the community had stopped, from the excitement of the moment." [1]

No orator ever met expectations more fully than Daniel Webster. He needed an audience and a crisis to bring out all his latent powers; and, when these were provided, he seldom

[1] *Figures of the Past*, pp. 46–48. Josiah Quincy (1802–82) was then a Senior at Harvard. At the trial he sat between President John Thornton Kirkland and Harrison Gray Otis.

failed. On this occasion, he refrained from melodrama, but, in a long and persuasive argument, maintained that the charges were not proved. No one had charged Judge Prescott with bribery or corruption, but it was alleged that he had accepted fees for official services to which no fee was attached by law. In his analysis, Webster stressed what seemed to him to be the real issue: whether, as the Managers contended, Judge Prescott was entitled to fees in office only by express grant of the Legislature; or whether, as the defense insisted, he had a general right "to receive reasonable compensation for services rendered and labor performed." Webster was insisting on a liberal interpretation of the functions and perquisites of a public official.

When his presentation of his client's cause was finished, Webster gratified his listeners by an appeal to their feelings. Turning to the presiding officer, he broke out: —

Sir, the prejudices of the day will soon be forgotten; the passions, if any there be, which have excited or favored this prosecution will subside; but the consequences of the judgment you are about to render will outlive both you and them. The respondent is now brought, a single, unprotected individual, to this formidable bar of judgment, to stand against the power and authority of the state. I know you can crush him, as he stands before you, and clothed as you now are with the sovereignty of the state. You have the power "to change his countenance and to send him away." Nor do I remind you, that your judgment is to be rejudged by the community; and, as you have summoned him for trial to this high tribunal, that you are soon to descend yourselves from these seats of justice, and stand before the higher tribunal of the world. . . . If you send away the respondent, condemned and sentenced, from your bar, you are yet to meet him in the world on which you cast him out. You will be called upon to behold him a disgrace to his family, a sorrow and shame to his children, a living fountain of grief and agony to himself.

No man could have done that kind of thing more effectively than Daniel Webster. The sentimental reference to family pride; the suggestion of the helplessness of the victim; the reminder that soon their own reputations would be at stake — all these were subtly conveyed to the senatorial conclave. Josiah Quincy declared that Webster's burning words gave him his "first idea of the electric force which might be wielded by a master of human speech." He added that, while the orator was concluding, his eloquence "seemed to sweep away all adverse testimony, and to render an acquittal by acclamation a simple necessity."

Judges, however, must be dispassionate, and they showed themselves unmoved by Webster's fervor. There were fifteen articles of impeachment against Prescott, on thirteen of which he was acquitted. On Number III, charging him with having received fees illegally from Benjamin Dix, and on Number XII, alleging corrupt practice in the case of the guardianship of an insane person, he was declared guilty, by votes of 16 to 9 and 19 to 6. Judgment was pronounced on April 27, removing him from his judicial position.

Spectacular incidents like Webster's speech in defense of Judge Prescott kept him before the public, and he was soon one of the most conspicuous figures in Boston. Within five years after his arrival, he would have been placed by unanimous consent among the foremost citizens of the town, and he was tacitly admitted to that inner circle of patricians who then actually directed the destinies of the community. There was nothing commonplace or drab about Daniel Webster. His dramatic qualities caught the fancy of the people, and he was, from then until his death, Boston's favorite son.

XII

THE GREAT ORATOR

New England's stateliest type of man,
In port and speech Olympian;
Whom no one met, at first, but took
A second awed and wondering look
(As turned, perchance, the eyes of Greece
On Phidias' unveiled masterpiece).
— WHITTIER, "The Lost Occasion"

Mr. Burke is no longer entitled to the praise, — the most consummate orator of modern times. . . . This oration will be read five hundred years hence with as much rapture as it was heard. It ought to be read at the end of every century, and indeed at the end of every year, for ever and ever.
— JOHN ADAMS to DANIEL WEBSTER, December 23, 1820

ON an unseasonably warm day just before Christmas, in 1820, the roads towards Cape Cod from the north and west had far more than the usual number of travelers, some ambling on horseback, but most of them comfortably seated in chaises or coaches. Just as Canterbury is located some sixty miles south-east of London, so Plymouth lies forty miles distant in the same direction from Boston; and the farmers along the route, in Quincy and Marshfield and Kingston, were not far wrong in thinking that they were watching a modern pilgrimage. But these devotees were on their way, not to visit the shrine of a saint, but to hear an address by the Honorable Daniel Webster, whose fame as an orator had aroused their curiosity.

Earlier in that year, with the approach of the two-hundredth anniversary of the arrival of the *Mayflower*, a "Pilgrim Society" had been formed by a group of patriots, who wished, as they said, "to commemorate the landing and to honor the memory of the intrepid men who first set foot on Plymouth Rock." A committee secured Webster's consent to be the chief speaker;

and, when December 22 drew near, although the Constitutional Convention was still sitting at the State House, he left its sessions and took the journey to Plymouth, where he delivered the discourse to which he himself gave the title, "The First Settlement of New England."

Webster was well aware of the opportunity presented to one of his peculiar gifts and latent ambitions. The argument in the Dartmouth College Case had established his prestige as an orator, but on a legal subject and before a limited audience. In Congress, too, he had been noticed for his forensic eloquence, which, however, had been logical rather than emotional. He was now, however, to compose and to deliver the first of those occasional addresses which have become classics in our language and which have led sound critics to rate him with Demosthenes, Cicero, and Burke.

Knowing that much was expected of him, Webster made careful preparation. His experience in Congress and in the courts had increased his self-confidence. Many years had passed since, as a Dartmouth Senior, he had spoken his first oration before a group of his fellow citizens. Now, in his prime, he was to thrill a larger public on a more exalted theme. In the edition of his works to which he himself gave his approval, this oration is placed at the beginning, as if he cherished it most of all.

With a small group of friends, among whom was George Ticknor, Mr. and Mrs. Webster set out, on Thursday, December 21, for Plymouth. Even behind fast horses, the trip filled most of a day, and the members of the party, with others who were also on the road, including Colonel Thomas Handasyd Perkins and young Edward Everett, had luncheon at "a little half-way house," where they were crowded uncomplainingly into two or three tiny rooms. After a morning spent in meditation, Webster became "as gay as any one." As they drove into historic Plymouth, the houses were illuminated, and a band of music was parading up and down the Main Street, serenading the distinguished guests, who had packed the three hotels. In the evening Webster received visitors at the home of his host, Barnabas Hedge, although he appeared "considerably agitated and oppressed."

The next morning dawned clear and mild, and it was later so warm that at least one Plymouth resident sat by his open window in his shirt sleeves.[1] The day was ushered in with a military salute, and flags waved from every porch. Long before noon, an expectant audience had gathered in the old First Church, filling it to the doors and even packing the aisles.[2] It was a square wooden structure, with a spire, holding about twelve hundred on the floor and three hundred in the gallery. After some preliminary experiments with the acoustics, Webster elected to stand on a table covered with a green baize cloth and placed in the "deaf pew" directly in front of and below the pulpit. He wore small clothes, with black silk stockings and buckled shoes, and a silk gown over all. He was briefly introduced by the Presiding Officer, President John Thornton Kirkland, of Harvard College, and spoke for an hour and fifty minutes, omitting some of the paragraphs which were later included in the published version.

When he had returned to his rooms, he was besieged by admiring friends, and seemed "full of animation and radiant with happiness." At the public dinner which followed later in the afternoon, at the Court House, more than five hundred guests sat down.[3] The Chairman, John Watson, Esquire, called for toasts, and Webster, in his turn, responded with, "The Rock of Plymouth, — May it be trodden two thousand years hence, by as worthy feet as leaped upon it two hundred years ago!" When the speakers, among whom were Levi

---

[1] See Davis's *Plymouth Memories of an Octogenarian* (1906) p. 358.

[2] This church building, erected about 1740, stood at the head of the Town Square, on approximately the same site as the present stone structure. The church in which Webster spoke was torn down in 1830, but the plans show that the ground floor was 71 feet by 67 feet, 8 inches, and that it had the usual oblong enclosed pews so common in colonial days. The parish is the oldest in New England. The pastor in 1820 was the Reverend James Kendall, D.D., who had been ordained January 1, 1800. The present pastor is the Reverend Alfred Rodman Hussey, who has greatly assisted my researches.

[3] At this dinner, parchment sheets were passed around for the signatures of the guests. These are now framed in Pilgrim Hall, in Plymouth.

Lincoln and Edward Everett,[1] had finished, there was a grand ball, which Webster also attended; and, at his host's afterwards, he was "as frolicsome as a schoolboy, laughing and talking, and making merry with Mrs. Webster, Mrs. Davis, and Mrs. Rotch, the daughter of his old friend Stockton, till two o'clock in the morning." [2] On the following Monday — Christmas Day — Webster was back in his seat at the Constitutional Convention, which held its sessions as usual, regardless of the holiday.

The effect which the oration produced upon the listeners was something which many of them remembered all their lives. Although Webster had been nervous during the morning, his preoccupation left him as he faced the audience, and he hardly glanced at his notes from beginning to end. The Boston *Daily Advertiser* reported that his address "filled the crowded audience with alternate emotions of sympathy, delight, and admiration." This might have been mere conventional eulogy, but there were other witnesses whose discrimination could not be questioned. George Ticknor, a man of cool judgment, not addicted to extravagance of statement, said, in a letter written that evening: —

I was never so excited by public speaking before in my life. Three or four times I thought my temples would burst with the gush of blood; for, after all, you must know that I am aware that it is no connected and compacted whole, but a collection of wonderful fragments of burning eloquence, to which his whole manner gave tenfold force. When I came out, I was almost afraid to come near him. It seemed to me as if he was like the mount that might not be touched and that burned with fire. I was beside myself, and am so still.

Edward Everett declared in his *Memoir of Webster* that it was "in some respects the most remarkable of his performances,"

[1] It had at first been planned to invite Everett to read a poem, and he had accepted. Webster, however, was not enthusiastic over the idea, and Everett eventually withdrew his acceptance, promising, at the same time, to deliver the oration in 1821.

[2] The quoted passages are taken from a manuscript account of the trip to Plymouth prepared by George Ticknor and quoted in Curtis's *Life of Daniel Webster*, I, 192–93. The other members of the Webster party were Mr. and Mrs. Isaac P. Davis, Miss Stockton, Mr. F. C. Gray, and Miss Mary Mason.

and added, "It is doubtful whether any extra-professional literary effort by a public man has attained equal celebrity."

There was in Webster's personality something which commanded the admiration, and even the awe, of those who saw and talked with him. Since his boyhood he had been striking in his physical appearance; but now, under the approbation of his friends, he seemed to expand to even larger proportions. That Olympian quality of which so many of his contemporaries speak apparently dates from the period of the Plymouth Oration, when he first became fully aware of his ability to sway masses of men. It was not merely his erect and imperial bearing, or his dome-like forehead, or his rich and glowing eyes. It was not altogether his mastiff jaw, set as if no obstacle could resist his will.[1] He seemed to radiate magnetism from a physique as rugged and tireless as granite Mount Cardigan —

> The hope of unaccomplished years
> Seemed large and lucid round his brow.

Not yet forty years old, Webster was at the zenith of his strength. "I never saw him at any time when he seemed to me to be more conscious of his powers, or to have a more true and natural enjoyment from their possession," wrote Ticknor. The adjectives which were applied to him, such as "grand," "imposing," "noble," "magnificent," "splendid," and "regal," would be ridiculously inappropriate for most statesmen, but they seemed to fit Webster. Nor did anyone smile when he was described in Hamlet's lines about his murdered father: —

> Hyperion's curls, the front of Jove himself,
> An eye like Mars, to threaten or command;
> A station like the herald Mercury
> New-lighted on a heaven-kissing hill;
> A combination and a form indeed,
> Where every god did seem to set his seal
> To give the world assurance of a man.

[1] Rufus Choate pointed out that Webster had " the *large mouth* which eloquence almost always gives its possessor."

It is impossible for us to-day to reproduce the voice and manner of the orator. The mellifluous cadences, the shifts of emphasis, the variety of gestures, have vanished like a summer's cloud. Only in imagination can we visualize his burning glance and the proud poise of the head. But from the words themselves an impression may be gained. We live in an age when many intelligent men are impatient of eloquence, feeling that most of it is "sound and fury, signifying nothing." It is so easy to lapse into platitudes and to disguise commonplaces with rhetoric, and the temptation to resort to buncombe is one which few public men can resist. Webster himself, especially in his later years, was not guiltless in this respect, and stock phrases appear again and again in his speeches. But the advantage which his greatest efforts have over the productions of lesser imitators is that they are animated by an unmistakable sincerity.

It is the special quality of the oration as a type of literary art that its appeal is rather to the emotions than to the reason. But Webster had something to say. He had been a careful student of history, both European and American, as well as Greek and Roman; his brain was for the moment replete with knowledge acquired in preparation for the Constitutional Convention; and the occasion itself led him naturally to meditate on the events of two centuries. Logically, the Plymouth Oration is a series of brilliant passages, strung like pearls upon an almost invisible cord. But it gives the impression of unity. Webster wisely did not attempt a systematic development of an elaborate theme. His ability to do that well had already been shown before the Supreme Court of the United States. At Plymouth, he had another plan in mind.

Beginning simply, he touched briefly on the momentous nature of the anniversary, analyzed the motives which drove the Pilgrims to our shores, described the history and character of the early settlements, dwelt at some length on the government and society of our country, — introducing several paragraphs on the importance of property repeated from his recent speech in the Constitutional Convention,[1] — emphasized the importance of free schools, denounced the African slave trade, called attention to "the religious character of our origin," and concluded with a greeting to future generations. In his early paragraphs, he reverted to the past; at the end, he seemed to be talking to posterity. Outlined in this fashion, the Oration seems to lack continuity. But those who heard him did not recognize this as a defect. They experienced the same delight which they might have received from a performance of *Hamlet* or an adequate rendition of Beethoven's Fifth Symphony. It was the emotional stimulus which afforded them pleasure. Such glorious "purple patches" as that picturing the debarkation of the Pilgrims or that paying a tribute to John Adams[2] were to them sufficient to make the Oration great.

Perhaps the climax was reached in those paragraphs towards the close, when Webster, in the midst of a discussion of the moral and religious aspect of the Puritan system of government, turned aside deliberately to assail the traffic in negro slaves. "The passage about the slave-trade," said Ticknor, "was delivered with a power of indignation such as I never witnessed on any other occasion." Even to-day, in cold type, the language seems to glow with the ardor of the speaker: —

Neither public sentiment, nor the law, has hitherto been able entirely to put an end to this odious and abominable trade. . . . In the sight of our law, the African slave-trader is a pirate and a felon; and in the sight of Heaven, an offender far beyond the ordinary depth of human guilt. . . . I pursue this topic no further, except again to say, that all Christendom, being now blest with peace, is bound by everything which belongs to its character, and to the character of the present age, to put a stop to this inhuman and disgraceful traffic.

There was no reason connected with the Pilgrim anniversary why Webster should thus have declared himself. It was because his heart was full that he burst out in these impassioned

---

[1] An interesting monograph might be written on the repetitions of the same idea, sometimes in the same phraseology, in Webster's public utterances. It was impossible for him, speaking as frequently as he did, to avoid saying the same thing more than once.

[2] Webster doubtless had in mind Adams's recent appearance at the Constitutional Convention.

phrases. That this section was the most stirring part of his address was due to the fact that he felt it the most strongly.

In the Plymouth Oration are to be found nearly all the stylistic qualities which, taken together, have set Webster above all other American orators. He understood, in the first place, the effective use of short and incisive sentences. Before Macaulay had published his *Essay on Milton*, Webster had learned the value of following a long periodic sentence with curt phrases, which fall upon the ear like the crack of gunshots. Here, for example, is an illustration of the peculiarity: —

But the great and leading observation, relative to these establishments, remains to be made. It is, that the owners of the soil and of the capital seldom consider themselves *at home* in the colony. A very great portion of the soil itself is usually owned in the mother country; a still greater is mortgaged for capital obtained there; and, in general, those who are to derive an interest from the products look to the parent country as the place for the enjoyment of their wealth. The population is therefore constantly fluctuating. Nobody comes but to return. A constant succession of owners, agents, and factors, takes place.

Secondly, Webster made a most effective use of verbal repetition — a device which may be overdone, but which, in the Plymouth Oration, seems to be the natural outcome of the speaker's desire to gain emphasis. He likes to open a series of sentences in the same manner — "They left behind them," or "They broke away," or "They came." The effect is like that in the refrain of such a poem as Tennyson's "Tears, Idle Tears." The mere recurrence of the same group of sounds provides an æsthetic pleasure like the delight of recognition which makes certain forms of musical composition — the fugue, for instance — attractive. Akin to this device is the piling up of phrases or clauses of much the same structure until the cumulative result almost overwhelms the listener. The paragraph near the beginning, opening, "There is a local feeling connected with this occasion too strong to be resisted,"[1] shows the vividness achieved by this method of repetition.

[1] National Edition, I, 183-84.

Understanding the virtue which lies in variety, Webster seldom allowed his auditors to be wearied by sameness. With a skill none the less admirable because of its artifice, he alternated the commonplace with the dramatic and shifted from one combination of words to another, varying his normal exposition with rhetorical questions and exclamations and instinctively following a compound sentence with one which was complex or simple. Even in its printed version, the oration bears the reader along without fatigue.

Webster had a strong, but not very subtle, sense of rhythm, and an ear for melodious cadences. At his best, the orator is akin to the poet, and Webster's sentences, if they lack the delicate music of Shelley, have the stately rhetoric of Byron or of Kipling. Consider, for instance, the swing of the following sentence : —

No sculptured marble, no enduring monument, no honorable inscription, no ever-burning taper that would drive away the darkness of the tomb, can soften our sense of the reality of death, and hallow to our feelings the ground that is to cover us, like the consciousness that we shall sleep, dust to dust, with the objects of our affections.

It is, of course, dangerous for an orator to become the slave of sound. Some speakers have been so entranced with the sweetness of their own voices that they have forgotten to say anything. With them, to quote E. P. Whipple, "thought and expression are supplanted by the lungs and the dictionary." This fault Webster usually, if not always, avoided, and it is not one of the defects of the Plymouth Oration.

Finally, there is Webster's diction, more Anglo-Saxon than Latin, all opinions to the contrary notwithstanding. He appreciated the magic of simple words, fraught with the connotation lent by ages of human experience.[1] In the entire oration, there is hardly a word which strikes us as rare. Often

---

[1] Henry Cabot Lodge, in an essay on " Daniel Webster " in the *Cambridge History of American Literature* (Vol. II, Chap. 16), said, " He cared for style and had strong preferences in the choice of words he used to express his thoughts." Lodge said also, " His rhetoric was always unimpeachable, but his peculiar power lay in the fact that he was able to give to it with ever-increasing ease the imperishable literary quality."

the phrasing is reminiscent of the Bible or Shakespeare or Milton, as in the sentence : —

Some actual tears they shed, as they left the pleasant abodes of their fathers, and some emotions they suppressed, when the white cliffs of their native country, now seen for the last time, grew dim to their sight.

His imagery, though not profuse, is discreetly employed, and is often peculiarly vivid, as in such phrases as "a glory as bright and as durable as the stars," or "whiten this coast with the canvas of a prosperous commerce." The quotations which he uses are such as clarify the thought, and are never for the ostentatious display of learning. He did not hesitate to cite the Roman classics, in a manner now obsolete even before scholarly gatherings, and he had no fear of being too literary for his audience. Latinists find in his manner many reminiscences of Cicero, but Webster is no servile imitator. Here and there are passages which seem turgid or verbose; but Chancellor Kent was generally right when he referred to the Plymouth Oration as marked by "purity, taste, and simplicity."

Exactly a century later, on December 21, 1920, there was a similar celebration at Plymouth. Senator Henry Cabot Lodge, Webster's biographer, was the orator of the day, and naturally referred frequently to his illustrious predecessor; thus historians and literary men had a favorable opportunity for comparing the utterances of two widely separated generations. Webster, buoyant and hopeful, had looked forward to a period of marvelous accomplishment; [1] Lodge, in a despondent mood, pointed out that "Webster expected too much; that the men of the nineteenth century thought they could at once effect changes which really might require ages for their fulfillment." In material progress, the United States had surpassed Webster's colorful dreams; but Lodge, listless in the shadow of the World War, could not feel that the country had

[1] Rufus Choate said, "One of the great characteristics of Webster's eloquence is that he glows and burns and rises with the tide of hopeful passion of a great young nation." (Parker, p. 294.)

progressed either morally or spiritually since Webster's time. Webster's was the utterance of youth, Lodge's of sophistication and disillusionment. In style also, the two were of course different. Webster spoke grandiloquently, in generalities which were not merely glittering, but golden; Lodge was straightforward, specific, and prosaic.[1]

Webster was perhaps the first man to make occasional oratory popular in the United States. At the date when the Plymouth Oration was delivered, there were no satisfactory models for him to follow. It is easy to forget how original in conception the address must have seemed to a scholar like George Ticknor. The almost unanimous praise of critics established his reputation as an orator — a reputation which he maintained for the next thirty years. He had numerous imitators, but no one in that field could vie with him successfully. Edward Everett, Rufus Choate, Caleb Cushing, and Wendell Phillips had their inspired moods, and Charles Sumner, in his florid and exasperating speech on "The True Grandeur of Nations," delivered in 1845, caused a sensation which made him seem a promising rival. But in spite of brilliant individual efforts by younger men, they all looked up to Webster. By universal agreement, he was called upon whenever it was necessary to voice the spirit of some great historic anniversary. And he did not fail those who trusted him. Not all of his orations were masterpieces, any more than all Shakespeare's tragedies were *Othellos*. But he rarely dropped below a high level of performance, and there were vivid moments, even in his old age, when the mantle of Burke seemed to have fallen on his capacious shoulders, and he spoke like a prophet swayed by a divine ecstasy.

Such a glorious moment was provided for Webster on June 17, 1825, at the laying of the corner stone of the Bunker Hill

[1] The day in 1920 was bitterly cold, and Senator Lodge, on the stage of the Old Colony Theatre, wore his overcoat and muffler until he rose to speak. Governor Calvin Coolidge was present, sitting in the chair of Governor Bradford, and, at a dramatic moment, was called on the telephone from San Francisco by Governor Stephens of California. With the audience listening intently, he replied, "Massachusetts and Plymouth Rock greet California and the Golden Gate."

Monument, at Charlestown, then just outside the limits of
Boston. At Plymouth, Webster's immediate audience had
been limited to the small number — about fifteen hundred —
who were privileged to have seats in the First Parish Church;
at Bunker Hill, the listeners included all those who could get
within the range of his powerful voice. Furthermore, the
proximity to Boston increased not only the crowd but also the
publicity which he received. Everybody who heard Webster
at Plymouth realized his preëminence as an orator, but his
supremacy was perhaps not universally conceded until after
the Bunker Hill Address.

When the project of a memorial at Bunker Hill was being
considered, Webster was chosen as a trustee of the Bunker
Hill Monument Association, and later succeeded Governor
John Brooks as its President. After funds had been collected
and a design prepared by the sculptor, Horatio Greenough, had
been approved, it was decided to lay the corner stone on the
fiftieth anniversary of the battle, and Webster's fellow trustees
unanimously requested him to deliver the address. The
importance of the event was heightened by the assurance of the
Marquis de Lafayette that he would be a guest.

Webster prepared himself with unusual care. Until the first
week in May he was detained in Washington on Congressional
business, but he had previously been aware of the honor which
was to be his. He was somewhat disturbed at learning that
Edward Everett was to speak at Concord on the same day, but
the conflict was easily adjusted, and Webster sought refuge on
Cape Cod in order to be free from interruption. There, while
walking about the countryside and fishing for trout, he composed the sentences with which so many generations of schoolboys have become familiar. Fletcher Webster, then almost
thirteen, remembered how, as they waded down the Mashpee
River, — a turbulent little brook in Barnstable County, —
his father, seeming quite abstracted and indifferent to his
sport, would sometimes let his line float carelessly over the
pebbles; and once, as the boy turned a bend, he saw him, as he
stood knee-high in midstream, advance one foot, extend his

right hand, and begin, "Venerable Men!"[1] It was his method of getting ready for the touching reference to the surviving veterans of the fight at Bunker Hill. Although he finished the speech in good season, he was far from being well satisfied with it, and wrote to Ticknor, "There is no more tone in it than in the weather in which it has been written."[2]

Showers on the preceding evening had laid the dust and cooled the air, and the morning of Friday, June 17, dawned with an unclouded sun. The day proved to be ideal for an outdoor ceremony. The city was thronged with visitors. At ten o'clock, from the State House, a colorful civil and military procession left for Charlestown, headed by a company of militia escorting about two hundred former soldiers of the Revolution in open barouches, followed by the Bunker Hill Monument Association, the Masonic Fraternity, in full regalia, with white aprons and blue scarfs, and General Lafayette, who was kept busy waving salutations to people on the sidewalks. Behind him came a long array of patriotic societies, dressed in gorgeous uniforms and carrying banners. Webster himself was in a carriage with the officers of the Bunker Hill Monument Association. So long was the parade that the van had reached the Charlestown Bridge before the rear had left the Common.[3]

The proceedings opened with the laying of the corner stone on the other side of the Hill. There, in accordance with Masonic tradition, the corn, wine, and oil were strewn, and Lafayette spread the cement over the stone, assisted by John Abbot, the Grand Master of the Order. The procession then continued to the other slope, at the foot of which was the platform. On either side, in a semicircle, were seats with awnings, reserved for more than a thousand ladies. On the hillside directly in front were places for the Revolutionary

[1] In his later life, Webster frequently made jocular references to this incident. See National Edition, XVIII, 375.

[2] Curtis, I, 251. Some of Webster's dissatisfaction was doubtless due to his fatigue, for he was a tired man.

[3] The route followed Park, Common, School, Washington, Union, Hanover, and Prince Streets to the Charles River Bridge.

veterans and for the multitude who had marched in the parade. Beyond the benches, in a mass extending to the top, stood countless men and women, eager to catch something, if only a few words, of what was being said. The spectacle was not unlike that which could have been observed in a Greek amphitheatre in the days of Athenian glory. At a conservative estimate there were twenty thousand people assembled on the elevation. Seldom has an orator had a finer audience. To-day, under similar conditions, amplifiers would carry the speaker's words to everybody within a radius of half a mile. Fortunately, Webster's voice had unusual volume and was pitched in a high key, so that it was audible for a considerable distance. George Ticknor Curtis, who, as a small boy, had a position on the outskirts of the throng, remembered that he could hear Webster distinctly.

When silence had been secured, the Reverend Joseph Thaxter, who had been chaplain of Prescott's regiment fifty years before, offered prayer in a tremulous and feeble voice; and then the vast throng, accompanied by a band, sang a hymn written by the Reverend John Pierpont, to the tune of "Old Hundred," beginning : —

> O, is not this a holy spot !
> 'T is the high place of Freedom's birth, —
> God of our Fathers ! Is it not
> The holiest spot on all the earth ?

Then Webster stepped forward, seeming to tower above those around him and to dominate the multitude. As he was about to begin, some of the hastily built seats gave way, and, in spite of all the ushers could do, there was a tumult of confusion. "It is impossible to restore order," said one of the committee in response to Webster's protests. "Nothing is impossible, sir !" thundered Webster, with lowering brow. "Let it be done !" Then, advancing to the front of the platform, he cried in stentorian tones to the marshals, "Be silent yourselves, and the people will obey !" It was as if Zeus had spoken. The edict had gone forth, "Let there be order" — and *there was order!* The commotion ceased.[1] When silence was restored, Webster, with that simplicity which he knew how to make so effective, opened his oration : —

This uncounted multitude before me and around me proves the feeling which the occasion has excited. These thousands of human faces, glowing with sympathy and joy, and from the impulses of a common gratitude turned reverently to heaven in this spacious temple of the firmament, proclaim that the day, the place, and the purpose of our assembling have made a deep impression on our hearts.

It was eminently fitting that Daniel Webster, the son of a Revolutionary veteran, should commemorate the achievements at Bunker Hill. As he confronted that surging mass of humanity, his mind must have turned back to winter evenings in the tavern on the upper Merrimack, when Captain Webster told stories of his campaigns under Washington.[2] Never had he spoken with more sincere emotion than when, with tears in his eyes, he paid his tribute of reverent praise, first to the survivors of Bunker Hill, — of whom forty were present, — then to the veterans of other Revolutionary battles, and finally to Lafayette, who, refusing to take a seat under the pavilion, had joined the old soldiers on their benches in front of the platform. Some of his impassioned sentences were followed by prolonged cheers from the audience, but few could refrain from weeping as he turned dramatically to the "Venerable Men" of Bunker Hill and said, "But, alas! you are not all here. Time and the sword have thinned your ranks." Then came the vivid summary of the changes during the preceding half-century. He closed with the familiar exhortation to his countrymen to enter courageously upon the tasks of defense, preservation, and improvement, and to cultivate a "true spirit of union and harmony."

[1] There are several different versions of this incident, the best of which is that given by Josiah Quincy in his *Figures of the Past*, pp. 136–37. Quincy's chapter entitled " Lafayette on Bunker Hill " is an admirable account of the events connected with the celebration as seen by a participant.

[2] Webster said to Quincy after the speech: " I never desire to behold again the awful spectacle of so many human faces all turned towards me. As I looked at them, a strange idea came into my mind. I thought of what Effie Deans said, in contemplating her execution, that there would be 'seas of faces' looking up at her. There was, indeed, a sea of faces before me at that moment." (*Ibid.*, p. 139.)

As he sat down, there was an impressive interval of silence. Then the applause seemed to come in waves from countless hands. The invited guests, to the number of four thousand, adjourned to a dinner under a broad pavilion at the summit of the hill, sitting at twelve tables each four hundred feet long. Amid noise and confusion, Lafayette, Webster, and many directors of the Bunker Hill Monument Association made brief speeches, and Webster gracefully proposed a toast, "Health and Long Life to General Lafayette!"

In the evening, at their house in Summer Street, the Websters held a grand reception, at which all the notabilities of Boston were present. Colonel Israel Thorndike, Webster's neighbor and friend, had cut a passage through the brick walls which separated the two mansions, and the guests passed freely from one to the other. The street was bright with illuminations, and a military band played selections in what is now called Webster Square. "It was deemed a happy circumstance," wrote Josiah Quincy, "that the intellect of the community in one of these adjoining houses should be backed by its purse in the other." [1] Strangers were there from all over the country — the eccentric Dr. Mitchell, from New York, the poet Hillhouse, — author of the forgotten *Hadad*, — and the reformer, Fanny Wright, with her bobbed hair and feminist theories. Mrs. Webster, although she was evidently pleased at the honors heaped upon her husband, "showed not the slightest symptom of vanity or elation." The costume which she wore on this occasion was the one in which she was painted by Chester Harding in 1827. Webster himself seemed to be the central figure. There may have been for him greater moments in his later life, but never one when his mind was less troubled by apprehension and his personality displayed to better advantage. It seemed a long way back to the intervale at Salisbury and the days when, as a farmer's lad, he had walked barefooted through the meadows.

However dubious Webster may have been at one time regard-

[1] *Figures of the Past*, p. 140. The chapter entitled " Daniel Webster at Home " gives a vivid description of Webster's reception.

ing the quality of the oration, he must have been pleased with its reception. Within a few days he went on a vacation trip with his wife and Justice and Mrs. Story to Niagara Falls, but, before he left, he turned over the manuscript to George Ticknor, who sold it to a publishing house for three hundred dollars, giving the proceeds to the Bunker Hill Monument Association. To its revision in galley proof he devoted much care, making many alterations in phraseology and completely remodeling the section relating to Colonel Prescott. When it finally appeared in a thin octavo volume, it was widely distributed and was later translated into French and other European languages.

Some critics have complained that the Bunker Hill Oration has no originality. One might, with equal justice, object to *Paradise Lost* or to *Macbeth* on the same ground. Webster was not aiming to produce a scholarly treatise, but rather a "patriotic discourse," in which he might sum up the natural emotions of his fellow citizens at a moment when national pride was at its height. It was not a fitting occasion for expounding new theories of government, or for assailing party policies. The references to the revolutions in Greece and in South America, with the suggestion of our sympathy with those downtrodden countries, were most timely and appropriate. Beyond that, Webster wisely did not care to go.

It has also been claimed that the Oration lacks unity — that the speaker wanders from one idea to another, with the result that his remarks have no continuity. But a careful study of Webster's thought and of his skillful methods of transition will show that he had constantly in his mind one central theme — the significance of the Battle of Bunker Hill, with peculiar emphasis on the duty of loyalty to the principles for which it was fought. Again, as in the Plymouth Oration, his optimism and his conservatism were conspicuous. He is sure that "if the true spark of religious and civil liberty be kindled, it will burn." He boasts of the benefit which the example of the United States "has produced, and is likely to produce, on human freedom and human happiness," and adds, with a complacency which is almost amusing, "The last hopes of mankind, therefore, rest with us." He does not urge reforms in our institutions but enjoins upon his fellow countrymen "the great duty of defense and preservation."

Webster's own preference for the Plymouth Oration has not been shared by his biographers, most of whom regard the Bunker Hill Oration as, on the whole, the finest of his occasional addresses. It has a massive grandeur and sweep of imagination which, together with its frequently intense emotional quality, place it beside the great speech of Demosthenes *On the Crown*. In style, also, it is not inferior to the earlier oration. The sentences are not merely rhetoric; "they are rhetoric" — to quote Lodge — "lifted up and illuminated." It is the rolling cadences of his periods, the precision and beauty of his diction, the splendor of his imagery, which have given Webster a legitimate place in American literature.

The Bunker Hill Oration, long studied and recited by children in our public schools, has been used also as a model by innumerable speakers on similar occasions. Some of its phrases have reached the dignity of "familiar quotations." But the fact that it is hackneyed must not obscure its vigor and charm. Although Webster did set the standard for a long succession of imitators, he has yet to be surpassed.

One more noteworthy oration was to round out the series of Webster's occasional addresses during this period of his career. By what was, perhaps, the most astounding coincidence in history, John Adams and Thomas Jefferson died within a few hours of one another on July 4, 1826, exactly half a century after that Declaration of Independence in the framing of which the two men had been inseparably joined. An event so remarkable could not be left uncommemorated; and it was inevitable that the municipality of Boston should turn to the orator of Bunker Hill as the citizen best qualified to do justice to the two Presidents whose almost simultaneous demise had stirred such emotions.

As the date of the ceremonies had been set for August 2, not much time was available, but Webster, under pressure, could work with unflagging rapidity. Again, as in the case of the

Bunker Hill Oration, he was far from pleased with the early drafts. The speech attributed to an opponent of the Declaration, and the supposititious reply made by John Adams, were written, according to Ticknor, on the forenoon of the day before the address was to be delivered. Webster summoned Ticknor to his Summer Street house and declaimed them to him, saying that he was not sure whether they were good enough to be kept. Reassured by his friend's favorable comments, Webster decided not to leave out the passages in question. To-day they are the most frequently quoted sections of the address.

In the morning there was a procession of the Young Men from the State House to the first Church, in Chauncy Street, where Samuel L. Knapp pronounced a discourse.[1] The hour of the chief meeting was twelve o'clock. For the first time in history, Faneuil Hall was draped in mourning, and, in the dim light which seeped through the shaded windows, the auditorium looked like a tomb. An official holiday had been declared, and all places of business were closed. On the platform were President John Quincy Adams, Governor Levi Lincoln, Mayor Josiah Quincy, President Kirkland, of Harvard, and representatives of learned and patriotic societies — a group of remarkably distinguished men. The seats in the body of the auditorium were soon filled, and the doors were closed. But the importunate crowd still left outside became so obstreperous that the programme was interrupted, in spite of all that the constables could do. At this embarrassing moment, Webster repeated what he had done at Bunker Hill. Acting promptly and decisively, he stepped to the front of the stage, and, in tones which carried to the farthest corners of the hall, cried, "Let the doors be opened!" Once again his commands were obeyed, and the portals were swung upon their hinges. The mob surged through, saw that no seats were available, and at once became calm.

---

[1] Samuel Lorenzo Knapp (1783–1838), a graduate of Dartmouth in 1804, studied law with Chief Justice Theophilus Parsons, and, after making a success in his profession, became an editor and author, chiefly of biographical subjects. He published a *Memoir of the Life of Daniel Webster* in 1835, and also wrote lives of De Witt Clinton, Aaron Burr, and Andrew Jackson.

It has been suggested that much of the effect of this and other similar orations of Webster can be explained by the fact that historians and biographers had not as yet covered adequately the early annals of the country. In a sense, Webster was the first in the field. Bancroft and Hildreth and Fiske and Channing were still to come. Incidents which to schoolboys to-day are commonplace had then the aspect of newly discovered truths. It was Webster's distinction in this case to be among the first in New England to summarize the dramatic careers of these two founders of our nation. In some degree, he had been acquainted with both statesmen. With Adams, he had conversed and corresponded on political topics. He had spent several days in December 1824 with George Ticknor as the guest of the venerable Jefferson at Monticello. He knew how each had looked and what views each had held. The account which he gave of their contribution to history was accurate and, allowing for his prejudices, complete and just.

But the address is not remembered mainly because of its value as biography. The sections with the most vitality are those in which Webster, with his creative imagination, carried his listeners back to the days of 1776, when Hancock was presiding over the gathering in Philadelphia. With no authority to justify him, but acting on his acquaintance with conditions as they were in the Continental Congress, he pictured an opponent of the Declaration as he rose to his place and began : "Let us pause! This step, once taken, cannot be retraced. This resolution, once passed, will cut off hope of reconciliation." And then he depicted John Adams, replying in a sentence which every American now knows, "Sink or swim, live or die, survive or perish, I give my hand and heart to this vote." It was this entirely fanciful speech attributed to John Adams which formed the climax of Webster's eloquence and thrilled the audience in Faneuil Hall.

In after days, people came to believe that Adams had actually made the speech which Webster attributed to him, and the latter was frequently obliged to explain the true circumstances. Answering a letter of inquiry on the matter, he said, on January

22, 1846: "So far as I know, there is not existing, in print or manuscript, the speech, or any part or fragment of the speech, delivered by Mr. Adams on the question of the Declaration of Independence. We only know, from the testimony of his auditors, that he spoke with remarkable ability and characteristic earnestness." [1] He once, in a moment of confession, said to President Millard Fillmore: "I will tell you what is not generally known. I wrote that speech one morning before breakfast, in my library, and when it was finished my paper was wet with my tears." [2]

Joseph Hopkinson, Webster's colleague in the Dartmouth College Case and other important legal causes, after praising the "Commemorative Discourse" highly, pointed out that Webster's imaginary argument against the adoption of the Declaration of Independence, though brief, was stronger in reasoning than Adams's supposed plea in its favor. In this shrewd comment, there was much truth. The caution which could lead a statesman to hesitate before venturing on a breach with the mother country was a feeling which Webster could understand. The thoughts which he placed in the mouth of the nameless objector were precisely those which would, under similar circumstances, have occurred to Webster. Just what course Webster would have followed if he had been in Philadelphia in 1776 it is, of course, impossible to surmise, but his conservatism might well have led him to say, "This step, once taken, cannot be retraced," and to add, "I shudder before this responsibility."

Before the end of August, the *Discourse on Adams and Jefferson* was printed in pamphlet form, and Webster was receiving the congratulations of his admirers. On August 3, Josiah Quincy wrote: "Your perfect success yesterday ought to be as satisfactory to you as it is to your friends. I think nothing has ever exceeded or perhaps equalled it." [3] Richard

---

[1] National Edition, I, 326.   [2] Curtis, I, 276.

[3] National Edition, XVII, 408. Quincy reported that some of Webster's auditors had gained the impression that the speech against the Declaration had been attributed to Hancock — which was not, of course, the case. Quincy himself devoted some space to showing that Hancock was probably not opposed to the Declaration.

Rush wrote a complimentary letter describing his delight in the perusal "of so admirable a specimen of discriminating and philosophical eulogy." [1] Jeremiah Mason added his praise to that of many others.

From the very nature of the subject, the *Discourse* was bound to be inferior to the two great orations which had preceded it.[2] The biographical sketches of the two men, outlining the chief facts in their careers, could not be highly emotional. But the eulogy contained one striking passage, which, coming from the most eloquent of Americans, was probably his own definition of what he was trying to do : —

True eloquence, indeed, does not consist in speech. It cannot be brought from far. Labor and learning may toil for it, but they will toil in vain. Words and phrases may be marshalled in every way, but they cannot compass it. It must exist in the man, the subject, and the occasion. Affected passion, intense expression, the pomp of declamation, all may aspire to it; they cannot reach it. It comes, if it comes at all, like the outbreaking of a fountain from the earth, or the bursting forth of volcanic fires, with spontaneous, original, native force. The graces taught in the schools, the costly ornaments and studied contrivances of speech, shock and disgust men, when their own lives, and the fate of their wives, their children, and their country, hang on the decision of the hour.[3]

As an exposition of the qualities of true oratory, this will stand for all time; and, in so far as oratory is an art, these are the attributes which it must possess. It is but just to Webster to add further that, in each of the three orations considered in this chapter, the man was fully equal to the subject and the occasion, great though they were. Ticknor, that invaluable reporter, tells us that on August 2, in Faneuil Hall, "he was in

[1] Curtis, I, 280.

[2] Rufus Choate, however, said to Parker: " Mr. Webster's best oratorical effort was the Adams and Jefferson eulogy. That produced an extraordinary effect." (Parker, p. 252.)

[3] Not long before, on January 17, 1825, Webster had written to Mrs. Ticknor: " The highest enjoyment, almost, which I have in life, is in hearing an able argument or speech. The development of *mind*, in those modes, is delightful. In books, we see the result of thought and of fancy. In the living speaker, we see the thought itself, as it rises in the speaker's own mind." (Curtis, I, 231.)

the perfection of his manly beauty and strength" and that his bearing was that "of absolute dignity and power." "I have never heard him," added Ticknor, "when his manner was so grand and appropriate." He himself did display "the high purpose, the firm resolve, the dauntless spirit, speaking on the tongue, beaming from the eye, informing every feature, and urging the whole man onward, right onward to his subject" — that eloquence of which he said, "It is something greater and higher than eloquence, it is action, noble, sublime, godlike action."

The *Commemorative Discourse* was the last for some years of Webster's formal occas onal addresses. After he became conspicuous in politics, he spoke more frequently in Congress, and, as a campaign "spellbinder," developed an informality which gave him a different style — less serious, more colloquial, and calculated by its ease and humor to appeal to the average voter. He could still, as in the replies to Hayne and Calhoun, display the grandeur of the *Plymouth Oration*, but he was more likely to trust to spontaneity and to the happy inspiration of the moment. The three orations considered in this chapter would, however, be sufficient in themselves to establish him as the foremost of modern American orators.

XIII

A RESTLESS LEGISLATOR

In the year 1820 he [Webster] was a frank disciple of Adam Smith and the *laissez faire* school. . . . His sympathies went strongly for free trade, individual initiative, and a competitive order, — sympathies which to the end of his life he never wholly outgrew.
— PARRINGTON, *The Romantic Revolution in America*

I never felt more down sick on all subjects connected with the public, than at the present moment.
— WEBSTER to JOSEPH STORY, May 12, 1823

WEBSTER was now forty years old. He had a large income, he was healthy and happy, and he had won an enviable professional reputation. Both as lawyer and orator, he was already famous. Yet, out of this contentment, he was slowly drawn into the hazardous vortex of politics. The merchants and bankers who were his clients respected his facile eloquence and insisted that it should not be lost to the community. He was personally so popular in his own neighborhood that he was never defeated for office until he became a candidate for the Presidency — and even then Massachusetts stood by him to the end.

In the autumn of 1820, Webster was chosen as a presidential elector from his district.[1] The electors from Massachusetts, although rated nominally as eight Federalists and seven Republicans, voted as a body for James Monroe. On the Vice Presidency, however, party differences were manifest. Webster

---

[1] At the election, on November 6, 1820, Webster received 3404 votes against 209 for his opponent, the venerable General Henry Dearborn (1751–1829), an uncompromising Democrat, who had a fine Revolutionary record and had been Jefferson's Secretary of War. The Massachusetts delegation, headed by William Phillips and William Gray as delegates-at-large, included John Adams, Benjamin W. Crowninshield, and Asahel Stearns.

and his seven Federalist colleagues refused to cast their ballots for the recognized Republican candidate, Daniel D. Tompkins,[1] but instead supported Richard Stockton, of New Jersey. It was a futile gesture, for Stockton received no other votes.

In 1822, Webster served for a few days in the Massachusetts House of Representatives, as a member from Suffolk County. When the session opened on May 29, Levi Lincoln [2] was elected Speaker. Webster qualified for his seat on the following day, but was appointed to no committees. While the General Court was sitting, he did not participate in the regular business, except by introducing and carrying through a bill making it illegal "to take or catch any pickerel or trout, in any of the rivers, streams, or ponds within this Commonwealth, by day or by night, in any other way or manner, than by hooks and lines."[3] When the Legislature assembled for its second session, Webster, having been elected to Congress, had resigned his place in the Lower House.

Meanwhile he had promoted the transformation of Boston into a city. During the Constitutional Convention of 1820, a resolution had been passed for an inquiry into the expediency of authorizing the Legislature to grant to towns charters of incorporation, with all the forms and privileges of municipal government. As chairman of the committee to which the matter was referred, Webster reported on it favorably. An

---

[1] Daniel D. Tompkins (1774–1825) had been Republican Governor of New York (1807–17) and represented a school of political thought with which Webster had no sympathy. The latter wrote Mason, November 12, 1820: "I have not been able to come to any definite conclusion, on the subject of votes for vice President. . . . There will be a number of us, of course, in this state, who will not vote for Mr. Tompkins, & we must therefore look up somebody to vote for." (National Edition, XVI, 59–60.)

[2] Levi Lincoln (1782–1868), of Worcester, after graduating from Harvard in 1802, had been admitted to the bar and had gradually entered politics, having served in both branches of the Legislature since 1812. He was to be Governor of Massachusetts from 1825 to 1834. He and Webster were almost exact contemporaries and were often thrown together.

[3] See *Laws of Massachusetts*, 1822, Chap. XXI. The measure was approved by Governor John Brooks on June 15. In responding to a toast at Syracuse, New York, in May 1851, Webster alluded to his service in the Massachusetts Legislature and to the bill which he had sponsored regarding fishing. "With that exception," he said, "I never was connected, for an hour, with any State Government in my life. I never held office, high or low, under any State Government." (National Edition, XIII, 422.)

amendment was promptly drafted, adopted by the Convention, and ratified within a few months by the people. It was time, for the census of 1820 gave Boston 43,298 inhabitants, and the rough-and-ready town meeting system was ridiculous for a population of that size. Webster next headed a committee for filing the necessary application to the General Court; and an act making Boston a city was signed by the Governor early in 1822. The charter was accepted on March 4, by a vote of 2797 to 1881. After some bickering between the adherents of Harrison Gray Otis and those of Josiah Quincy, a compromise candidate, John Phillips, was chosen Mayor, and the municipal government was formally inaugurated.

Webster's election to Congress in the autumn of 1822 is proof that, even in a democracy, the office sometimes seeks the man. Representative Benjamin Gorham,[1] tired of Washington life, had refused to accept the honor again, and the Boston journals were assailed with letters calling for the choice of the right person to represent "this commercial and wealthy district." A convention of the "Middling Interest" — composed of small shopkeepers and mechanics, in revolt against the Federalist machine — named Jesse Putnam as their candidate; and three days later, a group of regular Federalist delegates from all the wards in the new city gave Webster a unanimous nomination. A committee, with the influential Colonel Thomas Handasyd Perkins [2] as chairman, and composed also of four other intimate friends of Webster, — William Sullivan, Benjamin Russell, William Sturgis, and J. W. T. Apthorp, — was designated to notify him. One of them, calling on him at his office, said: "Mr. Webster, I come to ask you to throw down your law books and enter the service of the public; for to the public you belong. I know what sacrifices

[1] Benjamin Gorham (1775–1855), son of the patriot, Nathaniel Gorham, had been drafted in 1820 to fill the vacancy left by the resignation of Jonathan Mason, and somewhat unwillingly, had allowed himself to be reëlected to the Seventeenth Congress.

[2] Thomas Handasyd Perkins (1764–1854), one of the most successful of Boston merchants, sat in the Massachusetts General Court for many years and exerted an immense influence on state politics. He was later especially distinguished for his generous philanthropies, including gifts to the Perkins Institute for the Blind, the Massachusetts General Hospital, and the Boston Athenæum.

we demand of you, but we must rely upon your patriotism. We cannot take a refusal." [1]

Such an appeal, from such men, was flattering and irresistible. For Webster, it was the parting of the ways. He had been paying off his father's debts, and his expenses had been heavy. To reënter Congress meant a large monetary sacrifice, for his salary would be only $1800. He liked the law, and was reluctant to abandon his lucrative practice; but with many misgivings, he yielded, and, in the exciting campaign which ensued, heard himself described as an "aristocrat" and a "theorist." On November 4, however, he received 2638 votes against 1557 for Putnam.[2] He was the only one of the thirteen Congressmen from Massachusetts who rose above mediocrity.

The months between his election and the opening of the Eighteenth Congress in December 1823 were, for Webster, a period of despondency on political matters. The success for the first time in many years of a Republican candidate for Governor, William Eustis, over the Nestor of the Federalists, Harrison Gray Otis, did not discourage him, for he had expected that result. But he was chagrined at the failure of Massachusetts leaders to unite on important issues. The Federalist Party had been lifeless since the War of 1812, and its flurried adherents were seeking a new allegiance. The Era of Good Feelings was degenerating into an Era of Discord, out of which a new party alignment was soon to develop. "There is," Webster wrote to Justice Story, "a Federal interest, a Democratic interest, a Bankrupt interest, an Orthodox interest, and a Middling interest, but I see no national interest, nor any national feeling in the whole matter." [3]

Webster, searching during the summer of 1823 for an issue on which he might make himself felt, turned, not to a domestic problem, but to foreign affairs. The revolt of the Greek patriots in 1821 against the tyranny of the Turkish Empire

[1] Curtis, I, 198.

[2] Emerson wrote prophetically in his Diary for that day, "A victory is achieved to-day for one, whose name perchance is written highest in the volume of futurity." (Journals, I, 175.)

[3] National Edition, XVII, 325.

had naturally aroused the sympathy of the American people, who were eager that the Hellenes should gain their independence. Seeing an opportunity for a great speech, Webster prepared himself thoroughly, especially by conferring with Edward Everett, who had recently been in Greece and had written an excellent article on that country in the *North American Review*.[1] Everett, who aspired to be our commissioner to Athens, helped Webster with statistical material and encouraged him to champion the Greek cause.[2]

Mrs. Webster and the children went to Washington and were with him through a winter "as mild as October." The Hall of Representatives had been reopened in the South Wing of the Capitol in 1819, after a complete renovation under the architect, Charles Bulfinch. It was a domed, semicircular chamber,[3] bordered with handsome pillars of Potomac marble, between which, in recesses, were sofas for the relaxation of the members. The canopied throne of the Speaker dominated the auditorium on the straight side. Representatives were furnished with mahogany desks, armchairs, and plenty of writing materials.

[1] October 1823.

[2] Since Webster had taught Everett in the Short Street School in the summer of 1804, the latter had shown an amazing precocity. After graduating from Harvard in 1811 as Valedictorian, he had become a clergyman, and, at nineteen, was elected pastor of the Church in Brattle Square. In 1815, he shifted his profession and was inaugurated as Professor of Greek Literature at Harvard, and set out at once for Europe, where he spent four years and seven months in travel and study. The first person to call upon him after his return to Cambridge in 1819 was Daniel Webster. He was a successful college lecturer, but his restlessness led him to assume, in 1820, the editorship of the *North American Review*. In 1822, he married Charlotte Gray Brooks, daughter of one of the most opulent merchants of Boston, and thus achieved financial independence. In the autumn of 1823, he was nervous and ambitious, eager to go to Greece if possible, and weary of the monotony of academic life. He had written to John Quincy Adams, then Secretary of State, soliciting his aid (Frothingham, *Edward Everett*, p. 77), and Webster himself had spoken about the appointment to Adams (Adams, *Memoirs*, VI, 227). Webster wrote Everett, in November 1823, " If nobody does it who can do it better, I shall certainly say something of the Greeks." (National Edition, XVII, 327.)

[3] This room, now called Statuary Hall, was abandoned for legislative purposes on September 16, 1857, when the present South Wing was completed. It is now filled with statues of more or less famous Americans, each state being allowed to contribute two. Webster's statue, a copy in marble by Carl Conrads of the original by Ball, in the State House Park at Concord, New Hampshire, stands by the door leading to the Capitol Rotunda, with that of General John Stark, New Hampshire's other worthy, on the opposite side of the entrance.

Although each had his individual spittoon, the fine carpet on the floor was streaked and blotched by tobacco juice.[1] The gallery was simply a platform raised a foot or two, with a section reserved for ladies. The acoustics of the hall were very poor, in spite of the experiments of physicists, and the room is still remarkable for its peculiar echoes.

Henry Clay, who had retired from public life in 1821, in order to rehabilitate his finances, had been chosen unopposed from the Lexington district and was elected Speaker. With a desire to propitiate former Federalists and to promote harmony, he named Webster as Chairman of the Committee on the Judiciary.[2] The latter's opportunity came very soon. President Monroe, in his Message, had expressed officially the hope of the United States that Greece might "become an independent power." On December 8, Webster moved a resolution that the expenses of a Commissioner to Greece ought to be defrayed whenever the President should deem it expedient to make such an appointment.

Gossip in the capital had predicted that Webster would signalize his reappearance in the House of Representatives by a brilliant oration; consequently a large and fashionable audience had packed the galleries on the morning of January 19, when he was scheduled to speak. Among them was Everett himself, with whom Webster had been corresponding[3] and who had taken the trip to Washington with his heart full of vague hopes.

The United States, after its altercations with France and England, had developed a strong national self-consciousness,

---

[1] Charles Dickens was astonished, in 1842, " to see an honorable gentleman leaning back in his tilted chair with his legs on the desk before him, shaping a convenient 'plug' with his pen-knife, and when it is quite ready for use, shooting the old one with his mouth as from a pop-gun, and clapping the new one in its place."

[2] William Plumer, who had been Chairman during the previous session, himself voluntarily withdrew and urged Clay to appoint Webster. (Plumer's "Reminiscences," National Edition, XVII, 549.)

[3] Webster wrote Everett, December 21, 1823: "I find your communications of the utmost utility. In regard to the history of the campaigns, I could have done nothing without your aid." (National Edition, XVII, 336.) On several occasions Webster made a handsome acknowledgment of his obligation to Everett for information. On December 6, Webster wrote Everett: "It was, or I am not well informed, stated, yesterday, that there ought to be a commission, and that you ought to be persuaded to go. Go you will and go you shall — if you choose to do so." (Frothingham, p. 78.)

which sometimes broke out in bluster and braggadocio. Only a few weeks had gone by since Monroe, in the historic doctrine associated with his name, had asserted "that the American continents, by the free and independent condition which they have assumed and maintain, are henceforth not to be considered as subjects for future colonization by any European powers." In plain language, he had warned Europe away from the Western Hemisphere. It was this moment which Daniel Webster selected to denounce the edicts of Old World monarchs. For a young country we were doing very well.

So obvious were the expectations of his hearers that Webster at once disclaimed any intention of dazzling them by rhetoric. Ignoring the temptation to sentimental appeal, he entered upon an analysis of the nature, extent, and motives of the Holy Alliance, pointing out that it had advanced two very dangerous principles: first, "that all popular or constitutional rights are held no otherwise than as grants from the crown"; and second, "the right of forcible interference in the affairs of other states." With regard to the specific issues involved in the Hellenic uprising, Webster declared that the Greeks had "awakened a sympathy throughout Europe and throughout America." He insisted that his resolution involved no breach of neutrality, but was intended solely to gain information. His object was not only to encourage the Greeks, but also to make a protest against "the doctrines of the Allied Powers. . . ." The really significant portion of the speech, however, was his contrast between our "regulated" government with the "absolute" governments of Europe, to the appalling disadvantage of the latter. The complacency which he all unconsciously displayed was a buoyant manifestation of our growing nationalism. It was the cry of a youthful and assertive people insisting on being heard.[1]

In his missionary zeal for guiding the world towards democracy, Webster glowed with romantic idealism. The theory that we should "stand aloof" while the Greeks struggled heroically against tyranny seemed to him unworthy of an

[1] The speech is printed in National Edition, V, 60–93.

enlightened government.[1]   It would be injudicious to interfere by means of armies or warships, but we could at least
bring to bear the mighty force of public opinion — a force
which military duress may silence, but which cannot be
permanently crushed.   Such was Webster's confident optimism
in 1824.

Webster's speech provoked a brisk discussion, in the course
of which he enjoyed the satisfaction of being supported by
Henry Clay.   Chivalry and humanitarianism and romance
were on his side, but the administration was against the
proposal.   John Randolph commented caustically on the
"Quixotism" of Webster and Clay, and the cooler heads in
the House shrank from bringing the question to vote.   Soon
the matter was quietly dropped.   But Webster, acting on the
advice of his friend, Joseph Hopkinson,[2] and others, revised
the proofs of his address, and it was translated into several
modern languages, including Greek and Spanish.   Webster
once declared that he was "more fond of this child than of any
of the family." [3]

The matter of the Greeks produced a torrent of oratory, but
the issue which precipitated the most lively discussion was
much less glamorous.   According to some gloomy observers,
the United States was undergoing a commercial depression,
from which the only relief was through higher tariff duties for
the creation of home markets and the stimulation of domestic
industry.   Under Clay's direction, what he called the "American System" was brought before Congress, its chief features
being increases in the duties on iron, hemp, and cotton and

[1] The Greeks had received outside assistance. Lord Byron had landed on the
peninsula on August 3, 1823, and his actions received wide publicity. He reached
Missolonghi on January 5, 1824, and died there of fever on April 19, 1824.

[2] Hopkinson wrote Webster, February 1, 1824: " You are generally too careless
of yourself and your reputation; and, content with doing a thing well, you have too
little solicitude about the proof of it to the world." (National Edition, XVII, 343.)

[3] Curtis, I, 205. Jeremiah Mason wrote to Webster, February 1, 1824: " In my
opinion your first speech is the best example of Parliamentary eloquence and statesmanlike reasoning that our country can show. You were eminently judicious in avoiding
all declamation on the ancient glories of Greece, to which the subject so obviously
led." (Cong. Lib. MSS. I.)

woolen goods. The avowed object was the special encouragement of manufacturing; and those districts devoted principally to shipping or to agriculture were alarmed. Since 1789, the needs of shipowners and importers had determined, in a large degree, our economic policy. The proposed change of beneficiaries, affecting the pocketbooks of both laborers and capitalist, was bound to stir up trouble. Ultimately — although such a result was probably not foreseen — it brought about a sectional division culminating in a serious breach between North and South.

Webster was a philosophical realist, with an intensely practical mind. His conviction that sound business prosperity is produced mainly by "freedom of commercial intercourse and unrestrained individual action" led him early to espouse the doctrine of *laissez faire*, and to make a public confession of his faith in 1820, at Faneuil Hall. Since then, he had seen no reason for modifying his views. Belief in free trade was, with him, less the consequence of idealistic speculation than of a feeling that enterprise should be untrammeled, dependent only upon certain well-understood natural laws, such as that of supply and demand. Webster was rarely a theorist. We do not find him consorting with the visionaries and prophets of Concord or Brook Farm. He and Emerson were, in their meditations, as far apart as Hamilton and Jefferson. Accepting mundane affairs as he found them, Webster exercised his statesmanship in ameliorating conditions in industry, improving methods of government, and framing a wiser code of laws. Furthermore he had a strong sense of the importance of private property and of its rights and privileges. Sitting around the shining mahogany of State Street financiers, he developed perhaps an exaggerated sense of their proportionate significance in our scheme of things. The tariff was to him a question not of morals but of expediency, and he was ready to shift his views with changed conditions. For the moment he was concerned about the disastrous consequences to the caulkers and riggers and rope-makers, as well as to the merchants and importers, of New England. His sense of its injustice to his constituents led him to assail Clay's "American System" wherever it was vulnerable.

Like most tariff measures, this was built up by concession and compromise, in an attempt to secure enough votes for its passage. Over its technical details the House battled week after week, with Webster entering only seldom into the debate.[1] Finally, on the last two days of March, Henry Clay, descending from the Speaker's rostrum, addressed the Committee of the Whole at some length, emphasizing the economic distress through the land and maintaining that it could easily be relieved if we would follow the example of England and adopt systematic protection. Such a policy would, he claimed, benefit all the diverse interests in the United States. His speech was ingenious, brilliant, and plausible, in spite of its superficiality and the speciousness of his reasoning, and Webster was aware that he was expected to answer it.[2]

No orator can be expected to become lyric over the tariff, but Webster, having displayed his emotional powers in his address on the Greeks, now showed that he was capable of close-knit, statistical argument. His speech, delivered on April 1 and 2, not only exposed Clay's sophistry, but also correlated all the most forceful evidence against the protective theory.[3] He asserted that it was absurd to describe as an "American policy" a practice which America had never

[1] In a letter to Everett, February 13, 1824, Webster described the tariff as " a tedious, disagreeable subject," and added, " I am aware that something is expected of me, much more than I shall perform." (National Edition, XVII, 345.) On March 14, he wrote to Ezekiel: " The tariff is yet undecided. It will not pass, I think, in its present shape, and I doubt if it will pass at all. As yet I have not interfered much in the debate, partly because there were others more desirous to discuss the details than I am, and partly because I have been so much in the court." (*Ibid.*, p. 347.) On April 10, he wrote to Justice Story, " My impression rather is, that the bill will hardly get through our House." (*Ibid.*, p. 349.)

[2] Afterwards, Webster wrote Mason, " I was not expecting to speak at that time, nor ready to do so. And from Mr. Clay's ending, I had but one night to prepare." (*Ibid.*, XVI, 84.)

[3] As soon as the bill was printed, Webster sent fifty copies to the best-informed merchants, manufacturers, and business men among his acquaintance, asking for their detailed criticism. From the statistics and comments which he received he derived the material for his argument. (Plumer's " Reminiscences," National Edition, XVII, 550.)

tried; that Clay's melancholy picture of business depression was much exaggerated; that British authorities were beginning to question the wisdom of high protective duties; and that there was a fundamental difference between affording "reasonable encouragement" to existing manufactures and, by the virtual prohibition of imports, raising up an artificial production of goods which would not normally be made. He closed by presenting specific objections to the proposed duties on iron, hemp, and copper, which were bound to augment greatly the cost of building ships. This speech, replete with statistics, showed a comprehensive understanding of the situation and established him as an authority on economic problems.[1]   In his final sentence, he summed up his conclusions: —

There are some parts of this bill which I highly approve; there are others in which I should acquiesce; but those to which I have now stated my objections appear to me so destitute of all justice, so burdensome and so dangerous to that interest which has steadily enriched, gallantly defended, and proudly distinguished us, that nothing can prevail upon me to give it my support.

As in every tariff debate, the disputants were actuated chiefly by their own selfish interests, or those of their constituents. The bill of 1824 was strongly assailed by Southern Congressmen and defended by those from New York, Pennsylvania, and Ohio. When, after a discussion lasting ten weeks, the matter was finally brought to a vote, several sick members were carried in on stretchers, and keen excitement reigned. It passed on April 16 by a vote of 107 to 102. A careful analysis made by Frederick J. Turner [2] shows that the Ohio Valley and the Middle states, where manufacturing flourished, were in

[1] Carl Schurz, in his *Henry Clay*, declared that Webster's speech "stands to-day as his strongest utterance upon economic subjects." Webster was not himself very proud of what he had done. He wrote Mason, April 19, 1824: "My speech will be printed, and you will get it. Whatever I have done in other cases, I must say that in this I have published it against my own judgment. . . . The ideas are right enough, I hope, but as a speech it is clumsy, wanting in method, and tedious." (National Edition, XVI, 84.) There is an excellent analysis of Webster's argument in Carey's *Daniel Webster as an Economist*, p. 134 ff.

[2] Turner, *The Rise of the New West*, p. 242.

alliance against the Southern states and New England.   Massachusetts was in an anomalous position.   Although textile
production had developed amazingly, the manufacturers
themselves were not yet active in demanding protection.
Shipowners and traders were, however, zealously guarding
their own interests, and it was for them that Webster was most
concerned.   In the end, he voted against the bill, as did all
but one of the Massachusetts delegation.   In spite of his
prediction, it was also approved by a small majority in the
Senate, although somewhat modified through the efforts of
the friends of navigation.

Daniel Webster had never had a busier spring.   His Committee on the Judiciary held protracted meetings, at which he
was always prepared for the business on hand, and he argued
several cases before the Supreme Court, including *Gibbons* v.
Ogden and some important causes involving the Bank of the
United States.   According to Plumer, he exerted on all important questions "a controlling influence which was felt and
acknowledged in every part of the House."   The "great business of the session" for him, however, was securing the passage
of an act for the payment, under the Florida Treaty of 1819,
of claims against Spain because of the depredations of Spanish
cruisers on American commerce in 1788–89.   Webster was chief
counsel for the claimants, and, when settlement was finally
made, he received fees amounting to more than $70,000.[1]   Even
after Congress adjourned on May 27,[2] he was detained as a

[1] Webster had made, on July 27, 1821, an agreement with several claimants, including Peter C. Brooks, Gorham Brooks, Stephen Higginson, and other well-known
Bostonians, stipulating that he should receive 5 per cent of the amount actually awarded,
provided this should not exceed $20,000.   This agreement was waived in 1823 so that
Webster's compensation would be increased.   The bill was opposed in the House by
Clay and Randolph, but was finally passed.   See National Edition, XVI, 84, 86, and 88,
and Curtis, I, 287.   Webster, in part payment of the claims, received a draft for
$777,426.29, dated June 12, 1824, and made out to him as attorney for the Boston
Marine Insurance Company and forty-two other claimants with whom settlement
was being made (Senate Exec. Doc. No. 74, 49th Congress, 1st Session).

[2] On the last evening of the session, Congressman Enoch Lincoln, of Maine, composed some verse couplets, beginning: —

> What guardian power my country's glory keeps,
> When Senates doze, and e'en her Webster sleeps?

For the full version, see National Edition, XVII, 337.

member of the Special Committee to investigate charges of official misconduct brought by Ninian Edwards, just appointed Minister to Mexico, against William H. Crawford, the Secretary of the Treasury.[1] Webster sent his family north in early June, and, on June 16, wrote to George Blake, "I trust I shall get away before the week is out. I am homesick — homesick — homesick." [2] He did not reach Boston, however, until the month was nearly over.

The complicated presidential contest of 1824, the entry list for which had been thrown open as soon as Monroe entered upon his second term, was now drawing to a close. The candidates, by a process of elimination, had been reduced to four Republicans: Henry Clay, John Quincy Adams (then Secretary of State), the imposing William H. Crawford, and General Andrew Jackson, a turbulent and ominous figure on the political horizon. Webster's first choice had been Calhoun, and, even after the latter's withdrawal, Webster advocated his nomination for second place on the ticket.[3]

It might have been supposed that Webster would turn naturally to Adams, as a fellow Massachusetts man. But the New England Federalists distrusted and disliked John Quincy Adams.[4] One of them by inheritance, he had turned Republican at the time of the Embargo, and, for this apostasy, had never been forgiven. Temperamentally the austere and unamiable Adams was far apart from Webster, and each was uncomfortable with the other. Webster and the Federalists

[1] On this committee was John Randolph, who, before its sittings were over, sailed for Europe, leaving an open letter addressed to his constituents in which he claimed the credit for having persuaded the committee to give Crawford an opportunity of replying to Edwards's accusations. When this was published, each member declared its statements to be unfounded. This episode led to Randolph's challenge to Webster in the following session. For fuller details see Benton, *Thirty Years in the U. S. Senate,* I, 34. Crawford was completely exonerated.

[2] National Edition, XVII, 353.

[3] Webster wrote Ezekiel, " I hope all New England will support Mr. Calhoun for the Vice-Presidency."

[4] Webster wrote Jeremiah Mason, in 1823, regarding Adams: " My impression of that Gentleman's character, though high and favorable, in some respects, is, in others, so little satisfactory, that I hardly know what to *wish,* in regard to the future." (National Edition, XVI, 75.)

had no intention of declaring for Adams unless they could be sure of generous treatment. The backing of the administration belonged to Crawford, but his attack of paralysis in September 1823 had made it seem doubtful whether he could endure a campaign. Webster seems not to have thought seriously of Clay's chances, and he regarded Jackson as wild and irresponsible.

Webster was not present at the Congressional caucus at which, on February 14, 1824, a small group of Republican members came out openly for Crawford and Gallatin. Although Adams suspected him to be quietly working for Crawford,[1] Webster was really moving with caution, taking pains not to commit himself. He was coming to realize that it would be fatal to his political future not to join the Adams ranks,[2] but he held back from any public declaration. At the election in November, he was chosen with no opposition for a second term in Congress, and the Adams ticket swept Massachusetts, 30,687 to 6616. In the nation at large, however, Jackson, to the dismay of incredulous conservatives, had the largest popular support, and could count on 99 electoral votes, against 84 for Adams, 41 for Crawford, and 37 for Clay.

The battle was now carried to the House of Representatives, where, with Clay automatically eliminated, it was narrowed to a three-cornered fight, with Jackson and Adams in the lead. Between these two, Webster could not long be in doubt, but he did not intend to announce his preference without securing from Adams some sort of pledge. He took care, through William Plumer, to let Adams know of his desire to be appointed Minister to England, but the Secretary of State did not warm to the suggestion.[3] In late January, Clay and Adams had a

[1] Adams, *Memoirs*, VI, 391.

[2] On June 5, 1824, Webster wrote Ezekiel: "Mr. Crawford is *sick — very sick*. And recent events have appeared very favorable to Mr. Adams. In the event of Mr. C.'s death, (which I anticipate) Mr. Adams will be chosen by the people & by a great vote. If Mr. Crawford survives, I still think Mr. Adams's chance the best, at present, greatly. Genl. Jackson's interest is evidently on the *wane*." (National Edition, XVI, 88.)

[3] On December 14, 1824, Adams wrote, "Plumer mentioned to me a late conversation that he had had with Webster, who is panting for the Mission to London,

conference, at which the former urged the propitiation of Webster.[1] At last Webster himself took a decisive step. When he was consulted by Henry R. Warfield, who held the determining vote in the Maryland delegation, Webster advised him to stand by Adams, saying: —

For myself, I am satisfied, and shall give him my support, cheerfully and steadily. And I am ready to say that I should not do so, if I did not believe that he would administer the government on liberal principles, not excluding Federalists, as such, from his regard and confidence.[2]

Webster next showed the above paragraph to Adams and extracted from him the vague promise that, if elected President, he should feel it his duty, by some appointment, to indicate his disregard of party distinctions. At once Webster became ardent in Adams's behalf.[3] Immediately after his interview, he wrote to Ticknor, "It is confidently believed that New England will give a President, *Kentucky concurrente*" — this last phrase referring to the probability that Clay would throw his votes to Adams.

The result was apparent in the House of Representatives, where the New Englander was chosen on the first ballot, carrying thirteen states, against seven for Jackson and four for Crawford. Webster voted for Adams, as did twelve of the thirteen in the Massachusetts delegation; he was one of the tellers, with John Randolph, of Roanoke, and was deputed to make the announcement of the election; and he was

---

and sounding Plumer's hopes and purposes"; and, on January 17, 1825, he made another entry: " Plumer spoke again about Webster, and his ambition to go as Minister to England, which I thought might be gratified, but not immediately." (Adams, VI, 442.) Plumer, in his Diary for December 7, 1824, recorded his conversation with Webster, and added: " I have known for the last eight months his wish to succeed Mr. Rush at the Court of London, though he never told me of it before. He would make an excellent minister; and I would gladly see him there; but he is not very likely to get the appointment." (National Edition, XVII, 553.)

[1] *Ibid.*, p. 483.
[2] *Ibid.*, p. 378.
[3] On February 16, Adams had a long talk with Webster, and made the entry: " He will serve the next Congress as a member, and not stand against J. W. Taylor as Speaker. Will be glad, at a proper time, to go abroad." (Adams, VI, 511.)

appointed chairman of the committee to notify Adams of the decision. Thus Daniel Webster was early identified with the new administration and became its recognized supporter.

In early December 1824, Webster was back in Washington, this time without his family, and took lodgings on Pennsylvania Avenue, where he rented two rooms and had a servant, Charles, to look after his needs. He at once set out, with Mr. and Mrs. George Ticknor, on a trip to the homes of Madison and Jefferson. They left the capital on December 9, by steamboat to Fredericksburg, and then by a carriage and four horses to Madison's estate, where they were received hospitably and remained four days. Madison and Webster, reconciled since their antagonism during the War of 1812, had much to discuss, and the latter was confirmed in his opinion that Madison was "the wisest of our Presidents, except Washington."

The travelers next rode thirty-two miles to Monticello, being greeted not far from the hill by Jefferson himself, on horseback, his appearance indicating "an extraordinary degree of health, vivacity, and spirit." There they lingered for five days, detained by heavy rains, which swelled the streams. The Ticknors and Webster joined in preparing a careful record of Jefferson's conversation, which was written down by Mrs. Ticknor, as amanuensis, at a tavern, on the night after leaving Monticello.[1] Jefferson was nearly eighty-one, but his mind was clear and his memory unimpaired.

Of all history's strange contrasts, few are more striking than that between Thomas Jefferson, Republican, of Virginia, and Daniel Webster, Federalist, of Massachusetts. The one was tall, rangy, and stooping, with protruding neck and long arms and legs; the other, while not short, was stocky, with broad chest and massive body. Jefferson was slovenly in dress, with a gray surtout coat, a kersey waistcoat, long and loose pantaloons, woolen stockings, and shoes run down at the heel;

[1] The original "Notes of Mr. Jefferson's Conversation" are extant in a neatly written pamphlet preserved in the archives of the New Hampshire Historical Society. George Ticknor, after Webster's death, furnished an account of the journey in a memorandum to George Ticknor Curtis. (Curtis, I, 222–26.)

Webster was the well-groomed and immaculate man of affairs. The older man was the representative of a group of idealistic founders of a new nation; the other, in his prime, was the leading figure of a generation facing problems undreamed of by the men of 1776 and 1789. Jefferson, the owner of countless acres, was the country gentleman, the spokesman of agrarian interests; Webster, the son of an impoverished farmer, owed his place in Congress and his financial welfare to bankers and merchants. Jefferson, an aristocrat by birth, had become the champion of the people; Webster, of humbler origin, was the favorite of the "upper classes." Jefferson had spent much of his career in defending the rights of the individual states; while Webster was the equally zealous advocate of the authority of the Federal Union.

Next to John Marshall, Webster had done, and was to do, more to overthrow Jefferson's theories than any one man. Their views on the Dartmouth College Case had been diametrically opposed; later, in several momentous causes, Webster had argued successfully for the supremacy of the Federal government over the states; and he was to assail doctrines which, to the Virginian, seemed vital. It was the first and last meeting between the two great Americans. They did not converse much on contemporary affairs, although Jefferson did declare that General Jackson was unfit for the Presidency.[1] But they discussed Revolutionary times, French society and literature, and particularly Jefferson's experiment with the University of Virginia, which they rode over to Charlottesville to see. Webster left with a genuine respect for the older statesman [2] — a respect which he was soon to express in his *Eulogy on Adams and Jefferson*.

While he was on this journey, Webster received news of the

[1] Jefferson's exact words were: "I feel much alarmed at the prospect of seeing General Jackson President. He is one of the most unfit men I know of for such a place. He has had very little respect for laws or constitutions and is, in fact, an able military chieftain. His passions are terrible." (National Edition, XVII, 371.)

[2] Writing to William Plumer, December 18, from Monticello, Webster said: "I have found my visit here very pleasant. It has not only gratified a natural desire to see a distinguished & extraordinary man, but allowed an opportunity for much interesting & instructive conversation." (*Ibid.*, XVI, 92.)

illness of his youngest son, Charles,[1] who was not quite two years old.   The boy died on December 18, while Webster was detained at Monticello by the bad weather, and he found the sad tidings awaiting him on his return.   It was a terrible shock, for, when he left Boston, the child was in normal health.   In his loneliness and gloom, he wrote, on a Saturday evening in January, some verses which are pathetically sincere: —

> The staff, on which my years should lean,
> Is broken, ere those years come o'er me;
> My funeral rites thou should'st have seen,
> But thou art in the tomb before me.
>
> Thou rear'st to me no filial stone,
> No parent's grave with tears beholdest;
> Thou art my ancestor, my son!
> And stand'st in Heaven's account the oldest.[2]

It was fortunate that Webster, oppressed by grief,[3] had his Congressional duties to occupy his mind.   The criminal code of the United States, unaltered since the First Congress, was badly in need of revision.   Justice Story had prepared in 1818 a bill which had been introduced in the House but not passed; and he now, with his friend, Webster, as Chairman of the Judiciary Committee, hoped for better results.   Apparently he drew up the necessary code and submitted it to Webster, who, after it had been somewhat modified in the Committee on the Judiciary, reported it to the House.[4]   The act "more

---

[1] Charles was said to bear a marked physical resemblance to his father.

[2] The entire nine stanzas are printed in the National Edition, XVII, 376–77.

[3] Webster missed the companionship of Mr. and Mrs. Ticknor, who left Washington in January 1825.   He wrote the latter, February 4, " I begin to see *home* at the end of no long prospect, and all these things create a little activity and bustle, which serve, in some poor measure, to fill up such portions of time as I usually passed in your house, while you remained here."   (*Ibid.*, XVI, 97.)

[4] According to William Wetmore Story, the entire 26 sections were drafted by Joseph Story (Story, I, 439–40), to whom Webster never assigned proper credit.   The fact that Justice Story and Webster remained intimate friends long after 1825 would seem to dispose of the idea that the former was unjustly treated.   Abner A. Goodell, in the Proceedings of the Massachusetts Historical Society, June 1901, wrote: " Webster did well to appreciate the erudition of this friend, not much his senior, and better still to cultivate a friendship by which he could readily avail himself of it."

effectually to provide for the punishment of certain crimes against the United States, and for other purposes," was passed and signed by the President on March 3, 1825, after Webster had guided it skillfully through Congress. A few amendments were made, making it more palatable to those who were jealous of the authority of the individual states, and it finally emerged as "one of the great monuments of constructive legislation," the merits of which have been especially appreciated by lawyers.[1] There need be no dispute regarding the responsibility for this measure. There is honor sufficient both for Story, who probably created it, and for Webster, who secured its passage.

Webster's conception of the Constitution led him to the conclusion that Congress had full power to carry out a policy of "internal improvements," and he had an opportunity to express himself on the subject in the course of a debate over a project for continuing the Cumberland Road — a great national highway starting at Baltimore and extending west — from Wheeling to Zanesville, Ohio. Interpreting the Constitution liberally, he maintained that it was the business of Congress to consider what would be of most benefit to the country as a whole. His object in urging the construction of the great highway was to open up the public lands of the West to Eastern settlement; and when McDuffie, of South Carolina, drew a doleful picture of the depletion of the population along the Atlantic Coast, Webster announced himself in favor of letting economic movements take their natural course. If any of his constituents wished to settle on the Kansas or the Missouri, they should be encouraged to go. Such doctrines raised Webster's prestige beyond the Alleghenies, and it was not long before he was identified in a financial way with the development of the Northwest. Plumer declared that Webster's influence exerted against this project would have been fatal to its success.

[1] Until this code was adopted, many crimes, including rape, burglary, and arson, were beyond the reach of punishment in the federal courts. Story and Webster, because of their practical experience in the courts, were exceptionally well qualified to know what the situation required.

In February, Webster was again drawn into a quarrel with that half-insane fanatic, John Randolph. Webster, on the floor of Congress, had denied the truth of Randolph's aspersions on the Special Committee for the investigation of the charges against Crawford; whereupon Randolph, on February 20, sent Colonel Thomas H. Benton to Webster, bearing a challenge to a duel.[1] The details of the affair were later mysteriously concealed, by agreement between the principals. Apparently, however, Webster drafted a reply in which he declined a meeting, and later Benton was able to effect an amicable adjustment, as a consequence of which Randolph's challenge was returned to Benton and Webster's answer was burned. Webster conducted himself with dignity and lost no credit in the affair. The matter was kept out of the newspapers, but was revived in 1831 through a gossipy letter sent to the New York *Commercial Advertiser* by its Washington correspondent, recounting the story of the original challenge. Randolph had evidently talked too much, and the facts had leaked out. Benton at once wrote to Webster, who disclaimed any responsibility for the published version, and, after Benton had sent to Webster two or three verbose and pompous communications, the latter declared that the correspondence was closed. The incident has received far more attention than it deserves.[2]

There was some talk of Webster as a member of Adams's cabinet, but he was only too well aware that it was baseless.[3] The place which he wanted was the English Mission,[4] but

[1] William Plumer saw Senator Benton deliver the challenge to Webster while the House was in session. Webster, who was sitting on a sofa in one of the recesses, read the letter, folded it up, paused a moment, and then opened it and perused it again, as if doubtful of its import. He answered Benton in a grave manner, and after a few moments of deep meditation returned to his desk as if nothing had happened. (Plumer's "Reminiscences," National Edition, XVII, 553.)

[2] Fisher, *The True Daniel Webster*, Preface, pp. viii–xii. For Webster's letters to Benton in 1832, see National Edition, XVI, 102–7.

[3] Webster wrote to Mason, February 14, 1825: "It is not necessary, in writing to you, to deny the rumor, or rumors, which the press has circulated, of a place provided for me. There is not a particle of probability of any such offer." (*Ibid.*, p. 100.)

[4] Webster wrote Clay, April 7, 1825: "I have heard nothing, since I left Washington, respecting the English mission. If any thing has occurred, not improper for me to know, I should be glad to learn it from you at your leisure; and I shall be gratified also to hear from you on other subjects and occasions." (*Ibid.*, p. 109.)

Adams never really trusted Webster and was not inclined to gratify his aspirations. When the cabinet was announced, the President retained Southard, McLean, and Wirt of the previous administration, and named Richard Rush as Secretary of the Treasury, Barbour as Secretary of War, and — to the delight of Jacksonian scandalmongers — Clay as Secretary of State. The charge of a corrupt coalition between Adams and Clay aroused no small amount of excitement in Washington, but Webster was not involved. He remained long enough in the capital to hear Adams read his inaugural address from the Speaker's desk, and then returned North, to prepare and deliver his Bunker Hill Oration and take a recreation trip to Niagara Falls. When he went back to Congress in the late autumn, he was accompanied by Mrs. Webster and their three children, Daniel, Julia, and Edward. Edward Everett had been elected to the Nineteenth Congress, and he and his wife were friendly with the Websters, who took them under their wing, and instructed them in the niceties of Washington etiquette.

Webster wanted to succeed Henry Clay as Speaker, and probably could have been elected if he had but said the word.[1] He had already, however, promised Adams that he would not be a candidate. The President apparently wished Webster to remain on the floor, where his ability in debate would be of service to the administration. Until the very day when Congress met, Webster was undecided what course to take, for he did not trust Adams's rather vague promises; but he finally decided not to begin by antagonizing the President, and John W. Taylor, a New York statesman opposed to the extension of slavery, was elected on the second ballot. It was soon apparent that party lines, almost obliterated since the war with England, were once more forming, and that the Adams administration was to have strong opposition. The President himself precipitated a battle by somewhat unnecessarily asserting, in his first message, his conviction that the Con-

[1] Webster wrote Mason, December 11, 1825: "Some of my friends thought that I might have obtained some votes for that place, but I wholly declined the attempt. If practicable to place me there, it would not have been prudent." (National Edition, XVI, 117.)

stitution should be liberally interpreted and that "internal improvements" were desirable. These were doctrines of which Webster approved, but their promulgation at that moment was not shrewd political strategy.

The judiciary system of the United States had long been in need of revision, and various efforts had been made, without success, in earlier Congresses to bring about some reform. As Chairman of the Judiciary Committee in the House, Webster now resolved to see what he could do. For many months Justice Story and he had discussed the matter, both in private conversation and by correspondence,[1] and they had undoubtedly talked it over fully during their journey to Niagara Falls during the preceding summer. Their familiarity with the procedure and personnel of the Federal Courts gave them an advantage over others who had undertaken the task; and Webster brought back with him to Washington a bill which they had carefully prepared.

There had been since 1807 seven justices on the Supreme Bench, each of whom was allotted to one of the circuit districts. As only one of these districts was outside the Atlantic states, Webster proposed to increase the number of judges to ten and to create three new circuits covering the Western states. So far as he could tell, the system was satisfactory in the East, but the West was not adequately served. He was also in favor of having the justices continue with their circuit duties, feeling that it offered them an opportunity of testing the nation's pulse.

Webster introduced his measure just before Christmas in 1825, and spoke for it on January 4, 1826, in an argument which, for fairness, lucidity, and frankness, shows him at his best. It was not a question on which party lines should have been drawn, and logic was of some avail. By sheer force of reason and the exercise of conciliation, he carried the plan

---

[1] Replying to queries, Story wrote Webster, January 4, 1824, giving him some excellent advice (Story, I, 435–37). On January 10 he continued his suggestions, saying, "The more I reflect, with regard to the dignity of the Court duty, and the permanent interest of the nation, the more I am satisfied that the best change will be by adding two Judges to the Supreme Court." (Story, I, 438–39.) Webster, who had the highest respect for Story's attainments and judgment, consulted him on all the details of the proposed measure.

through the House,[1] and, in his elation, felt confident that it would also pass the Senate.[2] But its progress was halted in the Upper House. The Jacksonians, distrusting any project from an administration source, were suspicious; they may, furthermore, have been reluctant to entrust Adams with the appointment of three additional Supreme Court justices. Even the Western Senators, representing the section which would chiefly benefit by the reorganization, were only lukewarm in their support. In his optimism, Webster underestimated the growing antagonism to Adams.[3] Certain amendments were proposed in the Senate to which the House would not agree;[4] no plan of compromise was feasible, and Webster's hopes of reform were frustrated by the obstinacy of politicians.

The smouldering flame of animosity between the Jacksonians and the President was fanned into a conflagration by what at first seemed a gentle breeze from the South. An invitation had been received from some of the Central American states to attend a Congress at Panama, one object of which, although not specifically announced, was a union of the new republics against a possible European foe. Clay, who had dreams of a league of American nations, believed that it was sound policy for us to send delegates; and he won over the President to his point of view. It was indeed an opportunity for the United States to assume the leadership in a Pan-American Alliance which should counterbalance the European "Holy Alliance." On December 26, 1825, Adams, in a Special Message to the Senate, announced that he had accepted the invitation and had nominated Richard C. Anderson, of Kentucky, and John Sergeant, of Pennsylvania, — both well-qualified men, — as

---

[1] Story wrote to Denison, March 15, 1826, regarding Webster's speeches, "Our friend Webster greatly distinguished himself on this occasion, and in the estimation of all competent judges, was *primus inter pares*." (Story, I, 494.)

[2] Webster wrote, January 29, 1826, to Ezekiel: "The judiciary bill will probably pass the Senate, as it left our House. There will be no difficulty in finding perfectly safe men for the new appointments." (National Edition, XVII, 401.)

[3] On May 2, Webster wrote Mason regarding the Judiciary Bill, "It may possibly be lost, but I think it will not be." (National Edition, XVI, 128.)

[4] On May 9, Webster wrote Edward Cutts: "The *Judiciary Bill* will be lost, I have no doubt. The Senate adhere to their amendments, & I have no expectation the H. R. will agree to them." (*Ibid.*, p. 132.)

envoys to Panama. Adams's statement was perfectly regular, and, for him, unusually tactful. It was an item of business which would ordinarily have passed without comment. But watchful eyes were seeking a possible issue. Webster saw the clash coming, for he wrote Justice Story, as the year ended: "An opposition is evidently brewing. It will show itself on the Panama question." [1] Soon it became — to quote Thomas H. Benton — "a master subject on the political theatre during its day." [2]

The true motives of the opposition are somewhat difficult to disentangle. Many Southerners wished our government to have nothing to do with the new republics, which had abolished negro servitude, were endeavoring to suppress the slave trade, and were even considering the recognition of the "black republic" of Haiti. Some statesmen felt quite honestly that we ought not to involve ourselves in the affairs of other nations, even upon this continent. There were also strategists who merely seized upon the occasion as favorable for bringing the administration into ill-repute. These divergent groups, united in their antagonism towards John Quincy Adams, made a considerable show of strength. They controlled the Committee on Foreign Relations in the Senate, but that body itself refused to concur in the Committee's adverse report, and the nominations of Anderson, Sergeant, and Rochester (the Secretary) were approved by a strict party vote of 24 to 19. The matter of an appropriation for expenses now reached the House, where it led to a prolonged debate. [3] The one topic which engrossed the attention of the Congressmen seemed to be Panama.

[1] National Edition, XVII, 401.

[2] Of its disastrous results, Benton wrote: "It agitated the people, made a violent debate in the two Houses of Congress, inflamed the passions of parties and individuals, raised a tempest before which Congress bent, made bad feeling between the President and the Senate; and led to the duel between Mr. Randolph and Mr. Clay." (Benton, *Thirty Years*, I, 65.)

[3] Webster wrote Ticknor, March 1, 1826: "All goes smoothly except the Panama Mission; that sticks in the Senate. The incongruous materials of opposition assimilate better on that subject than they are likely to on most others. . . . In our House we shall have a debate on it, and I shall make a short speech, for certain reasons, provided I can get out of court, and provided better reflection should not change my purpose." (National Edition, XVI, 120.)

Webster detected a conspiracy, headed by Calhoun, of which the object was the dismissal of Clay as Secretary of State.[1] Modern historians look upon the affair as an early phase of the struggle over slavery between the North and South.[2] Webster called the session a *"talking winter."* [3]

Webster's own contribution to the discussion was made on April 14. To the resolution appropriating funds, amendments had been proposed, instructing our delegates as to what topics they should or should not discuss. Webster now arose to point out that the House had no constitutional right to advise or direct our envoys, and that there were certain matters which the latter could not help debating if they were brought before the Panama Congress. He characterized Monroe's message of December 1823, enunciating the "Monroe Doctrine," as "wise, seasonable, and patriotic." He closed with an eloquent appeal to the generosity of his countrymen, and said of the Latin-American republics: —

In their emergencies, they have looked to our experience; in their political institutions, they have followed our models; in their deliberations, they have invoked the presiding spirit of our own liberty. They have looked steadily, in every adversity, to the *great Northern light.* In the hour of bloody conflict, they have remembered the fields which have been consecrated by the blood of our own fathers; and when they have fallen, they have wished only to be remembered with them, as men who had acted their parts bravely for the cause of liberty in the Western World.

Webster's speech — which was really an authoritative treatise on international affairs — undoubtedly had its influ-

[1] Webster wrote an interesting letter to Mason on March 27, summarizing the conditions and prophesying, " In the House of Representatives it is likely the necessary money will be voted by thirty or forty majority." (*Ibid.*, p. 126.)

[2] See Morse, *John Quincy Adams*, pp. 188–92, and Turner, *The Rise of the New West*, pp. 284–85.

[3] Webster, on May 3, sent his English friend, J. Evelyn Denison, a summary of the facts, saying: "The measure has met with much opposition, by which more was intended than the defeat of the measure itself. Various parties, not likely to act together often, united, on this occasion, in a close phalanx of *opposition*." (National Edition, XVI, 129.) Story wrote Fay, March 15, " The Panama Mission is the great point on which the opposition now hinges, and it has met with every sort of delay." (Story, I, 492.)

ence in the House, which passed the appropriation by the decisive vote of 134 to 60 — a larger majority than he had expected.[1] The controversy, however, proved to be "much ado about nothing." Anderson, one of our envoys, died on his journey south, and Sergeant, on reaching Panama, discovered that the conference had adjourned. At the date when the delegates were to reassemble at Tacubaya, Mexico, new quarrels had broken out in Central America, and nobody appeared. The dream of a Pan-American Conclave was still to be nothing but a dream.

Webster had certainly by this time merited some recognition by the administration. Yet, when the venerable Rufus King, who had been induced by Adams to accept the Ministry to the Court of St. James's, broke down in health and was obliged to resign, the President refrained from offering the vacant post to Webster, who wanted it badly. He was told that he could not be spared from the House of Representatives,[2] but this was small solace to his thwarted ambition.

In August, Webster delivered his masterly *Eulogy on Adams and Jefferson*, and, in November, he was almost unanimously reëlected to Congress, a few scattered votes being wasted on E. B. Smith, who called himself the "democratic" candidate. Shortly after his return to Washington, he reported, as Chairman of the Judiciary Committee, a bill providing for a uniform national system of bankruptcy. It was a period when the problem was being considered by the Supreme Court, and Webster had hoped, while there was some public interest in

[1] Throughout this debate, Webster was a leading factor. Story wrote Denison, March 15, " A majority, powerful in talents, numbers, and public confidence, aids the administration in the most unequivocal manner, and you may depend that Mr. Webster is, and will continue to be, their leader." (Story, I, 494.) Regarding Webster's great speech, Sergeant wrote, May 2, " Mr. Clay owes you a great deal for bringing out the true colours of his conduct from under the dust and cobwebs they have been covered with by his opponents." (Cong. Lib. MSS. II.)

[2] Webster consulted several of his friends as to the policy which he should follow. Mason, writing on May 7, replied: " It seems to me that you cannot, under existing circumstances, assert your claim at the present time. Should the Government offer you the appointment, I think you ought not to refuse it. But, if I mistake not, it will be thought you cannot at this time be spared from the House of Representatives." (Curtis, I, 273.)

the matter, to settle it by appropriate legislation.[1] But the House was not disposed to debate the question, and Webster's well-drawn act, although read for a second time, was never brought to a vote.

On the vital issue of the conflict of authority between an individual state and the Federal Government, Webster, who had already expressed himself in arguments before the Supreme Court, had an opportunity to speak during the violent controversy which developed during the spring of 1827 between the State of Georgia and the United States. Through its fiery Governor, George M. Troup, Georgia had asserted its claim to certain lands originally the property of the Cherokee Indians. Georgia had threatened to use military force in seizing the territory in dispute, had defied the President, and had declared herself prepared to resist the Federal Government. Adams, after warning the Governor that he should not hesitate to employ all the means under his control to "maintain the faith of the nation," sent a special message to Congress on February 5, 1827.

This shameful bickering was allowed to drag along, while the Georgians took possession of the Indian lands in defiance of protests from Washington. Webster courageously undertook to rise in the House as the spokesman of the President. When Adams's Message was read, certain Southern members, headed by Forsyth, of Georgia, tried to block its reference to any committee, but especially to the Judiciary Committee, of which Webster was still Chairman. Having been denounced as the tool of the administration, Webster declared that he was not to be frightened by "high words" or "loud declamation"; that he would not submit to dictation from any state or its Representative; that states would act on their own responsi-

---

[1] Ever since his reappearance in Congress in 1823, Webster had had this matter on his mind. During the preceding session, he had actually prepared a suitable measure, but Congress was lethargic. On December 31, 1825, he wrote Justice Story: " By direction of our committee I brought in to-day a resolution for a bankrupt law. I think there is some chance for it if we get a good bill." (National Edition, XVII, 400.) He was even more confident a month later, when he wrote Ezekiel, " The bankrupt bill will be introduced, and has a fair chance of being passed." (*Ibid.*, p. 402.)

bility, and at their own peril, if they undertook to extend their legislation to lands where the Indian title had not been extinguished; and that there were numerous citizens, both in the House and the country at large, who would take the part of the Indians if their rights needed defense. The debate was bitter.[1] Adams, however, was not prepared to back up his threatening words. The ground in dispute was seized by Georgia in spite of all the administration could do. But Webster had at least told Congress where he stood. The voice had spoken which was soon to reverberate through the nation in the *Reply to Hayne*.

In the late spring of 1827, Daniel Webster was elected to the United States Senate, with which he was to be identified for many years. The circumstances leading to this promotion are not easy to trace. An analysis of the mental processes of an ambitious statesman is difficult, and it is possible to interpret Webster's conduct as that of either an unselfish patriot or a self-seeking politician. Probably his underlying motives, like those of most mortals, were confused, and he was frequently perplexed and irresolute.

As we have seen, Massachusetts, in the autumn of 1824, was overwhelmingly for Adams. The once respectable Federalist Party had dwindled to a shadow, and its spirit survived only in scattered local elections. In 1825, Levi Lincoln, an Adams Republican, was chosen Governor by a vote almost unanimous; and in the following year, when the Federalists, in a dying outburst of vitality, decided to give Lincoln a battle, he received 27,884 votes as against 12,108 for all his opponents combined.[2] Although the anti-administration men were elsewhere enlisting under the Democratic-Republican banner,[3] Jacksonism made

[1] Webster wrote Plumer, February 11, 1827: " In my little experience, I have never witnessed such extreme heat and violence of opposition, as now exists in Congress. Our *war* debates were cool and temperate compared to the *manner* of our discussions now." (Cong. Lib. MSS. II.)

[2] The vicissitudes of Massachusetts politics during this period are covered in Professor Arthur B. Darling's *Political Changes in Massachusetts, 1824-48*, an interesting and scholarly monograph emphasizing the trend towards Jacksonism and the rise of the Democratic Party.

[3] Clay wrote to Webster, November 10, 1826, from Washington, " Names may be gotten up or kept up in particular states for local or personal purposes, but at this time

slow progress in Massachusetts. Even in 1828, when Adams was so badly beaten in the country at large, Lincoln was continued in office, with 27,981 votes against 4423 for Marcus Morton, the Democratic candidate. The National Republicans were still dominant in the Old Bay State.

During the winter of 1826–27, there was much doubt as to whether the health of Senator Elijah H. Mills [1] would allow him to be a candidate to succeed himself. Mills, who was a Federalist, would not commit himself openly, but appeared in the Senate in early January, and it was reported in the press that he was daily attending to his legislative duties. As the hour drew near for the General Court to choose a Senator, Webster was approached from several quarters, but he replied to Joseph E. Sprague recommending Mills, on the ground that the latter was "second to no man in the Senate among our friends." The Legislature was unable to agree. The House, on January 16, gave Senator Mills 106 votes against 67 for William C. Jarvis (the Jacksonian candidate), 21 for John Mills (a Springfield politician), and 3 for Levi Lincoln. On the following day, the Senate cast 26 votes for John Mills, 9 for Elijah Mills, 2 for Jarvis, and 1 for Lincoln. As the branches had to concur, the deadlock continued from week to week, the Senate doing its best to break it by turning first to James T. Austin and then to Lincoln. Neither man, however, was agreeable to the House, which persisted, by varying majorities, in standing by Senator Mills. At last, on February 16, the House voted to postpone the election indefinitely, and the matter was left to the incoming Legislature, which was to meet in May. Meanwhile Governor Lincoln had publicly declined to let his name be considered, and the politicians, bewildered,

there are but two parties in the Union, that of the Administration and the opposition." (Cong. Lib. MSS. II.)

[1] Elijah Hunt Mills (1776–1829), a graduate of Williams College, studied law and settled in Northampton, from which district he served two terms in Congress. He was then appointed to a vacancy in the United States Senate and was reëlected, his entire period in that body extending from December 1, 1820, to March 3, 1827. The word " venerable " applied to him by one of Webster's biographers is not precisely accurate, for he died at fifty-three. Politically he was an old-school Federalist and a supporter of Adams.

sat down to talk the situation over.   During this long period of balloting, not a single vote was cast for Daniel Webster.

Senator Mills now decided to withdraw from the contest, and renewed pressure was brought to bear upon Lincoln.   For the first time, also, Webster was openly mentioned as a candidate on whom all could unite.   Henry Clay wrote Webster that President Adams preferred Lincoln, but was ready to accept Webster as his second choice.   Nathaniel Silsbee,[1] the other Senator from Massachusetts, informed Clay that the majority of the Bostonians preferred Lincoln, mainly on the ground that they were afraid that they could not find the right kind of man to replace Webster in the House of Representatives. Doubtless Webster had now reached the conclusion that he had done a great deal for Adams without receiving any reward, and he made up his mind that he and Lincoln could settle the matter without outside interference.   With what seemed to be perfect candor, he wrote to the Governor, urging the latter to accept the Senatorship, and saying that there were many reasons why he himself ought to decline the place if it were offered to him.   Lincoln replied with equal courtesy, regretting that he could not yield to Webster's importunities, and declaring that the latter must sacrifice his private affairs, if necessary, in order to go into the Senate.[2]   After this interchange of civilities, Webster responded, admitting that Lincoln's arguments were not without weight, and concluding, "Under existing circumstances, I feel it my duty to leave it to others to decide how the place shall be filled."[3]   This meant simply that Daniel Webster wanted to be Senator from Massachusetts.

From that moment, all went smoothly with Webster. Edward Everett, it is true, had Senatorial ambitions and had sounded the President on the subject without receiving encour-

[1] Nathaniel Silsbee (1773–1850), a shipowner of Salem, after building up a fortune in foreign trade, entered politics as a Republican, serving in the State Legislature, then for two terms in Congress (1817–21), and again in the State Senate.   He had become a vigorous supporter of the Adams administration and was elected to the United States Senate, taking his seat on December 4, 1826.   Later he was an influential Whig.   He sat in the Senate until March 2, 1835.

[2] Curtis, I, 295.

[3] Ibid., 296.

agement.[1] He had also discussed the situation with Webster in early May, at which time the latter had ostensibly favored Lincoln. To a friend in Boston, Everett wrote, "The opinion is, so far as I know, universal here, that Webster ought not to leave the House of Representatives. It is also, however, a prevalent impression, that he wishes to go into the Senate." [2] This view was undoubtedly correct. On June 7, the new House declared overwhelmingly for Webster, and, on the following day, the Senate concurred.[3]

If we accept Webster's language literally, he was not altogether happy over his promotion.[4] As a Senator, he would have less opportunity for practice in the Supreme Court. Furthermore he was abandoning a position of leadership and influence in the House of Representatives for the doubtful vicissitudes of the Upper Chamber. But he could not ignore the prestige attached to the Senatorship. He was succeeded in the House of Representatives by Benjamin Gorham, who had also been his predecessor; and he was sworn into the Senate in December, having served no portion of the third term in the House to which he had been elected.

It cannot be said that Webster, during his second period in the House, had achieved much in the way of constructive legislation. Some of the matters to which he had devoted himself most assiduously, such as the cause of the Greeks, the Panama Mission, and the reform of the judiciary, had resulted

[1] With delightful disingenuousness, Everett had managed, in this communication, to suggest his own name, hoping undoubtedly for a favorable reaction from Adams. Everett, one of the most ambitious statesmen of his generation, was not above artful methods in attempting to gratify his aims.

[2] Frothingham, p. 112.

[3] The vote in the House was: Webster, 282; John Mills, 82; Elijah H. Mills, 22; Jarvis, 8; Everett, 6; and Lincoln, 3. In the Senate, it was: Webster, 26; John Mills, 11; Lincoln, 1; and Everett, 1. The Boston *Centinel*, on June 9, said editorially: "This appointment affords additional evidence of the patriotic policy which distinguishes the majorities of the two Houses; and is honorable to the gentleman who has received this new proof of the high confidence of the immediate Representatives of the people."

[4] Webster wrote Denison, July 28: "The good people here have seen fit to transfer me from the House of Representatives to the Senate. This was not according to my wishes; but a state of things had arisen which, in the judgment of friends, rendered the measure expedient, and I yielded to their will. I do not expect to find the situation as agreeable as that which I left." (National Edition, XVI, 169.)

unsatisfactorily. He had the Crimes Act to his credit, but he had been defeated on the tariff. If he had succeeded on the Cumberland Road, he had failed on the Bankruptcy Act. . . . Nevertheless he was regarded in 1827 as one of the most promising young statesmen in the country. Josiah Quincy, visiting Washington in 1826, heard Webster speak extemporaneously in the House on a movement for putting a breakwater in the Delaware River, and was astonished at the ease with which he exposed the selfish localism of the supporters of the measure.[1] William Plumer, once his bitter critic, now confessed that Webster was "forcible and authoritative," and that, on the issue of the tariff, he "in the pride of conscious power came into the field beating down as with a giant's club, the whole array of his opponents' force."[2] Barbour, once the Speaker of the House, told Plumer that he considered Webster the most powerful man "ever sent from the North."[3] He had helped to raise money for the anti-administration forces, at Clay's personal request,[4] and, although he had failed to secure the Mission to England, the party leaders knew that he could not be ignored.

Once, under the silvery moonlight in the Capitol grounds, Webster, walking with William Plumer, broke out into a passionate confession of his desire for fame. In one of those rare moments when a man bares his soul, he admitted that his hope was to say or do something which would be remembered. When Plumer reminded him of his accomplishment, Webster cried, "I have done absolutely nothing!" Later, as Webster's enthusiasm swept him on, Plumer smiled, and his companion said: "You laugh at me, Plumer! Your quiet way of looking at things may be the best, after all; but I have sometimes such glorious dreams! And sometimes too, I half believe that they will one day wake into glorious realities." Here was the true Daniel Webster — restless, unsatisfied, ambitious, craving always an immortality in the hearts of his countrymen.

[1] Quincy, pp. 280–83.
[2] Plumer's "Reminiscences," National Edition, XVII, 549–50.
[3] Ibid., p. 549.
[4] Cong. Lib. MSS. II.

XIV

SLINGS AND ARROWS

He [Webster] was on the happiest terms with the world, which had crowned him with its choicest blessing, and stood forth in all respects as an example and a hero among men.
— JOSIAH QUINCY, "Washington Society in 1826," from *Figures of the Past*

I confess the world, at present, has for me an aspect anything but cheerful. With a multitude of acquaintance, I have few friends; my nearest intimacies are broken, and a sad void is made in the objects of affection.
— DANIEL WEBSTER, Letter to Mason, April 19, 1829

RESIDENTS of Summer Street, in Boston, saw on a dismal Saturday morning in January, 1829, a "touching and solemn procession" setting out from Mr. Paige's house. Close behind a funeral hearse, there walked through the mist and melting snow a proud man bowed with grief, with a boy and girl by his side, all three garbed in black. Although he had been urged to ride in one of the carriages provided for the mourners, he refused, saying, "My children and I must follow their mother to the grave on foot." They were proceeding to St. Paul's Church, where Daniel Webster, excessively pale, was to watch while his beloved wife was laid in the crypt near the son and daughter who had preceded her. It was one of the saddest moments of his life, the sadder because the blow had fallen at a time when he had seemed to be a favorite of fortune.

As a Congressman from Massachusetts, Webster had been a happy man, with a reputation steadily growing and congenial work to keep him busy. His health was excellent, his only illnesses being the catarrhal ailments so prevalent in our northern climate during the winter months. His habits were temperate, even when he was in bachelor's quarters in the convivial capital. Under prosperity, he had acquired poise and assurance, and he bore himself with dignity. "No man of mark ever satisfied the imagination so completely," wrote Josiah Quincy of the Webster of 1826. He had a host of admiring friends, and as yet had made few enemies. If success can bring contentment, Daniel Webster must have been at peace.

There were moments, however, when he was troubled by financial embarrassments. The story of his money affairs will always be somewhat of a mystery. He first became a capitalist, apparently, in 1807, when he bought two shares of the Concord Bank. After his marriage, his income was ample to provide for his family all the comforts and many of the luxuries of existence, and they lived modestly both in Portsmouth and Boston; yet, even in his Portsmouth days, he was notoriously dilatory about paying his bills. He was temperamentally incapable not only of saving money but even of keeping a regular account of receipts and disbursements, and his investments, usually selected on the advice of acquaintances, were seldom profitable. He liked to deal with money in a large and lavish way, as if it were a negligible commodity, easily obtainable and intended to be spent. His wife, brought up in a clergyman's frugal household, exercised a restraining influence upon him while she lived, but he never regarded thrift as a virtue.

After he settled in Boston, his professional income increased, and he behaved as if its source were inexhaustible. He was not yet a landowner, and it is difficult to see how his routine expenditures could have been very large; but he was both generous and careless, and he made no effort to set aside a fund for the future. When, at the solicitation of his friends, he entered Congress, he had less time for the law, and was obliged to resort to loans from his supporters to compensate for his reduced revenue. Among his papers are documents showing that, in 1823, he borrowed $3254.25 from Alfred Curtis, and that Curtis lent him in the following year $6030.33, in two separate drafts. From then on, there was no period in his career when he was not under financial obligation to friends.

He accepted their help as a feudal lord received tribute from his retainers, and he was not punctilious about repaying his debts.

More and more in the 1820's Webster was allying himself with the bankers and mill-owners of Boston and its vicinity. The Lawrences and the Lowells were among his intimate associates, as were many of the other entrepreneurs who were presciently turning their capital into manufacturing, especially the making of textiles. When the Merrimack Manufacturing Company was incorporated at Lowell in 1822, Webster was allowed to subscribe to four shares,[1] and the desirability of a protective tariff for New England industry was thus brought home to him through his pocketbook. Both capital and labor in Massachusetts were convinced of the efficacy of protection as a basic economic principle, and they had sound practical reasons for wishing to retain Daniel Webster in Congress.

Beset with maternal cares, Mrs. Webster often found it difficult to leave her home. She did, however, take Julia and Edward with her to Washington during the winter of 1823–24, leaving Daniel and Charles at "Mr. Green's," in Jamaica Plain. In November 1825, the entire family made the journey to Washington. It was a fatiguing experience, for the trip by stagecoach from Boston to New York occupied from Friday morning to Monday evening, with stops for the night at Ashford, New Haven, and Stamford.

The Washington season of 1826 was exceedingly gay, and Webster wrote, "As to parties, dinners, etc., we have enough and to spare. My wife is a good deal dissipated." [2] In January, they dined at the White House, where they had "a very good dinner and a very good time," although Webster confessed that he did not like such large parties. He was much less constrained at informal dinners in his own house, such as one described by Josiah Quincy, when Henry R.

---

[1] Appleton, *Introduction of the Power Loom, and Origin of Lowell* (1858). The first power loom in Massachusetts was set up at Waltham in 1814.

[2] Webster to Ticknor, National Edition, XVI, 120.

Storrs, Rufus Greene Amory, and Quincy were the only guests, and Webster himself carved the roast and passed the wine.[1] Webster is quoted by Quincy as having said that "dinners were agreeable in inverse ratio to their state and formality," and the latter mentioned, as illustrating this point, a dinner which he attended given by the gentlemen lodgers at "Miss Hyer's boarding-house," at which Webster was a guest, and, after the Bordeaux wine was added to the customary Madeira, the conversation was "easy and animated." [2] There were many balls during the winter, and Quincy saw the waltz introduced into society for the first time. Webster seems to have cared nothing for gambling, one of the favorite pastimes of his political contemporaries, and he danced only under compulsion.

It was a time when fashionable assemblies opened at eight o'clock; when gentlemen wore ruffled linen, and frock coats, of gay colors, with large gilded buttons, over voluminous trousers tucked into high Hessian boots; when ladies had ball dresses of white India silk and wide flounced skirts revealing a bit of ankle; when Senators took snuff, and punch was plentiful at every home in Washington; when quarrels between statesmen often resulted in fisticuffs and sometimes in bloodshed; when negro girls were sold by the auctioneer in the open market; and when rooms were lighted by gas and heated by stoves, and modern plumbing was unknown.

To Daniel Webster's ancestors, men and women who spent their lives in manual toil, the idea of a recreative vacation would have seemed preposterous. But, after the heavy office and court work of the winter, he found fresh air and physical exercise essential, and he restored his energy by getting back to mother earth. For several years he sought diversion by short journeys in New England. In the summer of 1817, he accompanied his wife and her brother, William Paige, on a visit to their mother, Mrs. Paige, at Roxbury, New Hamp-

---

[1] *Figures of the Past*, pp. 254–60. Webster was "in a charming humor" and told "some good lawyer's stories."

[2] *Ibid.*, p. 265.

shire,[1] where he climbed Monadnock, the mountain to which he was compared by Emerson in the latter's Phi Beta Kappa poem in 1834 : —

> Not on its base Monadnoc surer stood,
> Than he to common sense and common good.

Not long after the birth of Edward Webster, on July 20, 1820, Webster took his wife to recuperate at Sandwich, a small coast village on Cape Cod. Here he found a comfortable boarding place, with a delightful climate, convenient sea bathing, and excellent fishing and hunting, and they returned for a few weeks during seven consecutive summers.[2] Often he made up parties of his friends, such as George Blake [3] and Isaac P. Davis,[4] and others, who enjoyed with him the pursuit

[1] Roxbury, a few miles east of Keene, was then a prosperous farming community, but is now an almost abandoned township, in which the roads have grown up to grass and the pastures have reverted to forest.

[2] The experiences of the Websters during the summer vacation periods can be followed from notes which Webster himself kept. In July 1821, Mrs. Paige died, and, after the funeral, the Websters went with the Storys to Portsmouth, where they joined the Masons, and the entire party drove to Lake Winnepesaukee, stopping for a night or two at The Elms. Later they were at Sandwich, and they spent some weeks in the late autumn at " Mr. Hall's," in Brookline. Not having settled as yet at any permanent home in Boston, Webster was free to move where he pleased. In 1822, leaving Edward and Charles with their aunt, Nancy Paige, in Dorchester, he and Mrs. Webster took Daniel and Julia, the older children, with them to the Cape. In 1823, both Grace and Daniel Webster attended the two-hundredth anniversary of the settlement of Portsmouth, observed on May 21, and signed their names to a guest register which is one of the treasures of the Portsmouth Athenæum. Webster responded to the first volunteer toast: —
" New Hampshire:
> Where'er I roam, whatever realms I see,
> My heart untravelled fondly turns to thee!"

[3] George Blake, a Boston lawyer somewhat Webster's senior, had a reputation for humorous exaggeration which made him famous among his contemporaries. Mrs. Blake was a charming woman, of whom Mrs. Webster was very fond, and the two families liked to be together. Blake, who had accumulated a comfortable fortune, had virtually retired from his profession, and could usually be counted upon for a hunting expedition. On June 9, 1824, Webster wrote to Mrs. Blake: " I pray you tell Mr. Blake, that after I get home, if I ever should do so, I expect to find him ready for play the residue of the summer. I am not yet so reduced but that I could walk with a bit of iron on my shoulder. Truth to tell I am extremely homesick; and I shall reckon it a happy day, when I set my face northward." (National Edition, XVII, 352.)

[4] Isaac P. Davis, at this period of Webster's life, was one of his most intimate friends, and they were often together. It was evidently Davis who first drew the attention of the Websters to the Thomas house, at Marshfield. (Harvey, p. 264.)

of deer and trout. The establishment of a large glass manu-
factory at Sandwich, however, brought to that district numerous workmen who, on their holidays, covered the neighborhood
with dog and gun, and reduced the opportunities for good
sport.

In September 1824, after Ezekiel Webster and his wife had
spent a month with them at Sandwich, Daniel and Grace
Webster, driving back to Boston, by chaise, in a leisurely fashion, happened to take a back road which ran by the farmhouse
of Captain John Thomas, in the town of Marshfield. It was
a picturesque old residence, built in 1774 by Nathaniel Roy
Thomas, a Royalist during the Revolution, who had fled to
Nova Scotia and whose property had been confiscated by the
Massachusetts General Court. After the war, his youngest
son, John Thomas, a staunch patriot, was able to establish a
claim to his mother's dowry, and, in this way, secured a title
to the homestead.

Mrs. Webster, impressed by the attractive location of the
Thomas farm, only about a mile from the sea, urged her husband to drive in for a call on the owner. The hospitality of
the Captain was so unstinted that the Websters remained for
two or three days; and after that they stopped there every
summer on the road to and from Sandwich. Webster, learning
that Captain Thomas's estate was mortgaged and that he was
without funds, did what he could to make the old gentleman's
lot less arduous; and, in 1832, after his second marriage, he
purchased the entire property under an arrangement which
permitted Captain Thomas and his wife to occupy the house
as long as they lived. Eventually it became Webster's real
home — the place on earth which he loved best.

As soon as the Bunker Hill Oration was over, in 1825, the
Websters joined Justice and Mrs. Story and Miss Eliza Buckminster [1] on an excursion to Niagara Falls. They drove from

[1] Eliza Buckminster, then thirty-two years old, was a sentimental but intelligent
spinster, who idolized Webster. Her unpublished letters in the New Hampshire
Historical Society Collection show that she regarded herself as occupying a very special,
although entirely platonic, relationship towards him. She wrote Mrs. Webster, April
13, 1817: "Remember me affectionately to Mr. Webster. Perhaps I should say

Boston to Worcester, where Webster called on Governor Lincoln, and then to Northampton, where he climbed Mount Holyoke. At Albany, they enjoyed a brief reunion with the tired General Lafayette. They visited the Catskills and Saratoga, and rode on a towboat from Canajoharie to Utica, on the Erie Canal, at a speed which made them dizzy. The Mohawk Valley seemed very much alive, — "new, growing, and highly excited," — and the inns and roads were crowded with travelers. After a few hours at Trenton Falls, they took a route by Onondaga Lake and through Geneva and Canandaigua to Buffalo. At Niagara Falls, Webster sent a long literary description in a letter to Mrs. George Blake.[1] They were thoroughgoing sight-seers. "We have been here now the whole or a part of three days," he said, "and although our eyes are not satisfied with seeing, yet some of us complain of weary limbs, from walking about so much, and going down and climbing up the banks so often." With the enthusiasm of the true angler, he even tried casting a line at the foot of the falls.

Through almost insufferable July heat, the party returned, by a route which included Rochester, Palmyra, Syracuse, Schoharie Bridge, Schenectady, Bennington, Brattleboro, and Concord. Justice Story was taken ill, and was obliged to rest along the way.[2] In a letter to Denison, he said, "We toiled very hard in order to see everything, and were amply repaid for our labor. . . . Mr. Webster has a giant's constitution, and can bear every sort of fatigue; but I was a good deal overcome and exhausted, and returned in very indifferent health."[3] The Websters sought retirement at Sandwich,

---

respectfully, but since I have known him so well I have seen so much to love I venture to say so." As late as 1827, she wrote to Webster, "Is it possible I am so absurd as to be writing sentiment to you, a statesman and a member of Congress?" She was accepted by the Webster children as a kind of maiden aunt, and was often very helpful to Mrs. Webster. In 1827, she was married to Thomas Lee.

[1] National Edition, XVII, 385–92. This letter was evidently intended to be passed around among Webster's friends.

[2] Story wrote July 16, 1825: "I have not time to write more, being exhausted in mind and body by the excessive heats. I long to be at home, to get some repose and some appetite, for I can truly say that I never felt so little of the one nor possessed so little of the other."

[3] Story, I, p. 487.

which Mrs. Webster described to her brother as "the most tranquil looking place in the world,"[1] and where Daniel was out hunting almost every day with George Blake. On the last day in 1825, he wrote from Washington, "My health is good, never better, not having worked off the strength obtained at Niagara, and at Sandwich."[2] The enervated Story must have read this sentence with an ironic smile upon his lips.

Webster's magnetism drew friends about him wherever he went. The Masons, the Storys, the Ticknors, and the Blakes often visited him, and the death of Mrs. Blake, on May 10, 1826, was mourned by the Websters as if she had been one of the family. Young men were peculiarly attracted to Webster. Edward Everett, emboldened by his encouragement, looked upon himself as his successor in the Massachusetts political dynasty. Caleb Cushing, of Newburyport, also had aspirations and became one of the great statesman's satellites.[3] Rufus Choate, who had first seen Webster at Dartmouth College in 1819, had chosen him as his model in law and oratory. These were, of course, his disciples. He also corresponded with most of the leading public men of his time, including Chancellor James Kent, James Madison, General Lafayette, Chief Justice Marshall, Henry Clay, and President John Quincy Adams. His letters, even to his closest friends, invariably opened with a stiff "My dear Sir," in the formal fashion of that age, but this conventionality did not persist beyond the salutation.

To foreigners, Webster was uniformly gracious. One of his boon companions in Washington was Julius von Wallenstein, an attaché in the Russian legation. In 1824, a party of young Englishmen — Mr. Stanley (later Earl of Derby), Mr. Stuart Wortley (later Lord Wharncliffe), Mr. Labouchere (after-

---

[1] Cong. Lib. MSS. II.

[2] National Edition, XVII, 401.

[3] Caleb Cushing (1800–79), after graduating at Harvard in 1817 and studying law, settled in his native town of Newburyport, where he quickly built up a large practice. In his *Diary* he records meeting Webster first at Ipswich in 1825, where he was opposed to him in a case and was much flattered when the latter invited him to walk and offered him some valuable advice.

wards Lord Taunton), and Mr. John Evelyn Denison (who was to become Speaker of the House of Commons) — came to the United States, recommended to Webster by Mr. Stratford Canning.[1] Webster entertained them during their visit, arranged for the necessary introductions, and acquainted them with the intricacies of American politics. After their departure, he corresponded with Denison, and resolved that he would go shortly to Europe as the latter's guest.[2] Not for fifteen years, however, was he able to renew his intimacy with his English friend.

Webster's married life was untroubled and happy. After seeing him in Washington in 1826, Josiah Quincy wrote: —

A congenial marriage seems to be essential to the best development of a man of genius, and this blessing rested upon that household. It was like organ-music to hear Webster speak to or of the being upon whom his affections reposed, and whom, alas! he was so soon to lose. I am sure that those who knew the man only when this tenderest relation had been terminated by death never knew him in his perfect symmetry. Whatever evil-speakers might choose to say about the subsequent career of Daniel Webster, he was at that time "whole as the marble, founded as the rock." [3]

He liked to have Mrs. Webster as his companion wherever he went, and, when they were parted, he wrote her most affectionate letters. Growing intellectually along with him, she could comprehend his problems and his needs, and she subordinated herself to her husband and rejoiced in his successes; but she had a mind and character entirely her own. Her influence upon him was salutary, both as a restraint and as an inspiration.

After a winter in bachelor's quarters at Washington, Webster returned to Boston in the late March of 1827. In June, Mrs. Webster fell ill with what was diagnosed as erysipelas,

---

[1] National Edition, XVI, 111.

[2] Webster wrote Denison, May 2, 1825: " I assure you, my dear sir, it is my fixed intention to see England within two or three years. No disappointment, not connected with my own health, or that of my family, can be allowed to prevent the accomplishment of this purpose." (*Ibid.*, p. 110.)

[3] *Figures of the Past*, p. 256.

but had recovered sufficiently on June 20 to be able to ride; and she went with her husband and their daughter, Julia, in early July to the island of Nantucket, where he had business at court. On July 20, he wrote Ezekiel that she was "getting well," and a few days later she drove with him in their chaise to Sandwich. There they spent a happy autumn, and planned to go with the Storys to Washington for the following winter.

On November 23, accompanied by Julia and Edward, the Websters started south. Their misfortunes now began, precipitated, no doubt, by the fatiguing stage journey. Mrs. Webster reached New York very ill and weak, and Webster was crippled by a painful attack of rheumatism, which confined him to his room in the house of his old college friend, Dr. Cyrus Perkins, at 176 Fulton Street, where they were staying. A consultation between Dr. Perkins and another eminent practitioner, Dr. Post, disclosed the fact that Mrs. Webster had an abdominal tumor, so extensive that it was inoperable. Webster immediately wrote to Mrs. Webster's brother, James W. Paige, asking him to come, if possible, to New York. Paige arrived on December 11; and Webster, although by no means recovered from his own illness, felt called upon by duty to set out for the capital. At the time when he left New York, Mrs. Webster's health was bad, but much better than it had been since her arrival in that city.

Apprehensive, weak, and sad at heart, Webster took his seat in the Senate Chamber, where he felt "new and strange" and where he drew a desk "nearest the chair on its left hand." [1] His rheumatism still persisted, and his Christmas dinner was "a handful of magnesia, a bowl of gruel." [2] In his despondency, he considered resigning from the Senate,[3] for he did not wish to remain away from Mrs. Webster. The reports became so alarming that he returned to New York after the New Year, to find her much more cheerful and comparatively free from pain. She had, however, lost flesh, and was very feeble. Webster now devoted himself entirely to her comfort, reading to her, buying her little delicacies, and sitting

---

[1] National Edition, XVII, 428.   [2] Ibid., p. 430.   [3] Ibid., pp. 430-31.

constantly by her side.[1] The case was hopeless, and she died on Monday, January 21, 1828, at quarter past two o'clock. Webster wrote to Mason, "The manner of the death . . . was, in all respects, such as her dearest friends would have wished." [2] Those to whom Webster wrote first were his brother, Ezekiel, George Ticknor, and Mrs. Lee.

Webster was reminded by his wise friend, Justice Story, "that the great secret of comfort must be sought, so far as human aid can go, in employment." [3] After the body had been placed in St. Paul's Church, arrangements had to be made for the care of his children. Daniel Fletcher Webster was a student in the Boston Latin School, and could safely be allowed to continue there, residing meanwhile with the Paiges. Julia went to the home of the kindly Mrs. Lee, and Edward was placed in the family of Mrs. Hale. It was understood that the three would dine on Sundays with their uncle, James W. Paige; and the Ticknors also promised to watch over their welfare. When these plans were completed, Webster, after a few days with George Blake, went back to Washington.

Bent beneath his sorrow, Webster for the first time showed signs of age. He seemed overcome by lassitude,[4] and even the suggestion, now renewed, that he go as Minister to England barely roused him from his melancholy lethargy. Whether or not the position was ever positively offered to Webster is doubtful. He had, of course, his children to consider; [5] and he wrote Ticknor in April that he could not afford the expense

[1] Harvey, pp. 320–22. Webster was himself taken ill, as a result of anxiety and exertion, and was obliged to keep to his room for some days.

[2] National Edition, XVII, 448.

[3] *Ibid.*, p. 446.

[4] He wrote Ticknor on February 22, from the Supreme Court: "I feel very little zeal or spirit in regard to the passing affairs. My most strong propensity is to sit down, and sit still; and, if I could have my wish, I think the writing of a letter would be the greatest effort I should put forth for the residue of the winter." (*Ibid.*, XVI, 172.)

[5] When Mrs. Lee wrote him, assuring him that, if he should wish to "cross the water," Julia would be taken care of in her household, Webster could only answer, "Even if what you allude to were supposed to be at my option, and however desirable it might be in itself, times and circumstances may nevertheless be such as 'give me pause.' That is all I can say about it at present; except that I am now too old to do anything in a hurry." (National Edition, XVII, 452.)

of maintaining the Legation. He did, however, consult Ezekiel Webster and Jeremiah Mason on the matter.[1] As conditions turned out, Webster's voice was badly needed in the Senate, and it was probably fortunate for him and for the country that he was not diverted into a diplomatic career.

Webster was now to make his début in the Senate Chamber, — to-day the room assigned to the Supreme Court, — with which his name will always be connected. It was a domed, semicircular auditorium, shaped as if a rotunda had been ruthlessly carved in half. Along the straight side were heavy marble pillars, some cylindrical, some square, and there were galleries above running completely around. It was not a large hall, but, when it was crowded on the floor and in the galleries, it could hold five or six hundred people. Along the straight side were the seats for the presiding officer and the clerks; while the Senators themselves sat at desks in three rows, each of which was divided by a centre aisle extending from the entrance, in the middle of the curved side, to the Vice President's platform. Behind this platform was a retiring vestibule, with a marble fireplace at either end, where the Senators might stroll when restless and from which windows overlooked the eastern end of the Capitol. It was a room in which even a light voice seemed loud, and in which Webster's deep tones resounded to the farthest corner.

On Monday, February 18, Webster resumed his seat in the Senate and received the condolences of his friends. Almost by accident, his attention was attracted to a bill, originally introduced by Hugh L. White, of Tennessee, regulating the supreme judicial process in the states admitted to the Union since 1789. Webster, hearing it read for the third time, went to the Clerk's desk and examined the details of the measure. He then gained the floor and explained in a few words why he was opposed to its provisions. When he sat down, he was attacked by Tazewell, Rowan, Hayne, McKinley, White, and others. He at once moved an adjournment, and, on the following day, was ready for his adversaries.

[1] National Edition, XVII, p. 453, and XVI, 175. See also Curtis, I, 323.

As soon as it was noised abroad that Senator Webster was to make his first speech in the Upper Chamber, official Washington was on edge with excitement. The hall was packed at an early hour, and he rose in an atmosphere of silent expectation. What he said was of no great importance, but his voice was far more impressive than it had been in the Hall of Representatives, where the acoustics were so inadequate. He spoke at some length, protesting against White's bill because it would disorganize and destroy the federal process in the original states; and, in the opinion of the reporters, he completely overthrew the arguments of Tazewell and Rowan. The latter attempted to answer, but the victory was clearly with Webster, and the measure was modified to meet his criticisms.

Around Webster in the Senate were some men with whose abilities he was to become well acquainted. The presiding officer was, of course, the Vice President, John C. Calhoun, who listened with an air of boredom to debates in which he would gladly have participated. From Missouri came Colonel Thomas H. Benton,[1] with his profusion of black curly hair and side whiskers and his thunderous voice, who was to be Webster's garrulous foe. Another of Webster's opponents was Martin Van Buren,[2] of New York, who concealed beneath his suave exterior a lofty ambition. Two other future Presidents were also among Webster's colleagues: William Henry Harrison, a tall, rather bewildered soldier, from Ohio; and John Tyler, with his long nose and obstinate chin, from Virginia. Levi Woodbury — "the rock of the New England Democracy" — was there from New Hampshire. There also were two men whose names were soon to be linked with Webster's through a

[1] Thomas Hart Benton (1782–1858), Webster's almost exact contemporary, served in the War of 1812, and was elected in 1820 as one of the first two Senators from the newly formed State of Missouri. A strong Democrat, he remained in the Senate for thirty consecutive years, the longest continuous service in that body up to that time. His *Thirty Years in the U. S. Senate* (1854) will be frequently quoted in this biography to show the Jacksonian point of view.

[2] Martin Van Buren (1782–1862) had entered the Senate on March 4, 1821, as a Democrat, and resigned December 20, 1828, to become Governor of New York.

great debate: Samuel A. Foote, of Connecticut, and Robert Y. Hayne, a slender patrician, from South Carolina.

Webster did not seek other occasions for speaking, but he was far from being silent during the remainder of the session. On March 21, he discussed the not very vital matter of granting the franking privilege to the Speaker of the House in the same degree as to the Vice President. On April 17, he had something to say in connection with Benton's bill for graduating the price of the public lands. He favored the graduation plan, but wished to apply it only to lands which had been on sale for ten years. A week later, when it looked as if a bill to provide pensions for the surviving officers of the Revolution were likely to be defeated, he spoke convincingly in its support, stating that it was "an act of discreet and careful bounty, drawn forth by meritorious services and by personal necessities." Mainly because of his impressive plea, the measure became a law.

Since 1824, active propaganda had been carried on, especially by the woolen industry, for further tariff protection. A vast amount of literature on the subject had been distributed; the Harrisburg Convention, held in the summer of 1827, had recommended a broad protective policy;[1] and the Twentieth Congress was soon engaged in a furious discussion of rates and schedules. Politicians, especially supporters of Andrew Jackson, saw an opportunity for causing trouble. A bill which upheld the theory of protection but which satisfied very few of its supposed beneficiaries was introduced in the House and advocated by leaders who were sure that it could not pass. Styled by its critics the "tariff of abominations," the measure was really a thing of "shreds and patches," framed unscientifically and with little regard to industrial needs. To the surprise even of its proponents, it passed the

[1] The Convention was called at Harrisburg, Pennsylvania, on July 30, 1827, and lasted five days. Among the delegates was Ezekiel Webster, who had been urged by Daniel to attend. (National Edition, XVII, 421, 422.) Abbott Lawrence, then one of Webster's closest friends, was a delegate from Massachusetts. For the proceedings of the Convention, see Stanwood, *American Tariff Controversies in the Nineteenth Century*, I, 264-68.

House on April 22, by a vote of 105 to 94, with eleven of the thirteen Massachusetts Congressmen in the opposition.

Webster had had nothing to do with the originating of the bill. Nevertheless he did, on May 9, make a brief and straightforward speech in its defense, and, in doing so, virtually abandoned free trade and accepted the protective theory. His explanation was interesting. He had fought the tariff in 1824 because he did not believe in its principles. But, when it was passed, New England investors wisely adjusted their plans to the new situation. Assured of protection, Massachusetts capitalists had invested their money in manufacturing, and it would be unjust to them if the system adopted in 1824 were unexpectedly reversed. The tariff of 1828, with all its weaknesses, did accord to woolens the protection which Congress had practically guaranteed four years previously, and Webster was unwilling to oppose a measure so beneficial to the industrial communities of his section.

Because he had, in 1814 and in 1820, questioned the constitutional power of Congress to enact duties for the protection of particular manufactures, Webster was now exposed to the charge of inconsistency. He himself, however, did not admit having changed his opinions. He pictured himself as a free trader, compelled by force of circumstances to yield to a policy which was for the good of his constituents. The simplest statement of what had happened was written by him, May 10, 1830, in a letter to his English friend, Denison : —

The New-England States, though not originally in favor of the protecting policy, having now become deeply interested in manufacturing establishments, are not inclined to change back again. All New England, or all with few exceptions, voted against the tariff of 1824. It is now nearly unanimous against repeal or reduction.[1]

Webster's conversion added a powerful ally to the supporters of the measure. In the end, a bill designed by scheming politicians, in the hope that it might affect the campaign of 1828, was passed by the Senate, 26 to 21, and signed by

[1] National Edition, XVI, 203.

President Adams six days later. Webster's Massachusetts colleague, Nathaniel Silsbee, who was identified with shipping rather than with manufacturing, voted against it.

The importance of this tariff controversy lies in the sectional struggle which it occasioned. Southern leaders saw in it a complete disregard of the interests of their part of the country. They regarded it as a device for transferring wealth and prosperity from the South to the North. Within a few months, the *South Carolina Exposition*, written by John C. Calhoun, was to declare that the Tariff of 1828 was unconstitutional, unjust, oppressive, and destructive of liberty,[1] and Calhoun, hitherto Webster's personal friend and political ally, was now to become his foe. In their attitude towards the tariff, both men were sectionalists, and local selfishness was behind the position which each one assumed.

In late May, Webster, still very despondent, returned to Boston. On May 18, he had written to Mrs. Lee: "You say Mr. Sullivan thought me depressed. It is true. I fear I grow more and more so. I feel a vacuum, an indifference, a want of motive, which I cannot well describe. I hope my children, and the society of my best friends, may rouse me; but I can never see such days as I have seen."[2] He was cheered by a public dinner held in his honor on June 5, in Faneuil Hall.[3] Most of Boston's prominent citizens were there to welcome their Senator, who was described by the chairman, Colonel Thomas H. Perkins, as "our distinguished guest, — worthy the noblest homage which freemen can give or a freeman receive, the homage of their hearts." Webster, in response, defended his vote on the tariff, on the ground that he was obliged to consider "the aggregate of all the

---

[1] Calhoun's original *Exposition* appears in his *Works*, VI, 1–57. It was later adopted, with some modifications, by the South Carolina Legislature. Webster wrote to Perry, April 10, 1833, " In December, 1828, I became thoroughly convinced that the plan of a southern confederacy had been received with favor, by a great many of the political men of the South." (National Edition, XVII, 535.)

[2] *Ibid.*, p. 458.

[3] Writing to Clay three days later, Webster said, " I do not think I have ever seen, in Boston, a meeting comprising so much character, talent, influence, and respectability. (*Ibid.*, XVI, 180.)

interests of the Commonwealth." [1] He drew attention also
to his advocacy of Revolutionary pensions, to his support of
"internal improvements," and to his vindication of New
England. His audience was with him, and responded with
applause when he declared that the government of the United
States could not be maintained "but by administering it on
principles as wide and broad as the country over which it
extends."

During the summer, Webster devoted himself to his motherless children, first at Boscawen, at Ezekiel's home, and later
at Sandwich, to which place his brother and his wife accompanied him. He attended the Dartmouth Commencement
and made a brief address, on July 28, to the faculty and the
graduating class.[2] It was, of course, a presidential year, but
Webster took no part in the campaign, although his influence
was given to Adams — or rather, against Jackson. As he
well knew, Adams was foredoomed to defeat. Inexpert in the
art of conciliation, the President had made many enemies,
and they had all joined in the cry, "Hurrah for Jackson!"
Conservative Massachusetts still stood firm, casting approximately 30,000 votes for Adams as compared with 6000 for
Jackson. But in the nation at large there was a different story.
Jackson received 178 votes out of 261 and was swept into
office on a wave of popular favor which did not pause to consider his qualifications.[3]

After delivering an introductory lecture on November 12
before the Boston Mechanics' Association and presiding a few
days later at a meeting for the organization of the Boston

[1] In referring to the fact that his colleague, Senator Silsbee, had voted on the opposite
side, Webster said: " We both saw in the measure something to approve, and something
to disapprove. . . . The only difference was, when the measure had assumed its final
shape, whether the good it contained so far preponderated over its acknowledged evil,
as to justify the reception and support of the whole altogether." (National Edition,
II, 15.)

[2] *Ibid.*, XIII, 31–34.

[3] Clay wrote Webster, November 30, 1828: " We are beaten. It is useless to dwell
on the causes. It is useless to repine at the result. . . . I think, in regard to the New
Administration, we should alike avoid profession of support or declarations of opposition, in advance. . . . Above all, I think *we* ought not to prematurely agitate the
question of the succession. The nation wants repose." (Cong. Lib. MSS. II.)

Society for the Diffusion of Useful Knowledge, Webster devoted himself assiduously to legal work, and did not return to Washington until January 12, 1829.[1] Little could be accomplished in Congress, for everybody was looking forward to the inauguration of General Jackson. On January 20, Webster reported from the Committee on the Judiciary a bill to relieve the Supreme Court, providing that, if fewer than four justices were present at the sitting of the Court, they might adjourn from day to day for twenty days from the opening of the term, at which time, if no quorum were present, they might adjourn for a year. Webster's common-sense solution of the problem commended itself to Congress and was quickly passed. He was in Washington for the inauguration, saw Jackson take the oath of office, and noted the "monstrous crowd" and the "thousand expectants for office" who thronged the city.[2] Although he confessed that he was indolent and "growing old," he remained in the capital until March 16, when the short special session closed and he was released for what he hoped would be a happy vacation with his children, who had been spending the winter with their uncle, Ezekiel, in Boscawen.

Ezekiel Webster had now gained distinction at the New Hampshire bar, and, though never ambitious as a public speaker, was highly thought of as a pleader in the courtroom. His wife, Alice Bridge, had died in 1821, leaving him with two daughters, Alice and Mary Ann.[3] On August 2, 1825, he married Achasa Ballard, of Concord, of whom Daniel Webster soon became very fond. Ezekiel had accumulated a considerable property and owned a fine mansion on the Main Street

[1] Webster to Ezekiel, January 17, 1829 (National Edition, XVII, 466).

[2] Webster wrote, February 5, 1829, that Jackson's health was so feeble that there was little chance of his "lasting long" (National Edition, XVI, 187), and he added, in writing to Ezekiel, February 23, the somewhat amusing prophecy: "My private opinion is, tho' I do not wish to be quoted for that, at present, that Genl. J. has not character enough to conduct his measures by his own strength. Somebody must and will lead him." (*Ibid.*, p. 188.)

[3] Alice married for her first husband Professor Jarvis Gregg, of Boscawen Academy, and, after his death, was married to the Reverend George Whipple, of Oberlin, Ohio. She died November 6, 1876. Mary Ann married Edwin D. Sanborn, later professor at Dartmouth College, and died in Hanover, December 30, 1864.

of Boscawen, of which village he was indisputably in 1829 the leading citizen. On his judgment Daniel Webster had learned to rely when decisions had to be made, and a sincere affection existed between the two brothers.

In the spring of 1829 Ezekiel Webster had been persuaded to accept a nomination for Congress by Daniel, who wanted him at Washington.[1] Ezekiel, however, was still an uncompromising Federalist, out of touch with the political spirit of the age, and he was, as Daniel expected, badly beaten. A few weeks later, on April 10, while he was addressing a jury at the Court House, in Concord, Ezekiel finished one section of his argument, and then, erect, and with his arms straight down at his sides, fell backwards without any attempt to save himself, evidently losing consciousness instantaneously. Although he was only forty-nine years old and in the prime of life, he had long been aware of a disease of the heart, and had told Daniel of his fears.

Daniel Webster had just arrived in Boston from Washington, and had been met there by Mrs. Ezekiel Webster. The news, carried by a messenger from Concord, reached Webster at three o'clock on the next morning,[2] and he set out immediately, with Mrs. Webster, for Boscawen. He saw his brother buried in the old Boscawen churchyard, overlooking the Merrimack River. With his sorrow unassuaged, he wrote to Dr. Perkins: "This event . . . has affected me very much. Coming so soon after another awful stroke, it seems to fall with double weight. He has been my reliance, through life, and I have derived much of its happiness from his fraternal affection. I am left the sole survivor of my family." [3]

Fortunately Webster had much to do in settling his brother's

[1] Webster wrote to Ezekiel, March 15, 1829: " If no change takes place in my own condition, of which I have not the slightest expectation, and if you are not elected, I shall not return. . . . Your company and that of your wife, would make a great difference." (National Edition, XVII, 474.)

[2] For an interesting description of how the news was carried to Boston by Ephraim Hutchins, see the address by Henry P. Rolfe printed in Dearborn's *History of Salisbury*, p. 865 ff. When notified, Webster said, " I thought that must be the errand you came on when I heard the wheels of your carriage stop in front of my door."

[3] National Edition, XVII, 476.

affairs. Edward Webster was left in Boscawen, with his cousins; Julia was entirely happy with Mrs. Lee; and Fletcher remained with his father, pursuing studies preparatory to entering college in August. Meanwhile Webster spent several weeks in Boscawen. Ultimately he purchased Ezekiel's interest in The Elms farm from Charles B. Haddock, who had been made guardian of Ezekiel's children, and thus became the sole owner of the old family homestead.[1]

During the summer and early autumn, Webster seriously contemplated withdrawing from public life.[2] Letters to his friends show that he was profoundly pessimistic, and that the future to him looked very dark. His wife and brother, on whom he had relied so much, were gone; the accession of President Jackson effectually blocked his hopes of an ambassadorship; and he could see no refuge except in devotion to a professional career.[3] He did not, however, take any decisive step, and the autumn of 1829 found him in New York very much occupied with legal work.

It was natural that Webster's friends should look with satisfaction upon a possible second marriage. His children were still in need of a mother's attention, and it was impossible for him to be with them throughout the year. One of his correspondents, William Tudor, wrote him from Rio Janeiro, suggesting "a young native woman of New Hampshire" as a desirable mate. Webster himself was lonely, and he went

[1] Of Ezekiel's affairs, Webster wrote, "He has left a competency to those dependent upon him; but it will require care and oversight to preserve it, and make the most of it." (National Edition, XVII, 476.) See also *Ibid.*, pp. 485-86.

[2] During this period he eagerly sought any opportunity for diversion. He was present at the dinner of Boston merchants given on October 16, on the occasion of the opening of Boston's new and luxurious hostelry, the Tremont House, at which every kind of delicacy, from terrapin soup to Chasselas grapes, was served. The Mayor of the city presided, and both Everett and Webster responded to toasts.

[3] On April 19, Webster wrote to Mason, "This occurrence is calculated to have effect on the future course of my own life, and to add to the inducements, already felt, to retire from a situation in which I am making daily sacrifices and doing little good to myself or others." (National Edition, XVII, 477.) To Mrs. Langdon Elwyn, he wrote in September: "I have lived to be the last of a pretty large circle of brothers and sisters. It not only fills me with wonder, but with melancholy, to look round about the places of my early acquaintance. Everybody is gone. While my brother lived, there was yet something to hold to; but now, the last attraction is gone." (*Ibid.*, p. 480.)

GRACE FLETCHER WEBSTER

CAROLINE LE ROY WEBSTER

into society in New York in order to forget his misery. There he was thrown into the company of Miss Caroline Le Roy, daughter of Herman Le Roy,[1] formerly Dutch Consul at New York and later one of the founders of the firm, of Le Roy, Bayard, and McEvers, from which, in 1828, he had retired. When and where Webster met her is not known. The courtship, however, must have progressed with some rapidity, for Webster wrote on November 18 to his old friend, Jacob McGaw, announcing his engagement,[2] and the marriage took place on Saturday, December 12, in the parlor of the Eastern Hotel, near the Battery, before only the bride's immediate family, and Julia Webster.[3] On the following Monday, Webster wrote to Fletcher announcing the event and sending an "elegant gold watch," a gift to the boy from his new mother.[4]

Webster was cautiously restrained in his descriptions of his new wife. He said of her to McGaw that she was "amiable, discreet, prudent, with enough of personal comeliness to satisfy me, and of the most excellent character and principles." He depicted her to Mrs. Ezekiel Webster as "amiable, affectionate, prudent, and agreeable," and he wrote to Fletcher, "The lady who is now to bear the relation of mother to you, and Julia, and Edward, I am sure will be found worthy of all your

---

[1] Herman Le Roy (1758–1841), son of Jacob Le Roy, married, October 19, 1786, Hannah Cornell, by whom he had twelve children, of whom Caroline, born September 28, 1797, was the eighth. Caroline's mother had died, December 25, 1818. Among her brothers was Daniel Le Roy (1799–1885), who was long engaged in business in New York City. The Le Roys were substantial people, who moved in the best social circles of the city.

[2] "I must tell you and Mrs. McGaw (in confidence) a little news, — nothing less than my expectation of being again married. The affair is not of long standing, but it looks so much like terminating in a marriage that I may venture to mention it to you, — to go no further until you shall hear it from other quarters. The lady is Miss Caroline Le Roy of New York, aged 31 years or thereabouts. She is the daughter of a highly reputable gentleman, now some years retired from the mercantile business." (National Edition, XVI, 191.)

[3] Announcement of the wedding was made in the New York *Evening Post* for Monday, December 14, and stated that the ceremony was performed by the " Rev. Dr. Wainwright." A similar notice was printed in the *Columbian Centinel*, in Boston, on December 16.

[4] Webster diplomatically enclosed in his letter a note from the new Mrs. Webster to Fletcher, and said himself, " The enclosed note you will of course answer. . . . Let it come enclosed to me." (National Edition, XVII, 482.)

affection and regard." If we are to judge from her portraits, she was slender and graceful but not beautiful. Her letters indicate that she was clever and witty, but we know nothing of her formal education. Skilled in social matters, she made an admirable hostess for Webster's household, but she never replaced in his heart the plain New Hampshire schoolmistress whom he had loved and lost.

His second marriage had a subtle but nevertheless profound effect upon Webster's character. Intellectually and politically, he continued to make steady advances; indeed, his ablest speeches were still to be delivered. But Caroline Webster, seventeen years younger than her husband, could not exercise any restraining influence upon him. She was a city woman, accustomed to receptions and balls, and pleased with the idea of being a leader in Washington society. With no one to warn him against extravagance, Webster lapsed deeper and deeper into debt. He indulged more freely in the pleasures of the table. He developed into a man of the world, who was tempted by good food and good drink. The effect was shown in certain physical and temperamental changes. He grew portly and slow in his movements; his solemnity became almost portentous; and he was accused by his enemies of pomposity. The old Webster was there, but the adulation of sycophants and his own realization of his importance to party and nation were corroding elements. Webster, after 1829, was both greater and smaller than he had been in 1825.

XV

THE BATTLE AGAINST NULLIFICATION

God fills the gaps of human need,
Each crisis brings its word and deed.
— WHITTIER, "The Lost Occasion"

The great rebellion of 1861 went down hardly more before the cannons of Grant and Farragut than the thunder of Webster's Reply to Hayne.
— JOHN D. LONG, February 15, 1882

I say, the right of a State to annul a law of Congress cannot be maintained, but on the ground of the inalienable right of man to resist oppression; that is to say, upon the ground of revolution.
— WEBSTER, Second Speech on Foote's Resolution

ON a cold and blustery morning in January 1830, little groups of people were hurrying up the steps of the Capitol. When the noon hour struck, the Senate Chamber was packed, not only with legislators, but with society ladies, many of whom had audaciously monopolized seats upon the floor, and, with their gay bonnets and colored gowns, gave the assembly a kaleidoscopic tinge. A stranger would have perceived that some event of importance was expected. After some routine business, the presiding officer — the spare, shaggy-haired, bushy-browed Calhoun — pounded with his gavel, and every eye was fixed on a robust figure who rose to address the conclave. He wore a long-tailed coat, with shiny gilt buttons, a buff waistcoat, and a high white cravat [1] — an old-fashioned uniform which distinguished him from his neighbors, but which nobody felt to be incongruous. With his proud head and deep-set, glowing eyes, he had the calmness of superior

---

[1] Poore, I, 116. Sargent, *Public Men and Events*, I, 172. Charles W. March, *Daniel Webster and His Contemporaries*, p. 135. Speaking of Webster's appearance on this occasion, Sargent referred to "his forehead broad and massive, towering above his large, dark, deep-set, wonderfully-powerful eyes."

strength. Daniel Webster, in the most crucial moment of his career, was about to answer Hayne, of South Carolina.

Although much had been predicted of Webster in the Senate, he had hitherto done little to justify his reputation. His double bereavement had left him listless, with his ambition cooled. When the Twenty-first Congress was called to order, he was among those recorded as absent. But he had a legitimate excuse, for he was then on his honeymoon, — which he spent in New York City, — and he did not leave until the day after Christmas. As he formally took his seat in the Senate on the last day of the year, his friends commented on his improved appearance. His marriage had banished his melancholy and made him healthier in body and spirits than he had been for many months. Tranquil, even buoyant, he was again the Webster who had declaimed so eloquently at Plymouth and Bunker Hill. It was a man in his prime, with all his splendid faculties unimpaired, who was roused to action in 1830.

For a few days, Webster was occupied with important cases before the Supreme Court. He had been assigned to the Committee on Naval Affairs, and to a Special Committee on Roads and Canals, but little business came before them. On January 6, he moved the consideration of a bill "to establish an uniform rule for the computation of the mileage of members of Congress" — a matter of slight importance. On the eighteenth, he presented a petition from the South Carolina Canal and Railroad Company, praying the Federal Government to subscribe to its capital stock, on the ground that the railroad which it was planning would promote the national welfare. Hayne and Smith, the Senators from South Carolina, who were opposed on constitutional principles to "internal improvements," would not sponsor the petition; and it was for this reason that Webster had been asked to become its advocate before the Senate. After brief explanatory remarks, he secured its reference to the Committee on Roads and Canals.[1]

---

[1] The petition was apparently handed to Webster by Hayne himself, at the request of the latter's constituents. (Curtis, I, 367.)

Meanwhile a crisis was approaching which was to bring Hayne and Webster into hostile relationship. Two days before the latter reached Washington, Senator Samuel A. Foote,[1] of Connecticut, had introduced a resolution on the subject of the public lands: —

Resolved, that the Committee on Public Lands be instructed to inquire into the expediency of limiting, for a certain period, the sales of the Public Lands to such lands as have heretofore been offered for sale, and are subject to entry at the *minimum price*. And also, whether the office of Surveyor General may not be abolished, without detriment to the public interest.

The West had been peculiarly sensitive regarding the management of the vast areas in the Mississippi Valley, and the topic had frequently been brought up in earlier Congresses. The general policy had been to dispose of them to the highest bidder, with a minimum price (since 1820) of $1.25 an acre; but, as Foote pointed out in explaining the motive for his resolution, the annual demand had never exceeded a million acres, and there were still many millions undistributed. Westerners, eager for an increase of population in their section, felt that the government should be more liberal in its attitude towards industrious pioneers and allow them to acquire lands at a low rate; and Congressmen from beyond the Alleghenies were quick to resent and denounce any legislation tending to discourage desirable settlers. The problem was delicate and complex, and inextricably entangled with such dangerous issues as internal improvements, the tariff, and negro slavery.

Foote's resolution met with opposition from Senator Thomas H. Benton, and a wrangle ensued, resulting in a postponement

[1] Samuel Augustus Foote (1780–1846), a Yale graduate and later a merchant in New Haven and a farmer in Cheshire, Connecticut, served for some years in the Legislature and also in the national House of Representatives. He was a Senator from Connecticut for one term, but was defeated for reëlection and was later Governor. His name is often printed as *Foot*, but the *Biographical Dictionary of the American Congress* uses the spelling *Foote*. March described him as " incapable of any particular distinction," and added, " Amiable in private life, respectable but never eminent in public, of no ill-regulated ambition, nor eccentric vanity, he was one of the last to have been suspected of designing to give character or intellectual vitality to thought or action." (March, p. 158.)

of its consideration. It was taken up on January 13, as a special order of the day, and the excitement could have been allayed but for the irrepressible Benton,[1] who, on January 18, in a carefully prepared speech, deliberately aimed to combine the West and the South against the Northeast. He declared that Foote's resolution was another manifestation of Eastern hostility towards the West — an attempt of Atlantic coast cities to block emigration to the interior river valleys. Accepting it as inimical to himself and his cherished Graduation Bill,[2] he searched history for grievances against New England and sought to inflame sectional animosities. It was Benton's speech — so fanatical and so provocative — which was responsible for the tone which the debate was to assume. His denunciation of New England for endeavoring "to prevent the settlement of the West" could not be left unanswered.

On the afternoon when Benton thus ignited the conflagration, Webster was in the Supreme Court Room below, awaiting the calling of the case of *Carver* v. *Jackson ex dem. Astor* (4 Pet. 1),[3] involving some highly technical points of law. His correspondence shows that, up to this time, he had paid little attention to Senate business. On the following day, however, as Senator Hayne[4] was rising to continue the discussion,

---

[1] Thomas Hart Benton (1782–1858), born in North Carolina, early moved with his mother to Tennessee, where he became the voice of the pioneer spirit. In 1815, he moved to Missouri, and, five years later, was elected one of the first Senators from that state. He retired in 1850, after thirty years in the Senate. He was a strong supporter of sound money and of Andrew Jackson. His fiery utterances, his inflated manner, and his incorruptible honesty made "Old Bullion," as he was called, a conspicuous figure in Congress. In spite of the interminable length of his speeches and of his self-conceit, he was respected, and was "a constructive force in legislation."

[2] Benton's Graduation Bill proposed to reduce the price of unsold waste land by twenty-five cents an acre each year until it was bought or reached the low limit of twenty-five cents.

[3] This case, pending over many years, determined the title to a vast area of more than 50,000 acres in New York State. Webster's argument is printed in National Edition, XV, 290 ff.

[4] Robert Young Hayne (1791–1839), grandnephew of a Revolutionary hero, began the practice of law in Charleston, served in the army during the Second War with England, and early became conspicuous in state politics. After several terms in the Legislature, he was chosen as United States Senator in 1823, when barely of legal age for that office. He became a friend and supporter of Calhoun and an able critic of the Tariff of 1828. In 1830, he was a tall and slender figure, of the patrician type, with

Webster, after the adjournment of the Supreme Court, dropped into the Senate Chamber.[1] He was just in season to hear the Carolinian announce that "the South would always sympathize with the West" and that the attitude of the Eastern states regarding the public lands was "selfish and unprincipled." Hayne advocated an alliance between the West and the South in opposition to the protective tariff. For the most part, he reiterated the ideas already advanced by Benton. As he drew to a close, however, he confessed to a fear lest the revenue accumulated from the sale of the public lands might tend to "consolidate the government" and be "fatal to the sovereignty and independence of the States." With a significance which Webster did not miss, he said, "Sir, I am one of those who believe that the very life of our system is the independence of the States, and that there is no evil more to be deprecated than the consolidation of this government." During Hayne's remarks, Webster listened attentively. He was urged by his friends to make an immediate reply, and he did secure the floor as soon as the South Carolinian had sat down. But darkness was falling, and Benton's motion to adjourn postponed the debate until the next day.

Those who had observed events could see what was coming. Sectionalism — so dreaded by leaders like Washington and Hamilton — was about to break out once more, and from its usual causes — economic need and greed. The South, made apprehensive by its declining commerce and its dwindling wealth and population, was jealous of the more prosperous North. Negro slavery, economically so wasteful and so obstructive to industry, was hampering progress south of the Potomac. The imposition of the protective tariff, beneficial to New England manufacturing, was not welcomed by planters

---

vivacious and captivating manners, and was described by Everett as "fluent, graceful and persuasive as a debater." In December 1831, he left the Senate to become Governor of South Carolina, in which position he openly defied the Federal Government. After retiring two years later, he was Mayor of Charleston and President of the Cincinnati and Charleston Railroad.

[1] Webster to Mason, February 27, 1830 (National Edition, XVII, 488), and Webster to Dutton, March 8, 1830 (*Ibid.*, p. 493).

and importers. Two civilizations, one industrial and the other agrarian, were face to face, the former having the whip hand. Chafing under the tyranny of a relentless majority, South Carolina took refuge in a theory of the Union through which she could defend her interests and resist encroachment by the Federal Government. It was economic pressure which was responsible for the doctrines taught by Hayne and Calhoun. The position adopted by South Carolina in 1830 differed only slightly from that assumed by the New England Federalists in 1808 and 1812, when Massachusetts and New Hampshire saw their commerce slipping away through embargo and war. Then the Northeast had been sectional, and the South and West had been national. Now the rôles were reversed.

The Great Debate of 1830, started over the public lands, was quickly carried into other fields, — the tariff, local patriotism, the Ordinance of 1787, and slavery, — but it eventually narrowed down, through Webster's clever strategy, to one question which every citizen could understand: "Where does the authority of a sovereign state cease and that of the national government begin?" Whatever may be the opinion to-day, this was not, in 1830, a one-sided controversy. It has been easy for Northern historians to insist that Webster's position was impregnable. But the practical men who sat in the Constitutional Convention of 1787 were not themselves sure about the intentions of that body. Some leading American statesmen had accepted different theories at different periods. Webster himself was assailable in this respect, and his sensitiveness to attack betrayed misgivings about his past. There was a pleasing irony in the spectacle of a Northern Federalist instructing a Charlestonian regarding the supremacy of the Union.

Thus the discussion, although participated in by lesser men, became in the eyes of the people a duel between Hayne and Webster, as gladiators of their respective sections. Benton, who had precipitated the clash, was ignored by Webster, who saw that he could succeed best by directly challenging the representative of the South. Benton was annoying, but

Hayne was the more dangerous enemy. The issue of nullification had been raised, not by Missouri, but by South Carolina; and behind the voice of Robert Y. Hayne was the acute intelligence and ingenious sophistry of John C. Calhoun.

The debate was fair and open, a collision of opinions in which each combatant had his opportunity for defense and rebuttal, and neither sought to evade the issue. Never had the proceedings of the Senate been of more positive educational value. The protagonists exemplified contrasted schools of political thought, and, although Webster's intellectual resources were richer than Hayne's, the two were not unevenly matched. The fair-complexioned Hayne was intrepid, mercurial, and resourceful; the swarthy Webster was firm, slow-moving, and phlegmatic.[1] They had already had an altercation during the closing hours of the preceding Congress,[2] and Hayne had won a victory. Now it was to be Cavalier against Roundhead, the fluid sea against the immovable rock Each was a perfect product of the type of culture from which he had sprung.

On Wednesday, January 20, when the Foote Resolution was called, it was modified by the addition of the following clause: —

Or whether it be expedient to adopt measures to hasten the sales and extend more rapidly the surveys of the public lands.[3]

Webster then addressed the Senate in a speech which, filling only twenty-one pages in the collected edition of his

[1] A correspondent of the Philadelphia *Gazette* noted: " Mr. Webster's countenance is generally cold, severe, and impressive, which makes the occasional sarcasm when accompanied by a sneer or a smile exceedingly effective. The face of Mr. Hayne, on the contrary, is constantly in play; every varying emotion rushes to his countenance, and is there distinctly legible."

[2] The controversy had arisen over a resolution offered by Webster on February 27, 1829, calling on the President to communicate to the Senate copies of instructions given to our representatives to the abortive Panama Congress. Hayne's opposition prevented its passage, and the two men exchanged words on the floor of the Senate. (Jervey, *Hayne*, pp. 224–25.)

[3] Senator Levi Woodbury, of New Hampshire, had moved to strike out the original resolution and insert the new clause; and then Senator Peleg Sprague had suggested the addition of it as an amendment. (National Edition, VI, 18–19.) These technical parliamentary details did not affect the real issue.

works,[1] was principally a refutation of the charge that the policy of the Federal Government towards the new states of the West had been harsh and severe. Hayne's biographer has declared that Webster's remarks were "clever, disingenuous, provocative," couched in a style which was "nonchalant, flippant, offensive." [2] Although he had been given almost no opportunity for preparation,[3] he ranged with ease over our national history. Answering specifically the attacks on his own section, he asserted that not a measure for the benefit of the West could have been passed in Congress without the backing of New England; and he pointed to the Ordinance of 1787,[4] drafted by Nathan Dane,[5] of Massachusetts, as a measure which must have failed without the support of Northern votes. His most eloquent passage was a contrast between Ohio, in 1794, — a "fresh, untouched, unbounded, magnificent wilderness," — and the same section in 1830, and he attributed its marked prosperity to the exclusion of negro slavery from its soil. Commenting on Hayne's fear that a permanent revenue might "consolidate" the government, Webster defended "constitutional consolidation," saying: —

I wish to see no new powers drawn to the general government; but I confess I rejoice in whatever tends to strengthen the bond that unites us, and encourages the hope that our Union may be perpetual.

[1] For the complete text of this speech, see National Edition, V, 248 ff.

[2] Jervey, pp. 238–39. Jervey adds: "It was an irritating speech, and doubtless meant to be. It was to tempt the one attacked to a reply, after which he would be overwhelmed by the real speech, with regard to which, as Benton might have expressed it, as he does insinuate, Webster was lying in, to be delivered of."

[3] As if in extenuation, Webster said, "Owing to other engagements, I could not employ even the interval between the adjournment of the Senate and its meeting the next morning, in attention to the subject of this debate." (National Edition, VI, 6.) He did, however, have time to fill three sheets of ordinary letter paper with notes — which, however, he did not follow very carefully. (Curtis, I, 356.)

[4] The Ordinance of 1787, providing for the administration of the section north of the Ohio and east of the Mississippi, had included a prohibition of negro servitude in that district. In stressing the responsibility of New England for this important act, Webster was led into minor errors, which Benton, with some glee, later corrected. When the Ordinance was finally passed, it was carried by the votes of three Northern and five Southern states.

[5] Dane, nearly eighty years old and almost totally deaf, was still living in Beverly, Massachusetts, at the time of Webster's speech.

He closed effectively by quoting from a speech in 1825, by the truculent George McDuffie, who had complained because Webster had advocated the construction of highways to the West. Before sitting down, he moved the indefinite postponement of Foote's amended resolution, which seemed to him unnecessary.

Thus far, the discussion had been like the manœuvring of skillful fencers, each endeavoring to place the other in an unfavorable position. Benton, unwilling to be disregarded, followed Webster in an able speech, claiming a victory on the ground that the latter's motion for an indefinite postponement was a confession of weakness.[1] On Thursday morning, January 21, Webster was to appear for his clients in the Supreme Court, and his friend, Senator Chambers, of Maryland, accordingly requested that the debate be deferred. Hayne, offended by some of Webster's remarks and burning to reply, refused, saying that he saw the gentleman from Massachusetts before him and presumed that the latter could be present through the day.[2] Webster, his arms folded across his chest, haughtily declared himself ready to receive his adversary's fire. The indefatigable Benton then spent an hour continuing the address which he had begun on the preceding afternoon, during which Webster, going downstairs, secured a postponement of his business in court. Benton at last sat down, and, after the Senate had rejected another motion to adjourn, Hayne opened his reply to Webster, speaking for about an hour and then stopping so that Webster could keep his engagement with his client. On the following Monday, Hayne continued his speech in the Senate, occupying two and one-half hours more.[3]

[1] Isaac Hill's New Hampshire *Patriot* published a letter from Washington dated January 23, which said, " Mr. Benton's speech was a splendid display of eloquence, and every way superior to Mr. Webster's."

[2] Describing these events to Dutton in a letter of March 8, 1830, Webster wrote of Hayne, " He was very angry, and when he rose to oppose a day or two's postponement, as I wished to be in the court, talked perhaps a little too largely of what he was going to do." (National Edition, XVII, 494.)

[3] Hayne's speech is printed in full in *The Great Debate*, edited by Lindsay Swift, in the Riverside Literature Series. The break in his argument is clearly indicated in

Hayne was above the average height, with light-brown hair, a sallow complexion, and grey eyes, full of animation and fire. Although he was not distinguished-looking, his features were expressive, his voice was well modulated, and his gestures were graceful and appropriate. His manner was impassioned, even vehement, and a jaunty air of self-confidence lent weight to his impetuous utterance. He had taken pains to study Webster's record, and he dealt some telling blows. In spite of its personalities, it was a brilliant performance, and, to his adherents, Hayne seemed unanswerable. As a public speaker, he was more pleasing and convincing than Calhoun.

Hayne was especially formidable in his criticism of Webster's conversion to protectionism and in his exposure of the hostility of Northern Federalists towards the Second War with England. With stinging sarcasm, he contrasted the patriotism of South Carolina with the recalcitrancy of Massachusetts, and quoted from Carey's *Olive Branch*[1] expressions of disunion sentiment by the Federalists of 1812–14. Hayne's arraignment of New England's disloyalty delighted the Democrats, who smiled their approval as the orator uncovered the inconsistencies of Webster's past. The latter sat through the tirade like a sphinx, his face completely immobile.[2]

Hayne would have been wiser if he had confined himself to destructive criticism, at which he was not markedly inferior to his rival. But, encouraged by Vice President Calhoun, — who, from his desk, sent him rather ostentatiously some notes of suggestion, — Hayne entered upon an explanation of the South Carolina theory of nullification, which he based

---

the text by the reading, on January 21, of a paragraph from Burke's *Speech on Conciliation*. When Hayne resumed, on January 25, he took up at once the matter of " the consolidation of this government." (*The Great Debate*, p. 53.)

[1] Mathew Carey (1760–1839), a Philadelphia editor, published in 1814 *The Olive Branch, or Faults on Both Sides, Federal and Democratic*, in which he undertook to reconcile the opposing parties during the War of 1812. It passed through ten editions and was widely read.

[2] Evidence on this point is conflicting. The reporter of the *New York Courier and Enquirer* said: " I will not pretend to give you even a hint of the tremendous punishment which, for one hour, Mr. Hayne inflicted on the 'god-like' man. . . . He turned, he twisted, he leaned back, leaned forward, took notes, sometimes audibly dissented, and appeared indeed to be put to the rack."

principally upon the language and the authority of the Virginia and Kentucky Resolutions of 1798. Some features of the doctrine were never quite clear, and its defenders hesitated to carry it to its logical conclusion. Fundamentally, however, it claimed that each state, in assenting to the Federal Constitution, reserved the right to interpret that document within its own borders. The people of any state, if they felt themselves aggrieved, could declare an act of the Federal Government not binding upon themselves; in other words, they could nullify Congressional legislation. Hayne, following Calhoun, directly denied the power of the Federal Judiciary [1] to settle problems in which a "sovereign state" was involved, and said explicitly: —

As to the doctrine that the federal government is the exclusive judge of the extent as well as the limitations of its powers, it seems to me utterly subversive of the sovereignty and independence of the States. It makes but little difference, in my estimation, whether Congress or the Supreme Court are invested with this power.

The doctrine of nullification, which for many months had occupied the minds of certain groups of South Carolinians,[2] was thus introduced on the floor of Congress [3] and upheld as having been first promulgated by "the fathers of the faith." Hayne said, "The South is acting on a principle she has always held sacred, — resistance to unauthorized taxation," and asserted then and later that his theory was that on which the Federal Government of 1789 was established. He did not,

[1] Attacks on the Supreme Court, both covert and open, had been made in Congress for some years. (Warren, *Supreme Court*, II, 112, ff.) The authority of that tribunal had been enhanced by sweeping decisions, and it was alleged by Democrats that it had encroached on the states and assumed a jurisdiction to which it was not entitled. In the Cherokee Land Cases, Georgia had openly flouted a mandate of the Supreme Court. (Beveridge, *Marshall*, IV, 539 ff.) On March 12, while the Great Debate was still in progress, the Court, in *Craig v. Missouri* (4 Pet. 410), held a Missouri statute to be invalid, to the disgust of Benton, who was the attorney for his state.

[2] The fact that there was, in 1830, a strong Unionist Party in South Carolina, headed by such statesmen as Joel R. Poinsett, Hugh S. Legaré, William Drayton, and James L. Petigru, has not always been brought out by historians. See Frederic Bancroft, *Calhoun and the South Carolina Nullification Movement*, pp. 90–126.

[3] Benton, who had been in the Senate for a decade, said that the topic of nullification was then (1830) " first broached in our national legislature."

however, advocate disunion,[1] but rather "a firm, manly, and steady resistance against usurpation."[2] As to what South Carolina would do in case force were employed by the national authorities, Hayne was silent; but he did plead that, if the South should be "hurried beyond the bounds of a cool and calculating prudence," something should be pardoned to the spirit of liberty.

Hayne's speech was regarded as exceedingly effective, and, unless its impression could be counteracted, the prestige of New England was sure to suffer. Webster could not, of course, allow the charges made against him to stand without a protest. As soon as Hayne had concluded, he rose to reply; but, since it was then almost dark, he consented to an adjournment, and the stage was thus properly set for the next day.

On that Monday evening Southerners were elated. Their champion had measured up to their hopes. Northerners, we are told, walked about with "timid anxious eyes and depressed bearing."[3] But Webster was little perturbed. When Story called on him and offered to help in looking up material, the latter replied: "Give yourself no uneasiness, Judge Story! I will grind him as fine as a pinch of snuff."[4] After dinner, he talked the situation over with Edward Everett, who remarked that he had never seen Webster "more calm and self-possessed, or in better spirits."[5] Everett asked him if he had

[1] Speaking of Hayne's attitude, Benton wrote, " Nor have I ever believed that Mr. Hayne contemplated disunion, in any contingency, as one of its results." (*Thirty Years*, I, 138.)

[2] According to Hayne's theory, a state deciding against Congress could compel that body to ask for an amendment to the Constitution, requiring the consent of three-fourths of the states. Thus one-quarter of the states could make any legislation invalid. Hayne's plan would, in operation, have made the Union no more closely knit than the old Confederation of 1781–89.

[3] Most accounts of the Great Debate rely to a large extent on the excellent but too highly colored narrative given by Charles W. March in his book, *Daniel Webster and His Contemporaries*. March was present in the Senate and gave vivid descriptions of the various personages in the audience as well as of the speakers themselves.

[4] Harvey, p. 156.

[5] March, p. 126. On the authority of one of his friends, March said that Webster, who had lain down on his sofa for a rest, was overheard laughing to himself. When somebody asked him why he was amused, he replied, " I have been thinking of what Col. Hayne said to-day about Banquo's ghost; and I am going to get up and make a note of it."

taken notes. "Yes," answered Webster, taking from his vest pocket a slip of paper no bigger than the palm of his hand, "I have it all: that is his speech." [1] Shrewd observers knew what was coming. To a friend of Hayne's, who was praising the latter's speech, Senator Iredell, of North Carolina, said, "He has started the lion, — but wait till we hear his roar, and feel his claws."

Although he had received but little warning, Webster found time to prepare twelve pages of notes, on loose unnumbered sheets, answering some of Hayne's specific accusations.[2] He could not have been caught unaware, for he was saturated with the subject. Ever since the Dartmouth College Case he had been expounding in the Supreme Court the authority of the Federal Constitution over individual states, and had declared that, as a last resort, the national government was dominant. Webster's arguments in *McCulloch* v. *Maryland* and *Gibbons* v. *Ogden* were the genesis of the Reply to Hayne. He merely adapted to legislative chambers and to a lay audience what he had said repeatedly in the presence of jurists and to friends of his own fireside.[3] He once told a clergyman, "The materials of that speech had been lying in my mind for eighteen months, though I had never committed my thoughts to paper, or arranged them in my memory." [4] To an admirer who inquired whether the Reply to Hayne was extemporaneous, Webster replied, in his oracular manner, "Young man, there is no such thing as extemporaneous acquisition." Benton thought that Webster had planned for the encounter long in

---

[1] Harvey, pp. 150–51.

[2] These notes are printed in the National Edition, VI, 287–92, from a manuscript, mainly in Webster's handwriting, in the archives of the New Hampshire Historical Society. They are difficult to decipher, and do not correspond to the order of thought in the speech itself. Some of them were not used.

[3] John Whipple, a lawyer from Providence, Rhode Island, while reading Webster's speech, was haunted by the feeling that he had heard it before. When he spoke of this to Webster, the latter replied, " Don't you remember our conversation during the long walks we took together last summer at Newport, while in attendance at Story's court?"

[4] Harvey, p. 154. Webster told Harvey in 1846 that he had prepared material on several of Hayne's topics, and added: " If he had tried to make a speech to fit my notes, he could not have hit it better. No man is inspired with the occasion. I never was."

advance, but the latter himself at a public dinner in New York [1] said : —

Seeing the true grounds of the Constitution thus attacked, I raised my voice in its favor, I must confess with no preparation or previous intention. I can hardly say that I embarked in the contest from a sense of duty. It was an instantaneous impulse of inclination, not acting against duty, I trust, but hardly waiting for its suggestions. I felt it to be a contest for the integrity of the Constitution, and I was ready to enter into it, not thinking, or caring, personally, how it might come out.

Like a warrior clad in full panoply, Webster, on the morning of Tuesday, January 26, walked up the steps of the Capitol. Calling Senator Bell into the robing room, he said, according to the long-established legend: "You know my constitutional opinions. There are, among my friends in the Senate, some who may not concur in them. What shall I do?" Bell, with much vigor, urged him to speak out. "It is a critical moment," he added, "and it is time, it is high time, that the people of this country should know what this Constitution *is*." "Then, by the blessing of Heaven," responded Webster solemnly, "they shall learn, this day, before the sun goes down, what I understand it to be." [2] Senator Clayton, who had dined with him on the previous evening, watched him as he entered, and, approaching him, asked, "Are you well charged?" "Seven fingers!" was the reply — a reference to the charge of a muzzle-loading gun, for which four fingers of powder were generally considered sufficient.

Under such circumstances, then, and before an audience which was well disposed towards him,[3] Webster rose for what was to be the noblest effort of his career — a speech of which

---

[1] The occasion was a dinner tendered to Webster on March 10, 1831. See National Edition, II, 61.

[2] March, p. 132. Harvey, pp. 150–51.

[3] It had been known for some days that a great speech was expected from Webster, and people had come even from as far as Boston especially for the occasion. Writing to Dutton, March 8, 1830, Webster said: "One thing is singular enough, and I can mention it to you without danger of your ascribing it to any wrong cause. I never spoke in the presence of an audience so eager and so sympathetic. The public feeling here was on our side almost universally." (National Edition, XVII, 494.)

WEBSTER REPLYING TO HAYNE

From a painting by George P. A. Healy now in Faneuil Hall, Boston

Lodge said, "He never surpassed it, he never equalled it afterwards." With due regard to the importance of the occasion, Webster had arranged to have his friend, Joseph Gales, take down his words in shorthand. Although his meagre notes lay on the desk by his side, he seldom referred to them, but went steadily on, his feet firmly set and his only gestures the up and down motions of his right arm. Characteristically, he set everybody at ease by calling, in a low, impressive tone, for a reading of the original resolution. He then spoke for three hours without a pause. At a fitting point, he stopped, and asked for an adjournment, and he concluded his speech on the following afternoon.

The scene in the Senate Chamber during those two days has been made familiar to most Americans through Healy's colossal painting, "Webster Replying to Hayne," now hanging over the platform in Faneuil Hall.[1] On this canvas, sixteen feet by thirty feet in size, appear portraits of more than one hundred and fifty persons, most of them drawn from life.[2] Webster himself stands erect, his left hand on his desk, staring fearlessly at Calhoun, with Hayne not far away, in front and on his right. It has not been possible to identify all the faces, but among them, besides Mrs. Webster, are those of Mr. and Mrs. Ticknor, Justice Story, Mr. and Mrs. Paige, Harrison Gray Otis, John Quincy Adams, Franklin Haven, Colonel Thomas H. Perkins, Isaac P. Davis, and Samuel Appleton — all Webster's personal friends. Among the Senators are the

---

[1] George P. A. Healy painted this picture in Paris, devoting to it most of seven years. It was exhibited in the United States in 1851, and was finally sold to the City of Boston for $40,000. In commenting on it, Healy wrote: "Webster was the very man for the center of a large picture. His friends and enemies, in various attitudes of attention, of admiration, or of indignation, set him off very well, and in the galleries I grouped all the prettiest women of the day, with their big bonnets trimmed with drooping plumes, and their oddly made dresses." (Healy, *Reminiscences of a Portrait Painter*.) Healy made several portraits of Webster, the last being at Marshfield in 1848.

[2] Healy wrote, "Each head on the vast canvas is a portrait," but he was not careful about historical accuracy, and did not scruple to introduce the faces of Thomas Couture, his artist friend, who never visited America; of Henry Wadsworth Longfellow, who was, in 1830, a professor in Bowdoin College, and did not attend the Debate; and of M. de Tocqueville, who did not arrive in the United States until 1831.

refined and scholarly Forsyth, the self-important Benton and his colleague, the dogmatic Barton, the thoughtful Woodbury, the majestic Clayton, and the austere John Tyler.[1] The artistic merit of the composition has been questioned, and its accuracy is not above criticism,[2] but it does perpetuate one of the most dramatic moments in our history.

Webster's speech fills seventy-three pages in the National Edition of his works.[3] In the presentation of his cause he resorted to virtually every oratorical device, including banter, irony, scorn, sarcasm, and pathos. With consummate artistry, he would not allow his audience to be bored, but entertained them by his infinite variety. During two-thirds of his remarks, filling the first day, he devoted himself to the vindication of himself and his section against the slurs of Hayne.[4] He had little difficulty in showing that the policy of New England had been, on the whole, favorable to the development of the West, and that there had been no deliberate attempt to retard emigration to the Mississippi Valley. Nor was it hard for him to demonstrate "*when*, and *how*, and *why* New England had supported measures favorable to the West." He also proved that he had advocated internal improvements and had argued for their constitutionality. Without violating parliamentary etiquette, he retaliated most effectively upon his opponent.

With the ominous problem of negro slavery, neither speaker

[1] There were, in 1830, forty-eight Senators: and we are told that, during the Debate, almost no business was transacted in the House.

[2] According to a letter from L. H. Machen to W. Slade, January 30, 1830 (*Letters of A. W. Machen*, p. 52), " to accommodate the ladies who thronged the vestibules, not only the lobbies and passages below were filled with chairs, but even Senators had the gallantry to yield their seats." The *National Intelligencer* said, January 27, " Already the Ladies, too numerous for the ordinary accommodation, have usurped the places of the members of the Senate." It was even stated that Webster, when he arose, gave his seat to a lady, but Healy's painting shows no women on the floor. According to March, Representative Dixon H. Lewis, of Alabama, who weighed almost five hundred pounds, was wedged in the crowd behind the Vice President's chair, and finally forced his way to a place behind one of the windows flanking the presiding officer's desk. Healy, however, put him on the opposite side of the hall.

[3] National Edition, VI, 3-75.

[4] Many of Calhoun's friends saw the injudiciousness of Hayne's attack on New England. Judge Richard Peters wrote Joseph Hopkinson, January 24, " There never was a course so ruinous as that which is now pursued by the Calhoun party in this violence towards Webster." (Meigs, I, 397.)

had been eager to deal. Webster had mentioned it casually during his earlier remarks upon the Ordinance of 1787; and Hayne, sensitive at one or two phrases, had requited him in a lengthy statement, explaining the Southern attitude. Now Webster spoke out more boldly, declaring domestic slavery to be "one of the greatest evils, both moral and political," but maintaining that there never had been "a disposition in the North to interfere with these interests of the South."

As Webster approached the question of the tariff, he assumed an air of confidence, and did his utmost to repel the accusations of inconsistency; but his defense was disingenuous rather than convincing. He admitted that he regarded the tariff as a matter of expediency, on which he had voted in accordance with the economic interests of his constituents, and that his conversion to protectionism had been simply "a change of position to meet new circumstances." But this plea could not eradicate his brilliant free trade speech of 1824, in which he had argued, on broad philosophical and social grounds, against the principle of protection.

In the midst of his discussion of the tariff, Webster broke off, and the Senate adjourned until the following day.[1] So far, his speech, although interesting, had not been remarkable, and he had displayed none of that power of uplifting an audience for which he was famous. Those who had hoped for

[1] The shorthand report of Joseph Gales indicates that Webster closed with a passage afterwards omitted from the published version. Gales's account for Tuesday ended: " Mr. Webster here illustrated his situation by that of his going a journey (say Georgetown) with another person, — they differing as to the mode of travelling, he preferring to walk and the other to ride, and he yielding to his companion, — suppose a wheel was to run off the carriage, was he to persist in attempting to go on with three wheels because he had been opposed to going at all? Or was he to lend a hand to repair the defect that they might at least go safely on?" No such analogy occurs in the speech as printed by the *National Intelligencer* from the manuscript corrected and rewritten by Webster himself. The point at which Webster broke off occurs in the published version at the close of the paragraph ending with the sentence, " And there is another sort to which I lay as little, and that is, a kind of consistency by which persons feel themselves as much bound to oppose a proposition after it has become a law of the land as before." (National Edition, VI, 39.) There is nothing whatever to indicate why Webster chose to omit the illustration of the carriage wheel or why he left off speaking in the very midst of his discussion of the tariff. For a full and interesting discussion of this problem see a letter by C. W. Lewis in the *Boston Evening Transcript*, July 13, 1882.

passages of highly emotional oratory had been decidedly disappointed.

At noon, on January 27, before a throng hushed with expectancy, Webster resumed his consideration of the tariff. Summing up his position in a few crisp sentences, he turned to the defense of New England Federalism. He had to move discreetly and cautiously, for he knew how vulnerable he was. While acknowledging that individuals had showed disunionist tendencies, he denied that the Federalists as a group, even in the fury of party antagonism, had advocated nullification,[1] and he suggested that disloyal utterances could be assembled from south of the Potomac as well as from east of the Hudson. He wisely did not attempt to justify the Hartford Convention, contenting himself by granting that, if that gathering had come together for "breaking up the Union," it was "obnoxious to censure." This section of the speech was not impressive and showed signs of heavy labor.

But, whatever its deficiencies, Webster, with intuitive psychology, offset them by the glorious paragraphs which followed. He had been dealing with prosaic facts. Now, as if set free from shackles, he turned to sentiment, and uttered the still remembered words, "Mr. President, I shall enter on no encomium upon Massachusetts; she needs none." As he continued, he glanced towards a little knot of Bay State men in a corner of the gallery, as if seeking their support; and, while they listened, they "shed tears like girls."[2] March has left a description — probably too highly colored — of the orator as he stood "swaying his right arm, like a huge tilt-hammer, up and down, his swarthy countenance lighted up with excitement . . . like Vulcan in his armory forging thoughts for the gods."[3] Emerson spoke of him as being in a "galvanized state," and he certainly seemed like a man

[1] Webster chose to leave unmentioned the Faneuil Hall Resolutions of March 30, 1811, which declared the Act of March 2, 1811, " *ex post facto*, and void, unjust and tyrannical," and which were as strongly against the Federal Government as any of the resolves of South Carolina.

[2] March, p. 142. Lyman, I, 59.

[3] March, p. 144; quoted also in Lyman, I, 61.

inspired. Those who had come hoping for "purple patches" had what they wanted in Webster's eulogy of his Commonwealth.

As if relieved by what seemed a spontaneous outburst, Webster now devoted himself with impressive seriousness to an explanation of the nature of the Federal Union. He first outlined what he conceived to be the "South Carolina doctrine" — that state legislatures had, under the Constitution, a right to interfere whenever, in their judgment, the Federal Government transcended its constitutional limits, and that any state could not only lawfully decide for itself whether a given act of the Federal Government was illegal, but could also, "by its own sovereign authority, annul an act of the general government which it deems plainly and palpably unconstitutional." In answer, Webster declared that the right of a state to annul an act of Congress could not be upheld except "upon the ground of revolution." The issue was drawn much more sharply than is usual in such public controversies, and neither contestant sought to evade it.

Webster's legalistic mind led him to a peculiar and too literal interpretation of the language of the Constitution. He contended that it was "the creature of the people," not of the state legislatures; that its Preamble, opening, "We, the people of the United States," indicated that it was not established by each of the states severally; but that the people, by ratifying the Constitution, had created a new governmental unit, with certain specified and restricted powers, superior in various respects to the state governments. His conception is best summarized in his own words: —

I hold it to be a popular government, erected by the people; those who administer it, responsible to the people; and itself capable of being amended and modified, just as the people may choose it should be. It is as popular, just as truly emanating from the people, as the State Governments. It is created for one purpose; the State governments for another. It has its own powers; they have theirs.

Webster did not deny that the people have the right of revolution against an oppressive or intolerable overlord; nor did he gainsay the privilege of any one citizen, or group of citizens, to assert that a law is unconstitutional. The real question was, "Whose prerogative is it to decide on the constitutionality or unconstitutionality of the laws?" Webster's answer — and with his record he could have made no other — was that the Constitution is supreme and that the final appeal lies with the judicial branch of the Federal Government. He believed in the ultimate authority of that Supreme Court before which he had so often argued and which had so often decided in his favor.

To illustrate the proper procedure in disputed cases, Webster showed that New England, feeling herself maltreated by the Embargo, had declared it to be unconstitutional and had, through memorials, vigorously protested to Congress. But, when the United States District Court pronounced this law constitutional, New England had acquiesced. For purposes of dramatic contrast, he sketched a picture of what would happen if South Carolina, convinced of the unconstitutionality of the protective tariff, should refuse to recognize the ruling of the Supreme Court and should instead resist the collection of customs duties. This, said Webster, would be treason; and, if South Carolina persisted, the result would be civil war.

It has been forcefully and correctly maintained that Webster's argument from history is untenable.[1] He was certainly wrong in his interpretation of the words "We, the people," and, although his view strengthened our government politically, it had no foundation in fact. Separate states, like New Hampshire and South Carolina, undoubtedly felt, when they voted to form the Union, that they were entering an improved confederacy, from which, if dissatisfied, they could withdraw. The new government was primarily an agreement for mutual convenience and benefit, in which each state retained its autonomy. Utterances of public men during the first quarter-century of the republic assumed that secession was within

[1] Warren, *The Making of the Constitution*, pp. 394–95. In a letter to the author, Warren makes the plausible suggestion that Webster's ideas were derived mainly from Judge Joseph Story, who developed this theory in his *Commentaries*.

the province of any state government. The facts indicate that the Constitution was by many tacitly regarded as a compact between the states; that the advisability of secession was more than once considered, not only by Virginia and Kentucky, but by Connecticut and Massachusetts; and that nothing but expediency prevented the breaking up of the United States into smaller units.

Gradually, however, a revised conception of the Federal Union had become popular. The admission of new states; the acquisition of Louisiana; the sense of harmony developed during the struggles with France and Great Britain; the growth of a healthy national self-consciousness — all these had contributed to weld the sections together. But more important than any of these had been the influence of Chief Justice John Marshall, aided by Joseph Story and Daniel Webster, in emphasizing the authority of the Constitution and the Supreme Court. In 1830, sensible Americans were less concerned with the question, "What did the framers of the Constitution intend?" than with the more pertinent query, "What is best for the United States to-day?" It was easy to demonstrate that the compact theory of the government held by Hayne, no matter how logical it might be, would, if persisted in, undo the progress of forty years. It was for this reason that the splendid peroration beginning, "I have not allowed myself, sir, to look beyond the Union, to see what might be hidden in the dark recess behind," is the most convincing passage in Webster's speech. His appeal to the sentiment of Union met with a spontaneous response from patriotic hearts. But it was its emotional quality, not its reasoning, which made it of historic significance. Whatever the Constitution makers had in their minds, it was Webster's conception of the government which was to prevail. Any other theory, no matter how well supported by precedent, would have been fatal.

As he drew to a climax, Webster's rich voice deepened, and his manner became more solemn. After his concluding words, "Liberty *and* Union, now and forever, one and inseparable!" his audience sat as if held by some mesmeric witchery. Then the gavel of John C. Calhoun broke the spell. The Senate resumed its normal routine, and the guests walked out into the gusty winter afternoon, conscious that they had been present at a dramatic moment in American history.

When quiet had been restored, Hayne made a brief reply, adhering closely to the constitutional question; and Webster, in his turn, entered upon a short rebuttal.[1] Nothing novel, however, was brought out. Hayne still regarded the Constitution as a "compact between the states." Webster once more described it as "a popular government, founded in popular election, directly responsible to the people themselves" — "not a confederacy, not a league, not a compact between the States, but a Constitution." Of this reply, Edward Everett said that "for condensation, precision, and force" it was a specimen of parliamentary logic never surpassed.

In the evening, at a fashionable levee in the White House, Hayne and Webster were both present, attracting far more attention than "Old Hickory" himself. With characteristic courtesy, Hayne approached his rival to extend his congratulations. "How are you this evening, Colonel Hayne?" asked Webster, extending his hand. "None the better for you, sir," was the gallant response.[2] On the next morning, Webster was back in the Supreme Court Chamber, delivering his argument in *Bell* v. *Cunningham*, as if his legal career had been only temporarily interrupted.

The immediate effect of Webster's speech upon his listeners was, of course, evident,[3] but it took some time for his words

[1] Hayne's remarks filled nineteen pages of the Congressional Debates; Webster's only three.

[2] March, p. 151.

[3] John Quincy Adams described the speech as " a remarkable instance of readiness in debate, — a reply of at least four hours to a speech of equal length. It demolishes the whole fabric of Hayne's speech, so that it leaves scarcely the wreck to be seen." (*Memoirs*, VIII, 193.) Another listener wrote: " At the close of his speech, but one sentiment of unmixed admiration pervaded the most numerous assemblage I had ever witnessed at any debate in the Senate. . . . A gentleman of great natural endowments, whose opinions are entitled to great respect as a scholar and a Christian, assured me that he had formed no just conception, until he heard Mr. Webster, of the capacity of the human mind." (*Letters of A. W. Machen*, p. 55.) A Virginian, hearing the speech, felt as " if looking at a mammoth treading his native canebrake, and, without apparent consciousness, crushing obstacles which nature had never designed as impediments to him." (Parker, p. 43.)

to reach the general public. Mrs. Joseph Gales, using her husband's very neat stenographic notes, prepared a transcript in longhand for Webster, who revised it with great care and with so many alterations that the published form was very different from that which he had spoken.[1] The Reply was first printed in the *National Intelligencer* in three installments, on February 23, 25, and 27. It was not published in Philadelphia until February 26 and in Boston until February 27 — almost exactly a month after its delivery. Soon it was being circulated everywhere. At the office of the *National Intelligencer* alone, forty thousand copies had been sent out before the close of May. Never before had a Congressional speech been in such great demand.

Meanwhile Webster, unwilling that posterity should receive a distorted or biased account of what had happened, prepared a narrative of the entire proceedings, which was later followed, with only slight modifications, by Edward Everett in his *Memoir*.[2]

In Boston and in Charleston, the debate was the big news of the day, and citizens awaited impatiently the arrival of complete reports.[3] It was at first regarded merely as a phase of

[1] In the Boston Public Library is a bound volume including the original shorthand report made by Gales, in double column on folio sheets; the speech as transcribed by Mrs. Gales, on one hundred folio pages; Webster's revised draft of eighty-five pages, mostly in his own handwriting, with many changes and interlineations; and various notes and newspaper clippings. This volume was purchased, April 26, 1877, from Mrs. Gales by Robert C. Winthrop, representing a group of Boston citizens, and presented by him to the Public Library. A detailed comparison between Mrs. Gale's version and that finally perfected by Webster shows that the latter, in preparing the speech for the press, omitted many sentences, added others, and modified his phraseology so that it was very different from the original. The concluding sentence, as taken down by Gales, was as follows: " I hope to see spread all over it, blazoned in letters of light, and proudly floating over land and sea, that other sentiment, dear to my heart, 'Union *and* Liberty, now and forever, one and inseparable.' " Even when allowance is made for the inevitable inaccuracies of the stenographer, it is obvious that the speech, in its generally accepted phrasing, is not that which was delivered on the floor of the Senate. See the letter of C. W. Lewis, *Boston Evening Transcript*, July 13, 1882.

[2] For this manuscript, now in the Congressional Library, see National Edition, VI, 293 ff.

[3] A correspondent of the *Columbian Centinel*, in a letter printed on January 30, 1830, said: " The debate in the Senate exceeds in interest every thing of the kind I have heard. . . . I hazard nothing in saying that Mr. W. will fully vindicate the East, throw Mr. H. on his back. Messrs. H. and B. combined are but a handful for him, — a *bonne bouche* that he can take on any time after dinner." On March 10, the same paper said, " The moral effect of the late speeches of Mr. Webster will probably be

the struggle between Federalists and Democrats, and, even in New England, strong groups of Democrats openly applauded Hayne;[1] while the Federalists of Charleston, guided by the *Courier*, thought Webster to be the victor and toasted him as a "true patriot."[2] It took some weeks for his indictment of nullification to be fully understood.

By the majority of Northerners, however, it was felt that Webster had been valiant for truth. The odds at first seemed much against him, and it was feared that he might be not only outnumbered but outclassed. Peter Harvey described the anxiety of old Captain Thomas at Marshfield regarding the result. After perusing Hayne's second brilliant speech, the Captain retired to his bed, convinced that its arguments were irrefutable. When Webster's Reply appeared as an "extra" in the *Centinel*, he dreaded to glance at it. Finally the other members of the household placed the newspaper and a candle in his chamber and retreated to the glow of the fire. Suddenly they were aroused by a cry from the bedroom and, rushing up, found the elderly gentleman sitting on the edge of his couch, the *Centinel* in one hand and the candle in the other, shouting, "Bring me my boots!" His confidence in his hero's prowess was restored.[3]

The Reply to Hayne made Webster one of the three or four leading statesmen of the nation. Hundreds of congratulatory letters piled up on his desk. Monroe and Madison and Clay wrote praising him for his patriotism. Ralph Waldo Emerson entered in his Diary for March 3, "Read with admiration and delight Mr. Webster's noble speech in answer to Hayne," and

---

greater and more salutary than anything of the kind since the days of the Revolution." In Charleston, on the other hand, the *Mercury* denounced Webster bitterly, charging that he had been a member of the Hartford Convention and declaring that he had been the aggressor. Its correspondent wrote, February 4, 1830, "I am anxious that in Carolina at least it should be well understood that this personal contest was commenced by Webster."

[1] The Democratic members of the Maine Legislature ordered the publication and distribution of 2000 copies of Hayne's Speech in pamphlet form. The New Hampshire *Patriot*, Isaac Hill's organ, was almost the only Northern journal not to print Webster's Speech in full. (Bowers, *Party Battles of the Jackson Period*, pp. 98–99.)

[2] Jervey, p. 269.

[3] Harvey, p. 269 ff.

he wrote to Carlyle four years later that it was "a speech which the Americans have never done praising." To meet a demand, a volume of his speeches, prepared by his nephew, Professor Haddock, was published, with his consent, within a year.[1] Early in 1831, a short biography, written by the versatile Samuel L. Knapp, appeared in Boston and had a considerable sale.[2] After 1830, the hope of becoming President was constantly in the back of Webster's mind.[3]

Although Hayne and Webster had ended their skirmish, the battle over Foote's Resolution continued through the winter and early spring, offering an opportunity for one Senator after another to express his views on a variety of controversial subjects. Webster himself was not often in the Senate Chamber,[4] but he did rise on January 28 to protest against an erroneous report in the *United States Telegraph* — edited by Duff Green, printer to the Senate — of what he had said on the preceding day.[5] Most of the speeches are now forgotten, but one delivered by Edward Livingston was historically more

[1] Charles Brickett Haddock (1796–1861), son of Webster's sister, Abigail, was his favorite nephew, over whose education he watched with much care. After graduating from Dartmouth in 1816 with high honors, Haddock returned to Hanover as Professor of Rhetoric (1819–38), and as Professor of Intellectual Philosophy (1826–51). He was United States chargé d'affaires in Portugal from 1850 to 1855. He was named as trustee of Ezekiel Webster's estate, and the latter's children were his wards. (National Edition, XVII, 485–86.) Regarding the volume of speeches, Webster wrote to Haddock: "The book, I have seen. It is well enough except the awful face, which seems to be placed in the front of the volume, like a scarecrow in a cornfield, to frighten off all intruders." (*Ibid.*, p. 508–9.)

[2] This book, published by Stimpson and Clapp, was a neat volume of 234 pages, bound in boards. Knapp, a graduate of Dartmouth in the class of 1804, had been a lawyer and journalist, and had written several biographies. Webster assisted Knapp in the project by supplying him with reminiscences.

[3] McMaster has well said, in speaking of Webster, "He became at once a truly national figure, saw the Presidency almost within his grasp, and from that day forth was animated by a ceaseless longing to become one of the temporary rulers of his country." (McMaster, *Webster*, p. 189.)

[4] On February 20, the *Centinel's* Washington correspondent wrote: "Mr. Webster has been engaged in the Supreme Court ever since he delivered his admirable speech; he is prepared to go into the Senate at a moment's warning to vote in case of emergency. What with his efforts in the Senate and his unwearied labor in Court, he looks almost overcome with mental fatigue; for the last four weeks his labor has been that of Hercules."

[5] Green had quoted Webster erroneously as having said that "the National Government was established by the people, who had imparted to it unlimited powers over the States and the Constitution." (March, pp. 161–62.)

accurate than Webster's, and was a powerful repudiation by a Southern Senator of the nullification doctrine.[1] Among the supporters of Hayne were Rowan, of Kentucky, Woodbury, of New Hampshire, Smith, of South Carolina, and Grundy, of Tennessee; while nationalism was upheld by Barton, of Missouri, Clayton, of Delaware, Johnston, of Louisiana, and Robbins, of Rhode Island. Each of these men spoke for parts at least of two days. Finally, on May 21, Benton and Hayne said a few concluding words; and then, on motion of Bell, Foote's Resolution was laid on the table. No legislation on the subject had been achieved, but Webster's theory of the Union had been sinking into the consciousness of thoughtful Americans, including the impulsive, dynamic figure who then occupied the White House and on whose support Calhoun and Hayne had probably relied.

After Hayne's first speech, Jackson had sent him a note of congratulation, but without mentioning the matter of State rights. When his "scout," Major Lewis, rushed from the Capitol to Lafayette Square to announce that Webster had overwhelmed Hayne, the President declared that he had expected that outcome. Jackson, whose direct mind swept aside the subtleties of Calhoun and Hayne, saw only one fact, — that the Union was in danger, — and prepared himself for action. Meanwhile certain astute Democrats had arranged for a subscription dinner, at Brown's Hotel, on April 13, — the birthday of Thomas Jefferson, — and had agreed in advance upon a series of toasts, nearly all bearing on the relationship of the individual states to the Federal Government. One was drunk to the Kentucky Resolutions of 1798; another to the Virginia Resolutions, which were carefully elucidated by Senator Barbour; and finally the grim-faced President, who had not betrayed what he was thinking, rose and, amid profound silence, read the significant words, "Our Federal Union: It must be preserved." [2] The shock to the conspirators, who

---

[1] See Bancroft, pp. 70–71. Livingston's speech, witty and cleverly phrased, was especially effective in overthrowing the theory that a state could veto an act of Congress which had been upheld by the Supreme Court.

[2] For an excellent description of this intensely dramatic occasion, see Bowers, *Jackson*

had hoped to force Jackson openly into their ranks, was stupendous.   The toast was drunk standing, while "Old Hickory" remained erect and inscrutable, completely master of the situation.   Calhoun, obviously discomfited, had risen with the others, and, when they were seated, did his best to counteract the President's influence by proposing as a toast, "The Union: next to our liberty, the most dear," following it in a few seconds with, "May we all remember that it can only be preserved by respecting the rights of the States and distributing equally the benefits and burdens of the Union."

But the damage was done.   Many years later, when Van Buren's *Autobiography* saw the light, it was revealed that he had talked the whole situation over with the President, and that the two schemers had deliberately planned the sensational climax to the evening's proceedings.[1]   As the assemblage slowly dwindled away after the fiasco, the artful Van Buren knew that his enemies were scattered.   Jackson's utterance was the prelude to his open break with Calhoun in the following year.   Webster, who was soon informed of what had occurred, wrote to Mason: "The thing did not go off very well. Many, very many of the party, found themselves taken in."[2] With Jackson as his ally, Webster was secure.

It was apparent that he had the support of the people.   He declined an invitation to a public dinner in Baltimore,[3] and wrote that he preferred not to be tendered a banquet or a ball in Boston.[4]   But the Massachusetts General Court passed resolutions of approval; Amos Lawrence, a Boston merchant, sent him in the autumn a service plate, as a testimony of his personal gratitude;[5] and a group of his friends joined in present-

---

Period, pp. 101–3.   For a discussion of the exact phrasing of the toast, see Van Buren, *Autobiography*, pp. 414–17, and Bassett, *Andrew Jackson*, II, 255. The *National Intelligencer* for April 20, 1830, gives it as "Our *Federal* Union: *it must be preserved.*" There is a full contemporary account of the episode in the *United States Telegraph* for April 17.

[1] Van Buren, *Autobiography*, pp. 414–15.   At the meeting at which the plot was determined upon, Major Donelson was also present.

[2] Webster to Mason, April 14, 1830 (National Edition, XVI, 201).

[3] *National Intelligencer*, June 5, 1830.

[4] National Edition, XVII, 502–3.

[5] Lawrence to Webster, October 23, 1830 (*Ibid.*, p. 507).

ing him with a chest of silver, appropriately engraved.   By this
time, he was accustomed to the homage which is the inevitable
accompaniment of greatness.   At a public dinner in New York,
on March 10, 1831, with Chancellor Kent presiding, Webster
expressed satisfaction that "the doctrines of nullification have
received a severe and stern rebuke from public opinion." [1]

The controversy, however, had not as yet been adjusted.
Ever since the passage of the Tariff of 1828, nullification had
been threatened by South Carolina extremists.   Jackson's
toast at the Jefferson Dinner temporarily halted the movement, but soon Calhoun's quarrel with the President drove the
former into a position where he was glad of an issue.   During
the summer of 1831, he published an *Address to the People of
South Carolina*, in which he vigorously reiterated his conception of the relationship between the states and the nation.
Calhoun, once the aggressive nationalistic leader, had now
been forced by circumstances into a viewpoint which was
wholly sectional.

Because of the shrinking of the national debt, it seemed
advisable, during the session of 1831–32, to take steps towards
the reduction of the revenue rather than to permit a treasury
surplus to accumulate.   In response to a suggestion from Jackson, Congress, after a prolonged debate in which Webster took
little part, passed, in July 1832, a measure by which the revenue
was to be lowered but the protective principle still preserved.
South Carolina steadily opposed this bill, and Calhoun released
his *Fort Hill Letter*,[2] dated August 28, 1832, to Governor James
Hamilton of that state, in which he once more defended the
rights of his section.

Under the guidance of Calhoun, South Carolina proceeded
to turn theories into actions.   A State Convention, called on

---

[1] *National Edition*, II, 43–65.   In this address, Webster also dwelt optimistically on
the influence of popular government and education in promoting civilization.

[2] Webster considered Calhoun's letter as " far the ablest and most plausible, and
therefore the most dangerous vindication of that particular form of revolution, which
has yet appeared," and planned to answer Calhoun in a letter addressed to Chancellor
Kent.   Kent readily granted his permission, but Webster never carried through his
plan.

November 19, at Columbia, passed an Ordinance of Nullification, declaring that the tariff measures of 1829 and 1832 were "null, void, and no law" and that the people would "not submit to the application of force on the part of the federal government to reduce this state to obedience." The Legislature, assembling shortly afterwards, took steps to carry out this Ordinance. Calhoun was elected United States Senator,[1] and Hayne was chosen as Governor. A respectable minority of South Carolina Unionists was ignored, and medals were struck bearing the legend, "John C. Calhoun, First President of the Southern Confederacy." The Palmetto State was mustering its strongest men for defiance of Andrew Jackson.

Meanwhile, at a National Republican Convention held on October 12, at Worcester, Webster dwelt on current political issues, criticizing the President for his sins of omission and commission.[2] While condemning nullification, Webster rejected the suggestion that military force be employed to bring South Carolina to terms. He was indeed in an embarrassing position. As a National Republican, he must stand by Henry Clay, then the candidate of that party for the Presidency; but, deep in Webster's heart, there must have been the conviction that "Old Hickory," with all his defects, was the man to be relied upon in a crisis.

What Jackson proposed to do was not long left in doubt. After his triumphant election in November, he made preparations in case South Carolina resisted the operation of the tariff, and, on December 10, after receiving the news of the Ordinance of Nullification, he issued a proclamation, written mainly by Secretary of State Livingston, in which, after denying the right of any state to nullify a federal law, he asserted without qualification his intention of suppressing any resistance to national authority — by arms, if necessary. Jackson's proclamation, the longest ever issued by a President, had a clarion ring in the words, "To say that any state may at pleasure recede from

[1] Calhoun was elected Senator on December 10, but did not resign as Vice President until December 28. He sent his resignation to the Secretary of State, Edward Livingston, not knowing to what authority it should be presented.

[2] National Edition, II, 87 ff.

the Union, is to say that the United States are not a nation."
Livingston's common sense was revealed by the sentence,
"The Constitution of the United States forms a government,
not a league; and whether it be formed by compact between
the states or in any other manner, its character is the same."
Everybody who knew Andrew Jackson was sure that he
meant precisely what he said. The Ordinance of Nullification was to take effect on February 1, 1833, and the critical
moment could not be long delayed.

When Jackson's Proclamation reached Boston, Webster
was still in that city, having been kept by private business from
setting out for Washington.[1] A meeting was at once held, on
December 17, in Faneuil Hall, with Mayor Charles Wells
presiding. It was a Monday morning, and bankers and
tradespeople in the downtown district abandoned their offices
to assemble in this historic room and listen to the venerable
Harrison Gray Otis, Attorney-General James T. Austin,
Colonel Thomas H. Perkins, and Daniel Webster, the last of
whom declared that nullification had now become "secession
by force," equivalent to civil war, and that he should give the
President his "entire and cordial support." [2]

On his way south a day or two later, Webster met Clay in
Philadelphia,[3] and learned that the latter, in his rôle of the

[1] Charles W. March, in his *Daniel Webster and His Contemporaries*, pp. 187–88 is
responsible for the legend that Webster first heard of Jackson's Proclamation while he
was on his way to Washington, from a passing traveler in New Jersey, who told him
that the President had just issued a Proclamation against nullification "taken altogether
from Webster's speech at Worcester." The same story is used in Curtis, I, 434, although the author does not mention the Worcester speech, and, in a variant form, in
Poore, I, 139–40, to say nothing of more recent biographies of Webster, which repeat it
without investigation. The facts prove that Webster had seen the Proclamation before
leaving Boston, and that March's tale is merely another Webster myth.

[2] According to the reminiscences of Dr. Thomas Ruggles Pincheon, of New Haven,
who was in 1832 a student at the Boston Latin School and attended this meeting,
Webster wore "black trousers, buff vest, blue coat with gilt buttons, buttoned from
the waist up pretty high," and his gestures "were numerous, but vertical, up and
down, not flowing from side to side." The day was very wet and dark. For Pincheon's
letter to Edward Everett Hale, see National Edition, XIII, 43. Writing seventy years
later, Pincheon not unnaturally confused the months and placed Webster's speech in
March instead of September.

[3] Curtis, I, 434. Clay was in Philadelphia on December 17, following a business
trip to New York, and probably remained there to meet Webster in conference.

"Great Compromiser," was preparing a plan for appeasing South Carolina by making concessions on the tariff. Shortly after he reached the capital, a bill providing for the gradual lowering of duties was introduced in the House by Verplanck, of New York, and, when it failed, Clay himself, on February 12, proposed a compromise measure which would, over a period of ten years, gradually reduce all duties of over 20 per cent and would place some articles immediately on the free list. As a virtual abandonment of the principle of protection, the measure was distasteful to Webster, who also felt that it was not a time for yielding to the threats of a state. Meanwhile, Jackson had asked Congress for authority to employ the military power in executing the revenue laws; and a Special Committee introduced, on January 21, what was commonly called the "Force Bill." South Carolinians watched these preparations with some alarm, and a public meeting in Charleston voted to suspend the Ordinance of Nullification until after the adjournment of Congress.

Calhoun, who seemed to his enemies like a defiant Catiline, took his oath as Senator on January 4, 1833, in a voice which was "serious and solemn." He was aware that he was in serious danger of arrest for treason. His anxiety showed itself in his feverish excitement and in the agitation of his manner when, after fifteen years of absence from legislative deliberations, he once more resumed public speaking. Webster also had been late in reporting, and, after his arrival in late December, had spent most of his time before the Supreme Court. The course which he would follow with regard to South Carolina was still a mystery, and the New York *Journal of Commerce*, in printing the political affiliations of the Senators, said: "Mr. Webster we do not mark at all. He belongs to no party." He himself, however, had already drafted a series of eight "Principles" which were to govern his conduct, the first of which was "to sustain the administration in executing the laws" and the second "not to give up, or compromise, the principle of protection." [1] Living-

---

[1] For the full text of these "Principles," preserved in Webster's handwriting, see National Edition, XV, 104–5.

ston, as an emissary of the administration, called at his house, asked for Webster's help, and left with the assurance that he could be relied upon. When Webster warned Clay that the Compromise Tariff would be "yielding great principles to faction," the former was dropped from Clay's councils, and later Calhoun and Clay were obviously working together. Soon it appeared as if an alliance between Jackson and Webster were imminent, and such a Democratic organ as the *Boston Post* was praising the latter for his conversion to administration policies.

On the day after the introduction of the "Force Bill," Calhoun proposed certain resolutions justifying nullification.[1] Webster, hitherto passive, was now stirred to action, and, on January 28, rose to deny Calhoun's allegations that the "Force Bill" created a dictator and established a military despotism and to announce that he planned, "at a proper time, to try conclusions with the gentleman on this point." On February 8, Webster entered the debate, pointing out that the dispute was between the Executive and his enemies, ridiculing the Democrats for opposing their own President, and adding that, for himself, "he was not at liberty to look on and be silent, while dangers threatened the Union, which existing laws were not competent, in his judgment, to avert."[2] When Clay, four days later, submitted the "Compromise Tariff," Webster announced himself as opposed to it.[3] Thus no one in Congress could have been in any doubt as to what course Webster intended to pursue. He was prepared to fight Calhoun as he had already fought Hayne.

Webster, with his customary thoroughness, had prepared an elaborate argument, but held back, hoping that Calhoun would take the offensive.[4] The latter, impatient of delay,

[1] These resolutions are printed in the National Edition, VI, 180–81.
[2] *Ibid.*, XIV, 152–55.
[3] *Ibid.*, pp. 156–59.
[4] Webster was inclined to underrate Calhoun. On February 9, he wrote Hopkinson, "He cannot, I am fully persuaded, make a coherent, able, argumentative speech"; and, on the evening following the first section of Calhoun's speech, he again wrote Hopkinson: "As a Constitutional argument, it is too inconsiderable for an answer, — truly there is nothing in it. Mr. Calhoun may say, ' Non sum qualis eram. ' "

finally rose on February 15, and, over two days, made the most ingenious justification of nullification ever made in the United States. He was an object of "fearful curiosity" — a spectral figure, with his hair, "not reposing on his head, but starting from it, like the Gorgon's," his inquisitive, penetrating eyes, his thin lips, and his pale, intellectual countenance. As an orator, he disappointed his friends, for he was hoarse, even indistinct, in his utterance; but his argument was carefully reasoned and much superior to that of Hayne.[1] With threatening tones, he announced that, should the bill pass and an attempt be made to enforce it, "it will be resisted at every hazard, — even that of death itself."[2]

Calhoun's theory differed only in minor details from that of Hayne. His method of reasoning was speculative, not practical, and very unlike Webster's reliance on history and law. Calhoun's speech has been called "metaphysical," and the adjective is not inapplicable. His deductions were sound, but his premises were untenable.

On that morning the White House carriage had called at Webster's lodgings, probably with a message from the President; and Webster rode to the Capitol in Andrew Jackson's equipage. The incident was ironic, but also symbolic. When Calhoun sat down, shortly after one o'clock, Webster secured the floor and began the speech which he entitled "The Constitution not a Compact between Sovereign States," covering fifty-six pages in the National Edition.[3] After he had spoken for an hour, the Senate declared a recess until five o'clock. In the interval on that Saturday afternoon, the news that Webster

[1] March said, " In his tempestuous eloquence, he tore to pieces the arguments of his opponents, as a hurricane rends the sails."

[2] The scene was enlivened by a ludicrous incident. In the midst of Calhoun's tirade, a man in the gallery shouted, " Mr. President," and, in the ensuing silence, continued, " Mr. President, something must be done, or I shall be squeezed to death!" He was hustled out by the guards, while the audience could not help smiling. But Calhoun, who had no sense of humor, remained with his features rigid and grave, and, after the interruption, continued as if nothing unusual had occurred. (March, p. 234.)

[3] For the full text of this speech, see National Edition, VI, 181–238. There is an excellent description of the Calhoun-Webster debate in March's *Daniel Webster and His Contemporaries*, Chap. XI.

was up spread around Washington, and, when the Senate reassembled, he faced one of those brilliant audiences which invariably stirred him to exert all his reserve powers. Justices of the Supreme Court, cabinet members, Representatives — all were there, including Major William B. Lewis, the "great father of wire-pullers," who was unofficial newsmonger to Andrew Jackson. For three hours more Webster went on, holding the attention of his auditors even when his argument was abstruse and technical. He closed with the words: —

I shall exert every faculty I possess in aiding to prevent the Constitution from being nullified, destroyed, or impaired; and even should I see it fall, I will still, with a voice feeble, perhaps, but earnest as ever issued from human lips, and with fidelity and zeal which nothing shall extinguish, call on the PEOPLE to come to its rescue.

As he finished at eight o'clock, the galleries burst spontaneously into applause — an unusual demonstration in the Senate. The presiding officer ordered them to be cleared, and, when order had been restored, the Chamber adjourned, and Major Lewis went back to explain to the old man in the White House how Webster had come to the defense of the administration.

Webster's Reply to Calhoun lacked the picturesqueness, the variety, and the rhetorical fervor of the Reply to Hayne. Calhoun had undertaken, by the exercise of logic, to demonstrate that the Constitution was a compact among the separate states, and that each state had a legal right to judge for itself of any violation of the Constitution by Congress, and, when offended, to choose its own method of redress. Webster met him squarely by asserting that the makers of the Constitution had no such theory in their minds. After dealing with the historical aspect of the matter, Webster contended that Calhoun's doctrine, if consistently followed out, would make the Union no better than the Confederacy which had preceded it, and would send the republic down to ruin. Calhoun's reasoning, in so far as it relied upon history, had been clever, subtle, and even plausible. But it fell to pieces under the discomposing blows of Webster's common sense. He asked,

"What will happen when nullification actually takes place?" and his hearers, in their hearts, answered, "The Federal Government must either crush it out or perish." Fundamentally a realist, Webster saw clearly what would happen if Calhoun and his adherents were not checked. He had touched on the emotional phase of the dispute in his Reply to Hayne. Now he made an appeal to the intelligence of the Senate and of the constituency which it represented. It was generally conceded that he had won another triumph.[1]

Although the debate still lingered, nothing new was added to the evidence. Calhoun, after a week of meditation, made a sharp response; and Webster answered him a few days later, prefacing his remarks with a tactful reference to the friendly private relations between himself and his rival. As he closed, Webster summed up the issues by saying, "According to the gentleman's view of the matter, the Constitution is a league; according to mine, it is a regular popular government."[2] Feeling was running very high. John Quincy Adams wrote on Washington's Birthday that he doubted the continuance of "this federative Union" for five years.[3] On the floor of the Senate, Poindexter, of Mississippi, made a violent attack on Webster for his record during the War of 1812, and, when Webster scornfully declined to take any notice of him, his assailant declared that he "felt the most perfect contempt for the Senator from Massachusetts."[4] Not until the last hour of the session was a reconciliation effected through the mediation of Henry Clay.

Two days before Webster's second speech, the Senate had passed the "Force Bill." Before the roll call, all those opposed to the measure had filed out of the Senate Chamber except the courageous John Tyler, whose vote was the only one recorded

[1] Jackson wrote to Poinsett, February 17: " Mr. Webster replied to Mr. Calhoun yesterday, and, it is said, demolished him. It is believed by more than one that Mr. Calhoun is in a state of dementation, — his speech was a perfect failure; and Mr. Webster handled him as a child." (Stille, *Life of Poinsett*.)

[2] This speech, printed in National Edition, XIV, 166–71, was Webster's last important utterance of the session.

[3] Adams, VIII, 479.

[4] Van Buren, p. 685.

in the negative. The Compromise Tariff was then taken up and passed, on March 1, by a vote of 29 to 16, Webster voting, as he had declared he would do, with the opposition. Both acts then passed the Lower House and were signed by the President as his first administration closed. Thus, in the imaginative language of Professor Sumner, "the olive branch and the rod were bound up together." [1]

The South Carolina Convention, meeting at Columbia as soon as the news arrived, rescinded the Ordinance of Nullification by an overwhelming vote, but, with a final gesture of defiance, adopted a resolution nullifying the "Force Bill" and requesting the Legislature to take steps to prevent its execution. Calhoun and his followers maintained that their policy had been a success. To their jaundiced eyes, it appeared as if the alarmed Federal Government had yielded to their threats by modifying the objectionable tariff. [2] Through their resistance, they had compelled Clay to renounce his "American System." They had not been persuaded by the reasoning of Webster or coerced by the strong right arm of Andrew Jackson.

Actually, however, although Calhoun did not realize it, the presentation of opposing arguments had resulted in a victory for Webster. At a moment when we, as a people, were becoming more conscious of our strength and more eager to take our proper rank in world affairs, he had given adequate expression to our nationalistic longings and ideals. The casuistry of Calhoun could never convince the average American that

[1] Webster was fairly well satisfied with the result. He wrote William Sullivan, April 19, 1833, "All things have not happened as I could wish; but on the whole, I think the events of the winter have tended to strengthen the union of the States, and to uphold the government." (National Edition, XVII, 537.) Jackson, also content, wrote, March 21, to Buchanan: "I met nullification at its threshold. My proclamation was well-timed. It opened the eyes of the people to wicked designs of the nullifiers aided by the union of Clay, Calhoun, the Bank, and the corrupt of all parties."

[2] Calhoun wrote, March 27, 1833: "We have upheld and successfully asserted our doctrine, and proved by actual experience, that the rejected and reviled right of nullification, is not, as its opponents asserted, revolution or disunion." (Meigs, *Calhoun*, II, 31–32.) On the other hand, Calhoun's biographer admits that, "outside of his own immediate section, the almost universal detestation of Nullification put a sort of stain on him henceforth as a public man." (*Ibid.*, p. 38.)

any issue could possibly arise which would justify breaking up our Union. It was under the inspiration of Webster's eloquence that the North, thirty years later, entered the conflict which settled by force of arms the doctrine which he advocated.

Politics were much jumbled during that winter of 1833, when the anti-Jackson forces were slowly moulding themselves into that amorphous body which was to constitute the Whig Party. The leaders were not sure what turn events might take, and each was playing his own game. Only the President, strongly entrenched in the White House, had a position of real security, for he knew that the people were behind him. Whatever alliances were formed, he, at least, was safe.

From the turmoil Webster emerged with honor and the title of "Defender of the Constitution." The debate on nullification was his supreme contribution to statesmanship. Abandoning all his other interests,[1] he came forward in an hour when the Constitution needed a new interpretation, and he fulfilled a function hardly less important than that performed by those who framed the original document. Everett did not exaggerate when he wrote, "The student of Constitutional law will ever resort to the speeches of Mr. Webster with the same deference that he pays to the numbers of the Federalist, and the opinions of Chief Justice Marshall." Against the plausible theories of Hayne and Calhoun, his was the most influential voice to be raised. He was not alone in upholding the integrity of the Union, but, by the sheer magnetism of his personality, he wrote his beliefs into the Constitution, irrevocably and forever. Those who feel, with Carlyle, that individual men settle the destinies of nations may well shudder as they try to imagine what might have happened if there had been no Daniel Webster in 1830. His arguments supported Andrew Jackson in his noble public declaration that the Union must be preserved. It was Webster's words which, three decades

---

[1] During the session of 1833, Webster almost forsook the law. In a memorandum of his fees, he wrote, September 9, 1833: "A very poor year's work. Nullification kept me out of the Supreme Court all last winter." (National Edition, XIII, 42.)

later, led Abraham Lincoln to say that it was his primary aim
to save the Union. And his utterances during the thrilling
months of the Great Debate are rightly cherished by Americans
as the finest statement of the true basis of our nationalism.

END OF VOLUME I